PETER

The WRONG WAY HOME

BANTAM BOOKS

LONDON • NEW YORK • TORONTO • SYDNEY • AUCKLAND

www.booksattransworld.co.uk

THE WRONG WAY HOME
A BANTAM BOOK : 0 553 81238 6

First publication in Great Britain

PRINTING HISTORY
Bantam Books edition published 1999

9 10

Set in Times New Roman by
Midland Typesetters.

Bantam Books are published by Transworld Publishers,
61-63 Uxbridge Road, London W5 5SA,
a division of The Random House Group Ltd,
in Australia by Random House Australia (Pty) Ltd,
20 Alfred Street, Milsons Point, Sydney, NSW 2061, Australia,
in New Zealand by Random House New Zealand Ltd,
18 Poland Road, Glenfield, Auckland 10, New Zealand
and in South Africa by Random House (Pty) Ltd
Endulini, 5a Jubilee Road, Parktown 2193, South Africa

Printed and bound in Great Britain by
Cox & Wyman Ltd, Reading, Berkshire.

Contents

ACKNOWLEDGMENTS

I'd like to thank the following people who all played a part in this book seeing the light of day.

Heather Curdie, as an editor and a friend. Jacqueline Barrett, for her unwavering love and support while I did this trip. My family for at least pretending not to worry too much while I'm away. Miranda Foster-Mitchell, my London research assistant. Keith Levett, faithful sidekick in Afghanistan and somewhere to stay while I'm in London. Sean Henry, a limitless font of knowledge—both useful and useless—and source of all my best jokes. Robert Viller, a patient sounding board for all my harebrained schemes. Tim Cox, ABC *uber*-DJ, for keeping my name in the public arena even when I'm off galivanting around the world. Jessica Adams, the dark haired lady spotted in my coffee cup in Ohrid. Simon Taylor for his sense of humour, incisive comments and impeccable taste in music (although I have to say I still don't see what all the fuss over *Attack of the Grey*

Lantern was about). Alison Tulett, for seeing something in this manuscript that may appeal to the Brits. My agents, Fiona Inglis and Jonny Geller. All the people who fed me, sheltered me and helped me on my journey like Martina, Mirindi, Skender and countless others on trains, boats and mini-vans everywhere.

Finally, I'd like to thank Vic Breglec, Alby Mangels' sidekick in *World Safari I* and *II*. He might not be much of a boxer. He's not too cluey with a fish gaff in a rubber inflatable boat. And he may not be much chop pulling the chicks. But he showed that even a big boofy bloke without much idea of anything can still go out and see the world. Thanks Vic.

INTRODUCTION

Why?

Ever since I drew moustaches on the pictures in Yvonne Vacslavik's project on Russia and then stuffed it up the manhole in the sports storeroom hoping no one would ever find out, people have been asking me 'What did you do that for?'

On that occasion it was Miss Dudley, my chain-smoking primary school principal. In the intervening 25 years she has been joined by my mother, my father, my employers and anyone silly enough to get into a relationship with me. Whether it's sabotaging a primary school rival's homework or spending joint savings on front row tickets to a Bruce Springsteen concert, people have always struggled to understand why I do certain things.

I guess I shouldn't have been surprised back in 1994 when no one could fathom why I wanted to travel from London to Sydney without flying.

The astrologer at the *Daily Telegraph* reckons it's because I have my moon in Aquarius, the sign of perversity. Well, maybe. Everyone was telling me it couldn't be done and that there were any number of ways I could fail. For one thing, I only had $5000, and Australian dollars at that. My research—a cursory glance through the appropriate *Lonely Planet*—suggested I would also have problems getting through the former Yugoslavia, securing a visa for Iran, crossing from Pakistan or Nepal into China, crossing from China back into Asia through Vietnam or Laos and finally, getting from Indonesia to Australia.

To be honest, perversity was only part of the reason, though. The rest was pure, unadulterated hippy envy. They had the best music. They had the best drugs. They could have sex with whoever they wanted to without worrying about their penises dropping off. But most of all, they had the best trips.

Ask any ageing hippy—they're the ones wielding extraordinary power in large law firms and banks—and they'll tell you that the greatest trip was the overland journey from London to the East, circa 1967. A guy could grab a chick—hell, he could grab three or four if he wanted to—and head off on a long, laidback odyssey to India and Nepal and Thailand and other places people only ever saw in *National Geographic*. Along the way he'd find enlightenment, a brightly coloured shirt to match the amulet he bought from a gypsy in Camden market and, if he was really lucky, a kilo of hash for the price of a packet of crisps.

Close to thirty years later I wanted to see if the trip could still be done. I was leaving my job as an advertising copywriter and putting my Filofax into storage. I wanted to travel home overland—without flying—as a way of blowing my mind and enriching my life.

Can you dig it?

Miss Dudley couldn't.

To Shana

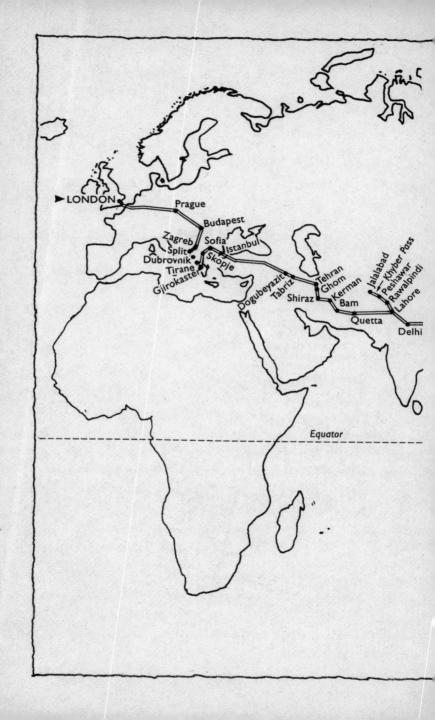

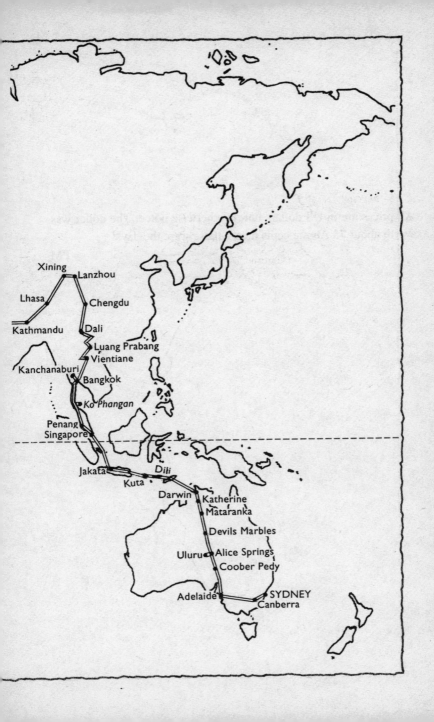

All prices are in US dollars unless otherwise noted. The dollar was worth about 75 Aussie cents then—those were the days!

PM

CHAPTER ONE

London

Soundtrack: 'Fat Bottomed Girls'—Queen

My journey back to Sydney began at London's Victoria Coach Station in the company of people with Billy Ray Cyrus haircuts. I hadn't planned it that way. I hadn't even imagined it could possibly *be* that way. But circumstances—well, OK, a severe lack of funds—meant that I would be catching a bus straight through from London to Prague. Those very same circumstances meant that the coach would be an Eastern European one.

The ticket had only cost £45, which I didn't think was too bad for a 22-hour trip across Europe. I bought it from a company that advertised in *TNT*, a magazine that mysteriously appears outside tube stations in places like Clapham and Ealing and Shepherds Bush, and other places cheap enough to attract slumming Aussie backpackers. It claims to be a 'guide to free-spirited adventure' but in reality it's more of a 'how to' guide to the debauched lifestyle that passes as living as an Aussie in London. The bus company certainly knew their demographic. Across the top of the ad, in bold print, was 'Don't forget. Beer only costs 12p a pint in Prague'. I considered myself lucky to get a seat.

I shouldn't have. Even the prospect of cheap alcohol hadn't lured any other travellers to use this particular bus company. There were only Eastern Europeans in shiny tracksuits, denim jackets and achy breaky coiffures. The really frightening thing was that they all had exactly the same haircut—the men, the women, the children, even the driver (although in all honesty his hair looked more like Eddie Van Halen circa 'Jump'). But instead of line dancing, they milled around the battered coach, guarding cheap red, white and blue striped plastic hessian bags loaded to bursting point with Marks and Spencers' undies and appliances from Woolworths.

Two of the girls—at least I think they were girls—passed the time practising a dance they had learned during their stay. It was an updated Charleston, done to an annoyingly catchy song called 'Doop'. They flapped their arms, shuffled their feet and waved their upturned palms with great vigour, moving aside only to let the conductress past as she dragged the bags full of contraband towards the open hatches on the side of the bus. Although the conductress was built like an East German swimmer (she had that slightly crazed look that comes from taking one too many growth hormones), she was struggling.

The coach spluttered to life, belching a cloud of black diesel smoke that hung ominously under the low roof of the coach station. The two Czech girls stayed outside long after the rest of us had boarded and busily continued to practise their dance steps. Eventually the conductress dragged them on board, a task that proved only marginally easier than manhandling the passengers' bags. We pulled out of Victoria Coach Station and inched our way through a cold, wet London night towards Vauxhall Bridge and Elephant & Castle, the girls continuing to practise in the aisle.

I was sad to be leaving London. I had spent close to a year there, and in many ways it felt like home. I had my favourite pub, the eccentric Prince of Wales near Clapham Common, where I would always find some startling new relic amongst the cluttered Steptoe and Son decor. I had my favourite cafe, the Northcote, where I seemed to spend every Sunday dining on greasy sausages, bacon and mushrooms and drinking from a Teenage Mutant Ninja Turtles glass (spookily, always the one with Leonardo on it). I had even come to appreciate the vagaries of the English weather. But if I were to be totally honest, what I had come to enjoy most was the drunken, wasteful, doleful existence that is the Antipodean scene in London.

My first taste of this Antipodean lifestyle came during my very first weekend in Britain. Barely off the plane from Turkey, I was invited to an expat cocktail party. Now before you getting ideas about me hobnobbing it with London's Aussie cultural elite in the Groucho Club, let me just point out that it was a little get-together thrown by two Kiwis, Wayne and Stuart, and that it was held in their backyard in Clapham. What's more, their idea of class and sophistication amounted to covering the backyard with hay.

Wayne and Stuart both looked like New Zealanders. They had that constantly startled look that all Kiwis seem to have, a look not dissimilar to that of a possum caught in headlights or a sheep getting an unexpected surprise from a farmer in gum boots. They both worked for a water cooler company, lugging twenty-five litre casks to offices all over London. They had stolen a number of water coolers for the party, and with the help of a number of their friends, emptied the huge plastic bottles of water and filled them instead with bulk versions of various cocktails. There was a Piña Colada cooler. There was a Margarita cooler and even a Black Russian cooler. Getting a cocktail was as easy as flipping back the toggle and filling your plastic cup.

I should point out right here and now that I am a very cheap drunk and that I have a penchant for sweet milky drinks. So when I found the Black Russian cooler, it was not a good thing. I knocked back four plastic cups full in a row and was ready to take on the world.

I guess I should also explain what my version of taking on the world involves. On this particular night, it meant linking arms with a dozen or so other similarly inebriated Antipodeans and dancing in a circle while trying to introduce ourselves to each other in time with 'Counting the Beat' by the Swingers. 'I'm Kylie' two three four five 'And I'm Sharon' two three four five 'And I'm ... ummm ... oh I forget' two three four five. Surprisingly, it was a lot of fun, or seemed to be at the time. But then I got something stuck on the sole of my boots.

I thought it was a stone and tried to flick it out with my finger while continuing to dance in a circle. It turned out to be a piece of glass from a broken bottle and I sliced open my finger. While it took me a few minutes to comprehend what had happened, a couple of girls, Kylie and her friend Sam, were more on the ball, and immediately took me up to the kitchen. After ferreting around in the fridge for a while, they found a piece of frozen chicken and applied it to the wound. They insisted that it would help stop the flow of blood, especially if I stood with my hand, and the frozen chicken, on my head.

It's amazing what an open wound will do—as long as it's not too horrific—for the maternal instincts. It wasn't long before I was surrounded by a gaggle of attractive but admittedly very drunk women clucking and fussing over me. Periodically one of them would take my hand off my head and check the wound under the tea towel, then carefully and tenderly replace my hand and the piece of chicken on top of my head. Back home, if I'd offered to buy them a drink or asked them to dance, these same girls would have told me to piss off. I think it was there and then that I decided I loved London.

Of course, it couldn't—and didn't—last. Just as Kylie was asking me if I would like her to keep an eye on my finger throughout the night, Tracy turned up. I had met Tracy in Africa a couple of years earlier, and it was thanks to her that I was at the party in the first place. She was a good friend but, unfortunately, she was also a nurse. She took one look at my finger, applied a band-aid from her purse and told me to stop being silly. Kylie was crestfallen. Her task gone, her duties over, she wandered back into the party. I went and passed out beside a bale of hay.

That party was pretty indicative of the Antipodean scene in London. Every night someone was having a party or there was a backpacker pub offering a pint for a pound. If you were really hard pressed, there was always an Australian band to see. (It was fun to think that they thought they had cracked it big time in the UK when in reality they were just playing to a gaggle of homesick yobbos.) Here's a scary fact. The British music magazine *Q* did a survey on the most requested songs on jukeboxes in London pubs and discovered that 'Khe Sanh' by Cold Chisel was the most popular by far. That's pretty unsettling considering that a) your average Brit thinks that a Cold Chisel is something you use to remove a stubborn piece of concrete, b) the English never fought in Vietnam and c) the song was never released as a single in the UK.

I spent my last Sunday in London as I did my first, getting drunk with my compatriots. This time I ventured to the true heart of Antipodean London, an abandoned warehouse behind Kings Cross Station called The Church. It was called The Church because the only time it opened was between 11 am and 3 pm on Sundays, but it was also a place where miraculous feats of alcoholic consumption occurred. I had heard about it in the furthest corners of Turkey and every week I had lived in London. But I had never been there.

The Church was worth visiting for the location alone. I wandered past lock-ups that looked like something that Arthur (out of 'Minder') would keep his dodgy gear in. And I passed the sort of guys that looked like the type Arthur was always having a run in with. Right down the back of the complex, beside a smelly canal, I came upon a rather dilapidated warehouse. There was a line of people outside, looking as if they were queuing up to get into a soup kitchen.

Inside, the floor was covered in sawdust and Church Wardens (they wore green T-shirts proclaiming their identity) sold six-packs of Victoria Bitter from plastic garbage bins packed with ice. Fifteen hundred sozzled backpackers stood beer gut to beer gut with each other and the odd British film crew keen to capture some Aussie youngster falling stylelessly into his own vomit.

The DJ, well aware of the dancing limitations of his audience, sensibly restricted himself to playing songs with moronic chants and a head-nodding beat. That way the average Aussie male could nod and sing along, his arms folded across his chest, a cold beer in one hand. Stuff like Simple Minds' 'Don't You Forget About Me', with the chorus 'hey, hey, hey, hey, oooohhh yeah!' or 'Walk Like an Egyptian'—'way-oh, way-oh, way ay ay ay-oh' or 'Working Class Man' by Barnsey—'woah oh oh he's a working class man'. Joan Jett's 'I Love Rock 'n' Roll' and Queen's 'We Will Rock You' also went down a treat, proving that the regulars weren't averse to a little bit of gratuitous riffing either.

For one of the faithful, a chubby girl wearing a floral dress and a brightly coloured sweater, it all proved too much. I had been a touch wary of her for a while; her eyes had gone a little glassy and she was shifting uneasily from one foot to the other. With a slurred yelp she threw her hands in the air and collapsed onto the floor, quickly assuming a crucifix position. A quick-thinking Warden rushed to her aid and, cradling her head in his arms, poured a little Victoria Bitter into her mouth. Revived, the girl got to her feet, a little unsteady at first, and shook the sawdust from her fleece.

'Awlright!' she slurred, holding her arms up weakly in triumph.

'Awlright!' she continued, this time with a little jig.

'Awlr ... ii ... urgh ... urgh.' She fell to the floor again, this time throwing up on my shoe.

I was singing along to 'Fat Bottomed Girls' at the time, so I didn't really notice.

>>>

That had been only the day before. I was barely 15 minutes into my grand journey and I was already getting all misty-eyed and nostalgic. Luckily, my head hit the headrest of the seat in front of me and I was brought back to reality with a thud. The bus had run up the back of a Morris Metro on the roundabout at Elephant & Castle. And there, sprinting across three lanes of London peak hour traffic in the rain to get away, was Eddie the bus driver.

The Czechs were nonplussed. They sat and chatted as if it were the most normal thing in the world. Which, in Prague, it probably was. The two girls got up and started practising the Doop again, moving aside momentarily when a policeman got on the bus looking for the driver. Back outside, the driver of the Metro gesticulated wildly at the conductress and the policeman, and then at the rest of us on the bus looking out at what was happening. The whole incident was eventually resolved when the hormone-enhanced conductress started unbuttoning her blouse. Both the driver and the policeman couldn't get away quickly enough.

With Eddie gone, it fell upon the broad shoulders of the conductress to get us safely to Prague. She settled behind the wheel— a little wet from the rain, but thankfully with her blouse re-buttoned—and inched tentatively back into the traffic. At first she was painfully cautious, but soon she got into the swing of things—running red lights, changing lanes without indicating, and mounting the occasional kerb. The only indication of what had happened was the piece of bumper that sat in the aisle beside her. Soon we were in Dover.

I remembered Dover from my first trip to the UK as a smallish seaside village with whitewashed houses and an impressive medieval castle on a cliff overlooking the channel. It was too dark to see all that this time, and besides, we by-passed it all anyway. My overwhelming memory of Dover this time was of a huge expanse of asphalt, floodlights that turned night into day and a bank of tollbooths that stretched as far as the eye could see. We joined a queue of other coaches—all much shinier and more luxurious than ours—and waited patiently for a ferry. Fifteen of P&O's finest departed before we were finally allowed to board one.

Our ferry, however, turned out to be rather like an aged luxury liner. There were rooms with tatty airline-style chairs, kiddies' rooms with Lego and Disney posters, cafeterias, and bars. There were duty-free stores, and even though it was well past 11 pm, they were packed, mainly with the Czechs from my bus.

I've always had an aversion to duty-free stores. They all seem to stock the same things—watches, perfume, cigarettes and alcohol—and at prices that seem to be an approximation of what the items will be selling for in the next century. I ended up following the Czechs anyway, partly to see what they would buy, but largely out of boredom.

The Czechs, and just about every other passenger on the ferry, judging by the crush at the till, chose the store that specialised in cigarettes and alcohol. Whereas a lot of the other duty-free stores on the ferry had gone for an up-market retail ambience, this establishment had all the charm and decorum of a discount cash and carry. Every imaginable brand of cigarettes and alcohol was stacked fifty deep and a metre high on shelves that looked as if they were made out of oversized Meccano pieces. Pimply youths in unflattering sky blue uniforms circled with trolleys of new stock, ready to replenish the shelves—stuff was disappearing at an alarming rate.

While I have never been impressed by the pricing at duty-free shops, the Czechs certainly seemed to be. They darted around the aisles, peering at prices and shaking their heads in disbelief. Then they called out to their friends on the other side of the store, beckoning them to come and check the prices. On having the price confirmed—preferably by two or three friends—they would grab a carton or two each and head for the till.

By the time we drove off the ferry on the other side of the Channel, at Calais, the inside of the bus had taken on the appearance of a customs and excise warehouse. The aisle was a solid wall of cigarette cartons and the overhead racks were stuffed with loose packets of cigarettes and clanking bottles of scotch and vodka. The Czechs sat obscured behind the pile of contraband on their laps, muffling their conversation and softening the impact of the inevitable collision. Even the driver had a stash of Marlboro and bottles of Stoli on top of her chunky thighs. The two Doop girls were trapped behind extra cartons of cigarettes that their parents had bought, frantic and restless at being unable to practise.

As the bus picked its way through the vast car park, with the driver juggling the bottles of Stoli and peering over a mountain of cigarettes on her lap, I got my passport out of my bag. Ever since Australia protested a little too loudly over the massacre of some Kanak rebels in New Caledonia a decade or so ago, the French have insisted that we need a visa to visit their country. The fact that I wasn't strictly visiting, but merely passing through, didn't seem to matter. I had to shell out £7 for the privilege of sitting on a bus for two hours as it travelled through their country.

Even getting my passport out made my blood boil, so when the bus stopped and I was forced to get out of my seat and visit immigration, I was determined to haughtily throw my passport to the desk in mute protest at the injustice of it all. It would have to be mute because I didn't know any appropriate French. Somehow, the only French I had managed to pick up in West Africa—une chambre, petit prix (one room, small price)—didn't seem to capture the anger I was feeling inside.

I needn't have worked myself up, though. I watched out the window as we left the oversized car park and went through the tollbooth. I watched as we travelled along a purpose-built approach road and finally around a roundabout and onto a French autoroute. And when we crossed into Belgium an hour or so later, my worst fears were confirmed. I had wasted £7. The bastards didn't even check.

With the ferry crossing over—and the possibility of being dragged off to have my passport checked by some gnarly French gendarme now well and truly passed—I decided to try and get some sleep. I was rather taken by the idea that while I slept, in the few hours left before dawn, the bus would travel through several countries and through more languages and dialects. It would sweep by the bland Belgians, pass momentarily the gruff Dutch and then speed through the industrious Germans. Back home, a similar bus journey would only get you from one sleepy small town to the next.

There was one small problem with my plan. The guy sitting next to me insisted on leaving his reading light on. I had christened him 'Ivanhoe' after the beat up Everyman edition of Sir Walter Scott's classic he was making quite a show of reading. He had a foppish Hugh Grant hairstyle and wore a turtleneck sweater and spent most of the time staring out of the window. At first I thought he was trying to catch a glimpse of the passing countryside—perhaps even contemplating the lives of those we passed, asleep in their quaint European cottages and neat city squares. Then I realised that the reading light made looking out the windows impossible. He was simply studying his own reflection.

When the sun weakly struggled through a leaden grey sky we were on an autobahn somewhere just out of Frankfurt. Gleaming BMWs and Mercedes hurtled by at breakneck speeds. So did the occasional Porsche. A convoy of trucks carrying tanks and armoured personnel carriers also overtook us. I wondered momentarily where they were going, as Germany was a neutral country. Were they heading down to the former Yugoslavia—maybe to Croatia, with whom the Germans seem particularly chummy—or were they heading to the recently absorbed East? Ivanhoe didn't seem to know any more about this than I did, but insisted that if they were heading to the Czech Republic they were in for a fight.

'The Czech Republic is a country ready for war,' he proclaimed knowledgeably. 'They have spent decades preparing for it, expecting it to come.'

Then, after checking to see if anyone was listening, he motioned me closer.

'Each apartment block,' he whispered, 'has been placed strategically so that in the case of invasion they could be knocked over and used as road blocks. That's why you should never take a room on the top floor.'

Ivanhoe had been teaching English in Prague for over 18 months and was returning there after a short break visiting his parents in Suffolk. He had adopted the bohemian ways of his new home a little too earnestly, so I nodded solemnly and pretended to make a mental note of his advice. If I had openly mocked him he may have become violent and, besides, Ivanhoe lived in Prague. He might yet prove to be useful.

Around 10 am the bus pulled off the autobahn and into one of those ubiquitous roadside petrol stations. Architecturally, aesthetically, it was no different from the same structures that lie beside the motorways in England and the freeways in Australia.

Well, no different from the outside, at least. Upon entering this monstrosity and inquiring after the price of a rather tired-looking sandwich and a can of Coke, I realised just why it was that I was bussing through Western Europe rather than taking a leisurely ramble through it. Those two items alone—let alone any subsequent costs, like accommodation and transport—would have eaten up a week or so of my budget. I went back to the bus hungry and watched a light snow fall on the trucks and coaches and crisp family sedans in the car park. I wasn't alone. The entire Czech contingent hadn't bought anything from the diner either. But at least they had been sensible enough to bring packed lunches.

About 80 kilometres from the Czech–German border, the autobahn gave way to a single road that wound its way rather circuitously through neat farmland and forests. Occasionally we slowed to pass through small villages lightly dusted with snow. The villages looked like something out of a Hans Christian Andersen story, with all the houses clustered around a town square, and each town square with a tower, a clock and a terracotta-coloured church topped by an onion-shaped dome. For the first time on the trip I felt as though I had reached Eastern Europe. It also changed my perception of my fellow passengers. All of a sudden they didn't seem so out of place.

Just after lunchtime we reached the border at Pozvadov. As far as borders go, it was a little disappointing. I had been expecting something right out of the Cold War, with towers and searchlights and barbed wire fences and Alsatians patrolling the perimeter ready to savage any Czech silly enough to make a dash for the West. Instead, there was a barrier and a group of bored looking soldiers standing around rubbing their hands together and trying to stay warm.

A burly guard wearing one of those furry Russian hats came onto the bus and disconsolately looked at everyone's passports. When he saw that I was an Australian he tutted disapprovingly and took my passport from me. I was fearful that there had been some diplomatic incident overnight, but Ivanhoe indicated it was something more serious.

'Well now you've done it. He only had to look at ours. The poor fellow actually has to go and do something with yours. I shouldn't try and upset him any more. I just hope your visa is in order.'

It was. It had cost me £13 in London and was good for a stay of up to 30 days. A few minutes later the guard got back onto the bus, tossed my passport to me from near the front door, then got off.

'My, that was quick!' said Ivanhoe, genuinely impressed. 'The computer must be working again. When I went to London a month ago it was down, and truck drivers had to wait three days to pass through the border. One even died waiting. The cold, you see.'

The conductress shifted the bus into gear and we headed off into the Czech countryside. I was excited to have a new stamp in my passport and busily flicked through the pages to find it. I have always loved visas. They always have a story to tell about the country they come from, and this one didn't disappoint. It had Poz-vadov, the date and, best of all, a little car to indicate that I had entered by road. Ivanhoe thought the car looked like the one from Monopoly, but with the tyre on the outside of the boot, I felt it looked more like a Nazi staff car from 'Hogan's Heroes'.

Almost immediately, the road deteriorated even more, into a single lane road barely wide enough for the bus, let alone any traffic foolish enough to be heading in the opposite direction. It wound its way higher into the hills, where the forests were thicker and the snow heavier. When we did come across farms, they were unkempt and dishevelled, many appearing to be abandoned. Ancient rusting electricity pylons lined the road. I was immediately struck by the fact that there were no fences. Ivanhoe said it was a legacy of Communism, which discouraged them because they implied own-ership. Personally, I think it was because they couldn't afford them.

That was certainly confirmed at our first stop after the border— a disintegrating restaurant rather sadly decked out as a Wild West cantina. The solid pine interior and the recurring logo of a rearing horse suggested that once, a long time ago, probably during the first flushes of freedom, someone had at least thought of spending a bit of money to spruce the place up. Now it just doled out stew to passing buses and beer to a few dishevelled regulars propping up the bar, where the varnish was already beginning to fade. The Doop girls, glad to be free of the confines of the bus, persuaded the owner to put on their tape and got in a few more minutes of practice. And all around, in the restaurant, outside in the car park and even the bus, was the smell of the smoke of brown coal.

The poor condition of the road meant that we would spend the rest of the afternoon travelling the 130 kilometres to Prague. We skirted Plzen, only catching a glimpse of the factories that surround it. During both World Wars it had been a huge centre for armaments—in fact, it was second in size only to Krupps in Germany. It was also the birthplace of bottom-fermented beer, named 'Pilsener' after the town, and made from premium Zatec hops and the soft local water. I asked Ivanhoe if the buildings we were passing were the breweries.

'No. They're closer to the town centre. See that logo?' he asked, pointing to the chimneystack of a particularly ugly industrial complex. 'It's the same as on a Skoda. It's the Skoda Engineering Works.'

'So that's where they make Skodas,' I said, trying to appear knowledgeable.

'No. That side of the business got sold to Volkswagen,' Ivanhoe corrected me. 'That's where they make all the nuclear reactors for the old Soviet Bloc.'

It was a sobering thought. The same standards of engineering excellence that went into your average Skoda car were applied to your average Warsaw Pact reactor. No wonder Chernobyl started making its way to the centre of the Earth.

'Do you know any Skoda jokes?' I asked Ivanhoe, trying to change the subject. 'They're quite funny. Look, there's a few in my guidebook. What's the difference between a Jehovah's Witness and a Skoda? You can close the door on a Jehovah's Witness! Ha, ha.'

Ivanhoe smiled weakly. Taking this as a sign of encouragement, I continued.

'Why do they put rear window demisters on Skodas? To keep your hands warm while you're pushing them! Ha, ha. How do you double the value of your Skoda? Fill it up with petrol! Ha, ha. What do you call a convertible . . .'

'Please,' interrupted Ivanhoe. 'I drive a Skoda. And really, they're not that bad. Now if you don't mind, I'd rather like to finish my book.'

The 90 kilometres to Prague passed in an uncomfortable silence. Which was fine by me.

CHAPTER TWO

Prague

Soundtrack: Anything by Tracy Chapman, it seems

I had very high expectations of Prague. Not because of the 12p pints. And not because *Time Out* had just declared it the coolest place in Europe either. (Nor, I should add, was it because the low sartorial standards on the bus suggested I would be the snappiest dresser in town.) No, I had far loftier reasons than that. By virtue of a rather conciliatory foreign policy during both World Wars, Prague was by far the most pristine example of 600 years of Mitteleuropa architecture. And when I entered it that sunny March afternoon, Prague didn't disappoint. It looked just like its postcards.

It has been my experience that whether you enter a city by air, land or sea, you get to see its ugly underbelly first—the industrial estates, the soulless apartment blocks or, in Sydney's case, the endless used car yards. It's not until you get to know a city a little better that it bothers to show you its best side. When you come to think about it, it's quite a refreshing approach. A city shows you its faults, and if you can accept that, you get to know it better. If you don't, you get the hell out of there.

Prague, however, was different. The coach had barely passed the 'Welcome to Prague' sign before vistas befitting very expensive coffee table books started popping up everywhere. To the left was Hradcany, crowned by the magnificent cathedral and palace. Ahead lay the Vltava River, winding its way past immaculately maintained baroque mansions and picturesque cobbled streets. When we crossed the Jiraskov Bridge I spotted the Gothic Charles Bridge before we plunged into Nove Mesto, Prague's most beautiful and exclusive suburb. When we made our way up Wilsonova, crossing the top of Wenceslas Square, looking particularly lovely in the golden afternoon sun, I had already seen more than most European cities offer in a week of intensive sightseeing. I could have jumped on a train out of Prague that night, convinced I had seen everything that the city had to offer.

As the bus turned off Wilsonova and headed towards a less salubrious part of town, Ivanhoe closed his book and sighed.

'I suppose you'll be looking for somewhere to stay,' he said wearily. 'You do know that accommodation in Prague is more expensive than Vienna, don't you?'

I said that I didn't. He reached into his leather satchel, and for one moment I thought he was going to offer me some money to help me get by. Instead, he pulled out a pen and a piece of paper and started drawing a map.

'This is the hostel I stayed in when I first arrived. It's not in the city centre. In fact it's on the other side of the river in Holesovice. But it is right near a subway station and it is cheap. And in the short time that I've known you, that seems to be the most important thing.'

I nodded, a little disturbed that he had read my character so well so quickly.

'And for what it is worth, here is the address of a small cafe called the Derby. It could be a little highbrow for you, but at least there are no Americans. And in Prague that is a very rare thing indeed.'

I had heard in London that Prague was crawling with Americans—street performers, mainly—and I wanted to question Ivanhoe at length about his experiences. But like everything with Ivanhoe, even this smallest of gestures had been planned with the greatest of precision. The coach pulled into a rather shabby bus station, and in one swift move he handed me the paper, grabbed his satchel and strolled off the bus. I watched from the window as he sauntered through the crowd, immediately at home yet completely alien. For a moment I envied his poise. He was off to teach English to eager students and sit in smoky cafes reading hardback editions of literary classics. But in the end I decided he was just a wanker.

I pocketed his note, convinced that I wouldn't have to use it. Everyone else I knew who'd been to Eastern Europe had been besieged by little old ladies offering them the use of their large, comfortable apartments for ridiculously small amounts of money. I just hoped they would let me get my bag before I sat down to play them off against each other to get an even more ridiculous price.

As it was, my bag was already waiting for me by the time I got off the bus. The conductress had been helped by some of the relatives who had come to greet the bus. The two girls were doing the Doop again, this time to a large and appreciative audience of friends and relatives. Some of the younger girls were already up beside them, copying the moves and begging for tuition. Someone—an aunty or an uncle, I couldn't really tell—grabbed their bags, and the girls reluctantly Dooped their way to a fleet of waiting Skodas.

Alarmingly, in my first minutes off the bus I wasn't approached by anyone, let alone a little old lady offering me a room overlooking Charles Bridge and unlimited access to her fridge for $3 a night.

For a moment I thought it might have been because no one realised I was a tourist—a frightening thought, considering the haircuts and fashion sense of the locals. Then I looked down at my bright red backpack with an embroidered badge of the Australian flag sewn on the front pocket and I realised it was much worse than that. There was nobody offering rooms. It looked as if I would have to venture to the other side of the river and check out the hostel suggested by Ivanhoe after all.

Holesovice was not the most attractive part of Prague. In fact, it looked a lot like the Eastern Europe you see in those arty foreign movies on late-night TV—dour, featureless apartment blocks and people scurrying by in big coats and scarves and hugging themselves against the cold. It was basically the kind of neighbourhood that makes people turn to vodka—in large quantities.

I followed Ivanhoe's crudely drawn instructions, turning left out of the Holesovice Nadrazi Metro station and then walking down a multi-lane highway where shabby trams rattled by, looking even shabbier in the dull grey light of the dying afternoon. At the first intersection, I crossed, turned left and walked towards the flyover underneath which, according to Ivanhoe's map, the hostel nestled. There was a cluster of buildings where his map indicated the hostel should be, but they looked more like the kind of buildings that would manufacture ball bearings—or at the very least, inconsequential parts for nuclear reactors—than like somewhere that would offer a clean and comfortable bed for the night.

Inside, the place was even more disconcerting. The building was a factory for something suitably Soviet. There were boxes of ugly grey things stacked high in the front office. But in keeping with the new spirit of commercialism, it was also letting out beds in the old workers' quarter. The foreman, after figuring out that it was a bed I was after and not a new crankshaft, set off down the hall, his cheap runners squeaking on the shiny linoleum, beckoning for me to follow.

At the end of a long, dark hall there was a door, which he proceeded to unlock and open. Inside were six camp beds, all freshly made with crisp white sheets, none showing any indication of having been slept in during the last year or two. He tossed me the key, turned and left the room. Just outside the window, workmen and little old ladies were picking their way along a disused railway line in the gloom. Watching them trudge along, stooped by the weight of toolboxes or groceries or the utter boredom of their lives, I suddenly felt weary myself. I drew the tattered curtains, threw myself on the bed nearest the window and fell into a deep sleep. I had just made the first step on my long journey home. Call me perverse, but it felt good.

>>>

The next morning I ventured into the centre of Prague, with some trepidation. From what I had seen coming into Prague the afternoon before, I knew it would be as beautiful as promised by the postcards, posters and coffee table books. But I'd be lying if I said I wasn't concerned about the little matter of the Americans. Apparently there were 40,000 of them.

Prague has become the new home for Americans with a bohemian bent. In the fifties they would don berets and cravats and rent a garret in Paris to write the great American novel or paint the great American painting. Now they were in Prague to become street performers. There was even an American Hospitality Center, no doubt to welcome the new arrivals and help them settle into their new bohemian lifestyle.

Ivanhoe had warned me I would find them at every turn, and he was right. A pair of bucktoothed girls strummed guitars under the vaulted arches of the shops lining the Old Town Square. A guy with the kind of jawline that advertises aftershave juggled knives in the courtyard of the great cathedral. And one guy, a little more dishevelled than the rest, sat on the Charles Bridge playing bongos. There were people on every corner carrying guitars and violins and harmonicas and flutes. And every one of them, it seemed, was an American.

I wandered up the cobbled streets that led up to Hradcany more than a little dismayed. Why were all these people coming to Prague? Wasn't there a city square closer to home they could busk on? Surely they didn't think they were going to make their fortune in the Czech Republic?! If their haircuts were anything to go by, the Czechs weren't particularly well off. They didn't look as if they could support a decent wardrobe, let alone thousands of romantic Americans with stars in their eyes.

I discovered the answer just outside the Loreto. The Loreto is a rather contrived baroque building up in Hradcany, constructed in an audaciously over-the-top fashion. Its primary purpose is to house the Santa Casa—the house supposedly belonging to Jesus's mum Mary, miraculously transported to Prague by angels from the Promised Land. Judging by the overly ornate stucco plastered all over the house, Mary had rather Mediterranean tastes in decorating. While there weren't any concrete lions and there was only a handful of pillars, there were more angels and cherubs than you could poke a stick at. Most importantly, the Loreto is also a popular spot on the American tour group itinerary. Knowing this, a fresh-faced American college kid stood just to the right of the entrance playing a violin.

In the short time I watched, three American tour groups entered the Loreto. I knew they were American because everyone on them looked like Frank and Estelle Costanza from 'Seinfeld'. Without exception, each member of each tour group placed a crumpled note into the young man's violin case as if it were part of the price of admission. One woman made quite a show of placing a 500 kroner note ($18) in the case. She didn't even flinch when the young man thanked her in perfect American-accented English. She just turned to her friend and said, 'Didn't *he* speak good English!'

At least the Americans were supporting their own. I'm not exactly sure what the Italian tourists were up to. They passed by in equally large numbers, but screaming and wailing and arguing as if Prague were their very own private asylum.

If there is one thing I've discovered in all my travels, it's that you can't take Italians anywhere. On Charles Bridge, one of them lay on the ground to take a photo and soon they were all doing it. Outside St George's Basilica, they started an impromptu volleyball match. Up at the castle, a group of Italian tourists walked out of the gates and down a pathway between cordoned-off crowds to see the changing of the guards. They strolled through leisurely, smiling and waving, convinced that the crowd had gathered to see them. The really annoying thing is that they look so damn stylish doing it.

Despite all the Italians and Americans, Prague still had its charms. And wandering around the castle district, soaking up the ambience, I must admit that I came over a little bohemian myself. I continued down in Mala Strana, a labyrinth of baroque houses painted in charming pastels, and on to Charles Bridge, with its eighteenth-century sculptures looking across the weir and towards the charming Old Town Square. The fact that the city has been left relatively untouched by natural catastrophes or war means that it was very easy to find a little corner and pretend that it was 1856 again.

Not being blessed with a beautiful singing voice or a natural ability with instruments, I decided to do what the less musically inclined of we bohemians do—go to a cafe and adopt a pose of quiet reflection over a cup of coffee. The first cafe I came upon was the Cafe Nouveau, just down from the Old Town Square. It looked like something out of a Toulouse-Lautrec painting—all heavy-handed art deco chintz and filigree. Inside, people dressed equally extravagantly sipped on coffee and waved at waiters wearing crisp white uniforms. The cafe also boasted a Celcobank Exchange Counter for those who found themselves a little short. My Visa card was still recovering from London, so I wandered on, catching a glimpse of the waiter who came across and immediately wiped off the greasy mark left on the window by my nose.

The *Time Out* feature on Prague made quite a big deal about a place called The Globe, an olde-worlde bohemian style bookshop and cafe that was the hot spot of the moment. There I would be able to sink into an armchair, read a book and knock back a long black. Apparently.

Tucked away off a main road in Prague 7, The Globe certainly looked the goods. The walls were lined with wooden bookshelves groaning under the weight of musty, leather-bound volumes and dog-eared paperbacks. Newer volumes were stacked in piles in corners, around the comfortable sofas that dotted the room. Unfortunately, the sofas were all occupied by fellow bohemians, silently reading books pretty much in the manner in which Ivanhoe had been reading his on the coach to Prague. Denied the opportunity to look similarly intelligent, I wandered over to the noticeboard to see if there were any garrets going.

'Hey You!' screamed the most prominent notice. 'Yes you with the face. Looking for talented uninhibited performers of all types (A, B, O-) to fill new performance space in Prague with laughter, screams of horror etc. Leave description of act/concept and contact # below.'

I was tempted to write that I was an American college student who specialised in singing Tracy Chapman songs but, concerned that they would probably take me seriously, I decided to check out the cafe attached to the bookshop instead. I walked through a wooden-framed doorway and gasped. It was a glass and chrome monstrosity, totally out of character with the bookshop it was attached to. A serving counter, not unlike those seen in university

cafeterias, doled out Black Forest cake and production-line cappuc-
cinos to Americans no doubt comforted by how clean it all was. I
immediately turned on my heel and left, but not quite quickly
enough to avoid a particularly loud college girl, a guitar leaning
against her table.

'You know, they just lurv 'Stairway to Heaven' here,' she
enthused.

I rummaged in my pocket for the address of the Derby, the cafe
recommended by Ivanhoe, hoping it would offer a more truly bohemian experience. It was just around the corner from The Globe,
but in every other respect it was a million miles away. It was like
something out of Paris in the sixties, a beat up beatnik place where
all the guys smoked cheroots and wore turtleneck sweaters. Pretty
girls with long legs and short skirts draped themselves over the
men's shoulders, wantonly trying to distract them from the poet in
the corner who was muttering incomprehensible verse and punc-
tuating it with equally discordant strums of his guitar.

It was a scene so perfectly bohemian that, as a pseudo-bohemian,
I immediately felt self-conscious and out of place. The way everyone looked at me when I entered—with disdain and suspicion—
didn't help matters either. No doubt they thought I was another
American, keen to find an undiscovered cafe and then win 'cool'
brownie points by telling all my friends about it. I asked for a box
of matches—smoking being a much more acceptable pastime in
Eastern Europe than it was in the UK or Australia—glanced dismissively towards the guitarist and wandered out again. If I'd been
a smoker, or even had a cigarette to pretend to light, it would have
been a perfect bohemian exit.

I spent a week in Prague trying to dodge American street performers and Italian tourists. I found a used car yard that also sold
second-hand howitzers, slightly scratched tanks and even an L29
Delfin fighter jet with one genuine owner. (If you're in the market
for a bit of pre-loved weaponry, the place is called Auto-moto Bazar

Okase, and you'll find it just near Holesovice Station.) I made a
day trip to Kutna Hora and checked out a pile of monks' bones at
the Cistercian Monastery and the largest tobacco factory in Europe
at Sedlec. I even made an effort to see the rather sad, scaled-down
version of the Eiffel Tower on the top of Petrin Hill. (Great view
of the city, by the way.)

There were other days when you'd find me just sitting on a
platform on the Metro, staring at the LED clock at the end of each
platform. Rather than tell commuters when the next train was due,
these clocks taunted commuters by telling them how long ago the
last train had left. I'd sit there, trying to figure out how I'd feel
looking at a clock that told me that I'd just missed the last train—
and probably the last chance of saving my job—by 35 seconds.

On my third day in Prague, I visited Franz Kafka's grave at
the Old Jewish Cemetery at Josefov. I don't know why. I've only
read one of his books, *The Trial*, and found it rather heavy going.
But I did, and what's more, I took a photo of myself standing
by his grave. I wondered if it was because I hoped that if I visited
the grave of a famous writer, some of his skills might rub off
on me. They didn't, but in the process I did discover that skullcaps
do not suit me and hence converting to Judaism was out of the
question.

By my last night in Prague I felt a little cheated. Prague was
undeniably a very pretty city, but I felt that I had been kept at arm's
length. I had not been able to get beneath its prissy, gentrified
surface. And every time I tried, there was a loud Italian tour party
or an American with some kind of instrument standing in my way.
That night I wandered around the city centre hoping it would be
different, but it wasn't. I turned a corner and found an American
girl singing Tracy Chapman songs with a large dog with a sign
saying 'Kafka' around its neck. More disturbingly, I found myself
stopping to listen and even singing along a little to 'Fast Cars'.
Knowing my sanity was in danger, I turned up the collar on my

coat, crossed the river and walked through the more depressed neighbourhoods back to my hostel.

About a kilometre or so before Holesovice, I passed a small, noisy pub. I stopped, entranced by the scene framed by the window and softened by the homely lace curtains—normal people tucking heartily into stolid broth and sucking on steins of Budvar brought to them by plain, solid waitresses with dour expressions. It was just what I had been searching for.

Inside, I immediately felt at home. The overhead lights were dim, and the dark wood panelling and orange tablecloths gave the room an inviting and comforting warmth that the cafe at The Globe sadly lacked. What's more, the diners didn't even bother looking up when I came in.

I made my way towards the table the waitress had gestured me towards, but before I could reach it I was waylaid by a table full of Czech soldiers. There were seven of them, all in Sherwood-green uniforms, all were 18 to 19 years old and all of them were very, very drunk. As one held me by the arm, the others lifted their steins and started singing.

'Harpee birtday to yew,' they sang discordantly. 'Harpee birtday to yew. Harpee birtday, harpee birtday, harpee birtday to yew!'

As it turned out, that was the extent of their English, but through a series of gestures, some bordering on the obscene, I gathered that they wanted me to sit with them and get exceedingly drunk. They had been on leave since 4.00 that afternoon, so they obviously had a good start on me, but as an exceptionally cheap drunk I knew it wouldn't be long before I would be in a similar state.

The early part of the evening consisted of us self-consciously nodding at each other and drinking toasts to incomprehensible phrases and people we didn't know. Periodically, a sour waitress (who turned out to be the best English speaker in the joint) came across and interpreted their questions before being hailed by other customers for another beer. 'Where are you from?', 'Do they have

National Service in Australia?' and the unanswerable 'Fuck the army!'

After each question, and barely after each of my answers was interpreted by the surly, not-so-long-suffering barmaid, the lads raised their glasses and shouted 'Long life to Mr Peter!'

While they waited for the barmaid to pass by again, the guys passed the time by showing me their army cards. The cards were austere, official-looking documents that listed their free time and marked the times they left barracks and when they were to return. They looked very Soviet and official, with entries in faded bleeding fountain pen, validated by equally faded and bled stamps. The exception was the rather crude 'Fuck off the army!' written in red pen next to the day their two years of National Service would be finally over. The fact that it was the same handwriting in each card made me suspect that it had been written by Josef, the only one in the group who spoke any semblance of English. The fact that he ended every toast with 'Fuck the army!' seemed to confirm it.

To mark the evening as the very special event that it was, the guys, in true macho fashion, all signed a beer coaster and gave it to me as a memento. They also gave me a handful of tacky brass insignia they wore on various epaulettes and on their elastically attached ties. But beyond that, I don't recall much else of the evening. From the half-filled-out application form I found in my coat pocket the next morning, I gather that I came very close to enlisting in the Czech army. And I have fuzzy memories of calling it a night outside a disco called Fantasy, despite the guys assuring me there were 'many good girls' inside.

I do remember the next morning, though. I woke up with a shocking hangover, 15 minutes before my train left for Budapest.

CHAPTER THREE

Budapest

**Soundtrack: Something suitably thrashy by the
Budapest Drinking Club**

The 5.58 am to Budapest via Brno and Bratislava pulled out of
Holesovice Station and into the grey misty dawn right on time. It
was filled with neatly dressed businessmen carrying briefcases,
setting out to do business in the brave new post-Communist world
of Eastern Europe. They all looked the part in their freshly pressed
business shirts and silk ties, but it wasn't long before they were
shifting uncomfortably in their suits, loosening their collars and
drumming their fingers on their briefcases. They were like high
school graduates on their way to their first job, not quite sure how
to carry off the whole charade of wearing suits and making money.

The train, on the other hand, harked back to more comfortable
times. It was ancient, green and battered, and had cabins with red
vinyl seats and pale lino floors dotted with black cigarette burns. It
also had faux wood-grain laminex on the walls and homey print

curtains on the windows. I settled into the seat beside the window, a rogue spring poking into my left buttock, and watched Prague pass me by in a mist that was partly meteorological, but mostly alcoholic.

At Kolin, a small town an hour or so from Prague, the businessmen all stood up at once and retired to the dining cabin to drink coffee and vodka. It was as if they had all received the same telepathic message that their bosses weren't watching any more, and that they could return to the old way of doing things by getting pissed. I celebrated having the cabin to myself by throwing open the window and hanging out like a Labrador in a station wagon. The cold air swept back my hair and snap froze my saliva, clearing the cabin of the stale warm air from the ageing Soviet heating system and discouraging any of the newly boarded passengers from choosing my cabin. It was a reckless, selfish and invigorating thing to do. I almost felt Italian.

Soon the train headed into the mountains and began winding its way through forests of fir trees crowned by a light covering of snow. For the next hour or so we passed burbling streams and log cabins and startled the occasional rabbit skittering across an icy lake. It was untouched and pure, like an illustration from my nieces' book of fairy tales. But it was soon shattered by the monumental ugliness of the factories and apartment blocks surrounding Brno, the Czech Republic's second largest city and, I would suggest, its ugliest.

Things didn't really pick up after Brno. We were heading into the Slovak Republic now, the heavy industrial half of the former Czechoslovakia, the ugly sister to the Czech Republic's Cinderella. It was dirtier. It was scruffier. And it was worn out. The towns became more squat and dark, filled with cancer-ridden concrete apartment blocks and scarred with signs in Soviet-style typefaces that seemed to oppress you the moment you looked at them. Even the fields and rivers looked overworked and in need of a good holiday.

I had never really understood why the Slovak Republic seceded from the Czech Republic. It didn't have any natural resources, and it didn't have a jewel like Prague to seduce foreign investors and lighten the pockets of tourists. In fact, every other traveller I had met intended to do exactly what I was doing—catching a train straight through to Budapest. It wasn't until the train passed through the heartland of the Slovak Republic and approached the rather sad-looking capital of Bratislava that it dawned on me—the Slovaks were just being realists. They knew that the Czech Republic didn't need them and would one day wake up to the fact. They just got in first, and saved themselves the trauma of having to deal with the inevitable rejection.

It was an attitude apparent in the immigration official strolling through the cabin issuing visas. He had that slouched-shoulder look of a charity collector already resigned to the fact that you're not going to give him any money. I'm sure if I had argued that I was only passing through and didn't really need a visa, he would have let it slide and maybe even apologised for disturbing me. But I coughed up the $26 regardless, and in the process brought a weary smile to the poor guy's face. Sure, I was on an extremely tight budget, but from what I'd seen of the Slovak Republic, it needed the money more than I did.

An hour later, the train passed into Hungary and, soon after that, by the stately towns of Esztergom and Visegrad on the Danube Bend. Contrary to what the song suggests, the Danube River here wasn't blue; it was a rather dirty brown. Nonetheless, it was extraordinarily beautiful; winding its way through pretty fields and around hills crowned by castles topped with green copper domes. I was moved to sing 'Blue Danube'—a bad habit of mine when passing through places mentioned in song—but I couldn't quite remember whether it even had words or if it was it one of those Tijuana Brass instrumentals like 'A Walk in the Black Forest'. All I remembered was my sister practising it over and over again on the piano. Even now, years later and on a train in the middle of Hungary hurtling towards Budapest, I could still hear that bum note she always hit when she got it wrong.

In the early afternoon, the train entered Budapest, through the heavy industrial suburbs in the north, and slowly made its way through shunting goods trains and countless railway lines and junctions to the iron and rivet monstrosity of Budapest's main railway station, Keleti. My guidebook thoughtfully suggested that on arrival I visit the office of the Hungarian National Tourist Bureau—or ISBUSZ, as it had been mysteriously acronymed. Here I would be able to buy a map, change money at the best rates in town and even line up a room for the night. What it failed to mention, however, was that I'd have to run the gauntlet of the little old ladies to get there.

These were the landladies I had been expecting to greet me in Prague: weathered and stooping, with headscarves and carrying shopping baskets. But they weren't as kindly or as gracious as I had imagined. They lined the corridor leading to ISBUSZ, shouting and waving and offering ridiculously cheap rooms with an intensity that was quite frightening. Any refusals were met with bloodcurdling wails and, more often than not, a fearsome gnashing of teeth. One woman clutched my shoulder and implored me to take a large apartment in the centre of the city for the cost of a Mars bar. When I said no, she reacted as if I had robbed her of her last chance of paying for her daughter's life-saving operation. I had to enlist the help of people passing by to prise open her grip.

Inside ISBUSZ it was quieter, but the rooms on offer proved a little too expensive for my budget. There's actually not much you can get within a budget of thirty Australian dollars a day, so I simply changed money and braced myself to leave. I had decided to take the first room offered, hoping that the women had some code of honour where, upon deciding on a landlady, a traveller would be allowed to pass unmolested by the others. Before I got out the door, however, a scruffy German whom I had assumed was a hobo handed me a brochure for a hostel called More Than Ways.

I hadn't planned to stay in a hostel in Budapest. My friend Sean had been to Budapest a couple of years before and had seduced me with tales of family homes with attentive hosts and Old Masters on the walls, all for only a few dollars a night. And unlike my arrival in Prague, here in Budapest I had little old landladies literally throwing themselves at me.

My resolve weakened, however, as I leafed through the brochure. The cover featured a cute, leggy blonde in tight cut-off denim shorts. She wore a tight white T-shirt with 'STAFF' emblazoned in red across her perky chest and, in suitably cursive script, the hostel motto 'More Than Ways—one way of life'. A starburst in the top right-hand corner of the brochure screamed 'Now with 24-hour bar!'. As a copywriter by trade, I was impressed by how quickly the Hungarians had realised that in advertising sex sells. As a weak-willed consumer, I simply said 'OK'.

More Than Ways was situated in a squat stone building opposite the Dozsa Gyorgy subway station, with an uninspiring view of a number of subway exits and a constant stream of Skodas and Tra-bants shuffling their way up Vaci ut and out of Budapest. It was dark and dull and looked as though it may have once housed a branch of the secret police or a sporting body charged with the task of feeding steroids to athletes. The German guy led me to the entrance of the hostel and then turned to leave.

'I must go back under ze cover,' he hissed loudly over his shoulder. 'Tell zem zat Hans sent you!'

My first impulse upon entering More Than Ways hostel was to turn around and leave. The place looked like a front for every vice imaginable, and a few I'm sure had never even been thought of. Sleazy guys with dark heavy features sat in the foyer drinking and playing cards, occasionally turning from their game to feel up the odd slapper ambling by. Travellers stumbled by drunk or stoned or both, drawn like moths to the squeals and the 'thump, thump, thump' coming from the bar at the bottom of the stairs below. A South African guy harangued the girl behind the reception desk, demanding his money back because he returned to the hostel at 3 am and found someone else in his bed. She gave him his money back before registering me and giving me a room key.

'You are lucky,' she said, looking frazzled—and nothing at all like the girl on the brochure. 'This is the last bed for the night.'

I nodded with what I hoped looked like gratitude.

'You'll have to wait for a pillow case, though,' she said. 'The girl who does the laundry has passed out down in the bar.'

I didn't sleep well that night. The dorm I had been sentenced to was directly above the bar and right beside the men's toilets. At 10 pm, two Canadian girls started complaining that there were crumbs in their beds. At midnight, the night manager came into the dorm with three late arrivals and only a combined revolt from all of us stopped him letting them sleep on the floor between the bunks. At 3 am, a young American guy thrashed about in his bed before screaming, 'I can't sleep with these fucking people!' At 7 am, just as the overnighting Eurailers were arriving from Vienna, I went to the bathroom and found a guy throwing up in the basin.

In spite of More Than Ways hostel, I decided on my first morning in Budapest that I liked it much better than Prague. Where Prague was prissy, Budapest was grubby and earthy and scarred by the kinds of buildings favoured by inner-city councils for housing the unemployed and by Sydney harbourside developers. The people were different, too. In Prague, the women dressed like they were heading off to the opera; in Budapest they dressed like they were going to work the streets. In Prague, the men looked like they all played in a chamber orchestra; in Budapest they looked like they were on their way to loot and torch some reactionary institution. And whenever I saw a man and woman together, they seemed to be attempting to shag each other senseless.

The preponderance of couples in amorous clinches was something I had noticed within minutes of arriving in Budapest. On park benches, on street corners, on grass verges—in fact in any place where large numbers of the general public could be counted on to pass by frequently—I invariably found a pair of Hungarians hard at it.

Take my first morning in Budapest, for example. I started the day catching the cable car up Gellert Hill, and found at least half a dozen Hungarian couples who thought that a rickety funicular railway carriage full of rotund tourists was a particularly good place to mate. Similarly, I was put off buying a little yellow can labelled 'The Last Breath of Communism' outside the entrance to the old stone Citadella by a couple whose rather athletic routine threatened to knock all the cans flying, as well as the card table they were resting on. I enjoyed a moment of respite in Matthias Church up in Varhegy, but as soon as I returned outside to the more secular, Disneyesque turrets and walls of the Fisherman's Bastion, it was on for young and old again.

Budapest's daily English-language newspaper had noticed the phenomenon too. That morning's edition featured the results of a street poll where people were asked for their opinion on the excessive smooching. One sour-faced matron said it was disgusting. A young guy said he couldn't see anything wrong with it. And a wrinkly 87-year-old said he was 'too young to be offended by such things'. Besides, he added, it was spring.

Thankfully, there was no one bonking outside the Iranian embassy or inside by the visa section. Getting a visa for Iran was crucial to the success of my entire journey. With it I could travel through Iran to Pakistan and then on to China. Without it, I'd have to turn around and fly home from London. The trouble was, securing an Iranian visa was a lottery. There were no hard and fast rules, and it depended largely on the diplomatic mood of the moment and the goodwill of the ambassador.

The news from the kind guy in charge of the visa section wasn't encouraging. If I wanted a tourist visa, I'd need someone in Iran to sponsor me. A transit visa had less stringent criteria, but would still involve telexing Tehran with my details. If my name didn't appear in the latest Debrett's *Enemies of Islam* a transit visa *might*—and he did stress *might*—be issued within a week. I filled in three tortuous forms that asked, among other things, for my father's mother's maiden name in Farsi. The fate of my entire journey was now in the hands of Allah. As Allah and I weren't really on talking terms—I had inadvertently walked into a mosque with my shoes on in Indonesia a few years before—things didn't look good.

I returned to More Than Ways a little despondent, but was cheered a little to notice that the American who had spent the night screaming was gone. In his place was Hans, the German who had brought me to More Than Ways in the first place. Touting, it seems, was only part of his gig. He was also in Budapest to get his teeth done.

It has been my experience that there are basically two types of people who go to the trouble of getting their teeth done in a foreign country. One, nerdy types with pencils in their top pockets who have extensively researched where the best dentists are. And two, sad individuals who, through circumstances that may or may not have been of their own making, are down on their luck and looking for the most cost-effective way of getting a necessary job done. Hans immediately struck me as the latter. Not only was his clothing more dishevelled and battered than mine, he was staying at More Than Ways. That was a dead give-away of insolvency if ever there was one.

It was cheaper for Hans to get his teeth done in Budapest than pay the 20 per cent excess he'd have to paying using insurance in Germany. He was therefore quite a regular visitor to Budapest, and during those visits had discovered the best clubs, the cheapest restaurants and the most captivating entertainments. That night he was going to Tiloz az A!, a club in Pest just around the corner from the National Museum. He invited me to come along.

Budapest Week, the essential English guide to what is happening in Budapest described Tilos az A! as 'the long time hide-out of Budapest anarcho-alternativos'. It had poorly painted murals of Manhattan on three of its four walls, mix-and-match tables and chairs, and stoned couples sleeping in all the corners. It seemed the Budapest anarcho-alternativos had a lot in common with the inner-city youth of Australia. The place had the ambience of a student house in the grungier sections of Newtown, an inner Sydney suburb.

To the right of the bar, just past a table where the Hare Krishna were doling out lentil soup as part of a Hungarian recruitment drive, a winding staircase of huge flagstone steps led to an underground brick cavern. Here, just about every Hungarian under the age of 30 was moshing, sweating and throwing up to a very loud thrash metal band. Hans and I forced our way through the heaving mass of Magyar youth to the sound desk, where Hans pulled out a tape recorder and asked if he could plug it into the mixer. The sound engineer agreed as if it was the most natural thing in the world to do.

'Iz for ze friend back home,' he yelled into my ear. 'He'z got radio show.'

The band that night was the Budapest Drinking Club. They were good musicians, and played with the kind of intensity that suggested they had deep-rooted psychological problems. The crowd loved them, as did Hans who stayed around until after they finished to speak to them and to exchange business cards. He spent the trip back on the train to More Than Ways listening to the tape he had made on his Walkman.

The next day I decided to collect the other visas I needed. The most sensible and direct route for my journey would be to catch a train from Budapest straight through to Sofia in Bulgaria, passing through Serbia but not stopping. That way, all I would need would be a Bulgarian visa and a transit visa for Serbia. Both embassies were near More Than Ways; in fact, both were just around the corner from the Iranian embassy.

That was the sensible thing to do. That morning, however, with the sky a crisp blue and my ears still ringing from the Budapest Drinking Club, I decided that it would be a good idea to go for a little jaunt through the war-torn Balkans instead. Why catch a train straight through to Bulgaria when I could amble through Croatia, pop into Albania and then cross into Macedonia? (I posed this as a purely rhetorical question to myself. Had I asked my mother—or any sane person, for that matter—I'm sure she could have rattled off a million reasons why it was a foolhardy plan.) Nor would it affect my plan to follow the hippie trail east—with the hippies coming from all over Europe, the trail didn't really start until Istanbul. So on a bright and sunny morning I found myself in the Buda Hills, in a little white cottage that acted as the Croatian embassy.

Any doubts I may have had about going through Croatia were dispelled by the lovely girl I met on the sofa in the lounge room that doubled as the embassy's foyer. Her name was Emese and she had long hair, long legs and the sort of accent that mesmerises men and convinces them to invade neighbouring countries. She listened to my planned itinerary as if it was the most interesting thing she had ever heard.

'Ahhh, if only you were going in summer,' she purred. 'My family have a holiday home near Dubrovnik. I could have shown you around.'

Before I could change my plans I was called to the counter to collect my visa. It was valid for a month, starting there and then.

Securing an Albanian visa was next on my list. Even if for some reason I didn't get to Albania, it would be a handsome visa just to have in my passport. The embassy was back in Pest and had turrets and shutters behind twisted leafless trees, just like the haunted houses in a Scooby Doo cartoon. From a flagpole, an Albanian flag hung tattered and limp—looking very much like it had been there ever since it had been first hoisted, 50 years earlier. The lawn was unmown. The garden was untended. And the pictures in the display cases were faded. By the look of it, I suspected that the ambassador had invested all the maintenance funds in an Albanian pyramid scheme and was now begging on the streets. The only sign of life was a Hungarian couple humping on the lawn. Judging by the X-rated nature of their antics, they must have thought that the grounds gave them some sort of diplomatic immunity.

I lingered at the entrance of the embassy, hoping that a guard would come along and challenge my right to be there and, after a meaningful game of charades, point me in the direction of the visa section. As it was, I wasn't challenged until I reached the ambassador's bedroom, and then only by a terrified maid brandishing a toilet brush. Thank heavens I had my passport handy—I was able to wave it around frantically, pleading 'Visa! Visa! Visa!' before she could land any serious blows. She frogmarched me to an even more remote corner of the embassy, where the ambassador was sitting at a desk in the dark. He stamped my passport immediately, without question or cost, and the maid escorted me to the gate.

My visit to the Serbian embassy was disappointingly less eventful. My visa application was processed promptly and efficiently, and the only entertainment was provided by a Canadian waiting in the same line who insisted on telling his friend about his father's strange sexual predilections.

'He's got hundreds of dog collars,' he said quite loudly. 'But he hates dogs, if you know what I mean.'

Disturbingly, half the line nodded that they did.

Three days, and I had all my visas—bar my Iranian one—sorted.

>>>

One afternoon later in the week I arranged to meet Hans at a cafe he had found across the road from the National Opera House. At first glance, I had an uneasy feeling that I had come to the wrong place. It looked, well, classy. It was like the Viennese coffee houses you see in Nescafé ads—all gilt and mirrors and chandeliers with waitresses in long black skirts and frilly shirts. In the cafes I usually go to—especially back home in Sydney's Newtown—the waitresses wear a scowl and a nose ring and have a dog on a rope. I turned to leave, trying to get out before suffering the indignity of the management asking me to. Hans waved to me from a table near the back.

The cafe had, in fact, quite a mixed clientele—some looked even more undesirable and disreputable than Hans and myself. There were old people, young people, rich, chic, Rasta and scruffy. In many ways the cafe was a cross-section of Hungarian society. At one table, a group of old men, no doubt Party cadres in their younger days, sat talking about football and the weather. At another, an American woman who looked remarkably like Linda Evans sat telling a tortured hunched Hungarian who looked remarkably like Yanni that her Arts Council wouldn't be funding his latest play. At the table next to us, a young man sat alone, alternately scribbling in a journal and then cupping his chin in a thoughtful pose. For one horrible moment I thought Ivanhoe had left Prague for the more bohemian vibes in Hungary.

It was a table of little old grannies, however, that caught my attention. They crowded around a tiny table, chatting and laughing and having a right old gossip. With their wisteria-coloured hair, sensible cardigans and costume jewellery, they were just like the grannies back home. But unlike the ones back home, these grannies had endured a hell of a lot of suffering. Sure, Australian grannies may have lost the odd husband or son to the wars—I know my grandmother did. But the difference was that these women had also endured first-hand the death and destruction of World War II, and brutally repressive governments that followed. What struck me was that looking at them on that sunny afternoon in Budapest, eating their biscuits and sipping their coffee, you wouldn't know it.

When night fell, Hans and I jumped on the Metro to Tilos az A! and watched a Dutch band called The Legendary Pink Dots. They had none of the passion of the Budapest Drinking Club. In fact, the only legendary thing about them was how insipid they were. I returned to More Than Ways to find a drunken Swede in my bed clutching a yellow 10-litre plastic container half full of cheap red wine. I rolled him onto the floor as if it was something I did every night of my life, and realised that perhaps I'd been in More Than Ways longer than any sane human being should be.

And so the week passed.

CHAPTER FOUR

Budapest, too

Soundtrack: 'What is Love?'—Haddaway

After already spending a week longer than I had planned to in
Budapest, just to get an Iranian visa, I arrived at the Iranian embassy
on the day they nominated, only to be told that my visa wouldn't
be ready for yet another week. They said there was a computer
problem in Tehran. On the face of it, this seemed probable enough.
But having dealt with bureaucracy in Arabic countries before, I also
knew that they could be trying to tell me I had as much of a chance
of getting a visa to Iran as Salman Rushdie.

One thing was for certain, I couldn't stay in Budapest and wait.
I'd already been up to the Fisherman's Bastion five times, and being
chased by little old gypsies selling sprigs of lavender and embroidered handkerchiefs was beginning to lose its charm. I had been
out to Nepstadion, the decaying grey sporting stadium on the edge
of the city, just for something to do. I had visited the Museum of
Agriculture, just behind the pretty boating lake in Varosliget, despite

my guidebook's assertion that it would make 'vegetarians blanch and everybody else yawn'. Worst of all, the staff at the world's largest Burger King at Oktogon were beginning to correctly antic- ipate my order.

I know a week doesn't sound like a long time, but patience has never been one of my strong points. As I child, I'd spend December snooping around the house to find all my presents, rather than waiting for Santa to deliver them on Christmas Day. So when it got to the stage where I was just hanging around the Iranian embassy with puppy-dog eyes, hoping the Iranian consul would take pity on me, I knew it was time for me to go on a little jaunt through Hungary.

My first foray was to Moloko, a rustic village where ISBUSZ subsidised the locals to gad about in colourful traditional costumes. The locals obliged, but only when the big tour buses were in town. As soon as the tourists left, they were back in their polyester shirts and jeans watching television. The highlight of my visit was staying in a little hut, down by the river, where I could listen to the cricket on Radio Australia next to a crackling open fire.

Next, I visited Pecs, a larger (but still attractive) old town in the far south of Hungary. The main attractions in Pecs are the very ugly radio tower (with revolving restaurant) on a hill overlooking the town and a rather sad zoo, where the animals would have made Kate Moss look well fed. Another notable feature was the incredible number of bicycle locks—just bicycle locks, no bicycles—which festooned every bit of wrought iron fencing in town. The highlight of my visit to Pecs was watching *Schindler's List* at the local cinema. The locals got quite a chuckle from the scene where the Russian soldier rides up and announces that Jewish prisoners have been 'liberated' by the Soviet army.

Finally, I went to Eger, famous for the thick red Hungarian wine known throughout Europe as Bull's Blood. According to my guide- book, it was one of the most beguiling towns in Hungary, thanks to 'a thousand years of invasions and bacchanalian revelry'. More interestingly, it was also home to Szepasszonyvolgy, or the Valley of Beautiful Women, which, after watching giggling college girls at More Than Ways getting extremely drunk before catching the last train out before their Eurail pass expired, sounded very beguiling indeed.

The valley looked the goods. It was surrounded by hills covered in vines and dotted with vineyards. And at the bottom of the hills, right next to a huge car park, were the smoky bars, cellars and taverns the valley was famous for.

Wandering bands of gypsies, handsomely accessorised with silver loop earrings and battered violins, patrolled the car park. It was their job to serenade the day-trippers from Budapest and lure them into the particular bar/tavern/brothel they were touting for. One couple had barely brought their Skoda to a standstill before half a dozen gypsies set upon them, fiddling madly and waving a plastic bag full of unlabelled bottles of red wine in their general direction. The terrified couple locked their doors and waited, rigid with fear, until the gypsies went away.

I'm afraid that set the tone for my whole 'Valley of Beautiful Women' experience. Rather than being full of beautiful women as the name suggested—and I had foolishly believed—the valley was full of tough-looking gypsy women in dirty embroidered skirts and greasy lambskin vests. They stood outside each tiny smoky cellar and manhandled passers-by into their establishments. Once inside, these poor souls sat at rickety tables, drinking dregs, in fear of the aggressive gypsy fiddlers, too frightened to move and dreading what the whole terrifying experience was going to cost them. I considered myself lucky to get away with one overpriced bottle of red with a vintage of a few minutes before I bought it.

The next day I was back in Budapest, hanging around the gate of the Iranian embassy with puppy-dog eyes again and making an embarrassment of myself. Inexplicably, I had found myself back at

More Than Ways. I figured I was suffering a backpacker variation of the Stockholm Syndrome. Stockholm Syndrome was first observed after a hostage situation in 1973 where four Swedes who were held in a bank vault for six days during a robbery became emotionally attached to their captors. The theory is that people who are intimidated, controlled, or made to suffer, begin to love, admire, and even sometimes sexually desire their captors. I had certainly suffered, and while I didn't have any unnatural desires related to More Than Ways, I did find myself becoming emotionally attached to the place. Recognising this, the receptionist bestowed upon me the rare privilege of a room to myself.

A few days later, on the day my visa was supposed to be issued, the guy at the embassy told me that it still wasn't ready and to come again in one more week. It was starting to get beyond a joke, and I was almost tempted to tell the guy to tear up my application form and forget the whole thing. The trouble was, the Iranian visa was vital to my trip. Not only was Iran an integral part of the hippie trail, it was also the only viable land passage to the subcontinent. I decided to give it one more week. If the visa didn't come through, I'd cut my losses and apply again in Istanbul.

>>>

While I had been away gallivanting around the countryside, Hans had made friends with a Pakistani shopkeeper from Manchester called Raz. There are some people you meet while travelling that you are convinced are having you on, and Raz was one them. He was a wiry little fellow, with a beaky face and milk-bottle glasses, and wore brown slacks and a zip-up jacket with Mazda embroidered on the breast pocket. He smoked a pipe with a mouthpiece that had seen better days and had left his cosmetic store in Manchester—

'some hardware as well, but not a general store'—to go to Bosnia, find a Muslim girl and marry her.

'Maybe she is a refugee,' he said, drawing on his pipe through the piece of yellow biro he had repaired the mouthpiece with. 'Maybe her husband has been killed. Either way, she will be living in poverty. I will take her to Karachi and she will live like a princess!'

Raz wasn't staying at More Than Ways. He had sensibly taken up an offer from a little old landlady who approached him as he got off the train. Her apartment was over an hour from the centre of town, but she had bought him a three-day rail pass, a cup of coffee and lent him a thousand florin, and he'd been in debt to her ever since. She even gave him a list of places to go when he was lonely. His favourite was the Szechenyi thermal baths in Varosliget, near the Museum of Agriculture.

'The water comes up to your neck and Hungarians play chess there,' he explained. 'My landlady says that I may meet another lonely person and we can go somewhere else. But she warned me. Always wear your swimmers!'

Things had changed at Tiloz az A! too. The one place that had (so far!) kept me sane during my extended sojourn in Budapest had been taken over by adolescent Italian girls.

There were at least thirty of them, all about 15 years old, dressed in skin-tight jeans, with tiny breasts squashed flat in lycra tops. They spent their time commandeering the small stage and bullying the DJ into playing one of their Euro-House tapes. He valiantly resisted but, like their breasts under the skin-tight lycra, he was eventually overwhelmed. Soon all the girls were squealing and dancing to the latest Euro-cheese from Real McCoy and Haddaway.

One of the songs had a distinctive Latin flavour and soon the girls were clapping and dancing like Flamenco dancers. They arched their arms above their heads in unison, clicking their fingers and yelping. Meanwhile, one girl sat on the edge of the stage, flicking her lustrous long hair from side to side and drinking beer straight from a bottle. She stared disdainfully at the old regulars sitting at their tables, who in turn stared back, a little shellshocked by what was happening to their club.

During a brief moment of silence, when the tape of Euro-House music was turned over under the threat of facial lacerations by long, red, Italian fingernails, I told Raz that I was planning to head south to Croatia and on to Albania. He suggested that I could go with him to a refugee camp in the south of Hungary.

'Maybe you can find a domestic girl too!' he said excitedly.

I pointed to the young Italian girls and suggested that perhaps he try his luck there.

'Slappers!' he exclaimed, turning up his nose.

We met up with Raz again a couple of mornings later for breakfast at the Cukraszda Espresso cafe. This had become a bit of ritual in the week after I got back from my jaunt through Hungary. Hans would come and knock on my door at about eight. We'd catch the Metro to Opera. We'd grab a table up the back—it gave us the best view of the assorted bits of humanity that began their day there— and ordered our coffee and croissants. About the time our coffees arrived, Raz would stroll in, wearing his blue Mazda jacket and sucking on his pipe. This particular morning, Raz was excited by a brochure he had been handed as he walked along the pedestrianised section of Vaci ut, the main shopping mall in central Budapest.

'It's an erotic club!' enthused Raz. 'They will pick you up, let you in the door and drop you home again for free!'

He pushed aside the coffee and croissants and laid the brochure on the table before us.

'Look!' he said thrusting his finger into the breasts of a spectacularly well-endowed dancer, 'the girls are very beautiful!'

He was right. They were very beautiful. But they weren't the dancers from the club. The *Playboy* logo and the page number at the bottom seemed to suggest that they had been lifted from a girlie magazine. Raz ignored my scepticism and concentrated his efforts on Hans.

Hans surprised me by agreeing to go along. I declined, and was a little upset that they didn't try to talk me into it. I was also a little miffed when they weren't particularly interested in visiting the sculpture park I had just read about in the latest issue of *Budapest Week*.

'Who needs sculptures when we'll have the real thing!' yelped Raz, unaware that the sculpture park had been set up to house old Soviet propaganda and not the Budapest government's private collection of erotic art. Unless I could convince Raz that he'd get some sort of illicit thrill, I knew I was fighting a losing battle.

The sculpture park was in an outlying suburb with the rather sinister sounding name of Sector 50, and had just been reopened for spring. The park had the distinction of being the world's first Communist memorial park and was the final resting place for the Soviet-era sculptures and memorials that used to adorn the streets of Budapest. Basically, tonnes of cast bronze that would have otherwise been sold as a job lot to Copperart and made into crappy brass towel rails.

Although it was officially spring, it was spring in name only that day. The sky was grey, a little drizzle fell and it was bitterly, bitterly cold. Even wrapped in every piece of clothing I owned, the cold seeped in. I passed through the grand red-brick entrance, under the watchful gaze of Lenin on the left and a cubist sculpture to the right, and looked for somewhere to huddle. The ticket office looked inviting, but the ticket seller was having none of it. In one swift motion he slid the window open, took my money, and slid the window closed again. Just as quickly, he wheeled his chair back to an electric heater.

Being a sculpture park, the pieces were left to the elements, pretty much as they were during the Communist regime. They were scattered across a couple of hectares of lawn, placed periodically along

a white central path and the six circular paths that came off it. There
were bronze boys waving flags. Metal people were punching the
air defiantly. And there were more metalworkers than you could
poke a stick at. All of them bore slogans and captions in chunky,
metallic letters in that solid, brutal typeface that the Soviets were
so fond of.

The best piece, and the most famous, was a huge bronze man
running, a coat draped over one arm and a flag held high in the
other. It was at least 10 or 12 metres tall and had previously stood
outside the Parliament buildings. Even from the back of the park it
dominated everything else around it. It has become a popular prop
for advertising shoots and PR photos for rock bands and it's easy
to see why. It had a poetry and spirit that was undeniable.

I wandered back to the entrance, pleased that the Hungarians had
the good sense to keep this stuff—not just as a reminder of what
they had suffered, but because it perfectly captured the mood and
spirit of a certain time in history. I was also thankful they had
equipped the park with clean, well-appointed toilets. I spent an hour
or so warming my hands—OK, my entire body—under the electric
hand-dryers.

In keeping with the Sovietness of my day, I decided to drop in
to Marxims, a sort of theme restaurant decorated in Soviet propaganda. I'd read about the place in *Budapest Week* as well, but in
the court reports rather than the restaurant reviews. The restaurant
had been in the courts—not because of low hygiene standards,
which were criminal throughout the city—but because its critics
said it was exhibiting symbols of tyranny. Apparently, in Hungary
it is against the law to go putting up the symbols of oppression—
whether they be swastikas, hammers and sickles, red stars or the
logo of the Australian Tax Department—and from all accounts,
Marxims was bathed in them.

The owner's defence—in the end a successful one—was that the
decor was ironic and in no way served propaganda purposes. I must

admit, the restaurant's setting was eminently ironic. After running the gauntlet of gnarled old cronies selling shirts, shawls and screw-drivers, I found myself wandering up a cobbled lane in the shadow of a Soviet-style factory and beside empty railway carriages shunted against concrete walls topped with barbed wire. Marxims was directly opposite the padlocked and chained factory gates, and was marked only by a red star and an illuminated advertisement for Stella Artois.

Inside, the place was bustling. The owner stood behind the bar grinning, taking drink orders and pointing newly arrived diners towards the grey and red booths that lined each wall. The booths all had their very own Soviet propaganda posters and were sepa-rated from each other by chicken wire and a loop of barbed wire. Mine had a poster proclaiming the joys of joining the Soviet navy. The lucky souls who got one of the booths lining the wall which looked up to the street got another special treat—grimy, barred windows with dismembered hands grabbing at the bars as if they were in a prison.

The menu was suitably ironic too. Each pizza was named after famous Soviet leaders and institutions. You could order a Lenin with mushrooms (because he was always kept in the dark), or an Anarchismo with mussels (because of the havoc they wreaked on your system). There was the Bolshoi with chicken and, my favour-ite, the ham and pineapple Gulag pizza, a Hawaiian pizza anywhere else in the world. In the end I ordered a Stalin, where the ham, cheese and mushrooms rather appropriately swam in a watery red sauce that looked suspiciously like blood.

It wasn't the best dining experience I'd ever had, but Marxims was certainly a lot of fun. The little white doves of peace, tangled and bleeding in the barbed wire above each booth, were a nice touch, as were the Communist banners and flags from all over the globe that hung from the ceiling. Most of the diners were locals who seemed to be thoroughly enjoying the experience, posing for photos in front of the two mannequins dressed as Russian guards. I remember thinking that they should enjoy it while they could. Soon the place would be full of every American college kid this side of Iowa, drinking Budweiser and insisting the owner play Steely Dan over the sound system.

From Marxims I rather imaginatively made my way to Tiloz az A! where, as fate would have it, it was an anti-fascist night. For those of you not altogether familiar with what constitutes an anti-fascist night in a former Eastern Bloc country, it goes a little like this. A group of students takes over a club, turns down the lights and huddles around an old 16 millimetre projector, laughing at grainy black and white propaganda films of balaclava-clad revolutionaries preaching worldwide liberation. Right up the front, chuckling hardest at the freedom fighters, was Hans.

'I thought you were going to the strip club,' I hissed at him, trying not to disturb those around us as I pulled up a chair in the half-light of the projector.

'I vaz. Ve did. Zey kicked us out.'

'And Raz?'

'He lost all his money buying drinks for prostitutes. He's gone back to the apartment to ask his landlady to lend him ze money to get back to England.'

I was sad for Raz, but I was also relieved. I hadn't been looking forward to him tagging along, dragging me along to every refugee camp between Budapest and Sarajevo. Now, the Iranian embassy willing, I would be able to continue my journey unhindered.

>>>

The day on which the Iranians had promised me my visa would be absolutely, definitely, no-doubts-about-it ready dawned rainy and cold. I hadn't slept well, partly because I was worried about whether or not my visa would come through, but mainly because an alarm had blared through the night from a burgled shop in the subway across the street. I staggered bleary-eyed to the Iranian embassy and found the gate chained and padlocked. I stood there, not altogether sure whether I should cry or throw rocks through their windows.

A few minutes before nine the embassy's guard arrived and took up his position in the dog box. He nodded—after my endless visits he probably counted me amongst his dearest friends—and offered me a hot cup of coffee from the thermos he kept on a shelf. Just after 9 am he unlocked the gate and accompanied me to the door of the visa section.

The office was still and quiet. The only indication of life beyond the sliding glass window was a distant rustle of paper and the creak of a floorboard. Finally, the man I had been dealing with strolled past the window. When he noticed me, he jumped with fright. I waved and smiled, and he waved back before disappearing. His smile had been weak and forced, and it worried me.

Fifteen minutes later he returned to the window and called me over. He pointed to the little red squiggles that indicated Iranian public holidays on his Arabic calendar.

'This,' he said, tracing a line of public holidays that went on unbroken for the past week or so. 'This has been your misfortune. Give me your passport and come back tomorrow.'

'Can I book my train?' I asked, a little unsure of whether this meant that my visa had come through or if it meant it would be ready the next day.

'Book your train, my friend!' he said with a grin, shaking my hand vigorously.

My Iranian visa was in the bag! I could finally leave More Than Ways and get on with my journey.

I'm not ashamed to say that it was one of the happiest moments of my life.

CHAPTER FIVE

Croatia

Soundtrack: 'Everybody Hurts'—REM

The morning I finally left Budapest, there was a spring in my step and in the weather's too. The sky was blue. Leaves were budding and flowers were beginning to bloom. It was as if the weather knew what I had been through and decided to join in the celebration. Of course, the weather had probably been good for weeks and I was only noticing it now because I wasn't walking around scowling, kicking over garbage cans and cursing the Ayatollah and all his kin. But hey, I had my Iranian visa. Spring was in the air. I felt great.

The people on my train were happy too. The train ran south alongside Lake Balaton, a huge expanse of milky blue popular with holidaying Hungarians and Germans. They were families, mainly, loaded up with fishing lines and hampers and rucksacks and whatever else it is that Hungarians take away when they go to the lake. They laughed and chatted and snacked on doorstep-sized sandwiches filled with dodgy-looking smallgoods. As we barrelled along beside the lake, they pointed animatedly at conifers and ducks and men wearing funny plastic wading pants.

All the families got off at Siofok, a small town only an hour or two south of Budapest. As they got off they gave me half-quizzical glances, wondering, no doubt, why I was staying on the train. Some gestured towards the platform and said 'Siofok', thinking that perhaps I hadn't realised that I'd reached my destination. When I answered 'Zagreb', alarm swept across their faces and they hurried off, shielding their children from me as if my madness was contagious.

From Siofok, the train continued along the lake, still dotted with holiday homes and camping grounds and cafes and souvenir shops. But the further south we went, the more they were shuttered and abandoned, either waiting for summer to come or the war in Yugo-slavia to end. By the time the train reached Balatonille, the mood was distinctly eerie and unnerving. Now I felt like I was in one of those really bad seventies cop shows where the final showdown happens in an abandoned amusement park. The kind of place where our hero, all polyester flares and mutton-chop sideburns, stalks through the ghost train, only to be distracted by the squeaking door banging in the wind. Here it was the train conductor slamming the toilet door. And instead of hearing the final gasps of a dying crim-inal, what I heard was the sound of the last moments of a partic-ularly troublesome stroganoff.

At the border, a succession of grey-uniformed people from both Hungary and Croatia got onto the train with the sole purpose of staring at my passport. They only ever looked at one page, and with an intensity that suggested that they were trying to turn the pages with the power of their minds alone. Exhausted, and seemingly defeated, they handed my passport back gruffly and got off the train. I amused myself through these lengthy psychic sessions by saying things like, 'I think you'll find my papers are in order, officer' and 'I'm here on business'.

Sometime during this process—and somewhere in the middle of a shunting yard—the train finally crossed into Croatia. It wasn't immediately apparent that I had entered a war zone. The border close to Hungary was relatively untouched by the war and didn't look any worse than some of more seedy parts of Budapest (or even More Than Ways, for that matter). But by the time the train reached the first station in Croatia, it did. Standing at other platforms were two trains. One was full of tired, hard-looking soldiers in battle fatigues. The other was loaded with shiny brand new cars.

I must admit, I did get a funny little feeling inside when it finally dawned on me that I had crossed into Croatia. For the first time on my trip I felt as if I was doing something adventurous. I was actually travelling in a country at war. I was doing something out of the ordinary. I made a mental note to call my Mum and tell her I was still in Hungary.

I sat congratulating myself on my daring and courage for a while, staring out the window with the kind of expression I imagine battle-weary foreign correspondents wear. You know, cool, detached, and with a slightly knitted brow that says, 'The horror, the horror'. Just as I was perfecting my Pulitzer Prize-winning pose—as described above but with the hand thoughtfully stroking the chin—the only other foreigner on the train burst into my carriage.

Now you might be thinking that 'burst' is a little too strong a word to use. After all, most people simply enter railway compartments, tentatively poking their heads in to see if there is a seat available. The more self-assured might stride in, confident that there is a seat available and, if not, in their ability to nonchalantly turn and leave. It is, I agree, very rare for someone to just burst in. But that's what Brad did. Burst. And with a rather large collection of plastic bags in tow.

Brad was an American and, to be quite frank, he was a pervert. Even before he started telling me stories about his weird sexual tastes, which he did almost immediately, there was something about his general demeanour that screamed, 'I'm sleazy, I'm greasy and I'm as horny as all hell'. In fact, within seconds of meeting him I would have bet money that somewhere in his collection of plastic bags, amongst the plates, the jars, the serviettes from McDonald's and the unwashed undies, was an inflatable doll and a collection of magazines displaying unnatural intimacies between man and beast.

Brad was heading south to broker an international arms deal that would make him enough money to pursue his other dream, starting an import-export business out of Albania. He would have secured the deal sooner if not for the little matter of being thrown into jail for six weeks in Prague for rubbing the breasts of 16-year-old school girls.

He had other equally salacious tales. Like the time he tag-teamed an ancient prostitute with a convicted murderer in a hostel in Skopje, or his kinky relationship with the 17-year-old virgin living with nuns in Romania. But none of them really sums up the person that was—and is—Brad as well as the one about the school girls.

Down on his luck in the Czech Republic—he was robbed whilst getting a blow-job in a laneway in Prague—Brad took up a teaching position in a girls' school. Some of his students complained that he rubbed their breasts while explaining the finer points of past participles. An unsympathetic judge didn't believe his defence that he was only massaging their shoulders (I must admit, I didn't either) and threw him into jail for six weeks. It was the worst six weeks of his life. He was spat on and beaten up. It was only by singing 'Everybody Hurts' by REM very loudly to himself that was he able to get through the ordeal. After telling me the story, he rifled through his plastic bags and proudly produced clippings on the trial that appeared in each of the English-language newspapers in Prague.

I don't know why Brad felt he had to tell me this story within minutes of meeting me. Perhaps he felt slighted that I was unaware of his minor celebrity status in the Czech Republic and that I hadn't recognised his photo from the paper or from the CNN report or something. Or maybe he wanted me to know that underneath that skinny bespectacled exterior beat the heart of a rampant love god. Whatever his reasons, I wish he hadn't.

I also wish he hadn't decided to spend the rest of the train journey to Zagreb telling me about a relationship dilemma he was facing. I didn't know whether he should choose the 17-year-old virgin in Romania or the 35-year-old slapper from Slovenia. Nor did I particularly want to know about the uniquely amazing sexual abilities each possessed and how difficult that made the decision. I just wanted him to shut up. I spent the remainder of the journey nodding and saying, 'Hmmm. That's a tough one', while secretly plotting ways of giving him the slip at Zagreb Station.

As it was, I planned in vain. He clung too close to my side to allow me to wander off into the Zagreb afternoon alone. And besides, I figured he might yet prove useful in helping me get a room. A Swedish guy staying at More Than Ways had claimed it was impossible to find accommodation in Zagreb because the hotels and hostels and pensions were full of UN staff and journalists reporting on the war. According to the Swede, I would probably end up sleeping on the streets or returning to Budapest.

As it turned out, Brad had a foolproof way of finding accommodation in a strange city. It entailed picking out the most attractive woman at the railway station of the said city, bowling up to her and asking to spend the night in her apartment. All in English. Of course it was a totally flexible plan. If you've just met someone on the train, you ask if it's all right if they come along too. That's how we ended up spending the night with Martina.

Martina was from Bratislava and worked in Zagreb as a stringer for the *Washington Post*. She was organising a ticket to Budapest to sit an English exam with the British Council and then hoped to get a work permit for the UK. She had a cute brown bob, a winsome smile and an accent that made you want to rush off to a chapel and marry her immediately. She was also surprisingly amenable to the idea of two smelly backpackers, one of whom was seriously and certifiably deranged, staying in her apartment.

Out on the street that ran beside the railway station I was surprised by how European Zagreb looked. I guess I had expected Croatia—in fact all of the former Yugoslavia—to be a little more primitive and chaotic. But here, just outside the railway station, was a stately park surrounded by stately buildings and dotted with ageing bronze statues of generals riding horses that wouldn't have looked out of place in London, Vienna or Paris. Travel is always surprising me like that; it can shatter my ignorant generalisations as well as confirm them.

Martina's apartment was deep in the suburbs, a long ride in one of the ancient yellow trams that trundled by the front of the station. Brad spent the entire journey trying to seduce her, while she sweetly ignored his advances by showing us the various points of interest along the way. We alighted amongst a cluster of identical tower blocks that looked as dishevelled and sleazy as Brad. The only difference was that the doors were a little less unhinged.

As soon as we got into the apartment, I started feeling a little protective towards Martina. The apartment was like her—clean and neat and homely. I was afraid she hadn't noticed Brad's lascivious manner and would be unsuspectingly pinned against the stove as she attempted to make us a cup of tea. When he started massaging her shoulders for no apparent reason, I felt compelled to cross my arms over my chest and mouth, silently, 'Cover your chest!' I immediately blushed, thinking she would misconstrue my concern as some kind of kinky come-on, but she just smiled and did as I suggested with the kind of look that said, 'I'm already one step ahead'. She deftly broke away from Brad's clutches and left to file a story at the InterContinental Hotel, where the UN and all the major news agencies hung out.

The next day Brad inexplicably headed off for Ljubljana—tellingly, in the opposite direction from Albania—and I explored

Zagreb alone. I traipsed through the town centre, admired the freshly gilded angels out the front of St Stephen's Cathedral and, after an unsatisfying lunch of greasy dumplings, wound my way along the tiny cobbled streets of the upper town to Gradec and the famous St Mark's Church. St Mark's is famous for the hand-painted tiles on the roof that form a rather elaborate coat of arms. They were indeed quite impressive, but the ambience was somewhat spoiled by two guys trying to convince me to head up the Australian side of an airline they were trying to get off the ground—ha, ha. I know it sounds tempting, especially when you consider that I was heading home to absolutely no prospects and a severely depleted bank account, but really, you have to question the business acumen of two guys who approach someone wearing tattered jeans and a beat up suede jacket and ask him to take on the likes of Qantas and BA.

I escaped from their plaintive offers of percentage points and limited liability in the case of a major air disaster, and headed off to the Lotrescak Tower nearby to get a little bit of elevation and hence get a better look at the tiles. To the right of the cathedral I spied a column of thick black smoke rising on the horizon. Once again I was reminded that the war wasn't far away. I found out that a munitions dump had caught fire the night before, and I also heard that a UN plane had been shot down over Bosnia. I probably should have turned around then, headed back to Budapest and taken the easy way to Turkey through Bulgaria. But instead, I spent another night in Martina's apartment—she had trustingly left me the spare key while she was in Budapest sitting the exam—then caught a bus to Split.

Getting to Split from Zagreb before the war was easy. You'd leave town on Branimirova, get onto the E59 expressway and, if there weren't too many German tourists swaying absent-mindedly from one lane to another in their overloaded BMWs and Mercedes, you'd be pulling up beside the Adriatic about three hours later.

Unfortunately, the war had turned the freeway into a war zone, and the journey down to the coast, staying entirely within Croatian territory, now took on the characteristics of an overlong and complicated car rally.

Almost immediately after leaving Zagreb, the bus turned up tiny mountain lanes, perversely ignoring signs that pointed down immaculately paved multi-lane freeways with signs that said things like, 'Stay right unless overtaking' and, alluringly, 'Split: 250 kilometres'. The lanes we were forced to take, on the other hand, were narrow and corrugated. The bus spent most of the time pulling to the side of the road, usually where the road was most precarious and the cliffs most steep, to let other vehicles pass. I was a little annoyed that our bus driver seemed to give way to every other vehicle on the road. It had been my experience that bus drivers use the bulk of their vehicles—and their often misguided confidence in their own driving skills—to bully everything else on the road into lay-bys and ravines. But as most of the other vehicles were armoured cars or troop carriers, I soon understood his reluctance.

Though long, the bus journey was incredibly engaging. The hills were dotted with goats and roughly built stone cottages and sturdy-looking women wearing heavy ankle-length skirts and scarves on their heads. Occasionally we plunged down beside ravines to discover hidden valleys or rushing streams and young boys with nothing better to do than throw rocks at passing buses. And, to the eternal credit of the Croatian army, they had gone to a lot of trouble to conceal each of the artillery points that dotted nearly every high point and hillock that overlooked these spectacular passes and had helped them blend in with the scenery.

The closer we got to the coast, however, the harder it became to hide the effects of war. Just about every house we passed had a broken window, a hole in the roof or a wall hen-pecked by machine-gun fire. In Maslenica, a stone-walled village with cobbled streets, every house had suffered all three. It had just been recaptured by the Croatians for the fifth time, and lay abandoned and empty, except for the occasional Croatian army patrol. Maslenica's misfortune was its proximity to Maslenica Bridge and a river that had been the source of its previous prosperity. As the bus crawled down the winding road through the town, grinding down through the gears and giving me ample opportunity to view the destruction up close, I found myself with my face pressed against the window muttering 'Fuck!' repeatedly. The other passengers simply continued to read their newspapers and sports magazines or catch up on a bit of sleep.

The bridge had been destroyed early in the war, so the bus was forced to sheepishly make its way across a pontoon bridge hastily thrown together out of tyres and forty-four gallon drums. The original bridge lay to the right, broken and half submerged, the approaches on either side leading to nothing more than a twisted mess of concrete and metal reinforcement. The whole scene looked like something out of one of those seventies disaster movies like *Earthquake* and I half expected Charlton Heston or Ernest Borgnine to pop out ahead and motion our bus to safety. They didn't. With a teeth-grinding crunch down to first, the bus simply crawled up a newly constructed incline and onto the road that had led to the original bridge. Within an hour we hit the Adriatic coast. Two hours after that, we were in Split.

The first thing that struck me about Split was the smell of salt air. It was the first time I'd got a whiff of the ocean since Dover, and it stirred something in me. Maybe it's because I'm a Cancerian, but to me the smell of brine and rotting fish is the smell of travel. It hints at adventure and at hidden vistas just over the horizon. Invigorated—and a little heady—I took the first offer of accommodation that came my way; a room in a house nearby for only three dollars a night, offered to me by an old guy wearing a grey pork pie hat.

After settling into my room, and noticing with alarm that the lumpy mattress was so soft that it nearly swallowed my pack whole,

I ventured onto the streets and noted that the other distinguishable feature about Split was a heavy UN presence. In Zagreb I had seen a few cars and soldiers. But here, every second car on the road was a white Land Rover Defender, and you couldn't walk along the streets without stumbling upon some fresh-faced Scandinavian wearing a poncy blue beret and eating an ice cream. It only took one visit to the bank for me to wish I was with the UN too. They had special queues that were marked by signs that said UNPRO-FOR, UNCOR, POMOC, UNHCR and half a dozen other acronyms like UNWANK. When I tried to join one, I was pointed towards a line of Croatians who, with their goats and chickens in tow, were still working on a barter system.

The bars and cafes were the same, especially down by the harbour. The promenade was a classic Kodak moment, especially at dusk when couples strolled arm in arm along the palm-lined marina. I sat at one of the tables that lined the promenade, soaking up the ambience, but the mood was spoiled by the UN soldiers nearby getting loudly drunk. I was obviously 'not one of them', and was treated accordingly by both the soldiers and the staff. When the waiter ignored me for the third time, choosing instead to serve a trestle-load of soldiers shamelessly waving about deutschmarks, I decided to spend the night annoying a gaggle of Canadians on the table next to me by asking them what part of the States they were from. When I tired of that, I went to a cheap cafeteria called the Bastion and ate tasteless gruel amongst people who talked to themselves and started fights with imaginary foes. There I composed a list of five things to do in Split on a slow Saturday night:

> Let the tyres down on the UN Land Rover
  Defenders and yell, 'The Serbs are coming! The
  Serbs are coming!'
> Spread a rumour that the UN has gone bankrupt

and that their cheques are not worth the paper they are printed on.

> Remark loudly that the war is over and they are all being posted back to Somalia.

> Report that as part of a cost-cutting measure, UN soldiers will now be paid in Albanian lek.

> Walk into the Bastion and say, 'The Serbs put on a better spread than this'.

There was one good thing about the UN presence, though. Down at the markets, amongst the forty-four gallon drums of sauerkraut, there were still a few stalls selling crappy souvenirs, a good many of them made out of shells. They bore tags that said 'Split, Yugoslavia' but with the 'Yugoslavia' part crudely scratched off. They had a host of other tasteless items as well, so I was able to haggle over a rather sad-looking snow dome, featuring two of Split's famous marlin gambolling on a seesaw. They also had postcards, but only ever a choice of two—one with Kylie Minogue and the other, the most common, a card that inexplicably featured a man leading a donkey. Make of that what you will.

Of course, Split is most famous for the ruins of Diocletian's palace that front the harbour. It was built from AD 295 to 305 to serve as the Emperor Diocletian's retirement palace and was one of the most impressive buildings of the Roman Empire. It was lined with marble imported from Italy and rose over three storeys high. Now it is but a shadow of its former self, a labyrinth of tiny alleyways full of shops and stalls. In its darkest corners it stinks of urine and harbours nests made from cardboard boxes and tattered clothing. The walls are covered in graffiti, some political but mostly stuff that proclaims the meaning of life like 'Sex! Deutschmarks! Beer!'

I bought a phrasebook—still titled a 'Serbo–Croatian' primer—from a small bookstall in the heart of the ruins. It was as if the language hadn't been ethnically cleansed yet. I don't know why I bother buying phrasebooks. My language prowess is such that whenever I try to speak a foreign language, people beg me to speak English, even if they don't understand it. My friend Sean, who I've travelled with extensively, and who has a natural ability with languages and the young women who use them, has rather unkindly christened me the 'Enemy of the Dialects'.

I purchased the phrasebook hoping it would help me with my rather audacious plan to travel south through Croatia along the Adriatic coast, cross into Serbia and then into Albania. With the war and all, I didn't know if it was possible, and needed information from the locals. Hence the phrasebook. Emese, the Croatian girl I'd met in Budapest, had assured me that I wouldn't have any problems, but now, well away from the spell of her undeniable charms, I began to doubt her words. I spent an afternoon poring over an old map of Yugoslavia with my landlord, trying to get an answer from him. But the only result of this was that the two of us drank a lot of cheap wine from old mineral water bottles, nodding at each other inanely, and came to the conclusion that the Serbs were bastards.

My visit to see the British consul (honorary) was equally fruitless. Captain Aleksij Mekjavic had a penchant for navy blue double-breasted suits with gold anchor buttons, and looked like a cross between Aristotle Onassis and Anthony Quinn. After giving me a rather cursory summation of the border situation—'not good, there is much tension'—he suggested I catch the boat to Albania. In the end I chose to ignore everyone's advice and catch a bus the next day to Dubrovnik, only 12 kilometres from the Croatian–Bosnian border, and take it from there.

The bus headed south past the airport and once again the UN was everywhere. Most of the vehicles in the car park were white UN staff cars, and on the tarmac a huge Hercules taxied beside mountains of aid—white bags of flour and grain stacked on pallets and covered in webbing. Soon we were winding our way along olive green bluffs overlooking startlingly blue water, and passing roadside signs that said, in English, 'Do the Right Thing. Holiday in Croatia'. We briefly passed through the small portion of coastline belonging to Bosnia, the borders marked by caravans, two kilometres apart, and reached Dubrovnik by mid afternoon.

Despite having had the crap bombed out of it, Dubrovnik was undeniably, unashamedly beautiful. The old walled city, Stari Grad, jutted out into the Adriatic, a medieval star in a pool of mystic blue. In fact, if no one had told me, I probably wouldn't have realised that the place had been shelled at all. Considering the age of the city, the holes in some of the red terracotta roofs seemed natural consequences of the wear and tear of nearly ten centuries.

Sure, there was also a lot of scaffolding, but anyone who has visited any of the great cities of Europe, particularly Italian ones like Venice and Florence, comes to expect a bit of scaffolding— especially over the most famous buildings and especially during peak tourist times. In fact, there was a time I was convinced that the city fathers of Venice kept St Mark's under scaffolding in a deliberate ploy to get tourists back to Venice when their natural inclination after being ripped off unnaturally for a single slice of pizza was to never visit again. So, really, the small mortar-shell craters on the marble slabs of the walled city's great walkway were the only signs of the war that were difficult to explain away.

Well, that and the total absence of German tourists. And, I guess, the fact that I could get a room within Stari Grad for only $4 a night. Sure, I had to put up with an overwhelming smell of mothballs. And sure, I had to ward off the unwanted advances of the landlady's rather insistent daughter. (Her boyfriend had been killed in the war and she was looking for a ticket out. She would have tried it on with Sir Les Patterson if for some inexplicable reason he had been spending the night in Dubrovnik.) But there was a time, not so long ago, before the war, when tourists were thick on the ground, when I would have been the one offering sexual favours just to get a room within 20 kilometres of Dubrovnik. So I put up with both mother and daughter with what I considered to be good grace and humour.

Stari Grad was similarly deserted when I went for a walk around the famous old city walls. The woman at the tourist information centre had told me that it would cost me two dollars, but when I got to the entrance the ticket booth was empty and the gate had been thoughtfully left open. I wandered two and a half kilometres around the wall, soaking up the atmosphere with nought to distract me but the cry of the occasional gull. I got nearly all the way around without seeing a single living soul. I say nearly, because just before completing the entire circuit, I startled a young girl looking out from one of the bastions onto waves crashing against rocks below.

She was in her early twenties and, although she was wearing thick stockings and thick glasses, there was something quite enticing about the way she turned and smiled at me. Now I should point out that picking up signals or reading body language is not one of my strong points. I spent most of my adolescence pining after girls I thought were not interested in me, only to find out years later— invariably just as they were about to get married—that they had been desperate for it and had supposedly been making the fact quite clear to me. But there was something about this girl that compelled me to actually say hello to her. It wasn't like she draped herself over the railing, hitched up her skirt and said 'Come and get it, big boy' either, although similar tactics have gone right over my head before. It must have been that she just looked friendly.

And she was. Her name was Natasha and she was a university student from Zagreb. She could speak English perfectly and was in Dubrovnik with her history lecturer and other students to attend lectures celebrating 900 years of Croatian history. She was just about to go on a tour of the Franciscan monastery and asked me to come along.

'I'll have to translate for you,' she said, 'It's usually closed to

the public. You'll be the only tourist in town to have seen it.' I
nearly replied that I was the only tourist in town, full stop, but
decided that that would make me seem ungrateful.

The monastery was close to where I had started my walk around
the city walls. It had been badly damaged during the war and its
entrance was heavily scaffolded. A group of people stood waiting
outside. They were the other students and Natasha introduced me
to them rather self-consciously. Most smiled and gave her the kind
of look that said, 'Natasha, we didn't know you had it in you!', but
one guy, Goran, appeared a little surly.

'Don't worry about him,' Natasha whispered conspiratorially,
'He's my boyfriend's best friend.'

'Well that's all right then,' I replied. I was going to say that I
thought he thought I was a Serb, but in a rare moment of diplomatic
aplomb, I decided not to. Instead, I noted with interest that my good
friend Sean's world view was once again right. Through years of
careful study and analysis he has concluded that all the nice girls
have boyfriends.

The monastery was amazing. Built in the early years of the
middle ages, it housed the third-oldest apothecary in Europe and,
appropriately, it was used by the Red Cross to store supplies during
the recent war. The apothecary survived the war relatively
unscathed, but the same could not be said of the library on the
upper levels of the monastery. It had been hit pretty badly, a mortar
tearing a huge hole in the roof. The hole was still covered with a
tarpaulin, and all the books, many of them priceless medieval manu-
scripts, had been put in boxes and stacked in the dining room.
Actually, the dining room was a bit of an all-purpose storeroom.
The main dining table had a life-sized carving of Christ on the cross
lying on it, forcing the monks to eat their bowls of gruel from
between the legs and under the armpits of their Lord and Saviour.

After the monastery tour, Natasha and her friends were going to
a lecture in the old cinema. She offered to translate again, but not

being a big fan of the works of Ivan Guudulie, a baroque Croatian poet, I decided to give it a miss. Instead, I agreed to meet up with them later that night in a small jazz club just outside the city walls. When Natasha kissed me goodbye I made sure it was on the cheek and that Goran didn't see.

I spent the rest of the afternoon walking around Dubrovnik startling myself with the sound of my own footfall. Before the war, Dubrovnik was one of the great tourist cities of Europe, vying with Venice and Florence for the title of most overcrowded, expensive and unpleasant tourist experience in Europe. Every summer it was full to bursting point with stout Germans in Bermuda shorts and similarly large Americans with zoom lenses as big as their voices. Now it felt like a ghost town. All the squares and plazas were deserted. Even the cafes, with their tables and chairs set invitingly out in the warm spring sun, were empty. At one, a waiter with clearly nothing better to do, sat at a table strumming a guitar and mournfully singing 'Under the Bridge' (by the Red Hot Chilli Peppers). I loved it.

I also loved the jazz club. It was small and smoky, and the walls were lined with old black and white photos of the people who had performed there over the last 50 years. The men in the photos all wore dark suits and thin black ties, the women slinky evening gowns. They were the Croatian equivalent of Dean Martin and Frank Sinatra and Ella Fitzgerald, and had obviously taken their cues from their American heroes. It showed in the clothes they wore, the poses they struck and even in the way they smoked their cigars. But where the clubs in the US had been bulldozed to make way for strip malls and Burger Kings, here, in the middle of a country at war, the spirit of the fifties lived on. I felt almost Bohemian.

Natasha and her friends certainly were. As a small ensemble belted out suitably jazzy and heartfelt numbers like 'Fever' and 'Let's Fall in Love' from the tiny stage, they spoke about politics with the kind of passion that only sport gets in Australia.

'When the war first started, we could not believe it would last long—one week, one month, one year,' Natasha told me as all her friends nodded in unison. 'Now I cannot see an end.' Elsewhere, her lecturer was deep in an animated discussion with the owner of the club about the evils of television.

To be honest, I was at a bit of a loss as to what to say. I didn't know much about the situation in the former Yugoslavia. And politics was not one of my strong points. But I knew there was only so long I could get away with just nodding my head, knitting my brows and scratching my chin thoughtfully before Natasha and her friends realised I was just another shallow Westerner concerned only with where my next Coca-Cola was coming from. As it was, help came from a most unexpected quarter. Goran started talking to me about music.

Goran was a DJ on the student radio station in Zagreb, and was surprisingly up to date with what was happening on the music scene. A friend of his had moved to London and was always sending him tapes and CDs and old copies of *Q* magazine. He asked me what I was listening to and was suitably impressed when I answered Pulp, a band he had only heard vaguely about. I was equally impressed that his knowledge of Australian bands extended beyond Air Supply and Men At Work, and that he had even heard of The Sunnyboys, one of my all-time favourite bands when I was at university.

'My friend has a radio program here in Dubrovnik,' he said enthusiastically, 'You must come on and talk about Australian music. But I must warn you, he will want to know about INXS.'

Goran and I ended the night the best of friends. His friend would interview me on the local radio station the next day about INXS (A sample question: 'Is INXS the most popular band in Australia?' My answer: 'No'.) And I would send him a tape of some more hip Australian bands when I got back home. Natasha, on the other hand, seemed a little miffed that I'd spent the night largely ignoring her.

To her credit, Natasha took me along to the police station the next day, as promised, to find out more about crossing the Croatian–Bosnian border. And it is largely thanks to her that I am not still waiting at the self-same spot. As a native speaker of Croatian she was able to ascertain that it was impossible for me to cross into Albania that way. There had been an incident down at the border the night before—a Serb soldier, drunk, had ventured into no-man's-land by mistake and had been shot by the Croatians. The border was closed, and if similar incidents in the past were anything to go by, it would stay closed for a couple of weeks or more. The policeman, through Natasha, suggested I go back to Split and catch a boat down to Albania.

So that's what I did.

CHAPTER SIX

Bosnia

Soundtrack: 'Led Zeppelin IV'—Led Zeppelin

There have been three times in my life when I have done something
really foolish and then spent a long time regretting it. The first was
in fourth class, when I pushed Linda Pickering over because she
told me she loved me. The second was when I bought *Sandinista*
by the Clash without realising that they'd gone reggae. The third
time was when I arrived back in Split from Dubrovnik and immediately jumped on a bus to Mostar.

Mostar is the capital of the Hercegovinian part of Bosnia–
Hercegovina, and only two weeks before had been the front line in
the war that had been festering between the Muslims and the Croats
since the break up of the former Yugoslavia. It's also one of those
ubiquitous 'east meets west' towns that seem to be everywhere once
you get on the wrong side of Paris—the kind of place where Eastern
orientalism meets Western classicism and produces the inevitable
'lively bazaar'.

As a former university student of all things old and irrelevant, Mostar had a special place in my heart. It was home to an ancient stone bridge that spanned the Neretva River, a river that divided Mostar's Muslims and Croats spiritually as well as physically. More importantly, the bridge had been the subject of a paragraph or two in one of my more appreciated history essays. And now it was only 155 kilometres away.

The bridge was thrown up by the visiting Turks sometime in the sixteenth century and was considered quite the engineering marvel, pretty much like the Sydney Opera House, in fact. From all accounts, it was stunningly beautiful, so when I saw a bus in Split with Mostar on its destination board, I thought 'What the heck?' If a bus was going there, and there were people boarding the bus, it must be OK. If there really were a problem, they wouldn't sell me a ticket. Right?

The bullet hole in the window next to my seat was perhaps the first indication that I had made a mistake. I had only ever seen a bullet hole in a bus window once before, and that had been in LA just after the riots. The bus had been going from Hollywood to Central and the guy sitting next to me spent the entire journey pointing out the territorial boundaries of all the different gangs and explaining which Barrio belonged to which Homies. He appeared quite knowledgeable and I had no reason to doubt him. In fact, his foot had been bandaged after catching a bullet during a drive-by shooting the night before.

On the bus to Mostar, my companion was a middle-aged woman in a headscarf. It wasn't red or blue and her foot wasn't bandaged, but she looked as though she knew her shit. I'm sure if I'd asked, she'd have been able to point out where the frontline had been during the various stages of the war and maybe even tell me the casualty figures for both sides.

The second sign that I was doing something foolish came at the Croatian–Bosnian border. There was a line of UN Land Rovers and

trucks and tanks a kilometre or so long. All the UN vehicles and
UN soldiers I had been trying to avoid in Split had simultaneously
decided that it was time to stop drinking beer and eating ice cream
and start moving the stockpiled humanitarian aid goodies out of
Split and into Bosnia, where they might actually do some good.
Small groups of UN soldiers stood around their vehicles, checking
straps or smoking nervously, while small groups of Croatian soldiers checked under the vehicles and under the tarpaulins on the
trucks carrying sacks of grain, just in case the UN had decided to
start running guns to the Muslims.

My bus was waved to the head of the queue by a bored-looking
Croatian soldier. There was no need for his fellow countrymen to
wait while the soldiers were having a bit of fun at the UN's expense.
At the border, another soldier, equally bored, jumped onto the bus
and strolled down the aisle looking at passports. Mine was the only
one he stamped. It said 'Granicni Prijelaz', 'Doljani', and the date—
April 24, my sister's birthday.

I probably should have called my sister. If I had still been in
Split I probably would have. But Mostar was another matter. I could
just imagine her reaction when the operator asked 'Will you except
a collect call from your brother in Bosnia?' Actually, my sister
would have been cool, but I don't think my mum needed to know
more than the fact that I was on my way to Bulgaria. When I'd
rung her the week before, I'd rather conveniently forgotten to
mention that I was going via the Balkans. A couple of kilometres
into Bosnia, and I forgot all about making a phone call anyway.
None of the houses looked liked they had running water, let alone
an ISD connection.

By early afternoon we reached Medugorje. Medugorje sits in the
desolate high passes of Hercegovina and is famous throughout the
Catholic world for being the site of one of the frequent miraculous
appearances of the Virgin Mary. Before the Virgin Mary showed
her face in 1981, the place was known for producing very little

apart from rocks, hard-headed people, and Ustasi (fascists). Now all it seemed to be producing was shoddily built hotels with names like The Vision Inn and The Virgin Hotel.

Before the war thousands of pilgrims travelled to the Hill of Apparitions, where the Virgin (or Gospa, as she is known to the locals) stopped by in 1981 and told six boys that God really did exist. Now, after years of a senseless civil war that begged to differ, the cheap hotels and restaurants that had miraculously sprung up to cater for the pilgrims were largely deserted. The only sign of life was the sandbagged chalet that housed the UN, and the video shop and post office the soldiers used.

An hour or so later we approached a major town via a Meccano-like bridge. It was a pretty spot, not unlike Taree in New South Wales, with poplars lining the banks of the broad river. But the concrete bridge that had previously serviced the town was broken in half and falling into the river, 500 metres downstream.

The town itself—Capljina—was completely shattered. Kids played in rubble and their mothers stood by with vacant stares. At the bus station, or what was left of it, there were no little old ladies in shawls or little old men in pork pie hats offering rooms, just burned-out shells of buses. Looking in my travel notebook some months later, I found just one entry next to the word Capljina— 'Completely fucked'. Now, though, I just felt like a ghoul.

The bus left Capljina and its shattered buildings and people and climbed up a hill and onto a scrubby plateau. A sign said Mostar 33 km. Then the bus headed in the opposite direction and into the Hercegovinian wilderness.

By late afternoon we had arrived at the last military checkpoint before Mostar, nestled in the grey mountains above the city. Although a cease-fire was in effect and the shelling had stopped, Mostar was still divided into Croatian and Muslim sections. Having entered Bosnia from Croatia, I was on the Croatian side of the city and would need permission from the Croatian military to enter the city. The cease-fire was barely a fortnight old, so things were still very tense. There was every likelihood that I would be turned back. And if I was going to be turned back anywhere, it would be here.

The checkpoint looked just like I imagined a checkpoint on the edge of a war zone would look. There was a large tent, a radio tower and plenty of heavy artillery pointing down at the city below. The personnel acted the way I imagined those in charge of a military checkpoint on the edge of a war zone would act. They walked around jutting their jaws out and talking aggressively into walkie-talkies, or saluted haggard commanders as they walked by barking orders to no one in particular. And a guy with a Serbian passport and I were dragged off the bus in a manner I imagined people who were in a place they had no business being were dragged off buses.

The man with the Serbian passport was dealt with pretty quickly. He had a letter from the department in Zagreb that specialises in writing letters for former/current enemies who have good ideas about turning misery into shit-loads of money for everyone. But when the battle-hardened commander turned his suspicious eyes on me and raised his eyebrow, I knew I was in for an interrogation. Not unreasonably, the first thing he asked me, in surprisingly good English, was why I was going to Mostar.

I knew that anything I said would sound suspicious, so I decided to answer truthfully. He would either believe that I was coming to Mostar on a silly whim to see what was left of a sixteenth-century bridge, or he wouldn't. And if he did decide to throw me into prison and torture me mercilessly, I would be able to look the visiting Amnesty International representative in the eye, knowing I had told the truth.

He didn't believe me and seemed convinced that I was a journalist, an arms dealer, a mercenary or member of some other similarly unsavoury profession. He snatched a walkie-talkie from one of his subordinates and tried to contact headquarters in Mostar. When no one answered, he turned his attention back to my passport.

Just as the commander found my Iranian visa—quite an incriminating find for someone who had been fighting Muslims only a fortnight before—a goofy Croatian policeman stumbled along. The policeman wore a blue uniform and, judging by his jinky little walk, was a little bit pissed. His breath stank and he had that silly smile people get when they've been on the turps and their tongue either hangs out or is bitten between their front teeth. He came up so close to me that our faces almost touched, then cocked his head to the side and smiled, eyelids fluttering. Then he snapped back to attention, walked around in a circle and did a little jig before starting the whole face thing all over again. It was as if he had never seen an Australian before.

The commander, meanwhile, continued to try and contact headquarters. His training had taught him what to do with a grenade-launcher and an oncoming Serb, but had obviously left him under-prepared on the classic 'Aussie backpacker turning up in a war zone with no particularly reason' scenario. The trouble was, he wasn't getting through. Well, I guessed he wasn't getting through. He kept slapping the walkie-talkie against his leg and cursing it.

Meanwhile, the policeman decided to spring to my defence.

'Peace, man?' he asked, putting his arm around my shoulder and flashing me the classic hippie 'V' with his free hand.

'Peace, man!' I replied, flashing him the 'V' back.

With a drunken flourish, he gave me back my passport and waved me onto the bus. The driver wasted no time in putting the bus into gear and driving off. The last thing I saw from the back window as we drove off was the commander poking his finger into the drunken policeman's chest.

Mostar was in a natural bowl-shaped valley surrounded by hills. With its high-rise apartment towers, it looked surprisingly modern. As the bus crawled its way into town, it all looked pretty peaceful and somehow less shattered than Capljina. There was snow on the distant high mountains, and all around trees were beginning to bud.

However, as the bus drew closer to the centre of town, the more convinced I became that I had been a little rash in coming to Mostar. The buildings *were* as shattered as those in Capljina, but had black stains where the walls had been burned out. Every park and grassy verge was being used as a cemetery, and I saw hundreds of freshly dug graves marked by small wooden crosses with dates written on them in marker pen. When we passed a bombed-out mosque, its minaret broken beside it, I began wishing that the drunken policeman had butted out and let the army commander send me back to Split after all.

At various points along the road passengers got off the bus with their shopping bags and shuffled towards the burned-out apartment blocks. The road was empty except for the bus and, closer to the town centre, a UN tank. The few people walking the streets barely gave the tank a second look as it rumbled by. But the blue-bereted soldier poking out of the manhole had that tentative kind of look on his face that said he was ready to duck any second.

At the end of the road, the bus made its final stop—at the skeletal remains of what had been the major bus terminal. I decided to stay on the bus and go back to Split. Then I noticed something. My backpack had been unloaded and was lying on the footpath beside the bus. When I quizzed the driver, I found out that the bus was terminating. And it wouldn't be returning to Split until 6.00 the next morning.

Generally, I regard myself as a pretty optimistic person. I like to think that, somehow, things will always work themselves out— whether that thing is a question in an exam on the only topic I'd had time to study or some work turning up just as the rent is due. But that evening, as I walked up the cratered main street of Mostar, I have to admit that even my indomitable optimism was tested. The few people I came upon—soldiers, mainly—simply laughed when I asked where I could find a room.

After walking 500 metres or so, I came upon a small general

store. It was neat and tidy and even stocked cans of Coke. I remembered thinking at the time that if they sold Coke, things couldn't have been too bad. When I asked the woman behind the counter if she knew of anywhere I could stay, however, she backed off as if I were a deranged rapist. When I begged her to let me sleep on the floor, for US dollars, she panicked and yelled to someone out the back. A small boy came to the counter and told me in perfect English that there were no rooms in Mostar and to stop frightening his mother. If I wanted a bed for the night, I'd have to go to the police station across the road or to the UN headquarters, closer to the centre of town.

Outside the shop I stumbled upon three young guys and asked them which building was the police station. They were just hanging out on the corner, smoking and slouching and making a pretty poor attempt at looking menacing. They were just like the guys who hang out in shopping malls in baggy shorts and beanies scaring little old ladies by riding their skateboards on handrails. Except these guys didn't have skateboards. They just had a basketball that they took turns sitting on.

'If you want room only,' said the smallest and most nuggety one, in faltering English, 'You can stay at our place. Free.'

I had a decision to make. I could cross the road and throw myself on the mercy of the police, and maybe spend the night in a cell. Or I could take my chances with three guys with scruffy goatees who looked like they were straight out of a Pepsi Max commercial and could very well lead me up a dark alley and steal everything I had. I made an instant character assessment and decided to trust them.

The ability to instantly assess the motives of people is a skill you learn pretty quickly when you travel. Nearly every day you are put in a situation where you have to decide whether or not to trust someone. You have to decide whether they're ripping you off or helping you out. And it's a fine line to walk. If you take it as read that everyone is trying to stiff you, you'll have a horrible time and rob yourself of some really wonderful moments of generosity and hospitality. Similarly, if you trust everyone blindly, you'll end up being robbed blind.

I haven't always got it right. The first time I went to Athens I trusted a guy who offered to shout me a beer. I ended up in a place called the Foxy Bar, buying every prostitute in the place drinks. But I learnt my lesson. I don't guilelessly follow strange men to places named after small furry creatures any more. Well, not unless I want to buy expensive cocktails for scantily clad women who insist on sitting on my lap.

Anyway, these guys' names were Slaven, Koca and Damir, and the apartment they were taking me to belonged to Damir's cousin. The cousin had quite sensibly run off to America at the start of the war and left the keys to the apartment with Damir. Damir didn't live in the apartment—he still lived with his mum—but the three of them used it as a place to have parties, smoke drugs or just sit around listening to music. Occasionally, it seemed, he also let the occasional backpacker doss there.

The apartment block had not been damaged much during the fighting. Most of the windows were unbroken and the scars of mortar fire were restricted to two of the four outside walls. The lifts didn't work, which is usual in any apartment block over ten years old, and the fire escape was full of sad 'nests' of families left homeless from the fighting. The cousin's apartment was on the third floor, and had a commanding view of the twisted remains of what had been a newer and swankier apartment block next door. Damir made quite a show of pointing out the bullet holes in the door where thieves had broken in to steal the television.

Inside, surprisingly, the apartment was quite homely. It wasn't exactly something you'd see in *Country Living*, but then it wasn't something you'd see in the latest edition of *Frontline Front Rooms* either. There were books on bookshelves, dishes and cutlery in the kitchen and a pair of souvenir salt and pepper shakers wearing tartan caps on the dining room table. In the bathroom there were robes on hooks, soap in the soap dish and bottles of shampoo on the floor. It was as if the owners had gone off to work that morning and were due home any moment. The only give-away that the place was really a den of iniquity for three male teenagers was the smell. The place stank of spilt beer, stale smoke and rancid bong water.

Damir gave me a quick tour of the apartment, showing me the bedroom where I would be sleeping and how to use the temperamental hot water heater. I was surprised that there was hot water or even electricity for that matter. But as the cassette player blasting out Led Zeppelin testified, the power was on, and so, it seems, was the gas.

'Who pays the bills?' I asked, naively.

The three guys all looked at each other and laughed.

'This is a war zone,' snorted Damir. 'There are no bills.'

Almost to prove the point, he turned up the cassette player full volume and played air guitar to Black Dog. Koca and Slaven looked up from the billy they were pulling and nodded in stoned appreciation. At 10 pm, just as the nightly curfew was about to come into effect, they left and went home to their mums. They agreed to take me to the bridge the next day.

I don't know why I wanted to see the bridge. It had been blown up early on in the war, so there wasn't much left of it. I remember seeing footage of its last moments on the news. It was incredible stuff, shot on a camcorder by one of the soldiers. There was a guy on the bridge, waving a Croatian flag at the Muslim gunners. A mortar was fired and the bridge was hit. The dust cleared and the guy was hanging on defiantly, waving the flag with his free hand. Another mortar was fired and he was gone. And so was the bridge.

At 7.30 the next morning the three guys came to collect me. To see what was left of the bridge meant going to the front line. They were quite nervous and were adamant that we always remained under cover. We darted from one deserted apartment block to another. And when we had to cross a park or road, we only did so behind the burned-out car bodies that had been overturned to provide safe passage. It seemed unreal to me, almost like a game. But if you lost, instead of being branded with a tennis ball, as in British Bulldog, you would be shot. I couldn't sense the danger, but the guys could. And soon enough their nervousness made me nervous.

Soon we were at the front line. Well, I guessed we were on the front line. There were blankets hanging from the trees to block the line of sight of snipers. And a plastic medical dummy, one of those ones that shows budding young medical students all the human entrails they are likely to come across in full gory colour, was hanging from a telegraph pole. A gaggle of soldiers in full battle fatigue sat on boxes of artillery drinking from hip flasks and playing cards.

One of the soldiers spotted us and, angry at being disturbed from his game of gin rummy, told us to piss off in no uncertain terms. (I should point out that I regard waving a loaded gun in my general direction as no uncertain terms.) When he found out I was from Australia, however, his mood changed and he insisted on taking me to the remains of the city's cathedral.

The cathedral was a mess. The roof was gone and so were one or two of its walls. The pulpit, miraculously untouched, looked out on to a pile of splintered pews. With a sweeping hand gesture and look of disdain, the soldier seemed to be saying, 'Look what these heathen bastards have done. Is nothing sacred?'

I almost mentioned the equally rooted mosque I had seen on the way into town, but as the soldier was carrying a semiautomatic rifle and had a few grenades attached to his belt, it didn't really seem appropriate. In the short time I had been in Mostar, it had become clear to me that both sides had reasons to want revenge. Back home, I had always felt that the antagonisms between Croat and Serb and

Muslim migrants seemed petty. I worked for a Croatian guy once, and when I asked him what part of Yugoslavia he was from, he spat back, 'I am not from Yugoslavia, I am from Croatia.' That was years before the current war—his hatred stemmed from a Serbian massacre in a Croatian village in 1564. I remember thinking it was all a bit melodramatic—dwelling on some atrocity from the Middle Ages when you were in a country that hadn't even been discovered at the time. But in Mostar, I could understand. I could see reasons in the destroyed apartment blocks and in the graves in the parks. I wondered how many centuries it would take before these atrocities would be forgotten.

The soldier wouldn't let us go past the cathedral. There had been some sniper activity that morning, and going any closer to the Muslim side of town, and the remains of the bridge, would have been foolhardy. The guys, sensing my disappointment, suggested we head back to the centre of town and get a pizza. As you do.

The centre of Mostar was a lively piazza of bars and cafes with names like The Cotton Club and Harlem, and seemed to have escaped the worst ravages of war. It was full of tables and chairs and battle-worn Croatian soldiers drinking beer and coffee in the warm April sun, their pistols lying on the table in front of them. Occasionally there was some shouting and a minor scuffle, but these incidents were quickly broken up by the soldiers who were still on duty. It was as if the Wild West had found a new home in the glitz and chrome of Mostar.

While we waited for our pizza, I asked the guys if they thought the war was really over. They weren't optimistic, particularly about the attempts to divide the country into Muslim, Croatian and Serbian enclaves.

'How do you divide people?' said Koca. 'I am half Serbian and half Croatian and so is Damir. Slaven here is half Muslim and half Serb and has an Italian grandfather. Are you going to cut us down the middle?'

They were equally ambivalent about the effectiveness of the UN.

'They are here, but they make no difference,' said Damir. 'If the fighting starts again, they won't stop it.' He waved towards a table of hard-looking Croatian soldiers. 'These guys love the fighting. They've got the taste for blood.'

The pizzas arrived and so did a constant stream of soldiers. At first I thought they might have been asking the guys about me and what I was doing in Mostar. But then I saw the surreptitious exchange of money for dope and realised that Damir, Koca and Slaven were dealers.

'My father and brothers were killed in the war,' said Damir. 'It's up to me to support my family. It's the same with Koca and Slaven, except Slaven still tries to study.'

'It gets us out of fighting,' said Slaven, a little miffed that he'd been painted as a bookworm. 'If we were at the front, these guys would have to get their dope from somewhere else. They trust us, so they don't hassle us into joining them.'

The guys laughed at the Zen neatness of all this, and ordered another pizza. When the bill came, they paid.

The day's business taken care of, Slaven excused himself and went off to school. With nothing better to do, Damir and Koca suggested we go up to Partisan Hill.

Partisan Hill sat high above the town, with commanding views over all parts of the city. It was crowned by a memorial to all the Partisans who had lost their lives liberating Mostar from the Germans and Italians during World War II. It was worn and unkempt and littered with empty bottles and charcoal from fires. The locals also used the space behind the marble honour list as a toilet. But the grass around it was clean and sprinkled with small flowers. We lay on our backs, chewing gum, watching the clouds floating by and enjoying the warm sun. It was a magic moment, but it was tainted by an underlying sense of gloom and pessimism.

As we chatted about life in general, I realised these guys were totally without hope.

It reminded me of my school days. I was a part of a group called the Tree People, who were equally apathetic. We were called the Tree People because we sat on a couple of park benches under a tree at the back of the school near the teachers' car park and just outside the principal's office. This was very handy for the principal when he drew up the infamous 'Drugs List', an honour roll of all the students he and other teachers felt were using illegal substances. He just looked out his window and wrote down all our names. A group of guys who had zero motivation and sat under a tree talking about Monty Python just had to be on drugs. What he didn't realise was that we didn't get involved in anything because we didn't see the point.

Yep, we had a good line in boredom and apathy. And with a little effort we could have had a pretty good stab at nihilism and pessimism. But we were just indulgent schoolboys. These guys were the real thing.

I asked where they would go if they could, and they half-heartedly answered Australia, Germany and Hawaii, before giving up and returning to silence. To three teenagers in Mostar, it was a waste of energy to even think about these things. Such dreams were as realistic as flying to the moon.

After an hour or so, just after a pair of Croatian jets screamed overhead doing a reconnaissance of the city, a dark-haired girl called Sandic joined us. She was a Muslim Serb, 19 years old and, in all honesty, quite stunning. She had the looks and the figure to turn heads anywhere in the world. But when it came to being bored and surly, she beat the guys hands down. She didn't smile—just recognised our presence with a resigned shrug and flopped down beside us.

Sandic's family lived on the Muslim side of Mostar, but she was stranded on the Croatian side of the city. Eighteen months before, she had been touring Italy with the Mostar junior volleyball team. She had tried to stay in Italy as a refugee, but was kicked out. Upon returning to Mostar, she found the city divided and herself on the wrong side. She hadn't seen her parents or brothers and sisters for a couple of years, and wasn't even sure if they were alive. The cease-fire offered some hope that she would be able to cross the city and find her family, but she wasn't holding her breath.

I remember thinking that Sandic was the sort of girl that Raz, the Pakistani shopkeeper, had been hoping to find in Bosnia to take back home with him as a princess. She didn't have a home or family or money or, most definitely, any hope for the future. But I doubt she would have been interested. She asked me a little about myself, but it didn't really go beyond my name and where I was from. When I told her how old I was, she asked me if I had been at Woodstock. I consoled myself by thinking that she meant Woodstock II. But I think Raz, as a middle-aged divorced shopkeeper would have had a hard time convincing her to marry him.

Soon early afternoon became late afternoon, and at dusk we made our way back into town. The soldiers would be changing shift, and those about to go on would want some drugs to get them through the night. The cafes were buzzing and business was good.

Back at the apartment, the guys pulled a few more billies and played music—*The Best of the Doors*, I think. I was amazed at how 'normal' they were. With all the shit these guys had seen—in fact, all the shit they were living through—they had every right to be total fuckwits, or at least vicious hard cases. But they weren't. They were just like teenagers the world over.

When 'The End' kicked in, I also found myself wondering what it is about dope that makes people listen to this music. When I was at high school it was the same. A bong would come out and so would The Doors or the Stones or Led Zeppelin or Hendrix. Now, years later, I was in an apartment in war-torn Bosnia and I was experiencing déjà vu. It's got to the stage now that when I smell marijuana, I automatically start singing the first few bars to 'Foxy Lady'.

Snooping around the bookshelves that evening I found Whitman's *Off Season Guide to Europe* and a souvenir photo album. I was pleased that the guidebook was off season—after all, you couldn't get more off season than after a bit of ethnic cleansing—and that it described the bridge in Mostar as 'an engineering marvel'. The photo album was the real find, though. It had a wooden cover with a vista of the bridge and its surrounds burnt onto it with a soldering iron.

That cover was fantastic, and I was immediately overwhelmed with a desire to keep it. It was tacky and touristy, but somehow it summed up my quest to see the bridge perfectly. I wouldn't see the bridge physically. But I could always have an illustrated version. I cut off the cover with my penknife and stuck it into my backpack, feeling elated but a little guilty. I rationalised my act of petty pilfering by telling myself the owners of the apartment would be more upset about the missing television than the cover of a dusty photo album they weren't even using.

By my third day in Mostar, I had fallen into a routine of sorts with the guys. Around ten we went down to the Cotton Club and drank coffee while they dealt drugs with soldiers. After dividing the takings equally amongst themselves, we'd go to the pizzeria, where they would shout me a pizza. After a half-hearted attempt to view the bridge from some bombed-out apartment that overlooked the river (or some other equally foolhardy vantage point), we would go back to The Harlem and have a beer.

That afternoon there was a group of Swedish journalists at The Harlem, knocking back a beer or two at the table beside us. They were in town to cover the visit of the head of the Red Cross, and were suitably attired in foreign correspondent war zone clobber—photographer vests and camel-coloured pants. One of them came up to our table and asked if I would take a photo for them. After

I took the photo, he complimented me on my English. I didn't correct him. To do so would have meant a long and drawn-out explanation of what the hell I was doing in Mostar and the inevitable questions about my sanity. I just thanked him and went back to my beer.

That night I had dinner at Slaven's house. Although the meal was only potatoes and a very grisly cut of steak, his mother put out the best crockery and hung a sheet over a hole in the wall where a mortar had hit during the worst of the fighting. We ate in silence, then watched a bit of television. It was a Croatian version of 'Sale of the Century'. When it was finished, Slaven walked me back to the apartment. When we got to the door, he gave me a plastic lighter with the Bosnian coat of arms on it.

'Souvenir,' he said.

I suddenly felt really guilty about the photo album I had butchered.

The next day, the guys decided to make one last attempt to see the bridge, this time from Hotel Mostar. On the way I asked them about the photocopied notices that were on most of the trees and buildings in Mostar. The notices invariably had a picture of a person (high school yearbook style), the Croatian coat of arms and a paragraph or two in Croatian. According to the guys, these were like obituaries, and had been put up by grieving families to mark the spot where a loved one had died. I was shaken by how many there were. In my short stay I had already seen hundreds of them.

As we stood looking at one photocopy nailed to the tree (one Zdravko Mihalj, a Croatian soldier who had been killed by sniper fire on this spot only two weeks earlier), a small boy approached the guys to buy some dope. The kid was only young, but he was hard—too hard—and his arms were covered in scars and cigarette burns. Amongst the scars and burns were home-carved ink tattoos of nothing in particular. He had the demeanour of someone who had spent his life inside jail.

When the guys said they didn't have any dope on them he pulled out a knife and started brandishing it wildly. He calmed down a little when they promised to meet him later, but left us cursing.

'He is only ten,' said Damir, 'but he is as dangerous as the soldiers. Since his parents were killed he has lived on the streets like a rat. Now he is a rat.'

Shortly after, Damir showed me the spot where he had been hit by shrapnel. He had just been hanging on a corner one day and 'kaboom', a mortar exploded and he copped it. I was surprised to find out that mortars don't whistle the way they do in the movies. They just explode.

'I left the shrapnel in,' he said, offering me the back of his head and the inside of his wrist to feel. 'It's a souvenir of what happened here.'

It made my stomach turn. Just under the skin I could feel the lumps of metal from an exploding mortar. I asked if it still hurt.

'Only when it is going to rain,' he replied nonchalantly.

Just around the corner, a basketball hung from a wall in one of those red hessian bags that oranges come in. Underneath were dozens of flowers. It marked the spot where two young brothers, only nine and seven years old, had been killed as they played a game of one-on-one in the courtyard of their apartment. Everywhere, it seemed, there were reminders of death and destruction.

None of this, however, prepared me for the Hotel Mostar. At the end of a cul de sac, the hotel was an eighteenth-century building only two or three storeys high. It was pink and white, and although most of its windows were shattered, it seemed structurally sound. Its sign was bent and broken and the foyer was knee-deep in debris, including instruction manuals—in Serbo–Croatian—on how to lay a land mine. A sweeping iron staircase to the left of the reception desk led to the upper floors.

With its commanding views of the river and the Muslim quarter on the other side, the Hotel Mostar had been a popular haunt for snipers. We slowly crept up the stairs, straining to hear any noise that might indicate they were still there. It was silent—eerily silent—so we cautiously made our way along the corridor on the second floor to one of the rooms overlooking the river. We entered Room 206.

The room was completely gutted, devoid of anything that may have suggested it was once a hotel room. In the bathroom, the copper piping had been looted, along with the basin and the bathtub. In the bedroom, amongst the rubble, sat a lone chair. It was hard up against three fist-sized holes that had been punched into the wall, and was surrounded by empty bullet shells. Weeks, days, maybe only hours before, it had been used by a sniper to pick off Muslims on the other side of the river. I looked through one of the holes and my heart sank. The sniper had had an uninterrupted line of sight to the Muslim market only 300 metres away.

Each room in the hotel was the same, looted and covered in debris and with that haunting single chair against the wall. Koca said that we could probably see the bridge from one of the rooms on the next floor, but I'm afraid my heart wasn't in it. I had seen enough, probably too much. I just wanted to go back to the apartment and so we did.

That night some particularly nasty-looking soldiers came around to the apartment to buy some drugs. They were already drunk or wired or both, and spent the evening asking me if I had a camera and where I kept my money. They talked amongst themselves in Croatian and laughed loudly, apparently at my expense. It was tense and I felt uneasy. So did the three young guys. They made excuses about having to get back before the curfew and hustled the soldiers out. It may have been paranoia, but I was convinced the soldiers had been planning to roll me.

The evening, and the visit to Hotel Mostar, had brought me back to reality with a thud. I had been lulled into a false sense of security hanging out with these guys. It was fun to pretend I could just hang out in a war zone with impunity, eating pizza and drinking beer and scampering about amongst ruins. But if a heavily armed, totally wired soldier decided to rob or kill me there was nothing that I, the three guys, or even the UN could do about it.

It was time to leave Bosnia and go back to Split. Albania awaited.

CHAPTER SEVEN

Albania

Soundtrack: *Saturday Night Fever* soundtrack

Back in the late eighties, there was a story doing the rounds in the hostels on the Greek Island of Corfu about a guy who wanted to go to Albania. At that time, Albania was one of the most isolated countries in the world—a backward, inward-looking Stalinist enclave that would rather eat its young than let in tourists. Getting an Albanian visa was about as likely as St George Rugby League team ever winning the premiership again.

This fellow, however, was persistent. Every day he turned up at the Albanian consulate in Corfu and asked for a visa. And every day the consul refused to give him one. Finally, after two months of daily visits, the Albanian consul relented and gave the guy a visa. But when the guy arrived at the Greek–Albanian border, he was bundled into a truck and taken to a potato farm. After a week of pulling spuds from the hard, dark soil, he was bundled into another truck and taken back to Greece.

I was impressed by a country that not only recognised persistence, but also rewarded it so perversely. It's probably the reason I'd always put Albania at the top of my fantasy destination wish list. (Which I guess tells you more about me than I should really be giving away.) In my mind, Albania was untouched and untouristed. Not only that, it would be an impressive destination to drop casually into any conversation.

Of course, I had already secured my Albanian visa while I was in Budapest. I had suffered a couple of blows from a toilet brush to get it, but I had it. And while it probably indicated to an Albanian border guard that I too was to be unceremoniously bundled off to a potato farm on arrival, I had a more immediate problem to overcome first. The ferry that everyone from Natasha through to Captain Aleksij Mekjavic through to the guy selling ice cream down on the waterfront had told me I could catch from Split to Durrës in Albania, only sold tickets to truck drivers.

The news was broken to me by the middle-aged receptionist at the harbour-side office of the Dalmacija–Kvarner shipping company in Split. To her credit, she seemed genuinely dismayed to tell me that the boat wasn't a passenger ferry but rather a vehicular one. It was operated for the express purpose of getting Croatian and Albanian truck drivers and their trucks around that troublesome stretch of Serbian coastline that would otherwise stymie trade between the two nations, just as it had stymied my plans to travel overland to Albania from Dubrovnik.

She rang the headquarters of the shipping company in Rijeka to see if there was any way around this impasse. She was transferred from one person to another, each time rolling her eyes at me in exasperation, and each time without success. Finally she was transferred to the big boss, who she spoke to for what seemed an eternity. 'They allow passengers in special circumstances!' she said excitedly, covering the mouthpiece with her hand.

'Am I a special circumstance?'

She laughed uproariously. Finally, choking back the tears, she spoke.

'Any stranger in our country is a special circumstance!'

The ticket cost me $90—four times my budgeted daily allowance—and gave me little else than passage on the SV *Josip* as it made its overnight journey from Split to Durres. I had hoped that for that sort of money I might have got a cabin, or at least a bunk bed in a shared one. But a quick tour of the SV *Josip* soon revealed that it was built to carry trucks, and not much else. There was a cramped, stale-smelling lounge just below the bridge where twenty or so truck drivers smoked, drank and watched TV. They all had tattoos and moustaches and wore denim jackets with the arms ripped out. A few wore leather caps. I felt I had stumbled on the planning committee for a sea shanty float in the Sydney Gay and Lesbian Mardi Gras.

The night's TV viewing charted our progress down the Dalmatian coast. As far as Dubrovnik we were treated to the soaps and movies of Croatian TV. As we passed Montenegro and Serbia we got dancing girls and propaganda featuring new Serbian recruits training for the front. Finally, one of the truck drivers changed the channel and we were subjected to the horrors of Italian game shows. It was a long and tiresome night, but when the truck drivers finally retired to their trucks below, I was able to stretch out over three of the seats and get a few hours' sleep.

The next morning a dolphin frolicked beside the boat. It was spotted by one of the truck drivers who had been strolling on deck having a smoke. He yelled out and soon all the truckies came running from all parts of the boat. They laughed and pointed like children, and I wondered what it was about dolphins that made these tough truck drivers behave like giggling school girls. I guessed that they didn't have a Marine World or Sea World in Albania. Either that or Flipper hadn't made it to the TV screens of Albania yet.

Just before lunch, and an hour or two after an unmarked white plane had buzzed the boat, we entered Durres harbour. Without wishing to appear ungracious, Albania's main harbour and window to the world looked like it had just been mistaken for Baghdad by a squadron of US Stealth bombers. Three rusting hulks leant against the breakwater like three drunks searching for support. A motley collection of boats and ships in various stages of disintegration were docked beside equally shabby cranes. This was the pride of Albania's military commercial fleet. The SV *Josip* looked the picture of modernity as it picked its way amongst half-submerged wrecks to a muddy bank, where it simply ran aground.

The cargo door was lowered onto the bank, and I walked off the boat along the planks they had put down in the mud for the trucks to drive along. No one asked to see my passport. No one wanted to check my bag. There wasn't even a welcoming committee from the local potato collective. I walked through the gates of the harbour entrance and onto the pot-holed streets of Durres unchallenged.

If you've ever seen photos from the Great Depression, you'll get a pretty good idea of what Albania looks like. All the buildings are worn out and in the process of falling down on themselves. Everyone wears clothes with patches. And just like in the thirties, there are an awful lot of people milling around with nothing to do and nowhere to go.

Albania's rather unfortunate financial state is well known, as is its penchant for pyramid schemes. Like North Korea, another country that closed the door on the rest of the world, it's been a long time since the country has had two coins to rub together. But unlike North Korea, Albania is relatively self-sufficient, and even has some oil reserves. (And here's something I'll bet you didn't know—Albania is the third-largest producer of chrome.) With its longstanding constitutional ban on borrowing foreign money, I had always wondered how Albania had got itself into such a state.

The answer seemed to present itself on the 35-kilometre trip from

Durres to the capital, Tirane. Freaked out by the Soviet invasion of Czechoslovakia in 1968, the Albanian government spent billions on building thousands of concrete igloo-shaped bunkers along every border and the approaches to their most important towns. On the road to Tirane they lined both sides of the street, barely 100 metres apart. It looked like the city was being defended by a line of sub-merged Daleks, a look that you pay for—big time.

On entering Tirane, it seemed that Albanians were still paying the price. I've never seen a more neglected and down-at-heel city in my life. Buildings were falling apart. Parks were dusty and des-olate. Everyone, including businessmen with briefcases, looked tired and undernourished. Horse and cart buggies shared the crumbling roads with buses that appeared to be disintegrating before my very eyes. The only thing that looked like it had been built this century was the Coca-Cola plant on the outskirts of town.

The bus terminated at Tirane's main railway station at the top of Stalin Boulevard, and here the wretched plight of the Albanians was even more apparent. The main entrance hall had been turned into a squatters' camp, with desperate families living in cardboard boxes and laying their washing in the sun on the tracks to dry. My guidebook, just a few photocopied pages out of any extremely out-of-date *Lonely Planet* Eastern Europe, indicated that the only place to stay was the Hotel Tirane, just off Skanderbeg Square. I set off down Stalin Boul-evard wondering if the hotel had also been converted into lodgings for retrenched factory workers and concrete bunker engineers.

I never found out. I was barely 200 metres down the boulevard when I was approached by a fellow who spoke very good English and introduced himself as Mirindi. With his tight, shiny slacks and reflector sunglasses he could have been a second-hand car dealer, but he turned out to be nothing more than a generous, friendly and funny guy looking to practise his English. What's more, when I asked him for directions to the Hotel Tirane, he insisted I stay the night at his place instead.

We caught a bus—or more precisely, the skeletal remains of a bus—to Mirindi's house, way out on the outskirts of town in the hills opposite an abandoned factory. The driver, to his eternal credit, was able to coax his dying bus most of the way, but a kilometre or so before our stop it belched, shuddered and then expired. Everyone got off and walked the rest of the way home without complaining, as if it were all part of their daily routine.

I doubt Mirindi would normally be in a rush to go home either. He and his family lived in a tiny single-roomed shack with whitewashed walls and a tin roof. With only one bed and not enough room to swing a cat, Mirindi sent his wife and small daughter to stay with the in-laws to make room for me. At first I thought he was setting me up for some kind of intimate encounter, but I was very wrong—he actually gave up his bed and slept on the verandah outside.

The most interesting part of Mirindi's house was the toilet. Not only was it the first hole-in-the-ground variety of my trip, it was also the most extraordinarily innovative English-language laboratory I had ever seen.

Ever since I spent nine months in Japan teaching unsuspecting businessmen how to speak English with a broad Australian accent, I've taken an interest in the various methods employed by others to teach the language. But I had never seen anything like Mirindi's. In his determination to learn English, Mirindi had papered the walls of the toilet with pages from English magazines and books. Interestingly, the only publications he had been able to get his hands on were the Book of Mormon and Penthouse Forum. On one wall, Jehoshaphat was telling the Mormons to come out of the desert. On the other, J.L. from Ohio was relating a tale that involved a brunette, crotchless panties and a carrot. I christened it the Mirindi method, and firmly believe that soon English language classes all over the world will employ it.

Mirindi also fancied himself as a bit of an artist, so most of the evening was spent flicking through his rather interesting interpretations of the Old Masters, including thirteen variations on the Mona Lisa alone. To be honest, I didn't mind sitting through this. It was a small price to pay for Mirindi's hospitality. And he at least had a sense of humour about his inability to paint hands properly.

The next day Mirindi showed me the sights of Tirane. In no particular order, they included the clock tower built in 1830, the mosque built in 1823 and the Palace of Culture built in 1966. Actually, I rather like the story behind the Palace of Culture. Construction of the Palace, a gift from the Soviet people, was started in 1960. However, after the Soviet–Albanian split in 1961, the Albanians were left to finish the building themselves; they didn't get around to completing it until five years later.

I have this great photo of Mirindi from that day. It's in Skanderbeg Square with the huge Socialist mural on the National Museum of History in the background. The mural is one of those typically Soviet things with the workers marching forward with a steely gaze and an Albanian flag. Mirindi, meanwhile, is wearing flashy sunglasses, white shoes, and the sort of used car salesman smile that makes you expect to see a glint of light come off the teeth. Enver Hoxha must have been turning in his grave.

Actually, Mirindi took me along to Enver's grave that night. What had formerly been the mausoleum of Dictator Enver Hoxha was now a disco. The mausoleum had cost $90 million to build, and I guess was a pretty good approximation of what a country that had been isolated from the rest of the world for over forty years might regard as a modern-looking building—that is, it looked like a space ship from a 1950s movie. When the Communists were finally toppled in late 1990, Enver's preserved body was tossed out, and coloured lights and a turntable were brought in. Put a $5 cover charge on the door, and hey presto, you have Albania's very first entrepreneurial venture.

Of course, that was the theory. The reality was that most

Albanians had more important things to do with a five-dollar bill than attempt the Macarena. The disco was full of Albanians who looked like Mirindi, with like-minded foreign businessmen who were in town to fleece the fledgling capitalist country. And amongst them wandered very tired-looking prostitutes.

For what was, in effect, the most expensively housed disco in the world, the sound system also left a lot to be desired. The turntable sat unevenly on the slab that had previously been home to the last mortal remains of one E. Hoxha. And the few speakers boomed unnaturally in a building that had been acoustically designed for hushed whispers, not disco beats. Worse still, the DJ only had one record—*Saturday Night Fever*—and he insisted on playing the album's obscure side, the one that featured Walter Murphy, David Shire and Ralph McDonald. After listening to the same tracks 10 times in a row, I convinced Mirindi to leave. It was obvious the guy wasn't going to play the side with 'Stayin' Alive' on it (perhaps it was too poignant for the Albanian audience) and besides, I had to be up early the next morning to catch a bus to Gjirokaster.

Although Gjirokaster is only 160 or so kilometres from Tirane, the last bus for the day left at 10 am. In fact, every bus out of Tirane left in the morning and stopped running soon after lunch. It wasn't laziness on the part of Albanian bus drivers, or lack of passengers, or even some obscure union rule. According to Mirindi, it was because there wasn't a single bus in Albania with working headlights. And they needed light so that the bus driver could find the vital engine part that was bound to fall off.

Personally, I was surprised that the bus to Gjirokaster even made it to the outskirts of Tirane. It coughed and spluttered like a tuberculosis victim, struggling from one mileage marker to the next. By the time it limped into Fier, a quick tinker from a roadside mechanic was in order before it continued its way south through the heart of Albania's oil industry.

Like everything else about Albania, the oil fields looked like something from another era. Actually, I half expected to find James Dean and Rock Hudson reprising their role from *Giant* amongst the grubby derricks.

Most of the fields and derricks appeared deserted and derelict. Oil oozed from the pumps and onto the fields that surrounded them and into the river that ran through them. Even the few houses that dotted the valley couldn't escape the grime. Imagine an earthbound version of the *Exxon Valdez* and you have a pretty good idea of what it's like around Fier. Except it's not otters that are covered from head to toe in slick, viscous oil; it's the poor Albanians.

Soon the bus crawled up some mountains and put the black oil fields behind us. After Tepelene, I could even honestly say, for the first time in Albania, that the scenery was pretty. It was here that the bus stopped for lunch at a roadside diner set in a wooded glen beside a sparkling mountain stream.

That diner is indelibly etched on my memory. It sat high on an embankment and beside a natural grotto where the stream briefly became a waterfall, spraying a cool mist of water across the tables on the terrace. It was really quite lovely, but that isn't why I remember it. I can honestly say that on that day I was served the most inedible bowl of gruel I've ever been offered.

If I'd had to give it a name, I would have said it was gizzard soup. It was a broth brimming with entrails and other animal parts that I had thought were never meant to be consumed. It had chilled slightly, so the top of the soup had congealed into a thick white layer of fat. I dipped thick, crusty bread into it, being careful not to disturb the gizzards, but even the taste of the broth made me retch. I can usually eat pretty much anything—the sparrow yakitori in Japan and the grilled monkey arm in Zaire are two meals that spring immediately to mind—but that day, despite knowing that there were Albanian families, probably even on my bus, who would kill for a meal like this, I left it. It took three bars of cheap Greek chocolate to get rid of the taste.

The bus was continuing on to Kakavia, a town on the Greek border, so I was unceremoniously dumped at a turn-off for Gjirokaster on the main road that by-passed the town. Gjirokaster is famous for two things: its old town centre, featuring three- or four-storey stone-roofed towers clinging to the mountainside, and the fact that Enver Hoxha was born there. While the Gjirokasterians are understandably proud of the old town—in fact, any new buildings must conform to strict historical preservation plans—they don't like to be reminded of Mr Hoxha. Indeed, the huge bronze statue that used to commemorate the fact that he was born here was one of the first things toppled over when the Communists were kicked out. But the old architecture remains. In fact, I could see it—sitting precariously high on a hill above the Drino Valley—a good three kilometres away.

It was a long walk, and as the weather was getting warmer the further south I was heading, I worked up a bit of a sweat. Once I hit the edges of town, the road began to become appreciably steeper, so I decided to get directions before I committed myself to any particular course of strenuous action. As luck would have it, I found myself outside a cafe, and sitting at the table closest to the road was the only person in the whole place who could speak English. His name was Skender and he invited me to stay in his house.

Skender was like Frank from Murphy Brown—thin, balding and slightly neurotic. He lived with his wife and mother in an old house that clung to the side of the hills and looked out across Gjirokaster. The house looked like a Swiss chalet, if Swiss chalets got rid of the flower boxes and were covered in grapevines instead. It belonged to Skender's mother, but as the eldest son—and in rec-ognition of looking after her in her old age—the house would pass to Skender.

'Then I will turn it into a guesthouse,' he said wistfully. 'But now my mother will only let me have one guest at a time.'

Skender's wife was named Berta, and she was the tourist officer up at the Hotel Cajupi, the only hotel in town. I wondered how she would react to my staying in her family home rather than patronising her employer's hotel. After all, from what Skender had told me, it was solely for the purpose of looking after people like me that she had been employed in the first place. It was her job to greet English-speaking guests, explain the hotel's services and ensure that they enjoyed their $60-a-night rooms. I thought perhaps she would be a little pissed off.

I needn't have worried. She was lovely; a rosy-cheeked beauty with porcelain skin and dancing, dark eyes. She seemed delighted that I was staying in her home and hanging out aimlessly with her unemployed husband. I think she hoped that Skender's English skills would benefit from spending time with a native English speaker, and he would thus become more employable. I hated to imagine what my dropping of g's, shortening of words and other dreadful Australian English habits would do to poor Skender's employment prospects.

My first day in Gjirokaster consisted of hanging around coffee shops and chewing the fat with Skender. In the course of the day I met pretty much everyone in Gjirokaster, including the mayor and the manager of the hotel, who had heard I was in town through Berta and tracked me down to practise his few words of English. This amounted to nothing more than 'What are you doing in Albania?' He didn't seem the slightest bit perturbed that I wasn't staying in his august establishment. Not for the last time, I found myself thinking what a weird and wonderful place Albania was.

Late in the afternoon, Skender took me up to the town's major tourist attraction, the fourteenth-century citadel. The citadel sat high above, dominating the town, and had spectacular views across to the mountains that ringed the Drino Valley. The citadel walls and

the large field behind them were largely deserted, with rusting lighting pylons that suggested the field might have once been used for
something other than a grazing ground for a few scraggly sheep.
My guidebook said that the citadel housed a Museum of Armaments, but we couldn't find anyone to let us in. I can't say I was
really disappointed. I don't really get off on looking at old guns,
but the two-seater US reconnaissance plane shot down over Albania
in 1957 (now the prime exhibit in the museum) would have been
interesting.

The next day Skender was busy—doing what exactly, I don't
know—so he introduced me to his brother-in-law, Ali. Ali was
more in the Mirindi mould, and ran a market stall selling anything
from women's clothing and toiletries to car batteries and padlocks.
The plan was that I would spend some time with him hanging at
his market stall, soaking up another facet of daily Albanian life. It
was a pretty uneventful day. Ali only had two customers: a girl
who bought a poorly reproduced poster of Jean-Claude Van Damme
and a guy who spent half an hour trying on sunglasses before
deciding he didn't like any of them. Ali didn't seem to mind. We
spent the day drinking coffee and debating the merits of his highly
dubious 'raki is life' philosophy.

Raki is an aniseed-flavoured grape brandy, not unlike Greek
ouzo, and Ali had extraordinary faith in its powers.

'Raki!' he'd say, lifting a glass and admiring it as he would a
pretty girl. 'It is what makes life worth living!'

Early in the afternoon, just as Ali was starting to live by his
philosophy a little too enthusiastically, and trying to get me to
adhere to it as well, Skender's brother, Argon, dropped by to see
if I wanted to come down to his clinic. Argon was a nurse at the
local hospital, but every Wednesday afternoon he supplemented his
meagre income by injecting people.

Basically, people didn't trust the hospital to use fresh needles and
fresh medicines. So they bought their own on the black market and

paid Argon a small amount of money to inject them. Frankly, from what I had seen of the hospital, I didn't blame them. Skender had taken me there the day before and, to be honest, it was disgusting. Used needles, bandages and swabs lay in piles in corners. The walls were smeared with blood and shit and god only knows what else. And patients lay on foam mattresses or blankets on the floor because the hospital couldn't afford beds. In fact, I suspect the hospital would have been closed by the local health authority but for the fact that it was the local health authority.

Argon's patients were mainly children, who seemed to take their medicine with a stoicism beyond their years. The only problem was a woman who yelped like a puppy when Argon went to give her an injection and a little old guy who insisted on asking me questions in Albanian with his pants around his ankles and a needle in his butt. Skender arrived, which pleased the old fellow immensely. Skender could now interpret his questions. It seems all he wanted to know was what the hell I was doing in Albania.

That night Argon was having a party for his four-year-old daughter. It was like family parties the world over, with the social strata within the family just as clearly defined. Ali and his wife were the nouveau riche, in flash clothes. Skender and Berta were the intellectuals. And Argon and his wife were the aspirers, trying to get ahead in their not-quite-finished unit on the edge of town. It was noisy and fun and very warm, with everyone laughing and screaming and Ali slowly getting very drunk. The room fell silent, however, when a song about Kosovo, the disputed territory with Serbia, interrupted the evening's entertainment on the TV. Everyone got sentimental and sang along with the guy on TV, who was wearing pointy shoes and a tuxedo a size or two too small. Skender interpreted for me.

'Oh Kosovo, beautiful Kosovo,' he sang, tears welling in his eyes. 'One day you will be back in the bosom of the motherland.'

It was my last night in Gjirokaster, so Skender, Argon and Ali took me to the town's only disco. It was in a large, cavernous hall made to look even more cavernous by the fact that there were only five other people in it, including the town's neurosurgeon. The DJ seemed to be stuck in some sort of fifties time warp and played the same three songs over and over again—'Great Balls of Fire' by Jerry Lee Lewis, 'Rock Around the Clock' by Bill Haley and the Comets and 'Tutti Frutti' by Little Richard. Ali continued his pursuit of the meaning of life and, just after midnight, found it, Albanian-style, when he passed out in the middle of the dance floor clutching a bottle of raki.

The next morning I caught a bus from Gjirokaster to Pogradec. I was sad to be leaving. In the short time I had been in Gjirokaster, I really felt I had become part of Skender's family. And judging by the teary three-cheek kisses goodbye, they did too. Just as I got onto the bus—an old German school bus totally unsuited for going from one end of the country to the other—Skender's mother stepped forward and gave me a packed lunch of bread, cheese and tomato. I don't mind admitting to wiping away a tear as the bus pulled away.

The countryside outside Gjirokaster was tired and haggard. In fact everything seemed to be affected—the cattle, the sheep, the people, the tractors, even the birds. Everything looked totally shagged out and too buggered to go on. Adding to it all, I noticed that Albania was the only country I'd been in where all the road signs were hand-painted.

Just after Permet, the road began winding its way close to the Greek border, and the concrete bunkers started appearing again. About halfway to Erseke, the bus erupted into wild cheering as passengers leapt to their feet and waved their arms frantically at half a dozen or so men walking up the side of the hill with white knapsacks tied to poles slung over their backs. I asked the man beside me who they were.

'Refugees,' he said.

'From where?' I asked, not altogether sure why any refugee would come to Albania.

'From Albania,' he said as if I were a moron. 'They are going to Greece to work.'

Judging by the army patrol and the contingent from the local police station on hand for the send-off, they were crossing the border illegally, but with the Albanian government's blessing.

The next time the bus stopped was at Korce. Following the lead of the other passengers, I got off to stretch my legs. After scouring a roadside vendor's table for something with a use-by date within a decade or so of the current date, I decided to look for a toilet. After a series of lewd gestures, I was pointed towards the town's only public toilet.

Albania being Albania, the place wasn't lit. And if the stench that greeted me hadn't physically knocked me back a metre or two I might have blithely plodded down the stairs to where the cubicles were situated. When my eyes adjusted to the light I realised that to have ventured any further would have been a very bad thing indeed, and had I done so, I might still have been in therapy. The entire floor, from corner to corner, was covered with at least six inches of shit.

I returned to the bus shaken, and a paler shade of white, and with a steely resolve never to travel on public transport in Albania again without visiting the little boys' room first. Not that I would have much chance to put my newly acquired knowledge into practice. Pogradec would be my last stop in Albania before crossing into Macedonia; the bus arrived just before dusk and well before nature called again. I took a room at the Guri I Kug Hotel, content in the knowledge that my sensibilities were safe.

I sat in my room overlooking Lake Ohrid, the concrete bunkers lining its shores staring passively towards Macedonia. The central heating rattled and the mattress was lumpy and uncomfortable. It suddenly dawned on me that this was the first time I'd actually paid for a room during my entire stay in Albania, and it was the worst one I had stayed in by far. For a pretty poor country, its people were extremely generous.

As I drifted off to sleep, something really quite poignant struck me. The only two Albanian phrases I had learnt during my stay were gezuar (cheers) and faleminderit (thank you).

CHAPTER EIGHT

Sofia

Soundtrack: *Nevermind*—Nirvana

I left Albania in a taxi with broken headlights and a missing rear windscreen. It drove beside the lake towards the Albanian–Macedonian border, past deserted fairgrounds and rusting ferris wheels, and alongside concrete bunkers that seemed to have formed a guard of honour to farewell me. Snotty-nosed children who'd spotted the taxi and figured that if I could afford a taxi I could afford to give them money ran beside the taxi with hands outstretched, begging. I sat in the back, with my Walkman on, gazing across the lake, and felt I was living out a scene in a movie.

I was listening to Nirvana's 'Something in the Way', which gave the whole scene an even deeper sense of poignancy. Everything seemed to be in slow motion—the children, the lake, the driver— and as if it had been shot in grainy black and white. I put it down to the deteriorating mechanical condition of the taxi, and the fact that we spent the final 300 metres to the border stuck behind a wizened old man on a donkey certainly didn't help either.

The Albanian border post was a little wooden shack that looked remarkably like an outback Aussie dunny. A guard stepped out— his uniform was crumpled and he was rubbing the sleep out of his eyes—and stamped me out of the country without asking me any questions or getting me to fill out any forms. The Macedonian border post was a couple of hundred metres up the road. It was brand new, a modern structure that looked like one of those fancy new BP petrol stations, but without the petrol bowsers or the 24-hour convenience store. Where the cashier should have been, half a dozen Macedonian border officials sat around in equally new brown uniforms doodling on freshly printed customs forms. The expected trade boom with Albania had not arrived, and they were just sitting around killing time.

Brad, the American pervert I had met on the train to Croatia, had told me that the Macedonians border officials here were thiev-ing, money-grubbing bastards, but I found them to be very pleasant individuals. They probably appreciated the fact that I didn't leer at them or try and talk them into a quick shag behind the foreign exchange counter. My visa was issued promptly and efficiently, and I was able to change money at a competitive rate. The girl respon-sible for foreign exchange even broke a US$100 note into smaller US notes for me so that I didn't get stuck with more Macedonian dinar than I needed. The only sour note in the whole proceedings was when they told me that the nearest town, St Naum, was 10 kilometres away and I'd have to walk.

It was a pleasant stroll, though, and it gave me time to appreciate just how pretty and neat and green Macedonia was. The road was immaculately paved and the grass on the verges was greener, thicker and healthier-looking than anything I had seen over the past week or so. The road signs were shiny and reflective and not hand-painted. I was amazed by the difference having even just a little bit of money in the national coffers made.

St Naum itself was a pretty and neat town that looked like something you'd be more likely to see in Germany than in the Balkans. The turn-off for the tenth-century monastery down by the lake was clearly signposted, and there was a bus stop with a timetable posted in a weatherproof cover. I noted with alarm that the last bus to Ohrid, my planned destination for that day, had already left. I had two options. I could stay the night in St Naum and catch a bus the next day, or I could attempt to hitch a ride to Ohrid. As St Naum was still a good kilometre or two away and I was too buggered to walk any further, I decided to stick my thumb out and see what happened.

I've never been a big fan of hitchhiking. And that morning reminded me why I disliked it so much. I sat on that corner for two and a half hours—forty minutes of which I spent sheltering from a rain squall—before the first car went by. Luckily, for my sanity, it stopped.

The driver and his two passengers were Albanian, and judging from the jerrycans in the back, they were in Macedonia to buy black market petrol. Buying black market petrol in Macedonia and smuggling it back into Albania was a lucrative and, apart from your car exploding into a fireball in the event of an accident, only slightly risky business. Although the Albanians had plenty of oil, they didn't have the technology to refine it. In the old days they'd send the oil off to the USSR, and it would come back as petrol. Now they sent men in flat caps and jackets with worn elbows in unroadworthy Trabants across international borders to forage for it.

The road from St Naum to Ohrid followed the lake and, with the snowcapped mountains on the right, was very beautiful. The Albanians had bought petrol in St Naum—where it was cheapest— and were returning around the lake, past Ohrid, to a border crossing more amenable to their line of business. Although the highly incendiary nature of the jerrycans full of petrol concerned me—particularly considering the driver's habit of cleaning his teeth with a toothpick as he drove—I eventually relaxed and let myself enjoy the ride. Just before Trpejca, however, the Albanians started arguing amongst themselves.

At first the argument was verbal. One of the passengers yelled at the other passenger, who then yelled back. After a few seconds of silence, the whole the process started all over again. Periodically, they would turn around and smile at me from the front seat, just in case I thought they were yelling about me.

The yelling didn't bother me. I had my Walkman and the scenery to distract me. But when the aggressive gesticulations that accompanied the yelling deteriorated into crow pecks on the head and thumps on the arm, I became a little concerned. I was worried that an ill-directed blow would catch the driver on the chin and send us careering down a cliff to the lake below as a rolling ball of flame.

The rougher it got, the more often they turned around to assure me, with forced smiles and raised eyebrows, that although they were trying to kick the shit out of each other, I was not in any danger personally. Soon the fighting deteriorated into a wrestling match. By Ohrid, the two passengers had each other in a headlock.

The Albanians weren't stopping in Ohrid. They were in a hurry to get around the lake to Struga and then on to Tirane with their fuel. They dropped me off at the tourist office and drove off, each waving to me with his free hand as he hit the other with his other hand.

Ohrid is a pretty lakeside town that first came to prominence when the Romans used it as a stopover on their way to Constantinople. The official Ohrid tourist literature claims that Ohrid is a place where you can hear the whisper of nature and feel the tameness of the people. They also seem to think that there is some touristic mileage in the fact that Lake Ohrid, on whose shores the town sits, is two thousand years old. I arranged to stay with a family in a flat just across the road from the tourist office and just on the edge of the old town, a protected UNESCO world heritage site.

I met the landlady, threw my pack in my room and hit the town.

I was really excited about being in Ohrid. Since my days as a student of medieval history, I've been a big fan of icons. If I were to be honest, they were probably the reason I took up medieval history in the first place. Well, them and the whole King Arthur and the Knights of the Round Table thing. For some reason, the naive, two-dimensional style and simple religious themes appealed to me. Perhaps it was because I figured that, given a bit of time, even I could make a pretty good fist of painting one. And here I was in Ohrid, a town that was basically a shrine to icons. The place even had an icon museum. The curator in the Icon Gallery up on Klimintov, beside the church of St Clement said that they had the best collection of icons in the Balkans, probably in Europe. After spending a couple of hours wandering around the collection, I believed him.

I shan't bore you with details but suffice it to say, with over 350 chapels in Ohrid, there were more icons than you could poke a stick at. I wandered from chapel to chapel, from St Sophia through to St Clement's, like a kid in a candy store. At St Bogorodica, a tiny Byzantine chapel tucked away behind Kosta Abros, workmen were fixing a beam in the roof and had simply leant a collection of priceless icons against the wall as they worked. Elsewhere, icons that would have been the pride of any collection, private or public, stood on crude stands gathering dust.

Ohrid . . . well, Ohrid is beautiful. Lying on the grass in front of St John's, soaking up the sun, gazing across the blue lake . . . swallows diving . . . yellow flowers with an overpowering perfume . . . insects buzzing. Down below, in a little grotto with a weeping willow and small fishing boats dragged up on the shore, two white swans swam serenely on the lake. It was archetypal spring and it was wonderful. It felt great to be alive.

Things were a bit more awkward that night at the home I was staying in. My landlady could not speak English and seemed to

have an aversion to putting the television on. Her idea of the ideal
night in, it seemed, was to hand me a coffee table book on Tito
and watch me read it. I flicked through the book, nodding appreciatively at pictures of Tito opening factories and meeting with
Soviet dignitaries, and hoping that the phone would ring so I could
sneak off to bed. The atmosphere was so tense that I jumped each
time the clock on the wall ticked.

At around 10 pm, the landlady's daughter arrived home. Her
name was Katrina and she was studying English at a private
college in the centre of Ohrid. She chastised her mother for not
offering me coffee and hustled her into the kitchen to make some.

'Don't mind her,' she smiled. 'She's never been the same since
Tito died.'

The coffee was thick and black and served in small cups. As I
reached the thick dregs, Katrina took the cup from me and turned
it upside down on its saucer.

'Spin it three times and I will read it for you,' she said, smiling.

I wasn't sure that I wanted to know what was ahead of me,
especially so early on in my trip, but I did as she said.

'There are many paths,' she said after a few minutes of peering
into the cup. 'A bird will follow you and bring you luck. But look!
A black snake! That means a man with black hair will try and harm
you. But you have much luck and good fortune.'

The dark-haired man reference wasn't much help to me. I was
heading towards the Middle East, India and Asia—just about every
man I came across for the rest of my trip would have dark hair. I
would have preferred it if Katrina had been a little more specific,
giving the guy a limp or a glass eye or some other more distinctive
physical feature.

After turning the cup to the left and the right to see if there was
anything she may have missed, Katrina told me to put my finger
in the cup and make a wish. She looked back into the cup and
gasped.

'Oh, you have very good fortune!' she exclaimed. 'Your finger has made a horse shape! And look! A dark lady will help your wish come true!'

That night I had a very bizarre dream that involved Tito, both his tin legs, and a dark-haired lady dressed as a dark-haired man. When I woke up, I didn't feel particularly lucky.

That morning I caught the bus to Skopje. Ohrid was beautiful, and I could have quite happily spent a week or two there, but I had a feeling deep down in the pit of my stomach that I should get a wriggle on. My jaunt through the Balkans had been a bit of an indulgence, and had eaten into resources that were already looking a little threadbare. It was time to put some serious kilometres under my belt.

Skopje is the capital of Macedonia and was one of those places that you want to leave as soon as you arrive. Although my guidebook described it as 'picturesque', I found it a rather nondescript place. Even the old town, described by my guidebook as 'beguiling' was full of UN soldiers from the US and restaurateurs determined to extract the very last red cent out of them. I decided to catch the first train out to Bulgaria.

The train left at 10.00 that night. It wasn't actually going to Sofia—in fact its final destination was Belgrade. But it connected—at Nis, a Serbian town halfway between Belgrade and Sofia—with a train that was heading to Bulgaria. That night, as the train sat darkened on the poorly lit platform at Skopje Railway Station, it didn't look as if it would be going anywhere.

I didn't have a good feeling about this train trip. It wasn't the train. Once it started its generator and the lights in the carriages flickered on, I could see that it was probably the best train I'd seen on my journey so far. It was relatively sleek and modern, with comfortable airline-style reclining seats in clumps of four facing each other. But there was something about the empty platforms and the empty carriages and the pervasive smell of stale urine that unnerved me.

Of course, it didn't help that my Serbian visa had expired six days before. Thanks to my little jaunt into Bosnia, it had taken me longer than I had expected to get to Serbia. I probably should have stayed in Skopje and got another one, but when the guy selling me the train ticket didn't notice that my visa had expired, even though he insisted I had a Serbian visa before he sold me the ticket, I figured I'd get away with it. That night, as the train pulled out of the darkened platform and into the even darker night, I wasn't so sure any more.

I had the entire carriage to myself, a phenomenon that made me even more certain that I was heading towards some disaster—or, at the very least, towards a deserted shunting yard. But after 20 minutes, a neatly dressed conductor wandered through the carriage. He checked my ticket and, as conductors are prone to do the world over, told me to take my feet off the seat in front of me. It was quite a petty act. There was no one else in the carriage and I had taken my boots off to make sure I wasn't rubbing piss or shit (or whatever else I had trodden in that day in Skopje) onto the seat. As soon as he left the carriage, I put my feet back up again.

Ten minutes later, two policeman wandered through the carriage and I instinctively took my feet of the seat. They didn't care; they were just wandering through to show that they were there. Half an hour later, a guy in a blue uniform came along and insisted on searching my bag. It seemed that on the Skopje-to-Nis Express, officials outnumbered passengers about four to one.

I'm not sure what branch of the police or armed services this guy was from, but he insisted on the most thorough search of my belongings since the time the guys at Sydney Airport were convinced that I was bringing back illicit substances from Thailand—first in my toothpaste, then in my shampoo and finally in my bowels. He placed each item on a seat and demanded, stony-faced, that I explain what each of them was. Within minutes, everything I was carrying was strewn over the closest seats and the four just on the other side of the aisle. After determining that I had nothing that could be used to derail the train, or hijack it and demand that it go to Libya, he rather ungraciously indicated that I should clean up the mess I'd made. As a final insult, he screwed up his nose and gestured towards my feet.

'And put your shoes on. Your feet stink!'

After repacking my bag, I spent the next hour or so staring out of the window into the dark. I remember thinking that everything seemed more mysterious and dangerous in the dark. Each time the train stopped, the darkness seemed overtly more sinister. During the day, there is always a platform or a red signal or a grazing cow to indicate why your train has come to a complete standstill. But at night, you can never be quite certain. These things are hidden from you, and your imagination takes over. And with me, that's not a good thing. That night I had our train stopping because of renegade bandits, Greek terrorists protesting at the Macedonians' insistence on using the name Macedonia, and a pack of drunken UN soldiers whose UN Land Rover had stalled on a level crossing.

We reached the border just after midnight. On the Macedonian side of the border, the formalities were cursory. A man in a brown uniform simply strolled into the carriage, stamped my passport and went on his way. But I knew I was in trouble when the Serbian immigration officials got on the train carrying automatic weapons and wearing blue-green camouflage pants. One of them flicked through my passport, then barked 'No visa!' When I pointed to the expired one, they motioned with their guns that I was to follow them. I went to get my bag—hell, that guy in the blue uniform might have seen something he liked and could return while I was away—but they would have none of it.

The train had stopped beside dark, vacant fields. There was only a small wooden shed beside the tracks. I was taken there and told to wait in the small, dusty waiting room with ragtag bunch of Romanian gypsies and an apparently terrified Croatian. At the end of the waiting room was an office, the only room lit.

About 10 minutes later I was called into the office. A tired and cranky-looking official sat a desk and an armed soldier stood beside him. The official had my passport in his hand. He pointed to my Serbian visa.

'Expired!' he said, angrily. 'This visa has expired!'

I gave him my dumb tourist look, which exasperated him. He raised his eyebrows and said something to his offsider in Serbian— no doubt something derogatory about the limited mental faculties of Australians—and then pulled out a dusty ledger.

'You have been to Croatia?' he asked, accusingly. I nodded. There was no use denying it. I had a Croatian visa in my passport.

He grumbled something under his breath and then grumpily wrote my details in his book, huffing and puffing and cursing the whole time. He stamped in a new visa and then dismissively tossed my passport towards me. I was free to leave. As I left, the gypsies and the Croatian in the waiting room looked at me expectantly, trying to get some sort of idea of what tortures lay ahead of them. I just shrugged my shoulders.

By the time the immigration official had processed us miscreants, and a gaggle of Serbian soldiers had checked every toilet and manhole, and under every seat on the train, we had spent over two hours at the border. When we finally got to Nis, my connecting train to Sofia was long gone. And the next one wasn't due for another 12 hours.

Desperate, I went up to the information officer and asked if there was any other way I could get to Sofia.

'There's a train going to Dimitrovgrad in 10 minutes,' he said. 'That will get you to the border, at least.'

At 4.35 in the morning, that sounded fine to me.

Of course I had to find the train to Dimitrovgrad first. The stationmaster at Nis had the same aversion to lighting as his counterpart in Skopje had had. I spent a good deal of time stumbling around in the dark, tripping over Serbian families who had made the station their home. I rushed up and down stairs, running from one platform to the other, following one dead lead after another, muttering 'Fuck! Fuck! Fuck!' Where the fuck was this train to Dimitrovgrad?

A male voice startled me from the dark. 'That's right, my friend,' the mystery man said. 'This is a fucking country!'

I eventually found the train to Dimitrovgrad, seconds before it departed, on the darkest and most distant platform. It was an old wooden train, with polished slatted seats and ornate wrought-iron luggage racks. With a caboose at the back, it looked like something out of the Wild West of America, not the wild east of the Balkans.

Once again I had a whole carriage to myself. But this time I was undisturbed by officials of any kind. As the train rocked and creaked through the Serbian countryside in the dark, I slept, for the first time since Ohrid.

When dawn broke, the train was rattling through a canyon of craggy rocks. It was not dissimilar to the one near the Ponderosa in 'Bonanza', and I wouldn't have been surprised at all if a 'Red Indian' had popped up and started taking pot shots at the train. But I arrived in Dimitrovgrad shortly after, with my scalp intact.

The streets of Dimitrovgrad were empty. The high street was like high streets throughout Europe—lined with newsagents, grocery stores and banks and the occasional betting shop. They were all closed, and the town centre soon gave way to the suburbs, which then thinned and became the less-populated outskirts. I asked a man walking his dog, the only sign of life I'd seen that morning, the way to Bulgaria. He pointed down an empty stretch of highway that seemed to be going nowhere in particular. I set off, not knowing that the longest known distance in the universe is that between the outskirts of Dimitrovgrad in Serbia and the Bulgarian border post at Kalotina. I was also to discover that it is the least used stretch of road in the world. Well, on that morning, anyway.

I'd hate to think what I looked like that morning when I finally stumbled up to the border. I hadn't showered since Macedonia, and my clothes were stiff with sweat. But I think my ghastly appearance may have led the officials there to take pity on me. Despite having a reputation for being viciously corrupt bastards, they stamped me in and waved me through with the minimum of hassle and the highest level of courtesy. In retrospect, I think they realised I had no chance of reaching the nearest Bulgarian settlement without suffering a major coronary, and wanted to make my last moments on this Earth as pleasant as possible.

I set off towards the first town in Bulgaria where I hoped to catch a train or bus the rest of the way to Sofia. There was no traffic on the road and the only signs of life were duty free shacks that dotted the road. Thankfully, they sold water, which I bought at duty free prices and drank voraciously. It was outside one of these shacks—the fourth I'd stopped at I think—that a car pulled up and I was asked if I wanted a lift to Sofia. It wasn't until I had closed the door and put on my seat belt that I realised that both the driver's legs were in plaster. More amazingly, the car was a manual.

I have to say, the way this guy, Dimitri, had figured out how to drive his car in this state was a testament to the innovative spirit of the Bulgarian people. He had pushed the driver's seat back as far as it would go so that his rigid legs, even when they were stretched straight out in front of him, barely touched the pedals. When he wanted to accelerate, he swivelled his hip so that leg was longer and could apply pressure to the accelerator. When he wanted to push in the clutch or apply the brake, he simply swivelled his hip the opposite way.

Dimitri had obviously been doing this for a while because he was quite adept. Soon we were on the road, zipping in and out of the traffic, on our way to Sofia.

If his car was anything to go by, Dimitri was a bit of a wide boy. It had a furry dashboard cover and a panel of switches he could flick to play different tunes on his horn. The sound system was pretty impressive too. It had enough flashing LED lights to illuminate a small town, and speakers big enough to let the rest of Bulgaria—and most of Eastern Europe—know what dreadful taste he had in music.

When I first got into the car, Dimitri was playing techno. I'm not a big fan of techno—it's a little too frantic for me—but I've got to say, it proved to be the perfect soundtrack to the way he drove. He changed lanes to the beat and honked his horn at a car dawdling in the overtaking lane so that it added to an appropriate musical hook. When I pointed at the stereo and nodded appreciatively, he thought I wanted something else on. Figuring perhaps that I was older (in my defence, I must say that I hadn't slept for 36 hours, and had just walked 30 odd kilometres) he changed it to Chris Rea.

The main railway station in Sofia, Tsentralna Gara, sits at the northern end of Boulevard Knyaginya Maria Luiza, the funnels of a nuclear reactor rising dramatically behind it. It was here that Dimitri dropped me off—as Chris Rea warbled something about being on a beach—and pointed me towards the Bulgarian tourist office, RILA. Before I got out, he handed me a pen and insisted that I sign his cast.

'How did you break your legs, anyway?' I asked as I handed back his pen.

'A car hit me,' he yelled, accelerating away recklessly into the afternoon traffic.

I went to the RILA office in the station and organised a room. After asking me how much I wanted to pay—my answer: as little as possible—the rather officious middle-aged man behind the counter flicked through a series of cards, then called a few numbers before he found someone who was home and would have me. After giving me instructions on how to get to the flat I was staying in, he motioned me closer.

'Do not make contact with people,' he warned sternly. 'They are cheats and they are liars and they'll always try to rob you.' I nodded my head and said (even though I had no such intentions) that I would try my best. I hadn't come to Bulgaria to stay holed up in a flat feeling paranoid.

'Nein contact!' he yelled after me as I left, apparently convinced that saying it in German would make it sink in.

Obviously, the guy at the tourist office had had dealings with my landlady before. Her flat was a short bus ride away, and I was barely in the door before she was helping me off with my backpack, running me a hot bath and imploring me to make myself comfortable. She immediately told me that she was in her early forties and that her husband had been killed in a factory accident five years before. When she asked me if there was anything she could do for me, she let her hand linger on my arm just a little too long. When I returned to my room after bathing, a robe was laid neatly on the bed and there was a chocolate egg on my pillow. She was probably just being hospitable, but I jammed a chair under the door handle anyway, then fell into an uneasy sleep.

I rose early the next morning and spent the day wandering around Sofia. In the old days of the Eastern Bloc, Sofia was described as a Communist Geneva, with its neat boulevards and monuments covered in fresh wreaths, and a police force one could imagine beating litterbugs or jaywalkers. And even now, years after the Communists had been overthrown, there was a certain grand Soviet-ness to the city. The boulevards were wide, the government buildings stately and squat. The only true sign that things had changed— apart from the Coca-Cola stalls that soldiers seemed to swarm around—was the derelict state of the mausoleum of the former leader, Georgi Dimitrov.

Dimitrov had once been Stalin's right hand, and his mausoleum had been one of the great shrines of the Socialist era. Now he was officially vilified and the mausoleum was covered in graffiti.

Amongst the various slogans about anarchism, Nazism and Communism, there was even a paean to Guns'n'Roses. In the new world of Bulgarian politics, it seems, Slash was playing Che Guevara to Axl Rose's Fidel Castro.

There was a market just down from the mausoleum selling the kind of stuff that was instrumental in bringing an end to European Communism—Russian cameras, torches that use 'B' size batteries, and watches that can't keep time but are heavy enough to make your knuckles drag along the ground. There were some icons, but they were cheap copies, nowhere near the quality of those in Ohrid. Still, my mum would have liked the markets. There were more lace tablecloths than even she could buy and store away for my sisters' glory boxes.

Actually, I decided that Sofia was a pretty good place to call Mum from. Bulgaria hardly rates a mention on the news in Australia, so I could probably tell her where I was without her worrying.

In my travels, I have found that buying a telephone card is usually the easiest and cheapest way to call home. Not only do you avoid the cost of using an operator, you can also use it on public phones at any time of day, an important consideration when you realise that Australia is in a time zone totally incompatible with the office hours of the rest of the world. I walked into the Sofia telephone office and bought the most expensive telephone card they had.

I soon discovered that telephone technology in Bulgaria had not advanced quite as rapidly as their taste in new political heroes. When I dialled Australia, I was greeted with a beep, a pop and a single drawn-out tone. When I went to the counter to complain, they told me that I couldn't call Australia with this card unless I dialled '2' for English instructions first. Instead of a helpful voice, all '2' got me was someone on the other side of Sofia, not my mother on the other side of the world. I hung up quickly, but not quickly enough. Ten units on my phonecard had been consumed.

After a discussion back at the counter, this time involving three other people, it was decided that I couldn't use this particular card at all to call Australia. And because I had already used 10 units, I couldn't get a refund. Naturally, I was a little agitated by this. Unless I spent the day randomly calling numbers out of the Sofia telephone book, the card would be a waste of 200 florin. In the end I decided to call Mum from Turkey instead, and I cut my losses by selling the card to an American tourist for 100 florin.

Feeling a little peckish—I had skipped the complimentary breakfast at the flat when I noticed the landlady cooking it in her negligee—I had lunch in an upstairs cafeteria just off Sveta Nedelya Place. Two old guys in their mid sixties spotted me coming in and invited me over to their table. One guy looked like Spencer Tracy, with thick white hair swept back with Brylcream. The other was a small, tubby, bald man with big round eyes that made him look like an owl. Spencer was an engineer and The Owl was a microbiologist. Both were already very, very drunk.

'Me anti-Communist,' said Spencer, patting his chest. 'Since child!'

'Me too!' hooted The Owl.

'All intelligent people in Bulgaria anti-Communist,' said Spencer.

'It is Mammon,' said The Owl soberly.

'No liberty,' said Spencer.

'Repression,' emphasised The Owl.

After a few more mouthfuls of his dumplings and a swig of vodka, Spencer returned to the point.

'Always anti-Communist,' said Spencer, poking himself in the chest as The Owl nodded his head in agreement. 'Always!'

Suddenly it dawned on them that they weren't really aware of Australia's political persuasion. Hell, we could still be old-school

Commies, for all they knew! The Owl turned to me, a little concerned.

'Australia? Communist?'

When I answered 'Australia no Communist', they launched themselves across the table and hugged me. Then they pinched my cheeks and slapped my face. Finally, they took turns in kissing my forehead.

'Three cheers to Australia!' they said, lifting their glasses of vodka and downing them in one gulp. 'Death to Communism!'

I would lay money on the fact that they were Party faithful. In fact, it wouldn't have surprised me if they had been in the ruling Politburo.

I have to say one thing for Sofia. It was bloody cheap. That meal cost me less than $2 and included two bottles of beer. I saw *The Getaway*, with Kim Bassinger and Alex Baldwin, at the cinema for 50 cents. (OK, I admit it. *That* was a rip-off.) And later, on Vitosha Boulevard, I found a record shop selling pirate tapes for $1.50. I bought Nirvana's *Nevermind* to supplement my already tiring compilation tapes. If it wasn't for the couple of extra Phil Collins tracks on the end, it would have hit the spot perfectly.

I returned to the flat, via the late Roman church ruins nestled at the back of the Sheraton, to find the lights dimmed and a candlelit dinner on the table. Luckily, I was coming down with the flu and was able to present a pretty good case—coughing and spluttering all over the fine china and silver cutlery—for calling it an early night.

I had planned to take a leisurely tour of Bulgaria, calling in at Trojanski Monastery and taking a stroll through the Valley of Roses. But I was genuinely getting the flu and feeling run-down. I know my landlady would have been more than happy to mop my brow and nurse me back to health but, to be honest, I was sick of Eastern Europe. I was getting sick of the depressing architecture and the nuclear reactors and the meals of greasy sausages. I was sick of meeting sleazy guys like Brad, who visited these countries from the West to look for women poor enough and desperate enough to give them a second look but still white enough to take home to mum. And I guess I was tired.

The next afternoon I caught an overnight express coach straight through to Istanbul. In the end, this part of my journey became somewhat of a Trafalgar Tours version of Eastern Europe—three countries in three days, through the windows of passing vehicles. But instead of a gay bus driver called Bernie, my tour guides had been a car-load of mad Albanians, a young Bulgarian with two broken legs and a lonely landlady with a penchant for frying eggs while wearing a see-through nightie.

CHAPTER NINE

Istanbul

Soundtrack: 'All That She Wants'—Ace of Base

I arrived at Topkapi Bus Station in Istanbul bleary-eyed and humming 'All That She Wants', by Ace of Base. It wasn't because I'd lost my mind—although humming a mock reggae song by a bunch of Swedes would have to rate pretty highly as an indication of an unsound mind. It's just that during an earlier visit to Turkey, that song had been indelibly planted in my psyche.

There was a time when I couldn't walk into a bar on the Mediterranean coast of Turkey without hearing it. Patara. Oludeniz. Kas. It was always the same. That haunting organ line and poxy reggae beat. It became the soundtrack to a time in my life that I am particularly fond of. It was a time when I was happy and carefree and held an inexplicable attraction for pretty English film students. The fact that I was always too drunk to do anything about it is the only stain on an otherwise Utopian period. I guess it wasn't surprising that 'All That She Wants' was the song that was playing in my mind when I arrived back in Turkey.

As I waited for my backpack to be unloaded, it struck me that not only is 'All That She Wants' one of those annoyingly catchy songs that lodge themselves like a limpet in your brain and refuse to leave, it's also got one of those lines you can't figure out for the life of you. It's the one in the first verse, after the heroine has woken up late as the day has just begun (interesting lyrics in themselves). She has decided that it's not a day for water, it's a day for catching . . . what? Sand? Man? Tan? Or is it 'sun', pronounced with a Swedish accent? I couldn't figure it out then and it still drives me mad now . . .

Not that there's anything wrong with misunderstanding song lyrics. Sometimes a misheard line can add immeasurably to the nuances of a song. I still believe that Alex the Seal would have been a much better name for the Go-Gos' 'Our Lips Are Sealed'. And a friend of mine is convinced that Steve Miller is talking about a Swiss cowboy, not a space cowboy, in 'The Joker'. I spent a good deal of a trip travelling around Africa trying to convince him of his mistake, but in the end I came around to his way of thinking. You've got to admit it; a Swiss cowboy called Maurice is a mighty powerful image.

I found my backpack amongst boxes of Bulgarian contraband and wandered off into the bus station. A lot of people get freaked out at the prospect of hundreds of tenacious Turkish bus touts trying to get them on their buses. But Istanbul's Topkapi Bus Station held no fears for me. The cacophony of horns, the persistent touts, the fumes, the dust—it was all quite comforting. A few years earlier I had spent close to three months in Turkey and had been to the bus station half a dozen times or more. Every time I wander around the Topkapi Bus Station I always feel as though I am about to embark upon a most incredible adventure.

It also helped that I knew exactly where I was and where I had to go to secure clean, cheap lodging and a tasty chicken kebab. I walked straight by the touts trying to drag me on their bus and off to some far-flung corner of Turkey for $10, and past the taxi drivers who would charge me roughly the same price to take me 200 metres up the road. I jumped on the tram out the front. I caught it up Millet Caddesi to the centre of town, got off just at the Blue Mosque, and followed the narrow streets of Sultanahmet to the Ilknur Pension, my hotel of choice in Istanbul. The whole journey—from getting off the bus from Bulgaria to slinging my bag down on my bed for the night—took less than 30 minutes.

My arrival in Istanbul hadn't always been like that. On my first visit to Turkey, I arrived at the Ataturk International Airport at 1 am after a 36-hour flight from Sydney via Amsterdam. My guidebook said that the fare from the airport to the centre of town shouldn't be any more than $10. After haggling for what seemed another 36 hours, the guy wouldn't budge from $15. In the end we broke the impasse when he agreed to put the meter on.

I got to see a lot of Istanbul that night. We skirted past the old city walls and crossed the Bosphorus two or three times before arriving in Sultanahmet with the meter sitting exactly on the Turkish lire equivalent of $15.

I'd been ripped off. But even that couldn't dim my excitement that morning or the palpable buzz I had from just being in Istanbul. I sat on a bench in front of the Blue Mosque just soaking up the atmosphere. Swallows flew around the minarets, swooping on the bugs that the lights had attracted. In the distance, on the Bosphorus somewhere, a boat blew its mournful foghorn. I knew that I should really find myself a room somewhere, but with the Blue Mosque in front of me and the equally beautiful Sancta Sophia behind me, I couldn't drag myself away. Then the morning call to prayer wafted across the city ... I've been addicted to Istanbul ever since.

The Ilknur Pension has a lot to do with my love affair with

Istanbul, too. That morning, when every other hotel and hostel in Sultanahmet was dark and shuttered, it had a bright welcoming light burning above its sign. I know now that it was because the owners of the hotel are mad and they had forgotten to turn it off. But when the 'Tache opened the door at 4.00 that morning, I was convinced he had been expecting me.

I never ever found out what the 'Tache's real name was. Neither he nor his wife could speak any semblance of English. He was called 'the 'Tache' by everyone staying at the Ilknur Pension simply because he had a moustache. For similar reasons, his wife was called 'Mrs 'Tache'. Both acted as if they were on day leave from an asylum, speaking in half-finished sentences and cackling dementedly for no apparent reason. If you were really unlucky, Mrs 'Tache would invite you into their bedroom to show you her unfinished needlepoint and offer you small fried fish.

The Ilknur Pension is not one of the great establishments of Istanbul. It's a narrow, three-storey house that has been converted into a rather shambling, chaotic guesthouse. There are limited views of the Bosphorus from the dorm room in the ceiling, but with a shared shower and the mindless nodding of the 'Taches, it doesn't really have a lot going for it. But like More Than Ways in Budapest, it is an establishment I find myself going back to.

And so it was this time. I made my way from the tram past the Blue Mosque and along past the weekly fruit market to a little lane and the Ilknur Pension. And I'm pleased to announce that it hadn't changed one iota in the few years since my last visit. The 'Taches were as mad as ever—Mrs 'Tache came to the door with what looked like a tea cosy on her head—and unbelievably, they hadn't changed the price of their rooms, despite rampant inflation in Turkey. The 25,000 lira room that had converted to $5 before came to only $1 now.

Boy, I was glad to be back in Istanbul! I just found the place invigorating—the sounds, the smells . . . even the call to prayer.

The skyline dotted by the bulbous mosques and their slender minarets. The Egyptian Bazaar, with its sacks of spices and dried fruits.
The Yeni Mosque down by Galata Bridge where for a couple of
cents you can buy seed to feed the millions of pigeons that have
made it their home. The bustling Bosphorus, with its ferries and
tug boats and little wooden fishing boats jostling for space on what
appears to be the busiest harbour in the world. Even those funny
little buses that rear up at the front and always look as if someone
has put too much weight into the back of them. For a place where
not much really gets done, Istanbul buzzes.

I have a list of five things that I absolutely must do whenever I
visit Istanbul. In no particular order, they are:

> Visit the Chora. A great little church out by the old
  city walls that chronicles the life of Mary in mosaics.
  I love the fact that she is born wearing a blue shawl
  and continues to wear one for the rest of her life.

> Wander around the underground Basilica Cistern.
  Huge thick columns, wanky classical music and the
  drip drip dripping of stagnant water. Sean Connery
  had a shoot-out here as James Bond in *From
  Russia with Love*.

> Grab a chicken kebab from Achmed, just down
  from the Blue Mosque, near the tacky souvenir
  shops. Complimentary yoghurt an absolute must.

> Spend a night in the upstairs bar at the Orient
  hostel. Thursday night is particularly good. The
  manager's ugly sister dresses up as a belly dancer
  and all the backpackers are too drunk to notice.

> Mill around the Old Book Bazaar. Dating from
  Byzantine times and run by members of an
  obscure dervish order, it's a great place just to
  hang around and at least look intellectual.

I also have to confess that I even love going to the Grand Bazaar, those ancient, vaulted undercover markets just off Yeniceriler Caddesi stuffed with spices, gold, carpets, leather jackets and silly embroidered shoes with turned-up toes and bells on the back. Sure, it's a labyrinth of tack and bad taste. And sure, it's touristy. But in April, before the hordes of summer arrive, it's possible to wander around the cluttered passages without being hassled too much and maybe even buy a Turkish carpet for a price something like what the locals might pay.

I think I can safely say that I am one of the few people in the world who has been to Turkey and hasn't bought a Turkish carpet. This is despite visiting the country a couple of times and despite being the most likely of the people I know to buy one. It's not that I didn't want to buy one. On the contrary, I was ripe for the picking. It's just that on my first morning in Turkey I picked the wrong guy to try and sell me one.

Actually, 'picked' is probably not the right word to use. It suggests I had some say in just which Turkish super salesman got to me first. And anyone who has wandered through the Grand Bazaar in Istanbul knows that that just isn't the case. You are spotted, and your destiny is decided, the moment you step inside the Bazaar. Mine was assigned to the most inept salesman in the Bazaar. It was apparent in his opening sales spiel. He told me I looked like Francis Rossi from Status Quo, which I guess I probably did with my long hair pulled back. But it was hardly a flattering comparison considering Francis is a good 20 years older than me. The carpet salesman must have been pleased with this line though because he followed it throughout the sales pitch.

'A here we go a here we go a here go, Here we go-ooO! Rockin' all over the world!' he said as he led me into his shop.

The shop was covered in carpets and other items that the Turkish seem to think tourists can't get enough of—fez hats and leather jackets cut along Eastern European lines. He sat me down on the floor, amongst hookah pipes and on loudly embroidered cushions, and brought me tea in a small tulip-shaped glass. I smiled weakly as he began the show.

'Whatever you want, whatever you like, you pay your money you take your choice,' he sang as he laid out a selection of carpets.

When I wasn't particularly interested in any of the carpets he had on offer, he went back to the pile of carpets he had at the back of the shop to see if he could find something more to my liking. 'Down, down, deeper and down,' he hummed.

I decided to make a break for it while his back was turned. I had a terrible feeling that he was about to start singing 'Roll Over Lay Down'. I scampered off into the markets and tried to blend in amongst the seventies-style suits and inlaid backgammon sets. Looking back, I can honestly say that this man is the sole reason I do not have a Turkish carpet on my lounge room floor. Well, him and the carpet seller who told me I looked like Phil Collins.

After a few days in Istanbul, my health and vigour were returning. The flu that had threatened to lay me low in Sofia had passed, knocked on the head by the fresh fruit I bought from the morning market just outside the Ilknur and a more positive state of mind. I walked around soaking up the warm spring sun, glad to be alive, smiling and chatting to everyone I met.

One morning, as I stood outside the bathroom waiting for the shower, I got talking to a Canadian guy who'd been in Gallipoli on Anzac Day. Anzac Day commemorates the landing of Australian and New Zealand troops on Gallipoli on April 25, 1915. The one thing that had disappointed me about my extended jaunt through the Balkans was that I arrived in Turkey too late to go back to Gallipoli for Anzac Day.

Gallipoli is a popular pilgrimage for Australians and New Zealanders. It is here, as legend has it, some 20,000 kilometres from our shores, that our young nations were born. Any Yanks or Brits who get dragged along can't understand what all the fuss is about.

Not only is it a rather barren peninsula, with nothing but a few war memorials to see, but they find it hard to believe that we celebrate and cherish what was effectively a humiliating defeat. To them it is as unfathomable as why we then spend the night in our hotel or pension in the area watching endless re-runs of Mel Gibson running through the trenches in the movie version of *Gallipoli*.

I've got to admit that I've never quite understood all this 'birth of the nation through bloody defeat' malarkey either. But the first time I visited Gallipoli, I found it a strangely moving experience. It was weird to see all the places whose names had been drummed into my subconscious as a kid—Lone Pine, Anzac Cove, Twelve-tree Copse—and walk around an area that was such an integral part of my nation's psyche.

It also gave me a different perspective on what actually happened. We've all been brought up to believe the British were absolute bastards—heartlessly sending the Aussies and Kiwis in to scramble up a steep incline, while they sat on the boats drinking Pimms. When you see the spot where they were supposed to land—a gentle slope all the way up to the Turkish lines—it all makes sense. Something, or someone, set the marker buoys adrift, though, and the soldiers were unwittingly dumped at the most awkward of spots. The place where they landed wasn't a cliff face as mighty as my imagination and a childhood of mythology had led me to believe; it was a crumbly embankment of eroded clay and rocks, but it would have been even more difficult to climb, if anything, than the cliff of my imagination.

I remember standing on the beach at Anzac Cove and looking back past the memorial and at the hill and being incredibly moved. It's about as mystical or spiritual a site as we have acquired in our 200-year history. And to my surprise, it stirred something deep inside me that felt suspiciously like national pride. It had been one of my aims on this trip to stand on the beach at Anzac Cove for the dawn service on Anzac Day—a real spiritual whammy, and the closest an Australian like me could get to finding his soul.

My disappointment at not reaching Turkey in time waned as I spoke to the Canadian. Apparently a group of Australians and New Zealanders had spent the night before Anzac Day on the beach at Anzac Cove sitting around campfires writing themselves off on raki. When dawn broke and the ceremony began at the memorial on the headland 100 metres or so above them, they all started singing 'Advance Australia Fair'. One of the drunken Australians realised that this was not very respectful, and staggered around the carousers going 'Shhhssshhh!'. When this didn't work, he started yelling 'Shut the fuck up!'. Ahhh, Aussies. We're a classy bunch.

As if to punctuate the story, there was a loud boom from the bathroom. The door opened, smoke poured out and the South African guy who had been showering came out, looking like something from a Bugs Bunny cartoon. His face and body were blackened with soot and his hair stood on end. The instantaneous gas heater on the wall had instantaneously exploded while he was washing the conditioner from his hair. The 'Tache rushed up the stairs to see what had happened and, after surveying the damage, simply shrugged his shoulders with a smile. From then on, we had to use the 'Tache's private bathroom downstairs. A lot of the guests started going to the Turkish baths instead.

I spent close to a week just wandering around Istanbul. In the evenings I would sit in front of the Blue Mosque and listen to the call to prayer, first from one mosque, then from another, until all the muezzins in the city seemed to be wailing to each other. In fact, I think the guy in the Blue Mosque and the smaller mosque just up the road were having a duel. One would start, then the other would answer. It was like an Islamic version of the duelling banjos from *Deliverance*.

They were magic days. The sky always seemed to be blue and the flowerbeds in front of the Sancta Sophia had just begun to bloom. I bought a few thin, long-sleeved cotton shirts from the market to make myself appear more respectable in Iran. I ticked off each of my five must-do events. And I was feeling a hell of a lot better. I was invigorated and recharged and ready for the next part of my trip. But before I left Istanbul I had one more thing to do: I had to visit the Pudding Shop.

The Pudding Shop was the legendary meeting point for travellers on the Overland Trail in the sixties and seventies, and it was here that the hippie trail really began. Istanbul was where travellers from all over the continent finally converged—at the crossroads of Europe and Asia—and set off on their common path. The Pudding Shop, in turn, was the gateway to nirvana, a place where seasoned hippies back from the East could sell their beat up VW Kombis to fresh-faced newcomers about to embark on their own journeys in search of enlightenment (or at least a shag or two). Over coffee, tea or something altogether a little stronger, travellers would swap information or leave notices on special boards for friends and acquaintances.

The Pudding Shop isn't called the Pudding Shop any more. It's the Lale Restaurant. But they realise the pulling power of the restaurant's illustrious heritage. They've plastered signs all over the front proclaiming that you are in fact passing the 'World Famous Pudding Shop'. Inside, it's a rather bland self-serve restaurant that doesn't look any different from the other establishments along Divanyolu Caddesi.

Despite the fact that the place had all the ambience of a Woolworths cafeteria, I felt I had to visit and even have a meal. I couldn't continue my grand journey east without spending some time at the Pudding Shop and having a pudding. In a rather pathetic attempt to appease the trail traditionalists, the Lale Restaurant had five puddings on the menu, including one with dry grapes, figs, beans and chickpeas. I ordered a chocolate pudding and ate it in near silence in an empty restaurant, the only sound being the hum of neon behind the plastic illuminated pictures of food. The Pudding Shop wasn't what it used to be, and I began to suspect that the Overland Trail wouldn't be either.

The evening I left Istanbul it was raining. The ferries to Haydarpasa Railway Station, on the other side of the Bosphorus, left from the docks near the Galata Bridge. Grizzled sea captains pulled their boats up to the docks and sold sandwiches filled with sea things straight off barbecues. Elsewhere, guys strolled along the waterfront selling mussels with freshly cut wedges of lemon. I sat at the back of the ferry, huddled against the rain, and watched Europe fade away, the mosques and minarets just grey silhouettes in the misty rain.

Haydarpasa Station was a grand railway station in the European tradition, built for the Sultan by Kaiser Wilhelm in the late nineteenth century as a token of appreciation for the Sultan's continued military and economic support. The grand entrance, and the ticket office it housed, looked straight out of Hamburg, but rather than being rudely ignored by a German ticket seller and being charged well over the odds for the privilege, a friendly Turkish gentleman told me I could get a first-class sleeper from one end of Turkey to the other for what amounted to just over $10.

I decided to catch the Dogu Express to Erzurum and make my way by bus to Dogubeyazit and the border crossing with Iran at Bazargan. The hippies used to catch the Van Golu Express to Van and on to the border at Qutur, where it would connect with the Tehran Express. The service was still listed on the huge wooden departure board at Haydarpasa Station, and still had Tehran as its ultimate destination, in gold paint. But it had not run past Tatvan (on the western shores of Lake Van Golu) since the Islamic revolution in Iran. I convinced myself that if the hippies were still around today, it would be the Dogu Express that they'd catch.

Paul Theroux describes riding on the Van Golu Express at the height of the hippie period in his book *The Great Railway Bazaar*. He is quite dismissive of the hippies. He described them as 'wild-haired boys with shoulder bags and sunburnt noses' and 'short-haired girls [with] the look of pouting catamites'. He despaired of their habit of copulating openly in every corner of the train, and of their dirty feet. And he cynically noted that the hippies, while disowning the stifling social order in their homelands, imposed one just as strict on their travels. They travelled in loose tribal groups with leaders marked by the amulets they wore and the number of women they shagged.

He was also quite dismissive of the Australians he met on this journey. In what is probably my favourite passage ever written about Australian travellers, Theroux describes being forced to share a second-class compartment with three Australians—'two boys and a pop-eyed girl'.

'It was a situation I grew to recognise over the next three months,' he wrote. 'At my lowest point, when things were at their most desperate and uncomfortable, I always found myself in the company of Australians, who were like a reminder that I'd touched bottom.'

I flattered myself by thinking that, twenty years later, I was continuing the tradition and marking the bottom again.

The Dogu Express pulled out of Haydarpasa at 10 pm and shuffled towards the steppes of Asia. After half an hour or so, a little man in a white coat pulled down my bed, fitted crisp white sheets and showed me the stainless steel basin that pulled out of the wall and had hot and cold running water. He left the cabin wishing me 'iyi geceler' (goodnight) and closing the door behind him. I don't remember much about the rest of that night other than that I had the most comfortable night's sleep I'd had in a long time.

I woke up the next day to vast open plains, brown hills and clear sunshine. The same cabin attendant brought me tea and made my bed while I retired to the dining cabin for a breakfast of fresh rolls, jams and yoghurt. It was all very civilised and, I must admit, I felt a little guilty about it. Hurtling across Turkey in the lap of luxury wasn't really in the spirit of the Great Overland Journey. The hippies wouldn't have had men in crisp white uniforms making their beds for them, and they certainly wouldn't have had such luxuries as hot and cold water. I made a promise that once I got to Erzurum I'd start roughing it again.

The dining cabin was charming and comfortable, except for a poster over the serving counter illustrating atrocities committed by the PKK rebels in their attempts to secure a Kurdish homeland. The border of the poster was made up of photos of victims of PKK terrorist attacks, taken minutes after they had been shot, blown up or stabbed. Underneath each picture was the name of the city in which each atrocity had taken place. Hakkari, Diyabakir and Sivas were well represented, but Mardin had the strongest showing. I found it a little off-putting, especially when I was brought my croissant and jam.

It's a little-known fact that I was once arrested as a suspected PKK terrorist. It was in Goreme, in Cappadocia. Cappadocia is the area of Turkey famed for its eerie troglodyte stone buildings hewn into weird conical formations. Like all visitors—well, all visitors who had spent a good part of their evenings drinking raki and listening to badly played bouzouki music—I thought it would be a good idea to sneak out into the Cappadocian wilderness and spend a night in one of these buildings. I was able to convince a group of other like-minded individuals to join me.

There were seven of us—a brother and sister from Melbourne, a girl from Sydney, an American guy who claimed to be a DJ on a college radio station, a Danish chap with a penchant for paisley shirts, a guy from Brisbane and me. We suspected that what we were doing was slightly illegal, so along with firewood, copious amounts of raki and a small cassette player, we also took blankets, to block the windows and hide the light from our fire. Within minutes of lighting the fire and nearly asphyxiating, we realised that the blankets were not a good idea and took them down.

Within half an hour, a couple of regiments from the Turkish army had our troglodyte building surrounded. One soldier nervously poked his head into the room and, relieved to see that we were just silly tourists, asked us to leave the building. We were then unceremoniously frogmarched across fields to a road, the main arterial to Nevsehir, where Land Rovers and police cars with flashing blue lights blocked the road.

I began to suspect that we weren't in too much trouble when the Turkish soldiers 'helped' the girls walk across the terraced fields and used the opportunity to feel their breasts. My suspicions were soon confirmed: when we stopped to take photos of our arrest— holding our hands held behind our heads like they do in the movies—the soldiers rushed back and insisted they be in the photos too. Finally, the army chief for the whole area dropped into the pension we were all staying in for a cup of tea and to check that we were all right.

By the second night, the Dogu Express had reached Kayseri. Kayseri was another dusty town set amongst brown hills, but on the outskirts of town there was a small patch of greenery beside a river where a bunch of moustachioed guys sat having a picnic beside the tracks. They raised a bottle of raki towards the train as a toast, maybe wishing us well on our journey, but probably because they were rolling drunk.

That night a fierce electrical storm raged over the steppes. The next morning I was in Erzurum.

The first time I visited in Erzurum they were celebrating Kurban Bayrami, or Bayram as it is commonly known. Bayram is a Turkish Islamic holiday celebrating the near-sacrifice of Isaac by Abraham on Mount Moriah. In the story, God orders Abraham to sacrifice the son of his old age, Isaac. While not happy with the order, Abraham does what he is told and gets as far as laying Isaac out on the alter and holding a knife high above his son. Just as he is about to plunge the knife into his son's chest, God stops him and congratulates him on his faithfulness. Then he tells him to sacrifice a ram tangled in some bushes nearby instead. In keeping with the tradition, the Turks sacrifice half a million rams on Kurban Bayrami each year. Erzurum is a conservative Muslim town, so on Bayram that year the streets were quite literally awash with blood.

Erzurum was also the first military garrison town I had visited. There were soldiers everywhere—on the streets and in trucks, being whisked off somewhere. They wandered about aimlessly in ill-fitting uniforms, not altogether sure why they were there or even if they wanted to be there. They came from all parts of the country, drafted into National Service and posted to the troubled eastern provinces. The postcard sellers were making a killing.

There were postcards for sale everywhere—on blankets on the pavement, on card tables, on special twirling stands—and they were invariably terrible. Judging by the subject matter, Turkish soldiers are the sookiest, purse-carryingest, most sentimental nancy boys ever to put on military uniforms. The really bad postcards were airbrushed, and featured Turkish soldiers writing to their girlfriends. The girlfriend would appear, rather tastefully, above the soldier's head in a thought bubble and was more often than not sprinkling rose petals on her loved one. It was enough to make you blanch.

This time I caught a bus straight to Dogubeyazit—the closest Turkish town to the Iranian border, and a four and a half hour journey through prime PKK stomping ground. It's a horse and cart, veiled women, army-tanked, moustachioed kind of town that sits below broken hills and is dominated by the conical hugeness of Mount Ararat—well, the conical hugeness of the clouds that perpetually shroud Mount Ararat. And before we finally arrived there, the bus was stopped and searched by fresh-faced shit-scared Turkish soldiers a grand total of seventeen times.

In Dogubeyazit I found myself staying at the Salman Hotel. Not only was it one of the cheapest hotels in town, it was also fun to shock the locals by telling them that I was staying at the Salman

Rushdie Hotel. It was a particularly nice irony that it was also full of Iranian shoe factory workers heading home from a stint making black money in Germany.

Of course when they found out I was going to Iran, they immediately took me under their collective wing. If they'd had any sisters with them I'm sure I would have been offered one as my wife. As it was, they'd just take turns to pop into my room unannounced with a handful of pistachio nuts and a burning desire to teach me Farsi. Within minutes of one leaving, there would be a timid knock on the door and my next Iranian chum would enter. It was like they were working shifts. I began to worry that I would start speaking Farsi in my sleep.

I escaped to the Gaziantepli Kepbap Salonu. It was on the main street, Belediye Caddesi, and had a sign that pronounced proudly in English 'All Kinds of Meal Found Here!'. The night before, patrons had spent the evening cowering under the tables as a gun battle raged between the army and some PKK rebels on the main street outside. Some of the rebels had been caught and were being held in the police station up the road. Tonight, aside from a few bullet holes in the glass and a bullet wedged in one of the tables closest to the front, you wouldn't have known. I was able to eat my kebab undisturbed by either gunplay or Farsi lessons.

I liked the music playing in the restaurant too. The only lyrics I understood were 'Kurdistan, Kurdistan, Kurdistan' but the music was suitably eastern and atmospheric, and made me feel I was somewhere exotic and different and dangerous. I got the guy to write the name of the tape in Turkish on a piece of paper and the next day I went to a tape shop to buy it. The guy was surprised by my choice, but pleased. It was a collection of Kurdish protest songs sung by a blind guy with a ukulele.

The next night I was back at the Gaziantepli Kepbap Salonu. Just on dusk, a huge white dog walked down the empty main street like a lone gunman from a B-grade Western. It had obviously been chained to something—remnants of the broken chain were still around its thick neck—but now it was jogging through the street wide-eyed and frothing at the mouth. It passed though the town and headed towards the army camp. In the background, just as night fell and for the first time in two days, Mount Ararat was clear, free of clouds.

The whole scene spooked me, and I was overcome by a particularly strong feeling that seeing the dog and Mount Ararat meant something. I had no idea what it meant, only that it did mean something. Either I'd been watching too many episodes of 'The X-Files', or the big guy upstairs was trying to tell me it was time to go to Iran.

CHAPTER TEN

Esfahan

Soundtrack: The theme from 'Skippy, the Bush Kangaroo'

My foray into Iran did not start auspiciously. It took me most of the morning to find a van that was heading to Bazargan, the dusty border post 30 kilometres from Dogubeyazit. Then it took another hour or so to convince the driver that I was not related to Bill Gates and could only afford to pay what the local Turks did. Then, when I finally arrived at the border post, scrambling through a hole in a mudbrick wall to finally reach it, the Turkish immigration official stamped me back into Turkey before he realised I was trying to leave.

The extra entry stamp caused a great deal of consternation among the staff on duty that day. No one seemed to quite know what to do about it. After a number of huddled meetings and telephone calls, it was decided that the best course of action was to ignore the new entry and just stamp the exit visa over the top of it. Two hours and numerous cups of sweet tea later, I was ushered into a cramped, airless room where I joined hundreds of other people waiting to be let into Iran.

I must admit I was surprised that so many people were trying to get into Iran. A cursory glance at Western newspapers would generally convince you that it was only trainee terrorists and ex-Soviet nuclear physicists who were keen to visit the country. Yet here on the border with Turkey there were literally throngs, all pounding on the huge metal doors with their fists, wailing and screaming and demanding to be let in. You might have thought a huge, scary monster was behind them and they were about to be consumed. In fact, we were about to run out of air.

The doors had a peephole, and periodically an Iranian guard would look through and choose who he would let in. It was a bit like waiting to be picked for a sports team at school. You stand there trying to look as useful as possible to the two kids lucky enough to have been chosen as captains. If they were picking you for footy you tried to look as tough as possible. For basketball, you tried to look as tall as possible. For cricket, as long-suffering and patient as possible. That day, every time the guard looked through the peephole, I tried to look as un-Great Satan-like as I could.

I must have been doing something right, because the third time the guard swung the door open, scanning the room with his AK-47 as he allowed the chosen few in, he chose me. I scampered through, pleased that I didn't have to suffer the indignity of being one of the last chosen. I flashed a smile to those left behind. They were muttering amongst themselves, complaining and wondering why I, an infidel, was chosen ahead of them. I guess sometimes it pays to be different.

After all the rigmarole I went through in Budapest to get my visa, the procedure at the border was pretty straightforward and hassle-free. A woman in a thick black chador (the capes that women in Iran are required to wear) tapped my details into a computer, another stamped my passport and that was it. I expected the customs official to at least go through my bag pretty thoroughly—to see if I was bringing any subversive stuff, such as a King James Bible or a copy of Penthouse, into the country—but he just waved me through with a generous flourish. It was mid afternoon, I was in Iran and my seven-day transit visa was ticking away. I was as happy as Larry.

After changing money at a dusty bank, I caught a taxi to Maku, the first Iranian town past the border. All the taxis at the border were white Buicks, with plush red velvet interiors and tinted electric windows. The drivers were all swarthy, and wore cheap polyester shirts with huge gull-wing collars. I could have been in some sort of Blaxpoitation movie, except that the scenery—jagged, broken mountains—was one hundred per cent Spaghetti Western.

If I had just ventured across the border into Iran, unsure of whether I wanted to continue or not, Maku was the kind of place that would have had me hotfooting it back to Turkey. It was a town of single-storey shopfronts full of mechanics, vulcanisers and every other profession prone to wallowing in oil, grease and rubber. To be fair, the good folk of Maku probably realised that nobody would ever stop for very long in their town. Most were simply passing through, either into Turkey or on to Tehran. Why bother?

The Buick dropped me off at the bus station and I bought a ticket to Tabriz from the Cooperative Bus Company No. 3. Even using rials I had changed at the official bank rate—well, you've got to make a show of legitimacy—the 242-kilometre bus journey cost me less than a dollar. If I'd used black market rials, which I could have got from the taxi driver, it would have cost me only 25 cents. I knew there and then I was going to like Iran.

I also liked Iranian buses. With their distinctive 'leaning forward' appearance—to give at least the impression of speed—they looked like they had been designed by a cartoonist, or a team of young school boys. My bus to Tabriz also had comfortable plush velvet seats and huge windows that reached from below the level of my knees to the roof. The huge expanse of glass made me feel like I was suspended precariously over the road, and that I would topple out at any moment. I felt exposed, but at the same time part of the scenery. It was like riding in a super wide-screen IMAX movie about Iranian highways.

The bus made its way along a well-sealed road through the usual jagged mountains, with the usual swirling wave-like fault lines. Every so often we passed huge hand-painted signs warning Iranians about the dangers facing Islam and the sacrifices to be made to protect it. In one, a caricature of a grotesquely monstrous Jew towered over a mosque, threatening to destroy it. Another featured grenades with roses growing out of them. As propaganda, they were extremely heavy-handed, but I remember thinking that if I let them, they could really freak me out. I think they unnerved the Iranians, too. Beside one sign, featuring the Ayatollah gazing out over a river of blood, lay two twisted burned-out buses.

Apart from the signs, the scenery along what was in fact Iran's main arterial road to the West didn't change much. Before each town there would be a little greenery, courtesy of irrigation or a well, and a few date palms and an orchard or two. And moments after leaving each town, everything was brown and dusty again. The mountains always stayed the same—broken, twisted and foreboding.

About an hour out of Tabriz, just after Sufian, I got a very real sense of foreboding in my bowels. I blamed it on the rather dodgy kebab I'd had for breakfast in Dogubeyazit. It was early; the guy hadn't even had time to turn on the spit-roast. He simply served up leftovers from the night before. Now, close to five hours later, my rectum was convinced that it was a whirling dervish.

It always surprises me how much energy it takes to fight the call of nature. There, on a bus in the middle of an Iranian desert, without a toilet stop in sight, I was sweating and concentrating like a weight-lifter about to attempt a clean and jerk.

Somehow, I managed to hold on until the bus arrived at the unkempt bus terminal at Tabriz. I was tempted to abandon my backpack and start my search for a toilet immediately, but as it contained my only other change of clothes, I decided against that, Instead, I lost precious seconds waiting for it to be unloaded from the bus. Then I ran around the terminal like a crazed animal that had just escaped from its cage, grabbing passers-by and yelling 'Dast shui! Dast shui!', Farsi for toilet.

Most of the people in the terminal turned from me in panic, realising with horror that the Ayatollah had been right all these years about drug-fucked Westerners. Eventually, just as I was to give up, a little man in a white flowing robe understood my plight and pointed me in the right direction. My dignity saved—well, at least partially—I sheepishly left the bus terminal and found a cheap hotel nearby.

That evening, I was the most interesting thing in Tabriz. Down at the old mud citadel, people stopped what they were doing and stared at me as I passed. On the dusty streets near the markets, two guys on a motorbike drove past pointing at me before nearly ploughing into a fruit stand. It was just like a Jackie Chan movie. Down in the bazaar, a labyrinth of alleys and passageways with red-brick vaulted ceilings, women in black chadors peeked out from behind sacks of brightly coloured spices and watched me go by.

Actually I was quite taken aback by just how blatantly the women checked me out. I had expected them to lower their eyes and maybe scurry off down an alleyway. But instead, they stopped and turned and watched me—wantonly, it seemed—as I wandered by. Some would yell out 'Hello Mister', and giggle when I smiled in reply. I felt like I was in a Diet Coke ad, not in one of the strictest Islamic countries in the world. Worse still, some yelled 'Dast shui' and made what I believed to be greatly exaggerated imitations of my arrival in Tabriz.

The next morning I caught a bus to Tehran. The scenery was

bleak and barren, and the trip went largely without incident. The driver skilfully manoeuvred around trucks and tractors and horse-drawn carts as he sipped tea and cracked sunflower seeds. Amazingly, he only put our lives in real danger four or five times. Just outside Tehran we passed a sign in English that said, 'Servitude is never accepted in an ideology that believes in Martyrdom'. Below was a picture of a white dove copping a bullet in the heart.

Tehran was nothing to write home about either. It was dirty and brown and sprawled from the Alborz Mountains in the north into the vast plains of emptiness to the south and east. It was a village that had grown into a teeming metropolis of 10 million people— 13 million according to some sources—and it showed. The only thing of note was the fact that every single car on the road was a Hillman Hunter.

The Iranians called them Paykans, and apart from a few concessions to modernity—velour bucket seats and carpet on the floor— they were identical to the Hillman Hunters that graced the streets of Australia more than two decades earlier. They were all proudly made in Iran, after the Republic bought the whole factory, lock, stock and barrel, from Hillman and transported it back to Persia. It was the Volkswagen Beetle of Iran, the People's Car of Persia. Somehow, the 10-storey murals of Khomeini that adorned nearly every city block seemed far less threatening when viewed across bumper-to-bumper Paykans.

Although the preponderance of Hillman Hunters gave an air of a time past to Tehran, it wasn't enough to keep me there. One and a half days of my transit visa were gone already and I wanted to spend more time in Esfahan and Bam, two ancient cities with something worth seeing. The only thing tempting me to linger in Tehran was a visit to the former US embassy. It had been renamed the US Den of Espionage by the new ruling mullahs, and from all accounts featured a stall selling various anti-US propaganda, including highly secret—and incriminating—documents painstakingly put back together after being shredded by the fleeing Americans. But my guidebook warned not to linger there. After the little I'd seen of Tehran, I decided to give the whole city a miss.

I caught a taxi from the Northern Bus Terminal to the Southern Bus Terminal. My taxi driver had just returned from working in Japan, and when he found out that I had lived in Tokyo for a year, he took me home to meet his wife and child. His wife brought us a cold, delicious lemon drink as we watched 'Skippy, the Bush Kangaroo' on a brand-new Sony Trinitron TV. It was the episode with Barry Crocker as a horse thief, and it was dubbed into Farsi. After it was finished, he drove me the rest of the way to the Southern Bus Terminal, refusing to take my fare at the end of it.

The Southern Bus Terminal was a huge concrete edifice in the south of the city, right beside the Tehran Institute for the Intellectual Development of Children and Young Adults. I was pleased to note that the bus I caught to Esfahan with the Cooperative Bus Company No. 1–17 had attained the status of 'beautiful bus'. It meant we had lace curtains, a plastic floral arrangement in the centre of the front windscreen and as much hot tea as we could drink.

I sat beside Mohammed, a serious young man wearing a turban. He was a student of religion, and was returning to Ghom, a conservative, fundamentalist town about halfway to Esfahan. He made quite a show of reading an English-language edition of the *Tehran Times*, which, I should point out, was describing Bill Clinton as that 'Gigolo cum President' well before the Monica Lewinsky affair.

Just past the Tehran city limits, we passed three trucks full of dancing soldiers. They seemed ecstatically happy and sprayed water at the bus as we passed them.

'They are on their way to the Khomeini Mosque,' said Mohammed, almost enviously. 'All soldiers must visit it before they go on their *situation*.'

Before I could ask Mohammed exactly what a 'situation' was,

the mosque came into view. Its size was staggering. It was a huge complex of golden domes and minarets, and housed the mortal remains of the Ayatollah Khomeini. It had become the most important religious site in Iran and also its busiest construction site. There were cranes and scaffolding and cement mixers as far as the eye could see. When it was finished, it would boast a university, a hotel and a supermarket. There were also plans for an international airport.

I can remember quite vividly seeing the news footage of Khomeini's body being brought to this place when he died in 1989. Ten million Iranians lined the streets, trying to catch a glimpse as his body passed. Some of them began grabbing inside the open coffin, trying to get a piece of clothing—or a piece of the Ayatollah, as it turned out—as some sort of memento or relic. I remember the coffin coming off the hearse and a helicopter coming in and firing on the crowd as soldiers attempted to retrieve what was left of the body. I had never seen anything like it. In Australia, we tend to prefer to rip our leaders apart while they are still alive.

That day, June 4, is a public holiday in Iran. It has the rather long-winded, but eminently colourful, name of 'Heart-Rending Departure of the Great Leader of the Islamic Republic of Iran Day'.

It was dark when we reached Ghom, and Mohammed asked me if I wanted to stay at his place. It would be late by the time I got to Esfahan, he argued, and I would have trouble finding accommodation. I was tired and still a little unsure of what my bowel might get up to, so I gratefully agreed. Everyone I had stayed with so far on this trip had proved generous and interesting. Mohammed would probably be the same.

Ghom is a heavily religious town. The Iranians regard the people from Ghom as the most fundamental of Hezbollah, and it was here that Khomeini studied the finer points of Islam. All the mullahs come here for day trips and most of the sights are religious, the most famous being the shrine of Fateme, the sister of Emam Reza. (If you're Shiite, that will mean something to you.)

Not that I'd be seeing anything that night. It was late and it was dark when Mohammed led me down windy dusty streets to his home. His mother rolled out a mat for me, brought me some food and went to bed. Mohammed stayed up late, studying by candle-light, silently mouthing verses from the *Koran* to himself. The next morning he woke me at dawn, walked me back to the bus station and put me on a bus to Esfahan. That was Ghom.

My bus to Esfahan had not attained the status of 'beautiful bus', but was cheap and comfortable nevertheless. It travelled for five hours through the flat, dry, dusty plains and dirty brown towns that seemed to be par for the course in Iran, and arrived in Esfahan just before lunch.

A sign on the outskirts of Esfahan declared that it was a science and technology town. I worry about towns that feel they have to tell you what they are. It indicates that although that's what they'd ideally like to be, or what the powers that be want them to be, in reality they are the exact opposite. Luckily, that was the case with Esfahan. Instead of being a haven of sterile laboratories and boffins in white coats, it was a picturesque town that sat serenely by the Zayande River with palm trees and mud-walled streets and mosques covered in pale blue tiles. It was as far as you could get from a science and technology town. Unless, of course, it was nominated a science and technology town sometime when Saladin was kicking around these parts.

I found a cheap, clean hotel just around the corner from where the bus dropped me off, on Chahar Bagh-e Pain. It was run by two brothers; one who spoke English well and another who didn't. Even when he was off duty, the English-speaking brother could be found in his room studying. Unlike a lot of the hotel managers, the broth-ers charged in rials. At black market rates, the rooms were extraor-dinarily cheap—$2 a night. After dumping my backpack in a bare (but clean) room, I ventured onto the streets, excited to finally be in the Iran I had always imagined.

If I was the most interesting thing Tabriz had seen in a day, I was the most fascinating thing Esfahan had seen since the revolution. Everywhere I went I seemed to cause a civil disturbance. If I stopped to look at the map in my guidebook, a gaggle of men would gather and peer over my shoulder. When I bought a felafel or a Coke from a stall, a group of Iranians would rush over and buy them too, as if I had given the place my official stamp of approval. As I walked down a street, black-shawled women would giggle and point and cry out 'Hello Mister'. Down at Meidun-e Emam, the massive Town Square surrounded by mosques, palaces and bazaars, a huge crowd assembled to watch me take a photo of the concrete table tennis tables that had been set up for the locals. Eventually, an army officer came along and, unable to disperse the crowd, suggested I go into the Emam Mosque.

The Emam Mosque is one of the most beautiful mosques in the world. It's set at the southern end of the square, just near one of the old goalposts from the time when the square was used as a polo ground. If you ever see any tourist literature on Iran, chances are it will feature a picture of this place. It was completed in 1638 by Shah Abbas I, and is covered inside and out with pale blue tiles. The entrance looks as though it has been sliced open like a medical dummy to give you a closer look at the intricate scalloped roof. Inside it was cool and quiet, a haven from the harsh afternoon sun. I sat quietly and soaked up the atmosphere, admiring the delicate designs on the tiles.

This mosque is unusual in that it features tiles that make up a picture of Khomeini. It has always been my understanding that the *Koran* expressly forbids the depiction of human form in religious art. I think it's the Islamic take on the 'though shalt not have any graven images' commandment. I remember visiting an old monastery high in the mountains behind the Black Sea in Turkey and being horrified that Islamic zealots had chipped out the faces of the Apostles and Jesus that featured in the beautiful frescoes there. Yet here were tiles bearing the human likeness of the old Ayatollah Khomeini. It crossed my mind that perhaps I should chip out *his* face. At just about the time I had this thought, I was grabbed from behind, wrestled to the ground and put into a headlock.

My first thought was that it was the Komite, the revolutionary guards given responsibility for enforcing the strict laws of Islam. I was fairly certain that my thoughts hadn't been read, but perhaps I had done something else to upset the regime. I went through a checklist in my head—arms covered by long-sleeved shirt, tick; legs covered by jeans, tick; long blonde hair and earrings, doh! I finally summoned the nerve to turn my head and face my accusers, and was surprised to see a bunch of big boofy blokes in shiny track suits and runners laughing at me. It was the All Tehran Wrestling Team.

I knew it was the All Tehran Wrestling Team because their suits had All Tehran Wrestling Team written on the back in English. They were obviously in town for a meet with the All Esfahan Wrestling Team, and were taking time out to do a bit of sightseeing. Well, I assumed that's what they were doing there. They didn't speak English, and apart from asking where the toilet was, I didn't speak Farsi. Our 'conversation' didn't progress much beyond them slapping me on the back and showing me their cauliflower ears. Worse still, each one of them had a camera and insisted I pose in their photos.

After thirty-odd photos, I figured my duty as the token foreigner was done, and I tried to leave. They disagreed, and instead rather forcefully insisted that I join their tour of the mosque. The up side was that I got to see parts of the mosque that I wouldn't otherwise have seen, including the theological colleges and the newly restored roof. The down side was that the guide only spoke Farsi. It didn't seem to dawn on the wrestlers that I couldn't understand, because after each of the guide's monologues they would look to me to see my reaction. Periodically, one of the wrestlers would come up and give me a bear hug. After an hour of this, I clutched my stomach, cried 'Dast shui!' and bolted.

I made my way through a maze of alleyways and ancient arcades to the river and the Si o Se Pol or Bridge of Thirty Three Arches. It was built in 1602 to link the upper and lower halves of the Chahar Bagh, was made of stone and had, surprisingly, thirty-three arches through which the Zayande River rushed.

The bridge was lovely. Although it was closed to motor vehicles, it was popular with pedestrians who, especially at dusk, would stroll across, either alone or with their families. I stood beside one of the niches and watched the river go by. Down on the north bank, just adjacent to the last pylon, I noticed a steady procession of men walking down some stone stairs and then disappearing under the bridge. Being a curious type, I followed.

Hidden under the bridge was a chaykhune. A chaykhune is a place where men go to escape the heat and to drink tea or suck on a hubble-bubble pipe. The bricked walls were decorated with pictures beaten out of brass and copper, exactly like the ones you see in Greek or Turkish restaurants back home, and had hookah pipes (and other weird attachments and accessories that aid the art of hubble-bubbling) hanging from the roof. A canary sat in a gilded cage, singing, beside an old man who took the money and gave out change from a roll of filthy notes he kept in a pouch under his fat belly. It was like stepping back a thousand years and into *The Arabian Nights*.

The heart of the chaykhune was a busy galley where the tea was made and the hookah pipes cleaned and prepared. The waiters were hyper, wearing the traditional black and whites of waiters the world over, but topped with a rather less traditional black fez. They milled around waiting impatiently for the tea to be prepared before swishing away with small cups of tea in tulip glasses on silver trays. Then they skilfully negotiated their way across planks, only inches above the rushing river, to a series of vaulted niches hidden in each of the arches. Here bearded men sat in small dusty rooms on carpets drinking and passing a hubble-bubble amongst themselves. It was a scene played out in every student household in the world. Except here they were drinking tea and the cone had nothing stronger than tobacco in it.

I wandered around, mesmerised. After the relentless heat and glare of the square and the busy streets that surrounded it, the chay-khune was an oasis of calm. A bunch of guys who looked like they'd just returned from planting a bomb on a 747 called me over to their table to drink some chai and, on their insistence, have a suck on their hookah pipe. I sat with them for an hour or so, drinking tea, spluttering uncontrollably and just relaxing. We couldn't speak to each other. They asked where I was from and left it at that. They were so mellow that I began to suspect that there was something stronger than tobacco in their pipes.

I returned to the hotel convinced that Esfahan was one of my favourite places in the entire world. I also met the four other Westerners who were staying there—a German couple, a Dutch guy and a Danish chap. We sat in the courtyard out the back playing sinful Western music on the non-English-speaking manager's portable cassette player and swapping information. The fat manager was pleased to have us there, and sent a young houseboy out to keep us supplied with felafels and Pipsi, the rather sad Iranian attempt at Pepsi. His brother told us that although he had permission to charge foreigners in dollars, he didn't, hoping that word would get around and travellers would come to his establishment. It was working. We were the only five foreigners in town—I didn't want to ask how he knew that—and we were all staying in his hotel.

In the course of the evening we discovered that we had all bought the same Khomeini postcards. They all featured the scowling countenance of the big fella, and we counted that we had bought 55 amongst us. I'm proud to say that I topped the individual count with 25. It's only now that ASIO (the Australian Secret Intelligence

Organisation for the uninitiated) has stopped surveillance on my friends' homes and places of business.

The next day I went for a walk through the parks that lined the Zayande River. They were the only greenery for miles, and were full of families picnicking and hiring those ubiquitous fibreglass paddleboats. I stood on the bank watching them and thinking that whoever had the patent for those boats must be a very rich person. A well-dressed young man in his mid twenties approached me confidently and introduced himself. His name was Maji and he was an Earnest Young English Speaker.

Earnest Young English Speakers are the linguistic equivalent of Born Again Christians. They are just as fervent, they dress the same and they wear that same beatific smile—except it's the English language, not Jesus, that they regard as their own personal lord and saviour. What's worse, they seem to be able to spot me as a native English speaker from miles off.

Maji, like all Earnest Young English Speakers, was unnervingly happy to have found me. In fact he spent the first ten minutes telling me so. He was studying English and he asked me—no, begged me—to let him follow me around for the day.

Experience has taught me that it is wellnigh impossible to shake an Earnest Young English Speaker once he or she has latched onto you. Experience has also taught me that, properly handled, they can also prove quite useful. I agreed that Maji could accompany me as long as he took me to the Rose Garden of the Martyrs, a place to which I would otherwise have been refused entry.

The Rose Garden of the Martyrs is a special cemetery for Iranians who lost their lives in the war against Iraq. I remembered seeing it on the TV news—metal-framed 'headstones' featuring pictures of the guys who died, surrounding fountains that seemed to be running with blood, courtesy of a little red food dye mixed in by the groundsman. As we walked amongst the graves, past hundreds and hundreds of photos of men who had given their lives to become martyrs, Maji voiced his disapproval of the war.

'The government was foolish,' he said. 'Our soldiers reclaimed the areas taken by Iraq in such a short time that our leaders thought we could keep going to Israel. But Iraq fought back. Three years later we were back where we started. It was a terrible waste of life.'

I could see what he meant. There were thousands of these unnerving photo headstones. Most were large portrait shots, obviously done professionally before they went off to the war. Some were action shots of the deceased on a motorbike or beside a cherished Paykan. One featured the victim, blurred, in the foreground, with Khomeini preaching on a balcony just behind him. The photos made the whole thing more personalised, and a little more horrific.

'Let's go,' said Maji, equally unnerved. 'I am very proud of these people. But it is also depressing.'

As we walked back to the centre of Esfahan, Maji was just as candid about the failings of the current leadership.

'Our salvation lies in science and technology!' he exclaimed. 'We must haunt the libraries!'

While a lot of his views were quite enlightened, his views on women were positively medieval.

'Women have become rash since the end of the war,' he said disapprovingly.

I must have pulled a face that said 'Rash? You call that rash?', because he seemed to feel he had to prove his point.

'Last week two women kidnapped a boy to satiate their lust,' he said with his eyes wide open for emphasis. 'They raped him so much he died!'

He was equally disapproving of the women we passed on the way from the cemetery. Without exception, each of them said 'Hello Mister'. Some even let their black capes flap open to show they were wearing jeans or white runners underneath. Some wore make-up, and another had blonde streaks. Maji was almost apoplectic with rage. 'Harlots!' he seethed.

The next morning, I wandered through the bazaar and checked out the 'Shaking Minarets' at Manar Jomban on the other side of town. (You climb up an old mudbrick minaret, brace yourself against the walls and push. It wobbles. Hours of harmless fun!) On the way back to town I passed a new car showroom selling Paykans and felt compelled to go in. It was extraordinary. The gaggle of brand-new Paykans sat in a special showroom with chandeliers and gilt-framed mirrors that wouldn't have looked out of place at Versailles.

The chubby, jolly salesman introduced himself as Sadik, and said that I could buy a brand-new Paykan with velour seats and an AM radio for only $4,000. For a moment I considered the option of buying one and driving it overland back to Australia. How cool would it have been to drive a Paykan through Pakistan and into India and finally down Parramatta Road home? The only problem was that I didn't have the $4,000.

Regardless, Sadik invited me back to his house for lunch. Business must have been good in the Paykan business, because his house was modern and large. It was fully carpeted and had a well-equipped kitchen with a shiny new microwave and dishwasher. He reheated a tuna and bean dish his wife had left in the fridge and motioned for me to go into the lounge room.

After drawing the blinds and locking the doors, Sadik put on a video he had smuggled illegally from the US. It was a grainy, 105th-generation copy of a middle-aged Persian woman in a linen suit singing a discordant song in Farsi. When she slipped off her jacket to reveal her bare shoulders and arms, Sadik whooped with delight. It was like a third-rate club act. But to Sadik it was hot as.

Sadik drove me back to Si o Se Pol, where I had agreed to meet Maji at 2 pm. Maji was waiting impatiently, and seemed a little miffed when I got out of the car and waved goodbye to my new friend.

As we walked across the bridge towards the steps that led

down to the teahouse, he asked if I would like to teach English at his school. Thinking it was one of those questions like 'If you had nothing better to do, would you fly to the moon?', I answered yes. In one swift move Maji hailed a cab, another Paykan as it turned out, and we were on our way to the Payoozi English Academy.

The school was in the suburbs, at the end of a dusty lane that looked like something out of a squalid medieval slum rather than part of a self-proclaimed science and technology town. On all the walls, on old-fashioned computer paper with holes down the side, were daisy-wheel printed signs saying 'English Only Spoken Here'. I was hustled into a bare concrete classroom and introduced to my class by the teacher who usually took them.

The Payoozi English Academy was a private school, and the students ranged in age from 10 to 60. They also ranged in attitude. There were the super-keen students who had saved up for months for just one lesson, and sat up the front of the class wide-eyed and enthusiastic. And there were the rich kids whose parents had paid for the lessons. They sat at the back slouching in their chairs and chewing gum.

The lesson began with them asking me questions. A guy up the front who looked like an Islamic scholar, all bushy-bearded and white-robed, started procedures by asking me about Australia's position on Bosnia. It didn't really improve after that. I was asked about my feelings about Khomeini and whether I fancied Iranian women. When an old guy up the back asked me how old I was when I lost my virginity, the teacher sensibly brought the question session to an end and handed me an English textbook. He indicated that I should lead the class in a selection of drills.

'They say the new movie is a comedy,' I read.

'They say ... the ... new movie ... is a ... comedy,' repeated the class.

'The floor show starts at nine and finishes at eleven.'

'The ... floor ... show starts at ... nine and ... finishes ... at eleven,' came the echo.

The selection of phrases that followed was just as bizarre. I couldn't help thinking what these students were making of these drills. These events were totally out of their realms of experience.

'I went to the night club/country club/drive-in with a group of friends,' they parroted. Without a smirk. Without a giggle. Without comprehension.

After the lessons, all the students brought up their textbooks and asked me to write my name. I started writing things like 'Study hard' and 'Good luck with your English' before Maji stepped in.

'No! No!' he said. 'They want your autograph.'

As I sat signing the textbooks like a movie star, one of the other English teachers came to the door. He waited for me to finish, standing nervously in the doorway. When I did, he dragged me into a corner to talk privately.

'Do not worry about Australia being attacked during a nuclear war,' he said, looking nervously over his shoulder. 'I have worked as an electronic engineer in America. Your country is safe.'

It was the perfect end to one of the most surreal experiences of my life.

CHAPTER ELEVEN

Bam

Soundtrack: 'You're the one for me, Fatty'—Morrissey

I woke up on my third day in Esfahan—my sixth in Iran proper—
and realised that I had less than two days left on my visa. The
sensible thing to do would have been to make my way calmly and
quickly to the border, cross into Pakistan and be done with it. But
the Pakistani border was still a good 1,244 kilometres—at least two
beautiful bus rides-away. Besides, I was rather enjoying my stay in
Iran.

I always had the option to extend my visa. Even though it was
only a transit visa, there was the remote possibility, Allah willing,
that I could visit the local Aliens' Bureau and get an extra few days
added. After my experiences in Budapest, however, I was a little
gun-shy with Iranian bureaucracy. It was arbitrary at the best of
times. Worse still, I had heard that the Aliens' Bureau in Esfahan
was the least likely one in the country to issue an extension.

But I was not totally without hope. The English-speaking

manager of my hotel told me that two Germans had been given a two-week extension just a week before. And earlier in the month, a Dutch guy had been given ten days. It all depended, he said, on the mood of the official on duty that day.

The Aliens' Bureau was on Kheyabun-e Khorshid, just around the corner from the central square, Meidun-e Emam. I felt a little weird going there—it was like I was looking for trouble, like the feeling you get walking past the principal's office at school or when you tell the boss you don't have much work on. I wore a long-sleeved shirt, took out my earrings, put my hair into a ponytail and tried to look respectable.

The Bureau was in an unassuming building, with a verandah on which two green-uniformed soldiers lounged around sipping tea. They didn't seem particularly surprised to see me, and certainly didn't make any effort to search me or inquire about my intentions. They simply pointed to a doorway with a sign in cursive Arabic script above it. Inside, a man in his forties, also in a green uniform and also sipping tea, sat behind a desk. He seemed to have guessed what I was there for, because he gave me a visa extension form to fill out before I asked for it. After I completed the form, he took my passport and told me to come back in an hour with 2,000 rials for the five-day extension.

I guess I should have been happy that I secured a five-day extension so easily. But as I left the compound, I had to find out why I had only been given a five-day extension when the Germans and the Dutch guy had been given more. I decided to go back and ask.

If I have learnt anything in my travels, it is some tips on how to deal with bureaucrats. They seem to bridle at smelly backpackers insisting on their 'rights' or telling them how to do their job. What a lot of backpackers don't seem to realise is that the whole notion of 'rights' is just as alien as they themselves are in some of these countries. You get a lot further by just being polite. Smiling also helps. I knocked on the door of the visa extension office with the sort of smile you see in toothpaste commercials.

'Is there a problem?' he asked, looking up from his paperwork, and clearly more than a little alarmed by my smile.

'No,' I said deferentially. 'I was just wondering why a German couple got a two-week extension, a Dutch guy got a ten-day extension, but I only got five. Is there a problem with Australia?'

He smiled and shook his head.

'No, there is no problem with Australia,' he said, chuckling. 'Because you have asked so nicely, I will give you a seven-day extension.'

'Ten,' I said quickly, with a smile so wide he could see my eyeteeth.

'OK, ten.'

When I came to pick up my visa an hour later he invited me to join him in a cup of tea. When I left, he said, 'Goodbye my friend, enjoy your journey'. So I left the Aliens' Bureau with a ten-day extension and another one of my preconceived notions about Iran turned on its head.

I spent another two days in Esfahan, mostly in the teashop under the bridge. It was starting to get hot now. By lunchtime, the asphalt roads began to melt and people and dogs took to sitting in the shade and panting. With summer coming, it would only get hotter—especially as I travelled through the deserts of eastern Iran and into Pakistan. But it was cool under the bridge. And the sound of the water rushing by only centimetres away made it seem even cooler.

It was tempting to stay under the bridge drinking tea and smoking hookah pipes even longer. There were a lot worse things I could be doing—doing the dishes, or working, for example. But even with the luxury of another ten days on my visa, the time had come for me to move on. The other travellers staying at my hotel had moved on and others had arrived to take their places, including a Dutch couple who had been in Dogubeyazit in Turkey two nights after me. (Apparently the rebels who had been caught while I was there tried to break out of jail. From all accounts, quite a melee broke out.) The next day I caught the Cooperative Bus Company No. 1 beautiful bus to Shiraz.

Shiraz was a nice enough town, with a pleasant climate and a fertile valley famed for its vineyards. (Yep, you guessed it. Shiraz is where the Shiraz grape came from.) Like all visitors to Shiraz, I ventured out to the ruins of the ancient Achaemenian capital at Persepolis, 57 kilometres out of town. Built in about 512 BC by Darius I, the huge palace complex was one of the most impressive cities in the ancient world. Although it was burned to the ground by a rather spiteful Alexander the Great 189 years later, in 323 BC, enough of the site remains to indicate its previous size and grandeur.

A lot of people get rather excited by the two seven-metre-high winged bulls guarding Xerxes' Gateway. I guess it might have something to do with the fact that they also have human heads and beards. But I was more taken by the reliefs that decorated what was left of the stairways. They featured people and animals bearing gifts to the king. Best of all, they were carved to look like they were walking up the stairs too. Little things like that impress me.

I was also quite taken by the shrine of Shah-e Chergh. I christened it the Saturday Night Fever Mosque because inside it looked more like a disco with multiple mirror balls than a place of worship. Every inch of its interior was covered in small mirror tiles, making it hard to focus on anything. When I took a photo, the light from my flash (which I'd forgotten to turn off) bounced off the tiles infinitely, confusing and dazing the worshippers. I backed out of the mosque, apologising profusely, making good my escape while they were still blinking.

The most bizarre sight I saw in Shiraz, however, was an Australian lawyer dressed in a shalwar qamiz, the baggy pantsuit that Pakistanis wear the world over. He hadn't shaved either, so he looked for all the world as if he'd just come down from fighting in the mountains with the mujaheddin in Afghanistan.

His name was Simon and he said he worked for one of the biggest merchant banks in Melbourne. As a rule, when I'm travelling, I tend to take what people claim to do for a living with a pinch of salt. After all, when you're thousands of kilometres from home, who is to know that you're not really the head of IBM, but rather the cleaner who mops the floor every weekend? The chances of running into someone who can disprove your story are pretty slim. In Iran, the chances are that you're not merely the sole representative of your company, but of your city, state and maybe country as well.

I must admit, I've also been a little colourful in describing my career while I've been on the road. I've never lied outright. It's just that through careful omission, vague shrugs of the shoulders and the other person's flights of fancy, a recruitment brochure I wrote for Kentucky Fried Chicken to encourage spotty-faced youth to clean out vats of fat can easily become a multi-million-dollar campaign featuring Elle Macpherson.

The point is, although I didn't believe Simon's story that he was high up in one of the largest merchant banks in Melbourne, I was prepared to give him the benefit of the doubt and accept that he worked there in some capacity. After all, there was nothing to be gained from getting him offside. He was the first Australian I'd seen since Budapest, and the first native English speaker I'd spoken to since Turkey. More importantly, he had just come from where I was heading. I hoped he would be able to give me some useful information about what lay ahead. Unfortunately, all Simon wanted to talk about was Australian Rules football.

Melburnians are a strange breed. They think that the rest of Australia—and indeed the rest of the world—is as obsessed about Aussie Rules as they are. When Simon heard that I had a short-wave radio, he was flabbergasted that I didn't know the scores from the weekend's matches or the standings on the league ladder. He had been checking newspapers in Australian embassies throughout

Asia and the subcontinent, but the papers were always three months old.

Sensing his agitation, I told him that I thought I'd heard something on my short-wave radio about his team, Richmond, leading the competition. It was a fantasy, of course, but he was thankful enough to give me a scrap of paper with the address of a place to stay in Bam written on it. It was called Ali Amri's Pension, and the scrap of paper also had a hand-drawn map of how to get there. According to Simon, it was the best place to stay in the whole of Iran. We said our goodbyes and I wished his team well, which he seemed to appreciate. My first encounter with a fellow countryman for a couple of months was over as quickly and as unexpectedly as it had begun.

From Shiraz I caught a bus to Kerman, 797 kilometres away. For the first time on my journey, I began to question my philosophy of not flying. Using rials changed at the black market rate, a flight from one end of Iran to the other would have cost me less than $15. A flight from Shiraz to Kerman would have only cost me $4. Yet here I was, travelling eight hours through unchanging desert just so I could say I travelled overland. I took heart from the fact that the bus had only cost the equivalent of 35 cents.

At a roadside diner about halfway to Kerman, I also got to try abgusht. Abgusht is a stodgy meal of fatty meat mashed together with maize, potatoes and lentils. The secret of the meal lies in the preparation. Luckily for me, a little old guy with grey stubble from the bus took pity on me and prepared it for me. He scraped the tender meat off the bone with his dirty and cracked fingernails and mashed it with the other ingredients in the metal bowl with great dexterity. Then he presented it to me proudly, watching me taking my first mouthful with a mixture of anxiety and anticipation. After I swallowed and smiled, he turned to me quite earnestly and spoke in English.

'Is it true that in England a man may marry another man in a church?'

I said that I didn't know and this seemed to disappoint him. He returned to his meal and didn't speak another word.

Kerman was a dusty collection of scruffy shops and half-finished houses. Every house had a flat roof and every roof was crowned with a series of concrete columns and protruding metal reinforcement. The columns suggested that sometime in the future a second storey would be built. Of course it never would be built, but I rather liked the optimism the columns represented. One day, 'Allah inshallah', the good folk of Kerman believed, they would find the money to extend.

I found a room in a tiny hotel near the bus station. The manager seemed unaccustomed to foreign guests and nervously scattered tiny terracotta prayer blocks around the room as he showed it to me. The blocks featured delicate Arabic script and I had found them in the corners of each of my hotel rooms in Iran. In fact, I was so taken by their delicate beauty that I had started collecting them as souvenirs. It was only now that I realised they were probably some sort of talisman to ward off the misfortune my evil Western presence would bring.

From Kerman I caught a bus to Bam, 194 kilometres away. I liked Bam the moment I arrived. Its streets were lined with trees and the mud houses looked clean and homely. Behind some of the homes in the more fashionable streets there were groves of date palms that added a welcome splash of green and lent a distinctly Arabian Nights ambience to the town. If the pension that Philip had recommended was even half as good as he said it was, I knew my stay here would be perfect.

The bus dropped me off at the Clock Square, a major landmark in Bam, and luckily one that featured prominently on my map to Ali Amri's Pension. I wandered down Pasdar Street and found the TV repair shop at which the map indicated I should turn right. A small boy, guessing where I was going, grabbed me and led me by my shirtsleeve down a dusty alleyway lined by smooth mudbrick walls.

When we reached a blue metal door set in a long mudbrick wall, the boy knocked on it then ran away smiling. For a moment I suspected that I may have been set up, and that an irate mullah would open the door and berate me for disturbing him. Instead, the door was opened by a pretty teenage girl who smiled and beckoned me in. She was not wearing a chador.

I seemed to be in one of those corny dream sequences you see in an Abbott and Costello movie. A beautiful girl was leading me into a beautiful courtyard surrounded by rooms that all looked out upon an abundant garden full of orange trees, date palms and vines laden with grapes. A murmur of Arabic music wafted from one of the rooms and mingled with the sound of lightly cascading water. It was cool, peaceful and, in a word, enchanting.

Sitting cross-legged on pillows at the far end of the courtyard was Joe, a redheaded Dutchman I had met in Esfahan. Someone had given him a map as well. An older woman was laying out plates full of exotic dishes before him and exhorting him to eat. We just smiled at each other, shrugging our shoulders in that goofy manner guys do when they know they don't deserve this kind of treatment but are going to lap it up anyway.

The young girl indicated for me to sit with Joe, and a minute or so later returned with a cold mint drink and food and another girl, aged probably in her early twenties.

'Hi, I'm Fatty,' she said, laying plates of food at our feet. 'Welcome to my home.'

The food was delicious, a selection of dips and stews and fruits cooked in herbs and spices I'd never tasted before. It was the first authentic Persian food I had eaten in Iran.

'The food is made by my grandmother,' explained Fatty. 'That's her in the kitchen over there. The girl who let you in is Rosie. She is my brother's youngest daughter. This is his place but, really, I run it. It's not a pension, really, just our family home.'

Fatty was the first woman I had spoken to in Iran, and she was a revelation. She was cheerful and vivacious and had a sly sense of humour. She was the kind of woman you could imagine having a few drinks with down at the pub, or livening up a party, when things got a bit boring, by dancing on a table. She had a collection of tapes that travellers had left her, including Woodstock and her favourite, *Nevermind* by Nirvana. She would play them on an ancient portable cassette as big as a suitcase and dance a strange hybrid dance that—not altogether successfully—combined elements of both belly dancing and moshing.

'My dream,' she sighed wistfully as she floated around the room to 'Something in the Way', 'is to go to Canada and see Nirvana in concert!'

Kicking back, an embroidered pillow under my head, my stomach full and content, it seemed churlish to tell her that Kurt Cobain was dead and that her chances of seeing Nirvana had thus been dashed. Instead, I just looked past the date palms at the moon and stars, and sighed. Fatty turned on a huge tap, allowing water to pour into the garden, and the cascading sound combined with a slight breeze to have a very soothing and cooling effect. It was as close to paradise as I had ever been.

The next morning I visited Arg-e Bam, the remains of an old medieval town sitting on a hill at the northern edge of town. It was at the end of a road lined by date palms, and looked like a set from 'The Legendary Journeys of Hercules'—a huge jumble of towers and fortifications and narrow, twisting lanes. In the Middle Ages, Arg-e Bam had been a thriving commercial and artistic centre, but now, because of war, pestilence and changing economic fortunes, it was a ghost town.

Despite its sturdy appearance, Arg-e Bam was not made of stone, but rather of a sand-coloured mudbrick. Incredibly, the high walls surrounding the city remained unbroken and the only way in was through the main gate in the south. I wandered around the city, past the ruins of mosques, military barracks, bazaars, squares and mansions, in awe of what it must once have been like here. From the citadel—the highest point of the city, complete with its own fortified residence, artillery store and stables—I gazed across what must have been one of the liveliest cities in the world. Now, the only signs of life I saw were the desert foxes that lived there and a mad Frenchman dressed as an Arab.

That night Fatty brought out the guest book to sign. Tradition dictated that everyone who stayed at Fatty's had to leave a photo and a message. I've never been any good at writing comments in guestbooks. I usually scribble 'ditto' or 'See above'. It's a legacy of writing for a living. If you are a copywriter in an advertising agency, everyone expects you to write the funniest, most urbane or most meaningful message in the cards that do the rounds on birthdays or when someone is leaving. You write something you think is witty and heartfelt, but inevitably someone with far too much time on their hands writes something better. Then the secretaries gather round like the witches from Macbeth and denigrate what you wrote.

'Wasn't Peter's message pathetic?' they mew. 'Bill's was better, and he's the accountant! Maybe he should be the writer!'

In the end, I refused to write messages in birthday or farewell cards. I just signed my name and hoped that would be interpreted as droll.

As it was, Fatty didn't really care what I wrote. She just wanted me to hurry so she could show me one of the earlier entries.

'Look at this!' she giggled, pointing to a photo. 'This is Tash and Andrew from Melbourne. They said they were married.'

She flicked through the pages of the guestbook, searching for a later entry.

'But look!' she said, barely controlling her fits of laughter.

'Matthew from Sydney visited two weeks later. That's a photo of him and his girlfriend in India. It's Tash too!'

Matthew had at least kept a sense of humour about it. His comment read, 'Sorry Andrew!'

I spent three days at Fatty's place in Bam. Each morning I would wander around Arg-e Bam pretending I was Hercules, or at least his trusty sidekick Aeolus, ready to help some maiden in distress. And each afternoon I would return to Fatty's and find a refreshing mint drink and a delicious snack waiting for me. Yep, it was a hard life staying at Fatty's. The only drawback was her brother, Ali.

Ali was round and fleshy with a bushy black beard and a lick of thin hair combed across his balding pate. Each night, if I wasn't quick enough, he would take up a position on a carpet in the main room and lecture me on religion and world politics. It was as exciting as the Queen's Christmas message.

'All the answers are in the *Koran*,' he would drone. 'What food we should eat, how we should marry . . .' (Fatty used this comment as her cue to make faces behind his back. Joe and I would have to try not to laugh.)

'It even mentions the atomic bomb!' he exclaimed.

I must have looked a little unsure, because he felt obliged to explain.

'Of course, it doesn't use the word *atomic*,' he back-pedalled. 'It says "Like the sun".'

On my last night in Bam he took a different tack. Instead of trying to convert me to Islam, he tried to sell me on his new business venture.

'I am building a new pension,' he said. 'A proper hotel, not like this. Each guest will have their own room and bathroom. Tell your friends when they come to Bam, they must stay at Ali's Pension.'

It was then that I realised that Ali had no idea what had made this place special. People weren't exchanging little hand-drawn maps to stay in a hotel with rooms with attached bathrooms. They were sharing the news of a place full of hospitality, great food and with a charming hostess. I remember rather ungraciously hoping that Ali's venture would fail and he would fall flat on his huge arse.

The bus to Zahedan left at 6.00 the next morning. Fatty woke me up and her grandmother made me breakfast and gave me some snacks to take with me. She then took me to the bus station, wearing her chador, of course, and made sure that I was given the best seat on the bus. I wanted to hug her and thank her for her wonderful hospitality. I wanted to tell her that for the first time on my journey I had really felt at home. But already some old women standing nearby were tutting at her for talking to a Western man. Instead, I gave her one of my compilation tapes with 'You're the one for me, Fatty' by Morrissey, on it. It was the least I could do.

An hour into the journey, one of the passengers, a dishevelled old man in a tattered blue suit and a thick bushy beard that seemed to be attached to his face by an elastic band, stood up and moved through the bus, singing. It was a sad and mournful tune and, to be brutally honest, quite painful to listen to. After a few verses, he cupped his hands and begged for money. Every passenger gave him something; indeed, most were exceedingly generous. I think they were afraid that if they didn't, he would sing for the whole 360 kilometres to Zahedan.

We pulled into Zahedan just after lunch. The sensible thing for me to do would have been to find a hotel and make my way to the border early the next morning. The border was still a good 90 kilometres away, and with the half-hour time difference between Iran and Pakistan, I figured I would be getting there just as the Pakistani border office was about to close. Zahedan, however, was one of those hot, dusty, featureless towns that encourages you to keep going. I wandered around the down-at-heel restaurants that lined the streets around the bus terminal until I found someone willing to take me to the border at Mirjaveh for what was left of my rials.

The guy's name was Joseph, and he drove an old Toyota ute with panels that were all different colours. Before the revolution he worked for Shell as a translator, but now he was forced to pick up the odd piece of work delivering sheep to market, drums of cooking oil to distant villages and tourists to isolated border posts. I threw my pack into the back and squeezed into the cab.

The road to the border, like every road in Iran, was smooth and flawless. The Iranian government, while unconvinced of the importance of religious freedom and human rights, was obviously a zealous proponent of maintaining immaculately paved public roads. To the left, a dramatic mountain range with jagged peaks rose sharply from the desert. It was at various times black, red, green and white, and looked as if it could be polished and set in pendants. We passed through a series of lonely military checkpoints where the young soldiers seemed more intent on eating the mangoes they had just 'liberated' from smugglers than checking my bag or my passport.

Just outside of Mirjaveh, a dust storm hit. Joseph stopped the ute and indicated for me to wind up the windows. We sat in the car for 15 minutes as winds buffeted it and rocked it from side to side. A fog of sand descended on the desert, turning the telegraph poles beside the road into silhouettes, then swallowing them completely. The air in the cabin became thick with sand and dust and we had trouble breathing.

The storm ended as quickly as it came. Joseph started the ute and we limped into Mirjaveh along a road covered in sand and past a sign that said 'Alms giving calms Allah's anger and sudden death prevents'. I remember thinking that perhaps the storm was Allah's way of saying that I should have given more to the singer on the bus earlier. It was my pack, though, that had taken the beating. I would be picking sand out of my toothpaste for weeks to come.

Mirjaveh was deserted in the kind of way that makes you think a few tumbleweeds are about to roll by, followed by Clint Eastwood, keen to dish out a bit of rough justice. Signs (in English) saying things like 'Down with USA! Down with USSR! Islam is victor!' and 'Sunni and Shia are like the fingers of the fist that knock the head off enemies or evil powers' creaked in the wind. If I had just come into Iran from Pakistan, I probably would have turned around and left. But after the friendliness and hospitality I had enjoyed during my time in Iran, it all seemed a bit of harmless bluster.

Joseph pointed me in the direction of the customs and immigration office. There were no queues. Nor were there any border officials. It was just an open-sided shed with sandy floors and benches covered in dust. Joseph wandered off and returned ten minutes later, with the news that the border official was having a nap and would be with me in an hour. I stretched out on one of the benches and slept.

The border official eventually came along and politely woke me up. He processed me quickly and took me (past a picture of the Ayatollah Khomeini's face hovering over an American flag turning into a river of blood) to a gate in the barbed wire fence that served as the border with Pakistan. A sign above the gate read, again in English: 'We hope you enjoyed your visit to the Islamic Republic of Iran and wish you a safe and comfortable journey back home.' It was typical of my experience of Iran—a serious attempt to keep you at arm's length brought undone by an uncontrollable, almost involuntary, urge to be polite and hospitable. When the guard unlocked the gate and indicated for me to go through, I didn't really want to, but I did.

CHAPTER TWELVE

Pakistan

Soundtrack: *Troublegum*—Therapy?

It only took one step to leave Iran and enter Pakistan. The border was quite literally a line in the sand, marked by a simple barbed wire fence dividing a featureless desert the two countries shared. Logically, the border shouldn't have made any difference. Both countries shared a common religion, Islam, and both were economic basket cases. But somehow, it did. With that one footstep I felt I was leaving civilisation behind me.

Taftan, the small settlement on the Pakistani side of the border, confirmed my fears. While the buildings on the Iranian side of the border appeared to have been built following some of the more generally accepted tenets of construction, the few shacks and humpies in Taftan looked to have been cobbled together by survivors of a nuclear holocaust. Where the streets had been neat and clean in Iran, in Taftan they were filthy. A hot wind swirled between the low mudbrick buildings, picking up litter that lay strewn everywhere and depositing it, flapping, onto the faces of the goats tethered helplessly in the sun.

It was also fucking hot. If the heat had been uncomfortable in Iran, especially in the last week of my stay, it seemed a good 10 or 20 degrees hotter here in Pakistan. In the short walk from the border to the immigration hut, I could feel my skin blister and hear my hair crackle. To make matters worse, every fly within 500 kilometres was trying to crawl up my nostril to find some shade.

The heat had affected the Pakistani border guard as well. He was a large, slothful man condemned to a job that seemed to consist of sleeping and occasionally noting, in a tattered exercise book, the passport numbers of people arriving and departing. After copying my details and stamping my passport, he took a swig of condensed milk from an opened can and lay back down to sleep. When I asked him where I could catch a bus to Quetta, he lazily lifted his head off the pillow and told me to wait beside the road to Quetta. When I asked him where the road to Quetta was, he pointed to a dusty track that wandered off into the desert before apparently petering out into nothing.

It dawned on me at that moment that the hard part of my journey was about to begin. Up until now, apart from a few moments in Albania and Bosnia, I had been cruising. I had descended into chaos, and suddenly, I felt tired.

The bus to Quetta arrived just after 6 pm, and I'm here to tell you it was no beautiful bus. It was brightly coloured, but in a manner aimed to distract potential passengers from its more serious shortcomings rather than to please the eye. Inside, the aisle was littered with food scraps, the seats were broken, and excruciatingly bad Pakistani pop music blared from the bus's totally inadequate sound system. The ticket cost $10, not a lot for a 12-hour journey, but expensive compared with Iran, where a similar journey would have cost only a dollar.

The bus sat in the heat for an hour. The driver and the conductor seemed more interested in changing money with the border guard than in starting the journey. I wandered off to get a warm Coke—I had long given up the idea of getting a cold one—and returned to find a village of colourfully dressed gypsies, and all their worldly possessions, including pots and pans, blankets and a tricycle, in my seat.

The gypsies knew they were sitting in my seat. I could tell by the way they avoided looking at me as I performed a series of elaborate charades to indicate that the seat was mine. When I did catch their eye, they simply gave me a look that said, 'Yeah, we know you paid over the odds for this seat and we paid nothing, but what are you going to do about it, buddy?'

And what could I do about it? One of the women was breast-feeding her child and the other pinched her baby so hard it cried, making sure I'd look like a right bastard whatever I did. But the bus driver noticed me standing helplessly in the aisle, and physically manhandled them out of my seat. It was a poisoned chalice I'd been handed, though. One of the children had shat on my seat.

At sunset, the bus finally headed off down the dusty track, picking its way through a shanty town of shops and houses made from cardboard, plastic, beds and tea chests. I figured that the bus made the journey from Taftan to Quetta across the Baluchistan desert at night because it was cooler. But even after the sun had dipped below the craggy mountains in the distance, the temperature was still hovering around the level needed to cook a leg of lamb. I opened my window to get a breeze, but instead was immediately coated with dust. When I tried to close it again, it stuck. I began to suspect that the gypsies had put a curse on me for having had them ejected from my seat.

It wasn't long before the last signs of civilisation disappeared, and only a vast dusty plain lay before us. A set of tyre tracks in the dirt was all that marked the road to Quetta. The tracks were badly corrugated and shook the bus with such a severity that bags and packages toppled from the overhead racks into the broth the gypsies were preparing on charcoal stoves in the aisle. I reclined my seat and tried to sleep, but it was as if I had been strapped into a vibrating massage chair that had somehow acquired a mind of its own and subsequently lost it. I gave up all hope of sleep, held on tight to the handles and concentrated on not being tossed into the aisle.

Just after midnight, the bus stopped at a roadside restaurant. It was little more than a tent in the middle of the desert, and sold nothing but tea and goats' meat and rice. We sat on rocks beside the bus and ate from battered metal bowls. It was eerily quiet and the sky above was vast and clear. The stars seemed close enough to touch. If I hadn't been so shaken, I might have been impressed.

From there, the road got worse. It wasn't a bus I was riding in now, but a bucking bronco determined to not only throw me off, but also turn around and trample me once it had.

By the time the bus crawled into Quetta, at 10.00 the next morning, I felt as though I'd gone ten rounds with Mike Tyson. My bones were jarred and sore and my sweat had mixed with dust into a thick paste that dried and cracked on my clothes and every exposed part of my skin. My hair had been matted (by rubbing against the back of my seat) into the sort of dreds Mick Hucknall from Simply Red pays good money for. And my eyes were red and wild from lack of sleep. I must have looked a sight, because the touts at the bus station backed away in fear as I passed. And I got a ride in an auto-rickshaw to the centre of town for the same price as the locals.

I stayed in the Muslim Hotel, not because it was anything special, but simply because my guidebook said it was cheap and 'almost clean'. It was also only 250 metres from the railway station. No offence intended to Quetta—from what I'd seen it had its charms— but I wanted to get out of there as soon as possible. I was heading

north, to the twin towns of Rawalpindi and Islamabad, to secure
visas for the next stage of my journey.

After the discomfort of my bus journey from Taftan, I was determined to travel north from Quetta in style. I strode into upper-class
ticket office—tellingly set in another building altogether from the
office selling lower-class tickets—and asked for an air-conditioned
sleeper on the first available train to Rawalpindi. A rather officious
man in a natty brown uniform told me there were none available
for a month. I lowered my standards to a first-class sleeper and was
told the same story. Second-class sleeper (soft)—still no joy. The
guy, sensing my rapid descent into abject despair, and possibly
fearing that I would commit suicide there and then in his office,
suggested I visit the Commercial Department of the Pakistan Railways office, across the way in the main railway building. He said
that sometimes they kept berths aside especially for foreigners.
Subject to availability—and on presenting my credentials as a foreigner—I may be able to secure a second-class sleeper (hard) on
the train leaving for Rawalpindi in two days' time.

The Commercial Department of the Pakistan Railways was situated at the far end of a bureaucratic rabbit-warren of offices with
mahogany doors sporting plaques that said things like 'Assistant to
the Assistant of the Financial Director'. People sat patiently outside
the offices on wooden chairs, waiting for the little signs beside the
door to flip over from 'engaged' to 'available'. The whole place
smelt of furniture wax and linoleum, and had a vague aroma of
decaying paperwork. I half expected a British officer to stroll
through, sipping a gin & tonic and castigating locals for doing
everything only in triplicate. It was as if the British had never left.

Having said that, getting a ticket was a relatively straightforward
process. I filled in three forms, presented my passport as proof of
my foreignness, then waited patiently as the Assistant to the Under
Secretary of the Commercial Department, Alien Ticket Issuance,
transcribed my details into a huge ledger. (I know that was his title

because he had a rather long plaque declaring it in cursive gold script on his desk.) Before giving me my ticket, he asked me a few questions about David Boon; specifically, what he was up to since he had retired as our number three batsman. I suspect he was just checking that I wasn't making it up about being an Australian.

The Pakistan Tourism Directory describes Quetta as 'a frontier town with no entertainment'. And to be frank, they were being kind. The only entertainment available to me during my stay in Quetta— apart from dodging auto-rickshaws and taking my chances with roadside falafel vendors—was the cinema next door to the Muslim Hotel. I hadn't been to the cinema since seeing *The Getaway* in Sofia, and I'm sorry to say that the cinematic offerings had not improved. The feature showing that night in Quetta was *Best of the Best II*, one of those kickboxing movies starring Julia Roberts' brother Eric.

The cinema was dirty and crowded and the biscuits sold by the hawker wandering up and down the aisles were stale. The movie wasn't anything special either, just your average boy-meets-girl, girl-gets-beaten-up, boy-seeks-revenge martial arts epic kind of thing. But to be honest, I didn't mind. I was just glad to be mind-lessly entertained by a movie in a language I could understand.

Just as one of the more elaborately choreographed fight sequences was about to reach its climax, there was a change in programming that I don't think the director had ever imagined. The trailers for two porno movies—*Swinging Wives* and *Bizarre Sixties*—had been spliced into the movie.

Both trailers involved lots of naked women; nothing too hard-core, just lots of bare breasts and bums. The audience—all male— erupted into a frenzy of cheering, hollering and stomping. When the trailers finished, the lights came on for intermission and the audience filed out for their peanuts and choctops in a quiet and orderly manner.

I was stunned. I was in the middle of a strict Islamic country and I had just seen more naked women in ten minutes than I had seen in all my years at university. I turned to the Pakistani guy sitting next to me and asked if this happened often.

'Only sometimes,' he sighed. 'The government shows us parts of these films so we can see how bad they are and why they will not let us watch them.'

That night as I lay in bed, I could tell when the pornographic teasers came on in the cinema next door; the walls shook from the cheers and stamping.

The Quetta Express, bound for Rawalpindi, left Quetta only half an hour late. Although the sun had barely risen, the temperature in my cabin had already hit thirty. I sat in a pool of sweat, wondering if I would ever get used to the heat. I was pleased to see that the chubby Pakistani sitting opposite me was sweating too, even though he was wearing a shalwar qamiz, the light cotton pant suit worn by most Pakistanis.

We had the two benches in our cabin to ourselves. They were bare and worn, with wooden, lacquered slats that bulged and protruded uncomfortably into the small of my back. The benches looked as though they had been ergonomically designed, but at a time when ergonomics was still a young and inexact science.

The windows were similarly dysfunctional. They were coated in grime and had wooden shutters that would fall down with a crash at the most inappropriate moments. My companion had obviously travelled on the Quetta Express before. He pulled out a piece of nylon rope from his bag and tied the shutter to the bunk above his head.

There was a single bunk above each bench, prized possessions of those lucky few amongst us who had been able to secure them. They were little more than wooden slats covered in tattered dark green vinyl, and looked as hard as the title 'hard sleeper' suggested they would be. Until night fell, they served as luggage racks for everyone else on the train.

The train made its way through dusty shantytowns (where small children amused themselves by throwing rocks at us) and into a vast dusty bowl of nothingness. A man riding a camel plodded towards the distant mountains. Half an hour later another man stood with a flock of sheep beside the tracks and watched the train pass, remaining motionless as he became consumed by the cloud of dust the train kicked up. And in the cabin, the temperature slowly climbed.

The man sitting opposite me bought a small snack from one of the young boys patrolling the carriages and introduced himself as Aflab Alam Bhatti. He was a sports writer and was heading back to Faisalabad after visiting his family in Quetta. He was delighted when he found out I was Australian.

'The people of Pakistan will always be grateful for your support in World Cup Final in 1992,' he said in a singsong tone. He handed me an intricately woven basket filled with small dates.

'Yes, it was like our boys were playing in Pakistan. Ninety thousand people in the Melbourne Cricket Ground cheering us on!'

I ate the dates and nodded, smiling inanely. I remembered that World Cup Final. Pakistan played England. People had bought tickets months ahead, expecting Australia to be in the final. I didn't have the heart to tell him that Australians would support anyone against England.

'Tell me, how is David Boon?' he asked as if the Australian batsman was probably my next door neighbour. 'I was very sad when he retired. A fine cricketer. An average of 43.6, I believe.'

I don't know what it is about the Pakistanis and David Boon, but if I were David Boon's publisher, I'd be getting boxes of his autobiography *Under the Southern Cross* over there as fast as I could.

By mid morning the heat in the cabin had become unbearable. Aflab sat mopping his face and the back of his neck with a handkerchief.

'The cooling system seems to have failed,' he said, pointing to an ancient ceiling fan that was clogged with grime. 'I shall find the guard and tell him.'

He returned with the guard who poked his pen through the grill and kick-started the blade. It span pathetically for a moment, barely raising a whisper of air, but died again as soon as the guard was out of sight. Aflab tried reviving it with his own pen, but soon gave up.

Just before noon, the train reached Sibi. Ice cream sellers wearing red turbans came to the window, as did boys in rags selling bottles of soft drink from metal buckets half filled with murky water. A goat wandered around the platform eating the food scraps thrown from the windows by passengers. Soon they all retreated to the shade offered by a scraggly tree, leaving the train baking in the open sun.

'You know, Sibi is the hottest place in Asia,' said Aflab proudly. 'In summer it reaches 60 degrees Celsius.'

'Well, it can only get cooler from here, then,' I said, perhaps a little too sharply. I was weak from the heat and getting a little annoyed with his endless chatter.

'Oh no!' he said. 'This whole area is hot. Dambooli is the hottest place in Asia too!'

I crawled up to my bunk and pretended to sleep. I could feel the heat radiating from the roof of the cabin, barely centimetres from my head. I could feel it crisping my skin. I tried to listen to my Walkman but I was sweating so much the headphones kept slipping out of my ears. Fearing he would be losing my undivided attention, Aflab yelled up after me.

'It won't get cooler up north, you know. They are having a heatwave there too,' he said, raising his eyebrows emphatically. 'Islamabad is running out of water. Soon they'll all go thirsty!'

When the train finally pulled out of Sibi half an hour later, I was sure I had lost half my body weight in sweat.

Aflab was right. It didn't get any cooler. I slept fitfully, waking up every time my arm brushed against the roof and was scalded by the hot metal. I'd rest on my elbow, my head in my hand, and watch the dry heart of Pakistan go by. Increasingly, the train passed medieval-looking brick factories where small children shovelled mudbricks into furnaces and then loaded the finished product onto carts pulled by decrepit looking donkeys. The children were grubby and dressed in tattered clothes, and when they looked up momentarily as the train passed, they had eyes a lot older than their nine or ten years.

By dusk I had long given up noting the names of stations and finding them on my map. It is never a good idea in a developing country anyway. The train is never going as fast as you imagine. And it is quite demoralising to discover that you are only a quarter of the way through a journey that by your calculations should be just about to end. On that train, and in that heat, it would have been downright dangerous. Instead, I took heart from the fact that I had a bunk where I could curl up and wallow in my own sweat, and not that of the whole carriage. It was a luxury that few others had.

That night I had a really weird dream. I was on the same train, in the same bunk, and I was being drugged with chloroform. I felt my bag being tugged away from under my head. I called out to Aflab to help, but he continued to sleep. I woke up from my dream with a start and found a gaggle of small children sitting on top of me on the bunk. Their mother and father had taken up residency on the bench below, and on seeing that I was awake, apologised and hustled their children onto the floor.

'There is nowhere else for them to sit on the train,' apologised Aflab. 'I told them that you were Australian and you would not mind.'

The man nudged Aflab, and said something to him in Urdu. After listening carefully, Aflab turned to me.

'He wants to know if it is true that in Australia they use kangaroos to lead blind people.'

Kangaroos leading blind people? Where the fuck do people get these ideas? As an Australian, these outlandish stories are something you just have to get used to. It's as if Australia is a giant freak show whose sole purpose is to provide weird and wacky copy for the newspapers and magazines of the world. I remember meeting a German woman in Turkey who was convinced that all the cities in Australia had air raid sirens that warned us when the hole in the ozone layer was overhead so we could rush indoors until the danger passed.

Perversely, I answered yes, it was true, kangaroos did lead blind people. We also used kangaroos as babysitters—they kept the smaller children in their pouches—and there would be a kangaroo on the next space shuttle. As I drifted off, I could hear the father relating my tales in whispers to his small children.

When I woke the next morning, I was in the middle of the Punjab. The family had gone, disappearing onto some darkened station we pulled into around 3 am, so I clambered down from my bunk and sat on the bench watching Pakistan come to life.

I have always liked the word 'Punjab'. It's one of those words that are fun to say just for the hell of it—the kind of word that feels good in the mouth and makes you feel better for having said it. In Urdu, it means five rivers, no doubt because five rivers run through the province. The rivers make the province the most fertile in the country, and the centre of the country's agriculture and industry. The train now ran beside one of the smaller rivers, the Sutlej, and its effects could be seen in the lush fields of corn and rice.

The Punjab is also home to more than half the population of Pakistan. The towns we passed were certainly getting bigger, and there was less open space between them. Changes were also apparent in more subtle ways. In Baluchistan and the Sind, the vendors on the station platforms only sold the bare essentials—food and drink. Now, in the more affluent Punjab, I was offered souvenirs such as a plaster plaque that said 'God Bless this House' and a game of snakes and ladders featuring Wasim Akram and other members of the Pakistani cricket team as the ladders, and cricketers from India as the snakes.

By mid morning we had reached Lahore. Lahore has been the capital of the Punjab for most of the last 1,000 years, and has long been the cultural, educational and artistic capital of Pakistan. It was also one of the most important British cities on the subcontinent. Lahore City Station was one of their greatest monuments; a huge fortress-like structure built in 1860 and designed to act as a last line of defence in an emergency.

The station was also where Aflab was leaving the Quetta Express to get a connecting train to Faisalabad. He had been a talkative bugger, but a good companion. If nothing else, he bought me snacks that I would not otherwise have tried for fear of being drugged or poisoned. As he left, he gave me a big sweaty hug.

'Tell David Boon the people of Pakistan wish him every success in his retirement!' he called out from the platform, wiping a tear from his eye.

After Lahore, the whole mood of the train changed. Now it was more of a commuter train, connecting two of the most important towns in Pakistan. There was a palpable buzz created by people with somewhere to go and something to do. Freshly scrubbed people in freshly pressed clothes bustled amongst the carriage, finding their seats and carefully brushing off the layer of dust that had settled on everything, including me. Those of us who had been on the train since Quetta were pushed into the corners and slowly ostracised. We were dirty and drained, too tired to get caught up in the faster pace of carriage life. At that moment, I thought I knew how country folk feel when they get to a big city.

The seven-hour leg between Lahore and Rawalpindi brought with it a new phenomenon—carriage singers. At first they were simple folk performing simple songs—a little old lady in a shawl moving through the carriage singing a mournful tune, a man with a deep baritone singing Pakistani sea shanties. But the closer we got to Rawalpindi, the more elaborate the acts of these performing beggars became. A young boy with a beautiful voice wandered through, accompanied by another small boy tapping on a jar. Another man strolled through playing a beat up sitar.

Finally, a boy of about fifteen bounced into the carriage with a set of metal maracas he had made himself. He had natural rhythm and the showmanship of a young Peter Allen. In fact, imagine Peter Allen in the 'I go to Rio' film clip and you have a pretty good idea of the show this guy put on. The crowd loved it. They were stuffing rupee notes into his collection tin like there was no tomorrow. He finished his final encore, with a flourish and a deep bow, just as the train pulled into Rawalpindi.

Rawalpindi was a sprawling patchwork of bazaars, beggars and brightly coloured vans. From the moment I stepped out of the station, I was caught up in the kind of manic energy that only comes from too many people with too little to eat and too little space to live in all trying to scrape by. It was filthy and chaotic and the air crackled. It was intoxicating and invigorating but I couldn't stay. I was heading to 'Pindi's straightlaced alter ego, Islamabad.

Islamabad, like Canberra in Australia, is a purpose-built capital. It stands on a spot that only 38 years ago was home to a few head of cattle and the odd nomadic tribe. Like Canberra, it has been planned to within an inch of its life. In Canberra, Walter Burley Griffin's vision was to build a city on expanding circles. In Islamabad, the architect was Konstantinos Doxiades, and his idea was to build a city based on squares, letting it grow sector by sector, following a grid. Circles or squares, the effect is the same in both cities—ordered, neat, but ultimately soulless environments full of politicians and bureaucrats.

In contrast, the bus I caught to Islamabad was prepared to make some sort of statement. It looked like a giant Hawaiian shirt and dropped me off at the city's grubbiest suburb, Aabpara. Here I found a cheap kebab restaurant, a general store that sold cold bottled water and the Islamabad Tourist Campsite.

The campsite was on the far side of a park that the locals used as a public toilet, and was surrounded by a neat waist-high hedge. It was dry and dusty and dotted with waist-high marijuana plants. At the back there was a grubby concrete amenities block with showers that never worked. Elsewhere, travellers had pitched tiny domed tents on purpose-built concrete slabs and sat outside them, smoking thick joints rolled from buds they had picked in the campsite and dried on the slabs during the day. I stayed in one of the concrete 'bungalows' for travellers without tents. At 3 rupees a night it was the cheapest accommodation I had come across in my travels so far.

These 'bungalows' were simply bare concrete rooms with dirty floors. Each one was cramped and airless, and packed with travellers who hadn't washed for weeks. The bungalow I was put in even came with its very own resident Iranian refugee.

You know the fellow who tried to shoot the Pope? Well, this guy looked just like him—a thin wiry bloke with close-cropped receding hair and a terminal dose of earnestness. He sat muttering in a corner of the bungalow, with a quilted blanket and a plastic bag filled with forms, books and various other scraps of paper. On my first night there I made the mistake of asking why he'd left Iran.

'Political complex!' he snapped. 'UN form! German! Good family! Problem!'

Sensing—correctly—that I didn't understand, he slowly repeated what he had said.

'Political . . . complex. UN . . . form . . . German . . . Good . . . family . . . problem!'

I tried to understand what he was saying, but I couldn't. I couldn't even understand what he was doing in Pakistan. Any self-respecting refugee looking for a better life or even a bit of political freedom would have headed to Europe, not Pakistan. I tried nodding my head sympathetically, but this only seemed to make him angrier.

'Political ... complex. UN ... form,' he said through gritted teeth. 'German ... Good ... family ... problem!'

I kept nodding, not altogether sure where all this was going or even if I would get out of it with my life. Seething with frustration, he fished around in his bag, found a form in a language that I didn't understand and thrust it in front of my face as if it would suddenly clear things up.

'Blessing on Boris Yeltsin!' he cried. 'Blessing on Boris Yeltsin. Boris Yeltsin he my friend!'

As if to emphasise his point, he poked his finger at the form and repeated, 'Boris Yeltsin! He my friend!'

I suggested he go to the Russian embassy.

'No! No! No!' he yelled. 'Political complex. Germany!'

To escape, I pretended I was going to have a shower. There wasn't any water, so I sat outside in the heat, listening to Therapy? on my Walkman, and returned to the bungalow only after he had fallen asleep.

For all its shortcomings—and it had many—the Islamabad Tourist Campsite was the best source of information on the Overland Trail in Pakistan. The travellers staying there had come from everywhere along the route. Some had travelled south from China over the Karakoram Highway. Others had travelled overland from India. Everyone had snippets of information that they would willingly exchange as they passed around a joint. As the only person at the camping ground who had been to Iran, I was particularly sought after. The Iranian embassy was only issuing three-day transit visas, and those heading east to Europe wanted to know how difficult it was to get an extension.

Chatting to a German guy one night, I found out it *was* possible to follow my dream of crossing from Nepal into Tibet. I had heard the Nepal–Tibet border was closed to independent travellers and I had resigned myself to the fact that I would have to enter China from Pakistan instead. According to this guy, however, if I got my Chinese visa in Pakistan, the Chinese border guards at the Nepal–Tibet border would let me cross. I would be able to travel overland through India and Nepal and visit the old hippy haunts of Varanasi and Kathmandu after all. It was news that called for a celebration.

Pakistan being a Muslim country, and quite a devout one at that, having a celebratory tipple was more difficult than I had imagined. There was a liquor store up in Aabpara, but I needed a liquor permit from the Excise and Taxation Department before I could buy anything. The big hotels were permitted to sell alcohol to non-Muslims, but they only sold alcohol to their guests. The only place in town I could get a cold drink, it turned out, was at the Australian embassy. To be precise, the Coolabah Club at the Australian embassy.

The Coolabah Club is held every Thursday night on the embassy grounds. With Friday being a religious holiday in Muslim countries, it is basically just an end of the working week piss-up. The embassy staff gather in the games room and drink beer smuggled into Pakistan in the diplomatic bag. Australia being the egalitarian society it is, the embassy kindly opens the door to its fellow countrymen. Judging by the reaction of the auto-rickshaw driver who dropped me off at the embassy just after dark, the Coolabah Club was a bit of an open secret. He took a swig from an imaginary can, gave me a nudge and wink and sped off into the night laughing.

The Coolabah Club had all the ambience of a country lawn bowls club. There was a bar at the end, with a tall fridge with glass doors and few posters depicting Australian scenes. For 200 rupees ($10) I got a book of vouchers that I could exchange for ice cold cans of Victoria Bitter, spirits or soft drinks. I got to mill around and talk about football and politics, while sensibly avoiding any discussion of religion. It was just like a barbecue back home. Except the groups weren't divided on sexual lines, but rather on vocational ones; the embassy crowd stayed down one end and the backpackers down the other.

I'd like to say that the whole evening degenerated into a typical Aussie party with the ambassador throwing up in the garden and the female trade advisor yelping topless on the shoulders of some young bronzed backpacker in the pool. But I honestly don't remember. I hadn't drunk anything alcoholic since Bulgaria, so the VBs went straight to my head. I rocketed through my early drunken stage of mischievousness—pulling the seat from under people as they are about to sit down and such—to the more dangerous stage of malevolence by my second can. Luckily, I was still sober enough to leave the embassy before I succumbed to my natural urge to draw moustaches on the portraits of the Queen and the Governor-General that hung on the back wall.

I managed to catch an auto-rickshaw back to the campsite, pleased that I had been able to celebrate the change in my plans in such an appropriate manner. I lay down on the hard floor in the concrete bungalow, my head spinning, and watched the patterns of mould on the ceiling swirl and form odd shapes—first a butterfly, then a flower, and finally, an apparition of Homer Simpson. And I'll swear to my dying day that he told me to go to Peshawar and try to get into Afghanistan.

CHAPTER THIRTEEN

Afghanistan

Soundtrack: I left my Walkman in Peshawar in case it got stolen

I caught a bus—decorated like a pair of Elton John's sunglasses—to Peshawar. It travelled east along the Grand Trunk Road like a giant cubic zirconium, reflecting light in a million directions, blinding other drivers and causing them to career off the road.

Peshawar is in the heart of Pakistan's Northwest Frontier, a lawless tribal area where the government has only tenuous control. The Northwest Frontier used to be the playing field for The Great Game, the cat-and-mouse shenanigans played by Britain and Russia in the late nineteenth century as each tried to get the upper hand in the region between the Hindu Kush and Pamir. British and Russian agents crisscrossed the road, posing as explorers, merchants and scholars, spying on each other and playing diplomatic chess with the local Pashtun tribes. In return for their support, tribal leaders were given money, guns and land. Back then, Peshawar was the number one hotbed of international intrigue and doublecross.

It doesn't take long in Peshawar to realise that things haven't changed much in the past 100 years. Amongst the plastic combs and mirrors and penlight batteries, the street hawkers sell vinyl covers for semiautomatic weapons and nasty looking knives. Shady looking characters in turbans stand on street corners looking like hired assassins, and women scurry across the road covered from head to toe in heavy, shapeless burqas. And in the slums on the outskirts of town, a few million Afghani refugees take a break from the constant fighting and plot a return to their homeland.

I decided immediately that I liked Peshawar. Where Islamabad had been ordered and relatively neat, Peshawar was an uncontrolled, chaotic mess. Potholed roads wandered in every direction before disappearing into a dark maze of alleyways and corridors. Bug-shaped auto-rickshaws buzzed round prospective customers like flies around a turd, the drivers haranguing them until they got in just to shut the drivers up. Huge hand-painted (in colours that don't occur in nature) movie posters, painted by people who are convinced that Bruce Willis is Chinese, hung from grey concrete buildings. In the old city, especially, I felt as though I could turn down a lane and never be seen again.

I stayed at the Tourists Inn Motel, a suitably shambolic hovel tucked behind a bakery in Saddar Bazaar. (The smell of freshly baked bread barely masked the smell of a pit toilet overflowing behind it.) It was run by a disreputable looking fellow with a wonky eye and an annoying habit of answering one question with another question. When I asked him if it was possible to go to Afghanistan, for instance, he looked over my head and slightly to the right and answered enigmatically, 'It is possible, but is it wise?' He suggested I visit the Afridi tribal town of Darra Adam Khel instead.

Darra was a scruffy, run-down town in the sandstone hills of the Kohat Frontier Region, 42 kilometres south of Peshawar. The main street was a series of connecting potholes of varying depths, lined on both sides by two-storey wood and adobe buildings. It could have been any town in northern Pakistan, except for the fact that nearly every shop lining the main road—and most of those on the side streets running off it—was a gun shop.

Darra has been a gun town since the 1890s. A Punjabi gunsmith on the run for murder set up shop here, and started making replicas of the guns used by the British soldiers stationed nearby. His handi-work was particularly sought after by the local tribesmen. They couldn't afford the real thing, but liked the prestige—and the power—the replicas gave them. A local industry was born, and now, close to 40,000 people in the area around Darra are pumping out pirate Kalashnikovs, M-16s and Smith & Wessons in workshops little bigger than broom closets.

I went to Darra with a Tasmanian guy called Keith. We walked down the main street browsing guns pretty much as you would browse the latest winter fashions back home. Small boys no older than nine years old struggled past us, dragging clutches of semi-automatic weapons behind them. The guns were made using tools that looked medieval, and occasionally, a gunsmith would take a pistol or rifle he had just finished out on to the street and fire it into the air to make sure it worked.

As we passed, the owners of the shops invited us in to look at their wares. In many ways, buying a gun in Darra was like buying a carpet in Turkey. The shop owner sits you down on a cushion, sends a boy for tea and proceeds to explain the relative merits of each piece, and like the carpets in Turkey, the merchandise is hanging on the wall behind him. He lets you handle the item that has caught your eye and praises your discernment and obvious ability to spot quality. But instead of numbers of knots, it's the calibre he is selling you on.

In one shop, the owner realised that we weren't really in a posi-tion to buy and offered us the opportunity to 'try' the weapons instead. For the princely sum of $10 we could fire off a clip on an AK-47. For $15 we could fire off two. For $100 we could fire an RPG grenade-launcher. For an extra $20, he'd throw in a goat to use as a target. While some deranged individuals may have been tempted to blow away a goat tethered to a stick, Keith and I decided on the clips. Each clip had 25 bullets.

The 'firing range' was in the stony mountains at the back of the town, just past the mudbrick hash factories where men stirred pots of resin over open fires. An old white-bearded man wearing a turban was waiting for us with two AK-47 replicas. After we stuck tissue paper in our ears, he tossed us the guns and pointed to the hills.

I fired my AK-47 one shot at a time, trying to hit a tree halfway up the mountain. After 15 shots I hadn't even got close, so I flicked it over to automatic and blasted the last 10 bullets in my clip in one violent spasm. Impressive as spraying 10 bullets into a mountainside in two seconds flat sounds, I'm afraid the whole experience left me kind of cold. I had expected some sort of Rambo-esque adrenaline rush but it just didn't happen.

Not so Keith. When I'd finished my clip he took both guns— one on each hip—switched to automatic, and let them rip. Most of the bullets ricocheted and zinged off the mountain, kicking up dust and making that cool 'pwong' sound. But where I had had a hard time even hitting a tree, Keith, to his credit, managed to shear a whole branch off.

If the old guy had been smart, that's when he should have tried to sell Keith the gun. His adrenaline was pumping, and if the price was right he might well have said, 'To hell with it! I don't care if I get caught and have to spend the rest of my life in a smelly Pakistani jail, I've just gotta have this muthafucka.' It was lucky he didn't. On the way back to Peshawar we were both dragged off the bus and searched at a police checkpoint just out of town. One guy forced me to take my shoes off and stand on the hot tarmac while he—bravely, I thought—sniffed them. I hoped he was looking for drugs.

It was on the bus back to Peshawar that I told Keith about my plans to go to Afghanistan. If he'd been from any other country, I may have hesitated. He probably would have exclaimed 'Are you mad?' and perhaps slapped me around and tried to talk me out of it. But Keith was an Australian and, as I suspected he would, he asked if he could come along. A Pakistani sitting in the seat in front of us overheard our conversation and wanted to come too. He introduced himself as Karman and said he could help us get there.

'I will not deceive you,' he said earnestly, talking loudly to be heard over the noise of the bus. 'There will be many hurdles and obstacles. The road to Kabul is broken and full of evil men who would rob you of your dominions. But I will protect you!'

Karman's plan was very simple. Keith and I would dress up in shalwar qamiz and pass ourselves off as locals. We would make our way up the Khyber Pass to the border with Afghanistan, where he would arrange for us to be smuggled across. Once inside Afghanistan, friendly locals would guard and nourish us and take us to Kabul. After we'd had a few days of dodging rockets and stray bullets, they would bring us back safely into Pakistan.

I considered the plan carefully and, to be honest, I couldn't see any flaws. I got to dress up and pretend I was Nick Danziger *and* visit Kabul, one of the great hippy haunts on the Overland Trail. I was almost afraid to ask how much it would all cost.

'I do not want anything for myself,' Karman said, unconvincingly. 'All I ask is that you buy a gift for your hosts in Kabul. A teapot, perhaps.' The adventure of a lifetime in exchange for a 300 rupee teapot? I was in, with bells on.

Keith and I spent the next couple of days haunting the tailor shops in Saddar Bazaar, each of us looking for a shalwar qamiz that would magically transform us from affluent Western tourists into Third World refugees. I finally settled for a subdued dark olive green one, and Keith went for one in a rather startling apricot. Having not shaved for a couple of days, I reckon I carried off the whole Pakistani–Afghani look quite well. But with his pale skin, blue eyes and ginger hair, Keith was less convincing. We decided in the end that he would have to pass himself off as a Russian defector.

By the third day, we were ready. Unfortunately, Karman's plans hadn't advanced much past the vague and inconclusive idea he expounded on the bus back from Darra. Over a meal in a restaurant—our shout, of course—he seemed more interested in explaining his extraordinary powers over women.

'You simply must make a fascination of oneself,' he explained. 'That way, wherever you go, you are sought after and admired.'

Part of what made him fascinating to women, he claimed, was the fact that he wrote poetry. Between mouthfuls of kebab and rice, he recited one of his favourites:

> Weather is fine, it's love sign.
> Sky is overcast but I am whine.
> For the satisfaction I took the support of wine.
>
> I recall those places
> Where we used to sit near vine.
> She is great oppressor
> But I can't incline.
> I pray for her success,
> I go to nearby shrine.

I think it was then that I realised the folly of going to Afghanistan with Karman. He was obviously a dangerous man. How could I entrust my life to someone with such a flagrant disrespect for the rhyming couplet? Keith and I decided to visit the consulate general of the Islamic State of Afghanistan in Peshawar the next day and try to get into Afghanistan the official way.

My guidebook said that only Pakistani and Afghani nationals and UN personnel were allowed to cross from Pakistan into Afghanistan. And the Tourists Inn Motel was full of travellers who had been denied a visa from the Afghanistan consulate and who had been turned back from the border when they turned up anyway. But now that I had the idea of going to Kabul in my head, there was no way of getting it out. I was convinced that visiting the city was crucial to the success of my journey. If the consulate knocked us back, then I would go ahead with Karman's plan. I just wouldn't take Karman.

The Afghanistan consulate was in University Town which, apart from the neat manicured ground of the university, was a sprawling shantytown of aid organisations and displaced Afghanis. The Afghanis ignored the sign outside the university imploring them to 'get education from craddle [sic] to grave', and instead continued going about their daily activities of trading guns and drugs and plotting the overthrow of their government.

The consulate was housed in a white two-storey building on a dusty alley just down from the Red Cross and Medicins Sans Frontieres. It was surrounded by a high wall topped with barbed wire and guarded by two guys who looked like they had just dusted themselves down after a street battle in Kabul. They confiscated Keith's penknife and placed it amongst the assault rifles and handguns that lay on a table waiting for their owners to finish their business inside.

The waiting room inside the consulate was surprisingly quiet and civil. International arms dealers and drug dealers sat quietly on the couch beside mujaheddin who were still wired and wide-eyed from battle. Amongst this motley bunch was Gi-Gi, a shifty looking Bosnian staying at the Tourists Inn Motel, and a Japanese guy he had befriended. We nodded at them, filled out a visa application form and waited. Within five minutes we were ushered in to see the consul.

The Afghani consul was a large and cheerful chap who wore a shirt and tie instead of the more traditional shalwar qamiz. He was seeing us before everyone else because his brother Achmed lived in Sydney. He asked me if I knew him and I lied and said I did. It was easier than explaining that Sydney was a city of four million people and that unless his brother lived next door to me—highly unlikely unless his brother had undergone a sex change operation and dyed his hair blonde—I had as much chance of knowing him as knowing the guy's mother in Kabul. It was the right answer, though, because he motioned us forward.

'I really shouldn't give you a visa,' he said. 'You do not have a letter from your embassy or the name of a sponsor in Afghanistan. But because you are a friend of my brother, I will tell you of a secret way to get a visa.'

He scribbled on a piece of paper and pushed it across the table to us, face down.

'This is the phone number for the Jalalabad Seura,' he explained. 'They are the mujaheddin group in control of the border and the area around Jalalabad. I don't know their address, but if you call them they will tell you. If they give you a letter saying they will take responsibility for you during your visit to my country, I will give you a visa.'

For a secret organisation, the Jalalabad Seura were surprisingly easy to find. The pharmacist in a drugstore across the road from the consulate called the number on his telephone, and the Seura gave him their address without question. The pharmacist told the rickshaw driver we had hailed to take us there. A few minutes later we were dropped out the front of an unassuming townhouse a couple of blocks away.

We were ushered into an office to meet the head of the Seura by a guy with a bushy beard and an AK-47 slung across his back. We explained who we were and where we wanted to go. He listened carefully to our story before asking us if we knew his brother,

Mohammed, in Hobart. He lived on Hampden Road in Battery Point. Keith said he lived five minutes up the road and we were invited to stay for lunch.

Lunch was served on the floor. It was a delicious selection of beans, rice and meat. There were no knives or forks. We followed the lead of our hosts and shovelled it into our mouths with fresh pita bread. After the plates were cleared and we had drunk a dozen or so cups of tea, an envelope was brought in by an acolyte and presented to us. We returned to the Afghani consulate and were ushered past Gi-Gi and the Japanese guy, who were still waiting on the couch, to see the consul immediately.

'There is one more formality before I can issue your visa,' the consul said, shaking our hands vigorously. 'I must get you to sign this letter.'

The letter was a legal document absolving the consulate of any responsibility should anything happen to us.

'I have been informed about the abnormal situation in Afghanistan but in spite of it I insist to go to Afghanistan,' it read. 'So I will be responsible of all consequences if occurred so the consulate of the Islamic State of Afghanistan Peshawar will not be responsible for one incident.'

We signed the letter and he stamped our passports.

It had been quite a day. In the space of less than six hours we had luxuriated in the air-conditioned office of the Afghani consul, enjoyed a delightful lunch with the leader of an armed militia, and secured a visa that everyone else had told us was impossible to get. And it was all thanks to Australia's liberal immigration policies. Now you know why you'll never catch me voting for Pauline Hanson and the One Nation Party.

The next day Keith and I donned our baggy pantsuits and chitral hats and headed off for Afghanistan. We caught a van outside a market in the Afghani part of town, where touts wandered amongst stalls selling vegetables yelling 'Kabul, Kabul, KABUL!' The van made its way through the shantytowns that ringed Peshawar, picking up extra passengers before heading east through dry jagged mountains towards the Khyber Pass. I felt like I was living out a story in a *Boy's Own Annual*.

A stone arch across the road at Jamrud Fort marked the official start of the Khyber Pass. It also marked the point where control changed from the Khalid tribe to the Afridi tribe. The Northwest Frontier is an autonomous region, and it is these tribes who are in control. They administer justice and collect taxes according to tribal traditions. The Pakistani government takes a cut of the taxes but otherwise leaves them pretty much to themselves. It's a model that the Scots have been trying to adopt for decades.

Soon we were climbing higher into the mountains on a road that wound its way underneath ridges lined with turrets and topped by forts. It was dry, brown and barren—there was not a speck of vegetation. I wondered what the British and Russians had wanted here. It was as godforsaken as any place on Earth could be. Even the goats by the side of the road stared quizzically at the boys who tended them, as if to ask what exactly they were supposed to be eating.

It is only 58 kilometres from Peshawar to the border at Torkham, but our progress was slowed by the inordinate number of trucks crawling up the windy mountain road towards Afghanistan. There were traditional trucks, gaily painted and covered with canvas, as well as modern semitrailers hauling shipping containers. They crawled up the mountain in a convoy, like a particularly languorous snake. I couldn't help wondering where they were going. Afghanistan is the third poorest country in the world—yet there were enough cargo trucks crawling along the Khyber Pass to service every mall in America. The mystery didn't become any clearer at Torkham. The border was closed for lunch, so the trucks parked in a huge dusty clearing, alongside UN trucks loaded with aid, and waited patiently to get into Afghanistan.

For those expecting an exotic border post crackling with intrigue and danger, Torkham is a major disappointment. It is simply a dusty, sleepy compound where the biggest threat is the heat. We spent our time posing for photos with the Pakistani guards, chatting with three Australian aid workers who had just fled Kabul because of the fighting, and searching for the 'alternative crossing' with a Japanese guy called Hiro who we met in a restaurant beside the border.

Hiro had heard about the alternative crossing when he got his visa in Tehran, and together we found it, barely 500 metres from the official one. It was a sandy path cut into the low hills, two metres wide and with rocky walls about three metres high on each side. There were no trucks or cars, just a long line of camels streaming into Pakistan from Afghanistan. It was the smugglers' route, and it was like stepping back five centuries to a quieter time before combustion engines. The only sounds were the plodding of camel feet in the sand, the clanging of bells and the groans of the camels when their drivers whipped them. But instead of spices and fabric, these camels were loaded high with Sony Trinitrons and car parts.

We walked against the stream, dodging camels loaded with radiators and differentials. Some of the more belligerent of the beasts spat and groaned, and one tried to bite us as we passed.

The path led to a dusty allotment with an overhead sign marking the border with Afghanistan. Three Pakistani customs officials sat in a small wooden hut beside the path, counting off the camels coming into Pakistan, but not checking their cargo or demanding any paperwork from the camel drivers. They simply tallied up what was coming in and calculated their cut from a deal struck earlier with the smugglers. They were not so easy going with us. After checking our paper work, they sent us back to the official border.

Lunch was over and the official border was open again. Where the smugglers' route had been orderly and peaceful, the official crossing was chaotic. Groups of men pounded on the metal gates on the Afghani side, while a ute full of Afghanis pushed against the gate, slowly forcing it open. Five Pakistani soldiers linked arms in front of the gate, trying to hold it shut as the ute revved and pushed harder against it.

Eventually, the soldiers couldn't hold on any longer and the gate flew open, knocking the soldiers off their feet in the process. The ute jerked through the gate and sped off into Pakistan. The soldiers chased after it before realising that they had left the gate unattended and hundreds of Afghanis were streaming into Pakistan unchecked. We slipped into Afghanistan as the Pakistani soldiers scrambled to close the gate. It seemed a highly appropriate way to enter the country.

The Afghani side of the border was even more chaotic—a cacophony of shouting, revving and horn blowing. Three Afghani officials were trying to stem the tide of people, trucks and cars scrambling to leave their country, and they were getting frustrated. It was like watching an old episode of the 'Keystone Cops'. They bashed on the side of the truck at the front of the queue with sticks, shouting at the driver to stop pushing forward. He stopped for a few moments, but soon started edging forward again, raising the ire of the guards once again.

The fourth time they went through this whole process, the guards lost their patience. They dragged the driver from the cabin and started beating him. He covered his face with his arms and pleaded with them in the name of Allah to stop. One of the guards looked up, spotted us watching in horror and pulled his punch, letting the guy fall to the ground. The guard looked at our letter and pointed towards a large green army tent 100 metres off the road. I'm pleased to report that the driver used the distraction we caused to scurry back into his truck and drive unmolested into Pakistan.

The tent was home to the local mujaheddin leader—the

commander in charge of the whole area from the border to Jalalabad—and was pitched in a pretty spot beside a leafy tree and a captured Russian tank. Inside, it was like Hawkeye and BJ's 'swamp' in 'M*A*S*H'—three camp beds, a cassette player, a few undershirts hanging to dry—but instead of a still, there was an urn from which the commander poured us a cup of tea. He read our letter and motioned for us to sit down.

We sat on the beds silently sipping tea while he arranged for an armed guard to accompany us to Jalalabad. As friends of the family, it seems we were to be afforded the very best in Afghani hospitality and protection. I began to suspect that we would need it. There was an AK-47 under the pillow of the bed I sat on, and I spied a bigger gun—probably an M-16—and enough ammunition to fight a small war under the bed opposite.

When the armed guard arrived, the commander insisted we pose for photos with him, with weaponry. They were simple photos. The armed guard looked as surly as possible, the commander held a whacking big M-60, and Keith, Hiro and I took turns holding the ammunition. I suspect the photos were some sort of insurance, should anything happen to us. He could show them to the head of the Jalalabad Seura and prove that not only did he send along his best man, he also loaded us up with enough weaponry to bring down a Russian helicopter. It was all for show. We had to leave the hardware behind.

We followed our armed guard from the tent to the main road, past groups of men sitting around drinking tea, their Kalashnikovs lying on the ground beside them. Two men, each with a grenade launcher strapped across his back, stood chatting in what looked to be a bus shelter. I posed for a photo beside a sign that said 'Welcome to the Islamic Republic of Afghanistan'. It had plastic, interchangeable letters—like the signs muffler shops use to highlight special prices or share a thought for the day—and even though some of the letters were broken or missing, it suddenly dawned on me where the fuck I was, and that Keith, Hiro and I were the only ones not armed. I made a mental note not to call my mother until I got back to Pakistan.

Fifty metres beyond the sign, the trucks we had followed up the Khyber Pass were unloading their cargo. Shipping containers were scattered across a vast empty plain like beer cans at an Australia–England Test match. Each had been cracked open, and the contents—TVs, small four-cylinder engines, refrigerators—were being loaded onto camels. It was like a huge dock, but without the water and without the cranes. The scope of the operation was astounding.

Watching the camels plodding off towards the smugglers' route and into Pakistan, it finally made sense. It was all a rather complicated and roundabout way of avoiding import duties. The containers were unloaded in Karachi, and since they were only transiting through Pakistan, no duty was payable. They were then trucked 1,750 kilometres to Afghanistan, where no duty was payable, if only because there wasn't a government to collect it. Fifty metres over the border, the containers are cracked open and all their contents are smuggled back over a border that the Pakistanis only had nominal control over. So next time you're in the market for a new wide-screen TV, forget your local electronic discount store; head straight to the Karkhanai Bazaar just outside Peshawar.

We travelled to Jalalabad in a Toyota Hiace covered in Kanji lettering that indicated it had spent its earlier life transporting kids to kindergarten in Japan. It was festooned with animal cartoon characters riding in a wooden carriage—a whole menagerie of them—each painted so that the head of a passenger became the head of an animal. It's not exactly how I imagined I would be getting around in Afghanistan. I guess I had a romantic vision of riding in on a tank, as you might in Bosnia, or in a ute with a machine-gun welded to the roof, as I once did in Somalia. I was coming into one of the most dangerous countries in the world as a giraffe, with an armed guard looking like an elephant, albeit an elephant with an AK-47.

The Afghani side of the Khyber Pass was little different from the Pakistani side. The road wound its way through a sandy valley that was desolate and empty, surrounded by mountains that were dry and broken. The first sign of life was a refugee camp, 20 kilometres from the border. It had been set up and was maintained by the UN, and its row upon row of white tents filled the entire valley. There were neat pathways between them and designated washing and cooking areas. It was like a small city, organised and ordered. It radiated a permanency that suggested it would still be there in 20 years, with a generation having lived all their lives there.

After the camp, the road was punctuated by deserted towns littered with burnt-out tanks and villages that had sprung up around the ruins of bombed houses. In the villages, people sat in the doorways of their temporary huts staring blankly, too exhausted or despondent to do anything. Their small children filled the potholes in the road with sand and demanded payment from passing drivers. Our driver rewarded their entrepreneurial spirit by tossing them a crumpled note.

Many of the buildings we passed were daubed with crude, hand-painted signs warning of the danger of landmines. An organisation called OMAR (Organisation for Mine Clearance and Afghani Rehabilitation) marked the areas that were safe and those that still had to be cleared. I had read somewhere that there are an estimated 10 million landmines in Afghanistan, and that at current rates of removal it will take 40 years to clear them.

Closer to Jalalabad, the battles had been more intense, and the damage to villages and settlements was more severe. In one town, only 10 kilometres from Jalalabad, every home had sustained some damage, and a petrol storage tank had a gaping hole in the side from taking a direct hit. On the football pitch, where young children had once played soccer, the burnt-out shells of four Russian tanks now sat, rusting.

So I was surprised to find that Jalalabad was a pleasant, tree-lined town surrounded by green fields and dramatic mountains. It seemed neat and clean, and the effects of the fighting were considerably less apparent. A tank graveyard outside the airport and a vomit yellow and green helicopter destroyed on the tarmac were the only signs that the city had been embroiled in the war at all.

All the hotels in Jalalabad were full. Most were booked solid by aid organisations. Others had been turned into hospitals for people who had lost their limbs stepping on landmines. At the Spingher Hotel, a rather grand establishment in the leafy suburbs at the back of the town, a man called Aabrar, from the Afghan Amputee Bicyclists for Rehabilitation and Recreation (I kid you not!), suggested we try the Mojahid Restaurant and Hotel on the main road.

The Mojahid was in the centre of town. Here Jalalabad was just another Third World town lined with dusty shops and restaurants. It could have been any small place in Pakistan or India, except that everyone walked around with a Kalashnikov or an RPG grenade launcher slung over their backs. Occasionally, a really wired looking fellow would walk by carrying both.

The most jittery of these guys—all of them bearded and dusty from fighting in the mountains—congregated at the Mojahid Restaurant. They sat dipping bread in sloppy soup, their eyes darting from side to side, waiting for someone to spring from the kitchen and try to slit their throats. By the look of the chef, they were probably right to be worried. He showed us to rooms that ran off the restaurant—no beds, just mats on the floor—and charged $2 for the three of us.

Once we had checked in, our armed guard bid us farewell (but not before getting us to sign a letter saying that he had delivered us safely). We were alone now, and we had to decide what we were going to do. Now that we were in Afghanistan, would we press on the 150 kilometres to Kabul?

Keith was particularly taken by the fact that it was a good deal higher—and therefore cooler—in Kabul than Jalalabad. For me, the allure of Kabul was that the city had been one of the big hippie towns on the Overland Trail. I would be able to check out what was left of the scene—the hash shops, the cafes and the hotels—and tick off another hippie icon. Hiro didn't really care, but pointed out to us that there were plenty of vans cruising the streets of Jalalabad looking for passengers to Kabul.

The major negative was the fact that there were seven different mujaheddin groups between us and Kabul, all controlling different parts of the road. The road from the Pakistani border to Jalalabad was controlled by one group—Jalalabad Seura—who, thanks to our friends in Peshawar, had let us pass unmolested. On the road to Kabul, however, we would have to take our chances with seven different rebel groups—without a letter and without a bodyguard.

Another problem was the rocket fire. From what the Australian aid workers had said, fighting in Kabul was particularly fierce. It was approaching summer, so all the mountain passes surrounding Kabul that had been blocked during winter were open now, allowing every tin-pot rebel who fancied taking the city to have a go.

In the end, the decision was taken out of our hands. That afternoon, as Keith and I sat on the roof drinking a black substance purporting to be Coke and debating the pros and cons of pushing on to Kabul, Hiro was dragged down an alleyway at gunpoint by a shell-shocked mujaheddin gunman. The gunman held his Kalashnikov against Hiro's head and screamed how much he hated foreigners. Luckily for Hiro, some locals begged the gunman not to shoot, thus rescuing him from a grisly death.

The incident made us realise that our safety was on a tight

hair-trigger in Afghanistan. It had been fun to think of Jalalabad as some sort of Wild West town. But there were too many crazy, drugged-out people wandering the streets with serious, heavy-duty weaponry. And there was no Clint Eastwood out there to put them in their places if they started causing trouble. If these guys wanted to rob us, kill us or truss us up just for the fun of it, there wasn't a damn thing we could do to stop them. Kabul was out of the question. Seeing the dusty ruins of a hash shop from the sixties was not worth losing my life over. We were going back to Pakistan. The trouble was, Keith and I needed Pakistani visas to get back in.

The news at the Pakistani consulate the next day, a Thursday, was not good. There were hundreds of Afghanis clamouring to get into the building and secure a visa, and each of them—including us—was told that visas would take three days to issue. We asked the harassed guy handling the applications if there was an express fee, a little extra something that would help matters along. We virtually begged him to take a bribe. It wasn't until we told him what had happened to Hiro that he said he'd speak to the consul and see what he could do. Twenty minutes later he returned. If we gave him two photos and the equivalent of $5 each, the consul would process our visas straight away.

Keith tugged on my shalwar qamiz and hissed, 'I don't have any photos!'

We had two options. Find a photographic shop in Jalalabad, have the photos taken, and come back to the consulate on Monday, or try palming off two different photos of me. (We figured that the photo of me with my hair out could be me, and the one with it slicked back and tucked into my collar could be Keith.) Neither Keith nor I remembered even seeing a photographic store in Jalalabad, so we gave the guy the photos. The guy was immediately suspicious.

'Which one is you and which one is him?' he asked.

'I'm the one with the long hair,' I said, turning around and showing him my ponytail. Of course that didn't explain why Keith didn't have the distinctive dark eyebrows that the person in the photo had, but the guy seemed satisfied with my answer and accepted the photos without any further questions. Either he thought all Australians looked the same or he really didn't give a shit. Ten minutes later he returned with our visas. Half an hour after that we were in a van heading to Pakistan.

I was heading east—and home—again. I had survived a rather foolhardy venture that, in all honesty, I probably shouldn't have attempted in the first place. I was relieved to be leaving Jalalabad and, after what had happened to Hiro, happy to have got out of Afghanistan alive.

So was my mum when I called her from Peshawar—without the distracting rocket fire.

CHAPTER FOURTEEN

Northern India

Soundtrack: 'Sexy, Sexy'—from the movie *Khuddar*

Keith and I returned to the Tourists Inn Motel from Afghanistan
like conquering heroes. Word of our journey spread throughout the
complex of grubby rooms, and soon everyone wanted to speak to
us and hear our stories. One Dutch guy insisted on taking our photo.
Even the wonky-eyed manager welcomed us warmly. 'Allah has
smiled upon you,' he said with a grin.

It was quite tempting to stay at the Tourists Inn Hotel for a while,
dispensing wisdom and reluctantly accepting offers of dinner from
travellers hoping to discover the 'secret way' to enter Afghanistan.
But it was hot. And now that I planned to head through India and
Nepal and into Tibet, I had the approaching monsoons to worry
about. If I got to Nepal too late, the road to Tibet would be washed
out and I'd be stranded.

Keith was flying home to Tasmania, so we exchanged addresses
and said our goodbyes. After all we had been through together, our

farewell was all rather low key, but I guess that's the way we Aussies do things. Besides, I knew I would keep in contact with Keith. I had enjoyed travelling with him and, unlike a lot of people I've been thrown together with on the road, I *could* imagine having a beer with him back home. In fact, that's exactly what I did when I ran into him, quite by chance, near Sydney Town Hall about nine months later.

From Peshawar I travelled quickly on to Islamabad, stopping only briefly to pick up my Indian visa. Part of the reason the Indian visa took so long to issue was that they telexed Australia to 'confirm my good character'. They must have spoken to the wrong people back in Australia because my character was reported to be free of blemish and the visa was issued.

I caught a GTS flying coach from Rawalpindi to Lahore. Despite its rather exotic name, the flying coach was disappointingly ordinary, and painted a drab grey. And it didn't fly, either. As I made my way across the top of Pakistan, I noticed that the closer I got to India, the less gaudy the buses became.

Lahore is perhaps Pakistan's most interesting city. It is the cultural and artistic heart of the nation. First the Moguls and then the British felt compelled to leave behind reminders of their rule. From the Moguls came the beautiful gardens and palaces and tombs that dot the city. From the British, the grand Imperial monuments of The Mall, Kim's Cannon, the Fort and, of course, the magnificent railway station. It was probably both empires that gave the people of Lahore a taste for doublecross and intrigue.

These days this manifests itself in ripping off tourists. Rather than just mugging somebody—which would seem to be the most straightforward way of availing oneself of a tourist's money—the good folk of Lahore have come up with all kinds of scams. There are the notorious police impersonators, well-dressed young men who drive around flashing fake ID at tourists and asking them to show them their money. And there are also the devious hotel managers down on Badrenath Road who will do anything short of poisoning you to get their hands on your moneybelt.

Even the more street-wise *Lonely Planet* guidebook to Pakistan is strident in its warnings about the dangers of being ripped off in Lahore. So it was with some disappointment that I found I was able to get off my bus, hail an auto-rickshaw and get to the Salvation Army Hostel out on Queens Road without being robbed, swindled or conned. Even the auto-rickshaw driver gave me the correct change. I must still have had my 'fuck off' vibes from Afghanistan.

The Salvation Army Hostel was pleasant enough in that camp-bed, national fitness camp sort of way. The sheets were clean and crisp, and the room smelt of linoleum floor wax. On one of the beds an Australian lady had laid out a huge map of the world; she was marking each country she had travelled in, and the routes. I pored over the map, tracing my route so far, and noticed with alarm that I was barely halfway home. The energy from con-quering Afghanistan deserted me. All of a sudden I felt tired again.

From Lahore I caught a crumpled van to get to the Indian border at Wagah. Although the approaches were dusty and disorderly, the border itself was neat and green and not very busy. Overweight Indian officials were hassling thin African guys from Ghana who, for some inexplicable reason, were trying to get into India. I was pointed towards a dusty shed—a one-armed porter offering to carry my bag—where an ancient X-ray machine was fired up especially for me. It was all very leisurely, and the simmering tension between the two countries was not at all apparent. There had been a time, not very long before, when the tensions were so great that the border only opened once a month, and if you missed that day you had to sit around kicking your heels for a month or fly. Now the place had the feel of a languid backwater.

From the border it was another 32 kilometres to Amritsar. I trav-elled this leg in relative discomfort, in a bus without any windows. I knew I was in India now. Amritsar was louder, noisier and more aggressive than any city I had travelled in so far. It was as though the sound level on everything had been turned up—the people, the cars, the markets, the sun—and I was being beaten about the head with a truncheon. As I attempted to get off the bus at the chaotic bus station, a rickshaw driver jumped on the bus and implored me to go with him. When I refused, he grabbed hold of the door of the bus and slammed it in my face. He wouldn't have been happy with me as a potential source of commission anyway. I was staying at the Golden Temple for free. And you can't get much of a cut on nothing.

The Golden Temple is the most famous building in Amritsar, a two-storey marble structure set amidst a pool of water and topped by a dome covered in 100 kilograms of pure gold. The temple is the holiest shrine of the Sikh religion, and for a time in the early 1980s was occupied by Sikh extremists who were evicted by the Indian Army in 1984 in a bloody and heavy-handed operation. For the more budget-conscious traveller, the Golden Temple is famous for other reasons. A central tenet of Sikhism is hospitality, so there is free food and free accommodation for everybody.

In many ways, the Golden Temple is just an extremely ornate, philanthropic Hilton. There are two buildings called gurdwaras—Sri Guru Ram Das Niwas and Sri Guru Nanak Niwas—where visitors can sleep for free for up to three days in double rooms, with bedding provided. (Toilets and a shower block are out in the open in the centre of a courtyard, but what do you expect for free?) Near the entrance to the bathing ghats is Guru Ka Langar, the dining hall, where volunteers dish up basic meals of chapatis and lentils, once again for free. Elsewhere in the complex are a post office, a bank and a railway booking agent.

I stayed in Amritsar for three days, enjoying the hospitality and the opportunity to rest. After months of travelling through strict Muslim countries, it was great to see men and women sitting together, studying the scriptures or just hanging out. At the back of the kitchen, volunteers—stripped down to their singlets but still wearing the distinctive Sikh turban—peeled vegetables. They would wave as I walked past. At night, usually sometime after midnight, I would wander down to the temple, dangle my feet into the pool that surrounded it and gaze upon the illuminated golden dome. It was cool and peaceful, and for the first time in a long while I felt content.

On my last day in Amritsar I took a tour of the Golden Temple complex. It was free, of course, and began at the tourist office just to the right of the Clock Tower and Museum. Our guide was Teja Singh, a big man with a bushy beard and friendly eyes that were magnified unnaturally by his milk-bottle glasses. We followed him down the stairs to the pool that surrounded the temple and stopped.

'You will notice that the dome of the temple is an inverted lotus flower,' he said. 'It is inverted, turning back to Earth, to symbolise our concerns with the problems of this world.'

He also pointed out the four priests (posted at various points in the complex) responsible for reading from the *Granth Sahib*, the Sikh holy book. The continuous reading, in Punjabi, was broadcast from loudspeakers. On the Gurus Bridge, the causeway across the pool to the temple itself, he explained how pilgrims offered sweet doughy parshad to attendants, who then distributed it to everyone leaving the temple.

He also spoke of the troubles in the 1980s. He pointed out the damage the Indian tanks had caused as they rumbled down the stairs beside the dining hall, as well as the cubbyholes, many of which have been sealed, in which the extremists hid.

'It was a terrible time,' he said. 'Imagine—it would be just like a tank firing at Mecca or St Peter's in Rome.'

We entered the temple, taking off our shoes and covering our heads with what appeared to be handkerchiefs. Inside, pilgrims sat praying, reading or talking quietly. Those on the second floor leant against the ornate marble railing and watched the faithful below.

'You will only see greetings and friendly eyes in this temple,' our guide said, sweeping his hand across the peaceful vista. And he was right.

I caught the 'superfast' train from Amritsar to Delhi (447 kilometres, 10 hours). It crawled between the two cities at a pace slower than the average residential-area speed limit, but still completed the journey in half the time the ordinary service would have taken. Speed, like personal space and hygiene—and everything else—in India, was a relative concept.

Most of the passengers spent the journey reading Indian movie magazines. Even the limbless beggars, rolling through the carriage on home-made skateboards, would take a few moments out from begging to flick through a copy of *Filmfare* or *Movie News*, using the stumps of their arms to turn the pages.

I spent the journey in the company of a Sikh gentleman (who I promptly and imaginatively christened Mr Sikh) and his two teenage daughters. Mr Sikh clearly regarded his daughters as princesses and they behaved accordingly. He spent most of the journey watching them adoringly, happily rushing off at every stop to buy them cold drinks and magazines.

It was quite entertaining to watch the whole charade unfold. As soon as the train pulled into a station, Mr Sikh rushed off and collared the first drink salesman he could find. After presenting the drinks to his daughters (and they always screwed up their noses at the flavours he had chosen) he would rush back onto the platform to tackle the much more daunting task of finding a new movie magazine for them. He would hop from one newsstand to another, frantically scouring the wire racks for a magazine they hadn't read.

Then when the whistle blew, indicating that the train was about to leave, he'd panic. I loved the startled look on his face—the same one game show contestants get when the buzzer goes and they've only completed half of their tasks. He'd snatch the nearest maga-zine, shove way too many rupees into the bemused hawker's hand and sprint to the train, jumping into the carriage just as the train pulled away. He'd plonk himself down, gasping for breath, and wipe away the sweat that formed on his brow just beneath his turban. And he'd always smile sweetly when his daughters whined about the magazines he had bought them.

I asked if I could read one of the magazines his daughters had carelessly tossed aside and he nodded his head wearily. It was called *Filmfare*, and it was all aflutter about the increasing vulgarity in Indian films. Now I don't know if you've ever seen an Indian movie, but vulgarity is not a word that immediately springs to mind. There's a lot of singing and dancing, and even a few longing glances. But at the slightest hint of even a kiss, the heroine invar-iably pirouettes off to a distant corner of the set.

According to *Filmfare*, however, Hindi movies were sinking into a mire of lewd wickedness. 'Double meaning dialogue' was the rule rather than the exception. And songs such as 'Sexy, Sexy', in the movie *Khuddar* and the 'hot pantalooney tune of Dulaara . . . pant be sexy . . . shirt be sexy', had—according to *Filmfare*—taken the tempers of the Indian nation to explosion point.

I had heard 'Sexy, Sexy'. It was hard not to, when the sound-tracks to Hindi movies had become just as big a business as the movies themselves. A catchy song meant bigger box office, and 'Sexy, Sexy' had been blasting out of every tinny transistor in Amritsar. In fact, it had got to the stage where I was finding myself singing the chorus—'sexy, sexy, sexy'—in mixed company at extremely inappropriate moments. But it hardly matched either Prince or Madonna in the lewdness stakes.

Yet questions were being asked about the song in parliament. I love it when that happens—it suggests that something serious is about to be done. But how many times have you ever heard of a question being *answered* in parliament? Never. And I suspect that the same would be true of the 'Sexy, Sexy' scandal in the Indian parliament.

In the end, the most important thing I learned about Indian movies by flicking through that magazine was that the Indian film industry was a lot like the computer and advertising industries back home—a lot of ugly men surrounding themselves with drop-dead gorgeous women.

The train arrived at the New Delhi railway station just before sunset and, being in a lazy mood, I decided to stay in one of the hotels on Main Bazaar, the road running west from the railway station. I had been to Delhi eight years before, so I knew I could find reasonably clean, cheap hotels only 300 metres or so from the station. I ignored the pleas of the auto-rickshaw drivers and plunged into the human scrum that is Main Bazaar and Paharganj. A few minutes later I was encamped in a relatively clean third-storey room with a bathroom, a fan and a view of the chaos below for less than $5 a night.

There was also a TV in my room, and that night I watched with interest as the weatherman on the evening news plotted the progress of the rain through India. Since arriving in India I had taken quite an interest in the coming of the monsoon. The success of my journey now depended on my staying ahead of it. It had reached Hyderabad and Bombay, in the middle of the country, and was making its way north, towards Bhopal and Calcutta. In a week or so it would reach Delhi.

In some ways, I would have welcomed the monsoon. I hadn't seen rain since Istanbul, and the temperature in Delhi was pushing 45 degrees Celsius. For close to three months now I had been travelling through heatwave conditions and, to be honest, the heat was beginning to sap my energy and resolve. By the time I hit Delhi, all I wanted to do was sleep.

Delhi was still large and noisy, but it seemed more tidy and relaxed than it had been on my last visit. Perhaps it was relative.

New Delhi had been my first introduction to the filth and squalor of the developing world, and I'd seen a lot more third world shitholes since. I also noticed a change in the type of people visiting the city. Where the streets around Paharganj and Main Bazaar had once been the haunts of hippies and backpackers, they were now teeming with large Russian women buying sack-loads of cheap polyester clothing.

The women squeezed themselves into tiny rickshaws and rode from one stall to another, even though many of the stalls were only a hundred metres or so apart. They haggled violently with the stall owners, pausing periodically to wipe sweat from their brows or to tug at sweaty dresses that stuck to their damp chests. The Russians were obviously the new buying force in town—their bleached blonde hair could be seen bobbing about everywhere. Even the signs for hotels and restaurants and moneychangers, which had previously been only in English and Hindi, were now in Russian as well. I was pleased to see that the Russians didn't feel the need to adopt Indian customs as their Western counterparts did. In all my time in Delhi, I only saw one Russian woman wearing a third eye. But even then it was a lurid blue, just like her shiny track suit.

I only left my room to eat. I'd make my way to a small restaurant that offered food that was one, edible, and two, stayed in my body long enough to provide some sort of sustenance. The street was always gridlocked, with a crush of people, bicycles and rickshaws all trying to go in different directions. I'd often find myself crushed against a wall or pressed into a compromising position with a chubby woman in a sari. One day I reached into my back pocket to get my notebook and found a hand in it.

The hand belonged to a rather startled Indian man. I promptly swung the guy's arm behind his back and pushed him up against a rickshaw, my fist drawn back to hit him. Not being a violent person—and having had zero experience in apprehending felons—

I was impressed by how smoothly it all went. I felt like Bodie out of 'The Professionals'.

The guy was in his late thirties. He stood there, shaking visibly and crying 'No! No! No!' His eyes were wide with panic, and he cringed at the sight of my raised fist. It struck me that he must have been new to this game. A hardened pickpocket gets surly with you or quickly points the finger at someone else. This guy was absolutely shitting himself. I felt like a right bastard, so I lowered my fist and let him go. He hadn't actually stolen anything. And his amateurism suggested that he been driven to theft out of desperation. Maybe he had a family to feed. Getting the police involved wouldn't have done anything except fuck his life up even more. He ran off into the crowd, nervously looking over his shoulder to see if I was following him.

I only stayed a couple of days in Delhi. I had seen the sights on my first visit. I had been to Jami Masjid, the great mosque of Old Delhi and the largest in the country. I had climbed the southern minaret and taken in the view of the Red Fort, the factories, the river and the new city rising to the south. I had visited Feroz Shah Kotla and failed to wrap my arms around the 13-metre pillar and hence prove my good spirit. I even visited the Prince of Dials—the huge sundial that is the centrepiece of the astronomical centre built by Maharaja Jai Singh in 1725. I had seen them all, and ticked them all off my list. There was nothing for me to do this time in Delhi but visit the Vietnamese embassy and have the consul refuse to give me a visa for his country.

The exchange with the consul—a short, stocky guy with a shorn head who wouldn't have looked out of place on the Ho Chi Minh Trail—went something like this:

Me: 'I would like to apply for a visa, please.'
Him: 'Can't issue tourist visa. Thank you! Goodbye!'

Me: 'But your government has changed its policy. You can issue tourist visas.'

Him: 'Yes. Thank you! Goodbye!'

Me: 'So you can issue a visa?'

Him: 'Maybe in two or three years. Thank you! Goodbye!'

The next evening I caught the overnight train to Varanasi. The train arrived at Varanasi Junction Station just as the first rains of the monsoon season started falling on the city. They were big, fat rain-drops that glistened in the sun as they fell and soaked everything they hit on impact. People huddled under cover in the entrance hall of the station and watched dispassionately as paths, lanes and roads instantly became rivers of filth and garbage. I stepped from the train and was immediately aware of an oppressive wall of humidity and the smell of human shit. This was the India I remembered, and I found it invigorating.

Outside the station I was besieged by a pack of rabid auto-rick-shaw drivers. In India, auto-rickshaw drivers are the equivalent of used car salesmen back home. They'll do anything and say anything to get your business, and don't mind telling you outright lies in the process. Their chief weapon is your ignorance. Just as a used car salesman knows that you don't know a carburettor from a universal joint, an auto-rickshaw driver knows that in Varanasi, you wouldn't know Godaulia from Lahurabir.

That's why it really upsets them when you do know where you're going. If they had their way, they'd drop you off at a hotel just up the road from the station, collect a massive commission and then charge you as if they had taken you from one end of the city to the other. They'd like it even better if they could get you to pay extra for your backpack or talk you into chartering the whole bloody thing for a week. I had decided to stay in the old part of the city, though, and this upset these guys immensely.

'It is filthy!' argued one.

'You will be robbed!' cried another.

'It is better you stay in the new part of town,' insisted the first, the picture of reason.

What they really meant to say was that the old city was a labyrinth of winding alleys no wider than one or two people— an area the rickshaws couldn't get into. They would have to drop me off on the edge of the old city, probably near St Thomas's Church, and watch helplessly as I wandered off down a tiny lane on my own. I could walk into a hotel of my choice, alone, and avoid having to pay a commission for the dubious honour of being dropped off at a hotel that I had insisted on being taken to in the first place.

Of course, the fact that a rickshaw driver agreed to take me to the old city didn't mean he would stop trying to take me to a hotel where he knew he would get a commission.

'Why won't you let me take you to a hotel, sir?' my chosen driver that afternoon said, not watching where he was going and nearly hitting a cow that strolled lazily across the main street. 'I know a very nice hotel. Very cheap!'

'But I'll have to pay for your commission,' I argued.

'Oh no, sir!' he said indignantly. 'I do not get commission!'

I looked at him in disbelief.

'Well, maybe I will get three rupee,' he admitted. 'Three rupee, that is all. It is better for you!'

I couldn't quite figure that one out. But before I could argue the point, we had arrived at St Thomas's Church. I paid my money and made my way down Dasaswamedh Ghat Road toward the Ganges.

'OK, sir!' he yelled after me. 'Only two rupee commission!'

Old Varanasi was chaotic, putrid and muddy. The rain had stopped but the roads and lanes were still running rivers of rotting vegetables and decomposing vermin. An oppressive mist had settled upon the disintegrating homes, shops and temples. The Ganges was the major landmark here, a silent muddy force. Upon finding it, I hoped to get my bearings and find a lodge I had read about in my guidebook. I followed the pilgrims heading down to the river in their brightly coloured saris for a swim. Their thongs flicked mud up their backs, but soon that mud, like their sins, would be washed away by the holy waters of the river.

The road led to Dasaswamedh Ghat, a large tiered staircase that led down to the Ganges. It was one of the most important ghats in Varanasi, and the centre of much of the riverside activity. Close to the ghat I discovered a myriad stalls selling flowers and incense, and Brahman priests offering cut-price absolution. The steps themselves were lined with identically weathered beggars, each wearing a sari as brown as himself. The only thing that distinguished one from another was their afflictions. People approached them and asked them to show their afflictions, checking them out—test driving them, if you will—before deciding who was the most worthy of their alms.

It was at the river, however, that all the action was. A mass of brightly saronged near-naked humanity milled about on the banks and in the river, getting up to all sorts of things. People washed clothes. Others had a bath. Some blasphemous individuals even took a dump. It was also where the devout were cremated, or simply tossed, when they died. I could have stayed for hours, just watching, but I had to find a room before the rain came again. I plunged into the muddy alleyways towards Manikarnika Ghat and, I hoped, a cheap hotel called Shanti Lodge.

Within seconds I was totally and hopelessly lost. Every muddy alley looked the same, each overhanging, shoddily constructed building a replica of the next. Even the tiny yoghurt stands were identical, and all seemed to be manned by cloned sellers with wispy moustaches and dirty shirts. Even the people I asked for directions were the same. They all wanted 50 rupees just to point me in the right direction.

After two hours of wandering hopelessly between the Dasas-wamedh and Manikarnika ghats and back again, I had seen more yoghurt stands, passed more poky little stalls selling snuff and trodden in more cow shit than any self-respecting backpacker should have to. I had also seen too many young boys playing Super Mario on ancient black and white TVs. I was about to offer someone 100 rupees to lead me by the hand to the nearest hotel when I spotted a sign pointing to Shanti Lodge. Within a minute, I was there.

If you're wondering whether Shanti Lodge was worth the losing three-quarters of my body weight in sweat to find, it wasn't. It was a rather ordinary concrete building with rooms that seemed to be modelled on prison cells. Its only saving grace, and the reason I had chosen it from the list in the guidebook, was a rooftop restaurant overlooking the Ganges.

It was here that I watched the end of my first day in the holy city of Varanasi. The leaden sky turned pink, then mauve, casting a rich hue over the river that flowed silently below. A single column of smoke rose from a nearby ghat, indicating that a body was being burnt. Monkeys scuttled in an ancient temple to the left. Even the more modern buildings, blackened prematurely with mould, looked charming in this light. I retired to my room for the evening and decided that despite—or maybe because of—all the filth, squalor, disease and death, I liked Varanasi. A lot.

At breakfast the next morning I discovered the Indian backpacker scene. A tribe of tanned Westerners sat on the floor eating yoghurt and lentils. In many ways they weren't very different from the hippies of the sixties and seventies in whose footsteps I was meant to be following. They all wore baggy pants and loose cheesecloth shirts, and decorated themselves with the same assortment of bangles, anklets, necklaces and earrings. All the girls—and most of the guys—had their noses pierced. And they all looked as if they had been in India for months, maybe even years.

It was funny—despite my long arduous journey along the old hippie trail, I felt very much removed from them. They'd had different experiences and had visited different places. They had probably got stoned in Goa and visited the Dalai Lama in Dharasalama. They had probably spent time on an ashram, in search of enlightenment. And more than likely, they were about to head to Delhi to pick up a cheap ticket home to their jobs as stockbrokers and lawyers.

I guess I was also a little cynical and suspicious about their search for spirituality. On my journey I'd seen most of the major religions, and what had struck me was that each was tailored to offer answers to the problems and needs of the cultures it originated from. It might be that I'm simple, but I just didn't see the relevance of a blue-faced God or an elephant with nine arms to a rich kid with a camera and a Walkman, and not a clue about what to do with his or her life. But then I've never been one for lighting incense, eating vegetarian food and wearing a beatific smile, either.

I couldn't stay long in Varanasi. The monsoon rains that were just starting to fall here would soon make their way north to Nepal, and eventually they would wash out the road leading to the border crossing into Tibet. I called my mum from one of the many international phone centres in the old city—each was basically a guy with a phone and a timer—and told her I was in India. (Thank heavens there hadn't been any natural disasters in the subcontinent featured on the news in Australia that week.) Then I booked a seat on an overnight bus heading to the Nepalese border the next evening.

I spent my last afternoon as I did my first, down at Dasaswamedh Ghat. It was just as colourful and hectic as ever. But this time, maybe 50 metres from where a group of elderly ladies were washing their smalls, a man floated by on his back. He was dead— mouth open, arms raised and fists clenched. In India, most people are cremated. But wood is expensive, so how much of your body is cremated depends on how much wood your relatives can afford. This guy wasn't even scorched.

As the little old ladies splashed at the man, trying to send his body back towards the centre of the river and towards nirvana, I noticed something quite extraordinary. His body was a deep shade of Vishnu blue. The hippies back at Shanti Lodge would have been green with envy.

CHAPTER FIFTEEN

Kathmandu

Soundtrack: *Connected*—Stereo MCs

My bus to the Nepalese border at Sunauli was supposed to be a deluxe bus, but it was as battered as any bus in India, with bench seats that were tattered and torn, and windows that were cracked and dirty. The only signs of added value for my extra 50 rupees were the crisp olive green uniform the driver wore and the Hindi film music he insisted on playing at deafening levels (and just a little below chipmunk speed).

My companion for the overnight journey was a middle-aged man from the Brahmin class. In the Hindu scheme of things, the Brahmin—the priests—are the top of the tree, kings of Vishnu's castle and superior in all things over the lower Kshatriyas (administrators), Vaisyas (artisans) and Sudras (peasants). Like all people lucky enough to have been born at the top of their society's pecking order, this guy had strong ideas about what was holding the lower classes back.

'The poor are poor because they won't work,' he proclaimed self-righteously. 'Only the other week I offered a Sudra (peasant) some money if he would come and work for my father and he refused!'

I nodded my head and wondered how I always got myself into circumstances like this. My journey seemed to be a litany of the rantings of bigots and racists. In Bulgaria it had been Spencer and The Owl, the drunken pair of ex-Communists. In Iran, it had been Fatty's rabid brother Ali. What really concerned me was that they all thought they had found a sympathetic ear.

'And the beggars! Don't get me started about the beggars,' he continued. 'They've all got millions of rupees squirrelled away in bank accounts. They're richer than most Brahmin.'

'It is big business, begging,' he went on. 'That's why the Sudras maim their children while they're young. More chance of making a living begging than on the land.'

It was like a Monty Python sketch. I made the mistake of saying that it helps if you are given all the breaks in life, as the Brahmin obviously were.

'Not so!' he lectured. 'They are the ones who get all the breaks in life. Sixty per cent of jobs in the civil service are reserved for the lower classes. It's no wonder this country is going backwards. Jobs are given to the untouchables and not on merit.'

He had similarly strong views on international politics.

'There is a conspiracy to keep India down,' he said. 'Why do you think the US supports Pakistan?'

I said I didn't know.

'To foment the troubles on our borders and keep India weak!'

His proof was the fact that at a recent meeting with the Indian Prime Minister, Clinton did not greet him correctly.

'Oh yes, Clinton is very charming,' he opined. 'But we saw the way he snubbed Rao!'

On and on it went. I yawned, hoping he would get the hint that

I wanted to go to sleep. He didn't. He rattled on about the need for India to develop a nuclear deterrent and the necessity of a war with Pakistan 'to sort things out once and for all'. In the end, I simply switched off, nodding my head automatically and staring off into the darkness. In my mind I was singing Bob Seger's classic hippie hit 'Kathmandu'. Trapped against the window, forced to listen to reactionary drivel, the lyrics were eminently appropriate. 'If ever I get out of here,' my mind sang, 'I'll go to Kathmandu.'

It was 4 am and it was raining when the bus arrived at the Indian border town of Sunauli. The town was still, and the only sound was the pounding of the monsoon rain on the tin roofs. The potholes in the broken road were already filled with water and the footpath had degenerated into a muddy goat track. I picked my way towards the border post by dashing from one covered shopfront to another, more often than not treading on some poor unfortunate beggar who was sheltering from the rain.

The Brahmin man had assured me that the border between India and Nepal was open 24 hours a day.

'It never closes,' he had said. 'It is a vibrant hubbub of commercial activity, the most important border between the two countries!'

I had visions of a floodlit area bustling with activity. Instead it was dark and deserted; the shops were all shuttered and the striped boom gate that served as the border was unattended. The Indians and Nepalese on my bus simply ducked under the boom gate and into Nepal. It was more complex for me. I didn't have a Nepalese visa, so I had to find the border officials, wake them up and get them to process me.

The Indian side of the border was easy enough. The immigration officer saved on rent by sleeping in a hammock on the balcony outside his office. After I shook him awake, he simply stamped my passport then rolled over and went back to sleep. It was only months later that I realised he had mistakenly stamped me into the country.

The Nepalese official, however, was more difficult to rouse. The doorway of the rather more elaborate Nepalese immigration building did not have a balcony. Worse, the rain running off the roof cascaded like a waterfall onto my head as I stood tapping on the glass door trying to wake the official. I could see him. He was curled up on the desk in a foetal position, sucking his thumb.

When he finally woke, he squinted at me, trying to make out what the bedraggled form at the door was. For a moment I thought he was going to turn over and go back to sleep, but he was just manoeuvring himself off the desk—knocking everything off it in the process. The Nepalese have a sticker visa, which he promptly stuck in upside down. After letting me out of the office, he slumped into the chair behind the desk before falling forward onto his arms on the desk and back to sleep.

The first bus to Kathmandu wasn't leaving until dawn, so I sat in a small restaurant—a puddle quickly forming around me—and ordered an omelette and toast. The rain was heavier now, pounding so solidly on the tin roof that the bored waitress had trouble taking my order. The rain was beginning to worry me. It was heavy and it was relentless. The bus station was already a sea of mud and dirty brown water. And so was the Siddhartha Highway, the main road leading north just outside. It was supposed to be an all-weather road. I wondered what state the more temperamental road into China would be in.

When dawn finally arrived it was grey, and came with a low rumble of thunder. The bus pulled out of the muddy bus station and onto the main road, creaking from side to side as it climbed through potholes that had become small lakes. Soon we were making good time through the fluorescent green tropical lowlands of the Terai.

For the first-time visitor to Nepal, the Terai comes as quite a surprise. Fed on brochures of barren grey mountains and snow-capped Himalayan peaks, they are surprised that at least half the country is hot and tropical, and as green as some parts of Southeast Asia. In fact, with its rice paddies and thatched huts, the Terai could quite easily have *been* Southeast Asia. It was certainly raining that way. My hope was that once we cleared this tropical region, we would leave the wetness behind us for a while—at least until I was safely over the Himalayas and into Tibet.

At Butwal the bus turned onto the Mahedra Highway and skirted the Chitwan National Park, famous for its tigers and elephant safaris. At Narayanghat the mountains began, and the bus began wheezing and spluttering past mudbrick villages that were starting to look like those in the tourist brochures.

By Mugling, my hopes that the heavy rain was confined to the more tropical Terai were well and truly dashed. A team of workers—men, women and children—were busy smashing stones and mixing cement to build a retaining wall to hold back a gushing torrent that had washed out part of the road ahead. The bus crawled along a small sliver of dirt—all that was left of the road—and past a ravine that plunged dramatically into mist. A brand new four-wheel drive from the Nepalese Road Maintenance Department was parked beside the road. A fair-haired European sat inside, his head in his hands, horrified at what he saw.

Rain fell heavily for most of the nine-hour journey up the mountains. Every ravine and cleft in the mountains seemed to have turned into a raging torrent. And every small village and town seemed to have a hive of people rebuilding the parts of the road that had been washed away by the weather. About an hour out of Kathmandu, the weather suddenly cleared and the rain stopped.

After struggling through a series of acute switchbacks, the bus reached Naubise, the highest point of its journey, and a point in the mountains that marks the southernmost point of the Kathmandu Valley. The mountains were now more like giant green hills, terraced into gardens of deep, rich soil, and the sun glinted off the tin roofs of the huts scattered about. A mist rose off the valley and there, on a long shallow plain, was the fabled city of Kathmandu.

I have to admit right here and now that I'm an absolute Kathmandu nut. My first visit there back in 1986 is one of my fondest travel memories. I flew into the airport, and just gawked at the cows grazing beside the runway and the snow-capped Himalayas, close enough to touch. My bag was searched by women in saris with a third eye on their foreheads and their bare bellies hanging over their sarongs. A beat up Trabant took me to the Ganga Path, near Freak Street, through intersections in the middle of which sat cows silently chewing their cud. Durbar Square was packed, and people swarmed through the alleyways. I was swept along with the mass of humanity, bobbing up and down, spinning around and smiling inanely, not knowing where I was going and not caring. I checked in at a mudbrick hovel, bought a colourful shirt and drank a yoghurt lassi. When I saw my first hippie, resplendent in white robes and sandals, I knew I had found my spiritual home.

I'm pleased to report that I got the same feeling on this visit. I caught a rickshaw from the bus station to near Durbar Square and was overwhelmed by the magic again.

I decided to stay in Freak Street, the area favoured by the hippies. Freak Street runs south off Basantapur Square, and in the late sixties and early seventies, it *was* Kathmandu. It was a collection of cheap hotels, far out restaurants, moneychangers and hashish shops. It was the place to unwind after the long journey east, to catch up with friends, and to find enlightenment.

The truth of the matter is that this part of Kathmandu has always been the heart of the city. The medieval temples, the muddy lanes, the mudbrick buildings with wooden balconies and views to distant jagged peaks, and the temperate climate are all conducive to spiritual awakening. Throw in a block of cut-price hash, legalise the smoking of it and it's damn near guaranteed.

Sadly, a lot of the old places have disappeared—places like the Eden Hashish Centre. It promised to meet 'all your hashish needs' and sold hash at retail and wholesale rates. When hashish was banned, during the run-up to King Birendra's coronation in 1972, one of the world's great hippie institutions received a wound from which it never really recovered.

Freak Street now felt like a ghost town. A few freaks still wandered around, but they were old and sad; pathetic individuals with nowhere else to go. The new travellers—the backpackers, the trekkers and the package tourists—had all migrated to Thamel, in the north of the city. Freak Street was just another sight to tick off. Spotting a hippie had become the equivalent of spotting a tiger down in Chitwan National Park.

The one thing Freak Street still had going for it was its proximity to Durbar Square. I could quite easily have spent a week just sitting on the steps of the Maju Deval. Built in 1690, the temple has one of those three-tiered roofs that are par for the course on temples in Nepal, as well as roof struts with lewd carvings that serve as the communal Karma Sutra. From high on the ninth step you also get a pretty good view of the surrounding temples and the square below.

Sitting on the steps of the Maju Deval was like watching a Nepalese soap opera—young lovers meeting beside the Garuda statue, shyly holding hands, hoping no one would see, a Nepalese Arthur Daley selling tourists 'genuine' thirteenth-century tangkas that he kept in a cardboard box, and old guys in robes, outside Shiva Temple, debating politics, religion and the price of melons. It would have been idyllic if a little fellow hadn't kept bugging me—he wanted to clean my ears of wax.

The ear cleaners are an annoying feature of visiting Kathmandu. They haunt all the major tourist sites and are more difficult to shake off than a Mormon on a bike. If you let them, they'll stick a long thin metal stick in your ear and then tap it against your eardrum to convince you that you have a 'stone' of wax in your ear. If you agree to proceed with the operation, he will twiddle the metal stick around your ear for ten minutes and scrape all the wax out. For the equivalent of a dollar you can get wax-free ears and a middle ear infection. When faced with one of these buggers it is best to do what I did—stymie his efforts by putting headphones in and listening to your Walkman.

I was listening to the Stereo MCs. Earlier in the day I'd had this uncontrollable urge to listen to *Connected*. I don't know why, but I did. Luckily, the pirate tapes on sale in Kathmandu were pretty ancient, so I was able to find it fairly easily.

'Oh yes, just in from London,' the guy said, dusting off a thick layer of dust.

From the first strains of the title track through to 'Step It Up', it fitted in perfectly with the tempo of the street scene below. The rickshaws, the hawkers, even the young lovers—all seemed to be moving to the beat.

Kathmandu has always had a strong musicality to it for me. Of course there's the classic Bob Seger song—I defy anyone to wander the dusty alleys around Durbar Square and not find themselves silently mouthing 'K-K-K-Kathmandu'—but I also remember that before I went anywhere near Kathmandu, I always wanted to look out across the Himalayas listening to the Hoodoo Gurus doing 'She': 'In the valley, secret worlds below'. I did, and it was cool. And when the small Burma Air aeroplane approached Kathmandu Airport, I also had a perverse compulsion to play 'Like Wow, Wipeout', also by the Hoodoos.

On my second day in Kathmandu, I wandered up along Makhan Tole to the north of the city, and into the new travellers' ghetto, Thamel. This is where all the restaurants and meeting places are now, as well as all the shops selling ridiculously colourful clothes, faux antique prayer wheels and tacky Nepalese jewellery. I passed Vishnu statues daubed in red and ancient temples covered in freshly washed sarongs. Every Nepalese person on the street, including small children, asked me if I wanted to change money. Most of them asked if I wanted to buy hashish. At first I took this as some kind of compliment—proof that I had that wearied world traveller look about me, the look that said I was the sort of guy who would deal in the nefarious world of black market currencies and illicit substances—but then I noticed them ask a middle-aged guy with a video camera around his neck the same questions, and realised that they simply asked everyone.

I've long had a theory that the continued appeal of Kathmandu is based on food, and the time I spent in Thamel proved it. Travellers don't come to Kathmandu for spirituality. Nor do they come here for the embroidered T-shirts saying 'Free Tibet'. They come to Kathmandu because it is the only place within 5,000 square kilometres where you can get a decent feed.

In the few days I was in Kathmandu, I stuffed my face with the best food of my trip so far. At Alice's Restaurant, I enjoyed a generous helping of Thai chicken. Not only was the chicken succulent and tender—and more than just a collection of bones—it came with vegetables that I'd had forgotten the look of: carrots, cauliflower, beans and squash. What's more, they were fresh and delicious. At the Everest Steak House, I tucked into buffalo steaks as thick as a guidebook, smothered in a rum sauce and cooked to perfection. At the Old Vienna Inn, I had Wiener schnitzel as good as any they serve in Austria. And I would start each day at the Pumpernickel Bakery, munching on bread so fresh it was still steaming.

The Pumpernickel Bakery had taken on the role of early cafes and restaurants in Freak Street as a source of information and gossip for travellers. It had a noticeboard full of printed fliers and handwritten messages. I browsed the noticeboard and realised that it was as good an indication as any of how things had changed. There were still notices for yoga lessons and crash courses on Buddhism. There was even a class offered by a Swedish Buddhist nun on how to be clearly in touch with your own thoughts, feelings and responses. But amongst them were more modern notices—a plethora of fliers for 'Eco-Friendly' tours, and an offer of a reward for information about a stolen computer. My favourite notice, from an 'established' writer, going to Tibet and Vietnam, told of how he was 'looking for a strong, financially independent, broad-minded female' to accompany him on his adventure. I wondered if he'd had many responses, but judging by the comments scribbled all over the notice—'You sexist wanker' being the most polite—I guessed not.

It was very tempting to hang out in Kathmandu for a while. The food was good, everyone spoke English, and I was developing quite a penchant for wearing brightly coloured shirts. But the rain was becoming more frequent, and heavier. If I wasn't careful, the road into China would be washed out and my journey would be over. But before I left for Kodari and the border with China, I had one more thing to. I had to visit Willie Bob.

>>>

Willie Bob was a Saddhu, a holy man, but he was a holy man who expressed his spirituality in a unique way. He praised the Gods by lifting heavy stones with his penis. I had first heard of Willie Bob in Indonesia, when an American guy showed me photos of his trip to Nepal. There, amongst the more standard trekking shots of snow-capped mountains and medieval town squares, were shots of a wild-haired man lifting rather sizeable stones with a rope tied to his old fella. It certainly gave new meaning to the weightlifting term 'clean and jerk', and I made a mental note to seek the guy out if I ever went back to Nepal.

Willie Bob was based in Pashupatinath, the most important Hindu temple in Nepal. It was about five kilometres from town, beside the Bagmati River, a river just as sacred to the Nepalese as the Ganges is to Indians. The road leading down to the river and the temple complex that spread over both banks of the river was lined with stalls selling all manner of beads, bangles, charms and flowers. Various holy men and charlatans sat amongst the stalls, selling fortunes and reading snake oil. There was even a small parrot that told your future by turning over cards with its beak. I passed them all by, dazzled by the colour and noise and followed by a group of grubby children yelling for sweets.

I asked one of the stall owners where I could find Willie Bob and she pointed me across a bridge towards a small compound surrounded by whitewashed walls. Like the Ganges, the Bagmati is a popular place to be cremated, as the locals believe that to have your ashes scattered into the river was, in effect, a short cut to heaven. On my first visit to Kathmandu and Pashupatinath, I had watched a cremation from this very same bridge. The guy getting burnt obviously couldn't afford enough wood, because his legs stuck out from under the firewood piled on top of him. After about half an hour, the guy tending the fire snapped the legs back and folded them into the fire. Today however, the charred concrete blocks beside the river that were the burning ghats were empty, and pilgrims were indulging in only the more sedate activities of washing clothes and bathing.

On the other side of the river, a group of gurus, holy men, drug addicts and drunks lounged under the whitewashed stupa that stepped down to the river. I asked them the way to Willie Bob, and they looked at me blankly.

'You know, Willie Bob,' I said again, this time doing a slightly obscene charade that saw me thrusting my pelvis back and forwards. 'I want . . . to see . . . Willie Bob!'

'You are too late,' said one guy, the smell of alcohol strong on his breath. 'He died last winter. Too many drugs!'

I was shocked. I would have thought that a guy who lifted rocks with his penis for a living would have a stronger constitution.

'If you follow me, I can show you where he used to live,' he said.

The guy led me to a small temple complex just off the path to the Goraknath Temple.

'This is where they found him,' he said, pointing to a small stone building. 'He had a needle in his arm and they found $10,000 US in his longavti [sarong].'

Then he led me to another corner of the complex.

'This is where they buried him. Babas are not cremated. They are buried holding a golden trident, sitting in the lotus position.'

Next he led me to a pile of rubble: Willie Bob's stage.

'He was called the Rock and Roll Baba,' said the guy. 'He would get stoned in the morning and lift rocks here in the afternoon.'

I asked who would come and see him.

'They would come from every corner of the globe,' he eulogised. 'But he was very popular with Spanish tourists. The Spanish girls would say "Oooh! Oooh! Do it Shayam Puri. Lift that rock!"'

I laughed. In my mind I saw a gallery of Latin lasses cheering the big guy on.

'The police would try to arrest him. But in Nepal there is no law against lifting rocks with your penis.'

I said he would be hard-pressed to find any country with such a law on their statute books.

'These are the rocks the disciples lift,' he spat, motioning to a pathetic pile of rubble. Then he pointed to a carved stone dome that had tumbled from a nearby temple and was resting against a wall. It would have weighed close to a tonne. 'Shayam would pick even that up easily!'

Now I knew he was getting carried away. He could sense my scepticism.

'Maybe you think I am telling funny story. But it is true.'

He turned for confirmation to a grey-haired guru sitting silently, reading a book. The guru nodded, as did a small boy walking by.

I nodded and put on my best 'I believe you!' face and made my excuses to leave. The guy sidled up beside me and whispered in my ear.

'If you like, I could lift a rock for you.'

I said that wasn't necessary, and anxiously moved away. As I left the compound and turned back towards the Bagmati, he called after me.

'Help me immigrate to your country!'

I told him I didn't like his chances. I was sure that somewhere on the statute books, probably up in Queensland, we *did* have a law against lifting a rock with your penis.

>>>

The next morning I caught a bus bound for Kodari. It had been raining heavily all through the night and the ticket seller couldn't assure me that the bus would get through. There had been reports of landslides blocking parts of the road. But if I had to return to Kathmandu, he promised he would see that the price of my ticket was refunded. I took some heart from the fact that we were carrying the mail. If anyone was going to get through, we would.

The bus headed north from Kathmandu, out past Bodhnath Stupa and Bhaktapur and onto the Arniko Highway. The Arniko Highway was built by the Chinese and, as far as Dhulikhel at least, was in reasonably good condition. From Dhulikhel, the road descended into the pretty Panchkhal Valley. In better weather the snowcapped peaks of the Himalayas are clearly visible, but that day they were shrouded by rain clouds and mist.

As we climbed out of the Panchkhal Valley, we passed a bus coming the opposite way, heading back to Kathmandu. Our driver signalled for him to stop, and asked him about the condition of the road ahead. I couldn't really understand what was being said but I knew that hand movements indicating gushing and rolling were not a good thing.

Now the road followed the spectacular Bhote Kosi River, and became a mixed bag of sealed and unsealed surfaces. When the Chinese first built the road, it was surfaced all the way to the border. The unsealed sections were the parts of the highway that had been destroyed by landslides, and now, in the drizzle of the first rains of the monsoons, they had become slippery mud patches determined, it seemed, to force the bus into a ravine.

At Barabise the bus stopped to change a flat tyre. All the passengers disembarked to mill around and stretch their legs. I stood in the drizzle throwing rocks into the river below. A small boy came up and asked me where I was going. I answered Tibet.

'Oh dear!' he said, genuinely alarmed. 'I heard on the radio last night that there was open warfare between the Tibetans and Chinese guards. Maybe it has stopped now.'

I would have liked to ask him what radio station he was listening to, but the bus was ready to go, and the driver honked the horn impatiently. There is a large expatriate community of Tibetans in Nepal and, if it were one of their radio stations, Radio Free Tibet or whatever, I wouldn't have worried. From what I'd experienced, those kinds of broadcasters tend to take minor incidents and blow them up into major ones—usually followed by pleas for donations for an appropriate fighting fund. But if the boy had been listening to the BBC World Service, I was in real trouble.

The road past Barabise was particularly prone to landslides, and especially after heavy rain. The scenery changed too, becoming more aggressively steep and dramatic. At one stage the bus was forced to edge around mud and rubble that had blocked three-quarters of the road; a ravine tumbling down to a river was on our other side. Once we had passed the debris, we saw three new Landcruisers, with Chinese plates and filled with well-dressed Chinese, waiting for their turn to traverse the blocked road. Now at least I knew the border was open.

The bus finally arrived at Kodari at 3 pm. The town was simply a road lined with wooden shacks beside a river and a bridge that marked the border between the two countries. The Chinese border post, however, was still 11 kilometres away, at the top of a road that snaked its way almost vertically up a mountain. The sensible thing to do would have been to stay the night in Kodari and enter China fresh and relaxed the next morning. But I had a fatalistic desire to get into China that afternoon.

If the Chinese were going to knock me back, I wanted to get it over and done with.

CHAPTER SIXTEEN

Lhasa

**Soundtrack: *Come On Feel The Lemonheads*—
The Lemonheads**

I wish now that someone had physically restrained me from attempting to walk the 11 kilometres from the Nepalese border post in Kodari to the Chinese one in Zhangmu. I wish the Nepalese guard on duty that day had roughly wrestled me to the ground, slapped me in the face and said, 'Good God, man, what do you think you're doing?' But he didn't. When I ignored his polite suggestion that I wait until the next morning and catch a truck up the side of the mountain, he just shrugged his shoulders in a resigned manner that said, 'Well, it's your funeral'. I'm here to tell you that it damn near was.

I could actually *see* Zhangmu—*that* was the problem. It was just above the cloud line, clinging desperately to the side of the mountain, just as Wile E. Coyote clings to a branch after he goes over a cliff chasing the Roadrunner. If anything, Zhangmu's grip looked even more tenuous. I set off with a determined gait, across a bridge and past a few shops selling cheap, crappy Chinese electronics and moonshine liquor, and along a road that climbed the mountain in a series of long 'S' bends.

At first I stuck to the road, but when I spotted some locals using a shortcut—a path that went straight up the mountain, dissecting the 'S' bends like the line in a dollar symbol—I decided to follow suit. That was my first mistake. Walking up the shortcut was like climbing up a ladder, except that instead of being able to grab the next rung to pull myself up, I was forced to hold onto rocks and small plants. My second mistake was refusing offers of help from Nepalese porters making their way back down the mountain. They scampered by, laughing at my discomfort and accidentally kicking dust and pebbles in my face. The prices they were quoting to carry my bag would have cleaned me out of my last US dollars, but what price do you put on your wellbeing?

I finally stumbled into Zhangmu at 7.38 pm precisely, wheezing like a man with a 60-a-day habit. The border guard tutted at me— disgusted by my tardiness and, no doubt, by the state I was in—and let me past the candy-striped boom gate even though the border was officially closed. But he didn't stamp me in. Instead, he confiscated my passport and told me to come back the next morning.

Zhangmu was a town full of ruddy-faced Tibetans wearing ornate silver belt buckles the size of world heavyweight title belts. Up close, the town's grip on the mountain seemed even more precarious than it had from Kodari. People, cars and even dogs inched along the road with their backs to buildings, looking as though at any moment they were going to go tumbling into Nepal below. I made my way cautiously up three twists in the road, past pool halls and bars, to a cheap, unsteady looking hotel. The view from my room—across the town and over the valley—was quite breathtaking. But then so was going down to one of the restaurants for a meal of noodles and Chinese beer.

The next morning I edged my way back down to the border post, still not sure whether or not I would be let into China. The immigration officer stared at my visa, turned it around as if he didn't know the top from the bottom, and then scratched at the page as if he were uncovering a forgery. Luckily, he soon tired of this, and grudgingly stamped me into Tibet. I was well pleased, not just because I was free to continue my journey, but also because the customs officer standing next to him didn't insist on seeing my pack. I had left it back up at the hotel.

Around lunchtime a fawn Toyota Landcruiser full of Westerners crawled into town. They were Europeans—I could tell by the designer trekking gear they wore and the bright, clean backpacks they carried. Most were heading to Nepal, but two dorky looking Germans in the group had travelled to Zhangmu to simply look at the border, and were returning to Lhasa with the driver. When they discovered I was looking for a ride to Lhasa, they suggested I talk to him.

Of course, with my natural affinity with languages, *talking* was the hard part. And it wasn't made any easier by the fact that the driver was Chinese, not Tibetan, and had an arrogant demeanour and a permanent scowl. Everywhere else in my travels I have been able to get away with a few stock phrases, a masterful ability at charades, and an overwhelming willingness on the part of the locals to at least try and understand what I was attempting to say. But in China, it seemed to be different. The people were brusque and not inclined to try to communicate with a scruffy foreigner. Considering the atrocities I was committing upon their language every time I opened my mouth, I can't say I altogether blame them.

Although the driver was only charging the Germans 200 yuan (about $35) for the journey back to Lhasa, he wanted 400 yuan from me. When I tried to haggle with him, he turned and walked away. I yelled out an offer of 250 at his back and he motioned me away as if I were a dog.

I don't know where this guy got his superior attitude—it was only a Landcruiser he owned, for Christ's sake, and one missing a windscreen at that. But I chased him up the street anyway, tapping him on the shoulder and keeping on tapping, more and more aggressively, until he turned around to face me. When I was sure I had his undivided attention, I gave him the single digit—my final offer, you see—and walked off. He must have thought my offer was a touch low, because he exploded into a fit of yelling, swearing and spitting and refused to take me to the top of the hill, let alone to Lhasa. I had to spend another day in Zhangmu. But it was worth it to see this guy burst a blood vessel.

Now I don't want you thinking that I make a habit out of giving the bird to people who annoy me. But Chinese four-wheel drivers have a reputation for upsetting even the most even-tempered of souls. I remember reading a posting on an Internet newsgroup—posted by an Australian, incidentally—that listed five reasons why you should consider renting a yak to get around in Tibet rather than hiring a Landcruiser/driver from CITS, the Chinese Tourist Company. I have reproduced it here in full, to help you understand the extent of the loathing Chinese drivers seem to inspire:

> Yaks speak more English than CITS drivers.
> You only have to kick a yak twice to get it to turn where you want it to.
> Yaks can't charge you more money after you pay for them.
> Yaks can't make up bullshit excuses about the road being impassable.
> Yaks aren't lazy.

The next morning I arranged a ride to Lhasa in a Toyota Coaster full of Tibetans, for 300 yuan. It fishtailed in the mud through Zhangmu as if it were being driven by a teenage joyrider. The mud was a reminder that the threat of monsoons and landslides was not quite behind me. I wouldn't be safe until we reached the dry Tibetan plateau at Nyalam.

The scenery leaving Zhangmu was a magical canvas of gorgeous green gorges and mountains covered in fir trees. The rain had turned each ravine into a thundering waterfall, covering the mountains in a fine mist. It was like driving through a Chinese watercolour painting, and I found myself smiling inanely at the beauty of it all. Two little furry monkeys sat on a rock beside the road, exciting my fellow passengers into a frenzy of yelping and finger pointing. Apparently they were a good omen for our journey.

The bus reached Nyalam without incident. We came upon our first line of prayer flags, and the driver stopped and tied a flag to the line, no doubt thanking the appropriate God for getting us this far. I guess I should have done the same. I was over the Himalayas now. The spectre of monsoons and landslides prematurely ending my journey was now banished.

The face of Tibet changed dramatically here. Now it was barren, grey and vast, and the thin air gave what few colours there were a startling intensity; the sky seemed unnaturally blue, and the sparse plants that grew alongside the river seemed a deeper, richer green. When we crossed the highest point of our journey, La Lungla Pass, the colours of the prayer flags looked like something out of an advertisement for Fuji film.

From here the road followed a dry riverbed across an immense dusty plain broken only by the snowcapped Himalayas on the horizon. It was a vast, unforgiving land, yet at no time was it without human presence. There were small clusters of low white-washed huts here, a solitary horseman there, and right in the middle of it all, where the land was its most bleak and inhospitable, stood a Canadian.

I knew he was a Canadian because he had an embroidered badge of the Canadian flag on his pack. His lips were cracked and his saliva had turned into a thick white paste. He was wide-eyed and crazy and he waved down the bus in a manner that suggested he was using the last of his energy to do it. Desperate and without water, he agreed to pay the driver a rather extortionate 200 yuan to take him to Tingri. His name was Doug and he had set out from Nyalam two days earlier without food and water and had failed to get a lift.

'Fuck, man!' he said. 'I thought I was gonna die! I saw all these Landcruisers but none of them stopped. One Chinese dude even gave me the finger!'

I was tempted to ask if that particular Landcruiser had been missing a windscreen, but decided to let it lie.

By 6 pm we had reached Tingri. After finding out I was paying 300 yuan to go all the way to Lhasa, Doug refused to pay 200 yuan, and gave the driver only 50 yuan. A verbal slinging match ensued—Doug yelling in English, the driver yelling in Tibetan—but it soon degenerated into fisticuffs when the driver lunged for Doug's watch as payment in lieu. After the driver had finished wiping the blood from his knuckles, I took him aside and paid my 300 yuan in advance.

From Tingri we travelled in darkness to Lhaze, another one-street town of low buildings made from concrete blocks. The bus stopped at a restaurant where I ate a tasteless bowl of noodles with the other passengers and watched a Chinese war movie on a battered black and white TV. After the meal we drove a further 200 metres down the road to a sad looking Chinese motel where we were divided into groups of four and assigned one of the rooms that looked out upon a dusty and abandoned compound. A small child spotted me and ran off screaming 'Gwailu! Gwailu!'—the Chinese word for foreigner that means something like 'white devil'. I thought nothing of it, but a few minutes later the manager came to the room with a hurricane lamp. After holding it centimetres from my nose, he confirmed that I was in fact a gwailu and insisted I pay double what everyone else was paying.

This policy of charging foreigners twice or even three times the price for everything is rampant in China. But this was my first dealing with it. While I regard it as a form of State-sanctioned racism, I was tired and ill-disposed to argue. I was prepared to pay the extra $2 and be done with it. The driver, however, was outraged. He collected all the other passengers together and we left to find another hotel.

I was genuinely touched and surprised. After the altercation with the Canadian, I thought the driver might have had his fill of Westerners. The support of the other passengers also surprised me. They had just been dragged out of bed, forced to pack and get back into the bus, but they still found it within themselves to give me murmurs of support. One even yelled out 'Fuck you!' in English to the bewildered Chinese hotel owner, left holding the hurricane lamp and scratching his head.

Luckily, we found another hotel just up the road. It was called the Happy Hotel, and we sat in the bus while the driver negotiated with the owner for a rate of 15 yuan each, same price for the gwailu. The rooms were brighter and the sheets cleaner, and I drifted off to sleep that night as a roommate chanted in a deep soothing manner. My faith in human nature was restored.

After breakfast at the Friendship Restaurant and the purchase of provisions at the Good Luck store (both with signs inexplicably in English) we left Lhaze and headed east along the Friendship Highway. By mid morning we had reached Shigatse, a bustling town in a fertile valley surrounded by barren mountains. Shigatse was little different from the other soulless concrete towns we had been passing through. Its only distinguishing features were a monastery with a gold roof and an inordinate number of red-robed monks slouching on its steps, and the pair of identical Tibetan twins we came across hitchhiking on the outskirts of town.

As is often the way with twins, both girls dressed exactly the same. Both wore thick green jumpers and combed their hair from one side of their head to the other like a man trying to cover a bald spot. Each had strands of cotton braided into her hair and a huge turquoise earring in her right ear. In keeping with the whole twin phenomenon, both girls reeked of the same perfume of sheep shit and three years' worth of body odour. Of all the bags and boxes in the aisle of the bus, they chose my backpack to sit on, punching it roughly to make it more cosy. But they flashed huge beaming smiles whenever they caught me looking at them, and I would have forgiven them anything.

The fertile valley of orchards and fields surrounding Shigatse gave way to a barren desert that seemed totally incapable of supporting even the smallest seedling. Chain gangs of Chinese soldiers from more hospitable corners of the empire busily shovelled sand that had been blown onto the road back onto the verges, to be blown back the next time the wind picked up. Soon we were in the mountains again, but making good time on the well-sealed, well-maintained road. For the first time in Tibet, the road was smooth enough for the driver to put a cassette in the cassette player, confident that it wasn't going to be chewed up.

I don't know what it is about bus drivers, but they invariably have the worst taste in music. You'd think that if you were responsible for the entertainment of a large, captive audience, you'd take the time to choose something that would appeal to a wide range of people. It has been my experience, though, that bus drivers go to one of two extremes. They either play ear-piercingly bad heavy metal music or sickeningly bland love ballads.

This guy chose the love ballads—soppy, sentimental sounding Chinese love ballads. Most of the passengers groaned when they heard the opening bars, and wrapped pieces of clothing around their heads to block out the noise. The guy sitting next to me, however, was so pleased with the driver's choice that he sang along. His voice was flat and off-key, but that didn't stop him giving it the full Celine Dion treatment. Periodically—for no apparent reason and in a manner in no way connected to the song that was being played—the twins would start yodelling. I spent the rest of the journey to Lhasa with the uneasy feeling that I was trapped in a lunatic asylum.

Just outside Lhasa, the bus was pulled over to the side of the road by soldiers in grey and mauve uniforms so it could be washed by girls wearing nylon straw hats. The girls set upon the bus wielding hoses, soapy brushes and brooms to reach the high spots, and attacked the mud and dust picked up on the long trip from Zhangmu. I never found out why—was it quarantine? A State-run money-making venture? Whatever the explanation, our bus was now glistening white and ready to enter the holy city of Lhasa.

The first landmark I spotted was the Potala, the former winter residence of the Dalai Lama. It sat on top of a hill, surveying all around it, down the end of a fertile river valley. The second was the dirty big TV tower the Chinese had built on the hill opposite. The bus followed the river that dissected the valley and entered Lhasa through the modern Chinese section in the west of the city.

Here Lhasa was a disappointing collection of tatty shopfronts, a squat five-storey skyscraper and a roundabout—the centrepiece of which was a statue of a huge golden yak. Chinese women in the latest nylon fashions from Beijing walked the streets past stores selling rice cookers and plastic shoes. If it weren't for the Potala sitting majestically above it—and the golden yak, of course—it could have been any town, anywhere. Thankfully, everyone on the bus was Tibetan, so we skirted the new town and went straight to the more aesthetically pleasing Tibetan part of Lhasa. It was older, more down at heel and altogether grungier. There were Tibetans in dark shawls, skinny dogs and garbage on the streets. The bus driver continued the kindness he showed in Lhaze by dropping me off right outside the Yak Hotel.

The Yak Hotel is something of a traveller's institution in Lhasa. It's cheap, clean and close to the Jokhang Temple, one of Tibet's holiest shrines and the focal point of Tibetan religious life. I was given a bed upstairs in a room that was painted as luridly as the trucks in Pakistan had been. Actually, I think it may have been painted by a Pakistani truck driver, because it featured the same elements you see on every truck in Pakistan—geometric patterns of no particular rhyme or reason complemented by a tranquil mountain scene quite unlike any landscape in the country in question. But at least it didn't feature another vital element of Pakistani truck art— the mandatory pair of F-15s screaming across the sky to drop a nuclear payload on India.

Before giving me the key to my room, the pretty Tibetan receptionist pointed to a framed notice on the wall from the Public Security Bureau. She indicated that reading it was part of the required registration process.

'Ladies and Gentlemen, welcome to Lhasa,' it started brightly. 'So that you have safe and enjoyable travels we would like you to be aware of the following government regulations:

1. Foreigners travelling in China must abide by Chinese law and must not endanger the national security of China, harm its public interests, disturb the public order or engage in any other activities incompatible with tourist status.
2. If Chinese citizens are holding a rally or demonstration it is strictly forbidden for foreigners to participate in, follow along with, take pictures or video film of any of these affairs. Foreigners are not allowed to interfere in Chinese internal affairs.
3. In accordance with regulations foreign tourists must go through all registration formalities and stay only at designated hotels. Without prior permission, travelling in unopened areas, using undesignated transport, operating individual business or privately taking up an occupation is forbidden.

Have a nice day.
The Public Security Bureau of Lhasa, China.'

I signed the registration form, disappointed that my plan to foment open rebellion, film it and then sell it to CNN had been thwarted so easily. I'd have to think of another way to top up my dwindling funds.

I ventured into the heart of the old town, not quite knowing what to expect. After a constant diet of Western propaganda and Richard Gere movies about this country I was kind of expecting Jokhang Temple to be shuttered and locked and the Barkhor, the religious circuit around the temple, to be awash with political agitation and tear gas. Instead, I found Tibetans buying prayer flags, prayer wheels and Buddhist scriptures in front of Chinese soldiers who looked bored and uninterested. Some pilgrims fed juniper bushes into a cone-shaped oven, creating an acrid, pungent smoke that engulfed the courtyard. Others prostrated themselves at the main entrance of the temple in a series of manoeuvres that wouldn't have looked out of place in an aerobics class. There were even a few stores selling what I had thought would be forbidden pictures of the Dalai Lama.

I wandered amongst the pilgrims, marvelling at the colours, the smells and sounds. The thin air at 3,683 metres slowed my usually brisk gait to more of a loping shuffle, and it wasn't long before I was feeling a little light-headed and giddy. After only one circuit of the Barkhor I was staggering into pilgrims and knocking over stalls as if I were on laughing gas. I retired to Tashi's, the legendary restaurant just off Beijing Donglu, to catch my breath.

Tashi's has long been the backpacker eating establishment of choice in Lhasa, but upon entering the low doorway and sitting at one of the low, dirty tables covered in floral-patterned Contact, I found myself wondering why. There is no immediately apparent reason for its ongoing success with the Tibetan tourist set. The dining rooms are dark and dingy. The food is basically a tasteless cornucopia of barley cooked three different ways and tea served in jam jars. And the waitress, lovely as she undoubtedly was, spoke

English in a breathless voice, as if she was barely in control, and got everyone's orders wrong.

It was the back room at Tashi's that annoyed me most. This was where the long-term travellers and their assorted groupies hung out, and you could only enter if you were invited. At any time of the day you could find a 'guru' sitting there pontificating about Tibetan politics to silly American college girls who sat leaning forward eagerly, with their chins in their hands and their eyes wide open, and saying things like 'Oh wow! Really? That's cool.' I guess what upset me most was that I was never invited in.

At first I ate all my meals at Tashi's. But I soon got sick and tired of eating bland bobis (unleavened bread) and thukpas (noodles with meat) and decided to try another restaurant I had heard about called the 'Pink Curtain'. It was called the Pink Curtain because it had a pink curtain covering the doorway. As its popularity grew, however, other less scrupulous restaurants started hanging pink curtains out the front of their establishments too. Finding the true 'Pink Curtain' became a quest not unlike searching for the Holy Grail. I was eventually shown the way by a tall German staying at the Yak Hotel as a trade for my tape of The Lemonheads. Some ungracious souls would argue that the poor guy had been gypped.

The Pink Curtain was even less extraordinary to look at than Tashi's, if such a thing were possible. It was bare and dusty, and most of the chairs were broken. But it was busy, and crowded with locals, which is always a good sign. The menu was in Chinese, so I just pointed at something another customer was eating that I liked the look of. The food was good. One day soon, I would choose someone to pass the information on to, and so it would go on until Lonely Planet got hold of it, and then the Tashi tossers would decamp.

After three days in Lhasa, I decided to visit the Potala fortress. I'd visited the Jokhang Temple nearly every day—poking about the shrines and galleries and breathing in the rancid fumes of the yak's butter candles—so I figured it was about time I popped over and visited what was once the centre of Tibetan government and the Dalai Lama's former winter hangout.

I have to say I found the Potala a bit of a disappointment. It was huge and empty and more like a museum than a living, breathing place of worship. While all the other Westerners were getting off on standing in the Dalai Lama's old bedroom and stroking his old silk dressing gown, I was getting bored. At the Jokhang Temple, every corner revealed something new—a group of rosy-cheeked youngsters making clay Buddhas or women embroidering curtains on old foot-pedal Singers. But here in the Potala, I only found endless 'donation' boxes and money-hungry monks with constantly outstretched hands. From the moment I paid the $15 entrance fee I felt like I was in the Tibetan equivalent of Disneyland.

The huge telecommunications tower on the hill directly opposite the Potala reminded me that perhaps I should give my ever-patient mother a call. I wandered down to the telephone office in the Chinese part of town, bought a 100-yuan telephone card and called her. Just as I was assuring her that I was nowhere near Tiananmen Square, the phone card cut out, short of funds for international calls but still with close to 20 yuan left on it. Rather than let the remaining yuan go to waste, I decided to use the credit left on the card to make a prank call to somewhere in China. Realising that a prank call isn't much fun unless the person at the other end understands you, I called the Australian embassy.

>>>

I should point out that I don't make a habit of making prank calls. In fact, the last time I made a prank call was when I fifteen and I was babysitting a kid called Gavin Hunt. We got bored watching telly and kicking a football around, so we decided to pass the time by ringing up his grandmother and putting on funny voices. (In defence of Gavin, he was only six. I should have known better.) It was nothing as witty as Bart's calls to Moe on 'The Simpsons', asking for someone called Al Coholic. We just put on silly high-pitched voices and hung up when we started laughing. I still feel guilty about the extra $10 Mrs Hunt gave me because her son had 'never been that well behaved for a babysitter before'.

In Lhasa, I put my lapse down to the thin air and the fact that every other Westerner in Lhasa was so goddamn pious. Most had visited Dharamsala, the northern Indian town where the Dalai Lama lives in exile, and wore T-shirts bought in Nepal saying 'Free Tibet'. All the pseudo-spiritual drivel and sanctimonious carping on about human rights and repression was driving me crazy. Earlier in the day I had wandered around the Grand Hall in the Potala, going up to the marble pillars and saying 'One, two, testing' after an earnest American college girl whispered to me that she had heard the Potala was bugged. Now I was going to call my embassy and pretend to be a farmer from west of the Great Dividing Range.

'G'day,' I said, in my broadest Australian accent, when a woman from the embassy in Beijing answered. 'I was wonderin' if I could speak to person who 'ands out visas. You know, the ambassador or someone.'

'May I ask what it's in relation to, sir?' said the sweet woman on the other end.

'Well, it's like this,' I drawled. 'Met a little lady and we're gettin' married this arvo. I was wonderin' if it'd be all right if I took her home with me.'

'Is she Australian, sir?' she asked.

'Oh God, no!' I exclaimed. 'She's a good cook, though. And she darned a hole in me socks in no time flat. I tell ya, she'll be a boon to the country.'

'Sir, as you can understand, we have regulations we must follow,' she said, still trying to figure me out.

'Oh, you don't have to worry,' I said earnestly, 'It's a marriage of love. We only met this morning and we haven't been out of each other's sight.'

'Look, I'm going to have to transfer you to someone else,' she said, bewildered. 'I'm afraid this is out of my jurisdiction.'

I barely heard the bells chiming on hold before I burst into laughter and hung up. Pathetic, really.

>>>

The next day was the Dalai Lama's birthday—not that anyone needed telling. Most Westerners were in town especially for the big day anyway. And just in case the increased presence of the Chinese army on the streets hadn't alerted the few people who didn't know that something was going on, some starry-eyed tourist had gone to every hotel and restaurant frequented by foreigners and stuck up a poster saying 'July 6 is the Dalai Lama's Birthday. May all his wishes be fulfilled!'

As it was, I reckon I had a better time on the Dalai Lama's birthday than he did. You see, while His Holiness was being bought some low-cholesterol, high-fibre birthday cake by some fawning movie star in Dharamsala, I was throwing flour at his loyal subjects.

Now I must say in my defence that they started it. For some reason I was never quite able to fathom, the Tibetans celebrate the Dalai Lama's birthday by throwing flour at people. I was hit three or four times just on my way down to the Pink Curtain for breakfast. Later in the morning I was clobbered by flour-packing pilgrims outside the Jokhang Temple. And I even suffered (with what I considered quiet dignity) a rather cheap shot from the chambermaid at the Yak Hotel. But there are only so many fistfuls of flour a man can endure before the urge to retaliate becomes too strong. If that's how the Tibetans wanted to celebrate the birthday of Tenzin Gyatso, the 14th Dalai Lama, spiritual and political leader of the Tibetan people and the latest incarnation of Avalokitesvara, the Buddha of Compassion, who was I to argue?

The Chinese don't stop the Tibetans from celebrating the birthday of the man many believe is a living God. In fact, July 6 is an official public holiday. Most businesses close for the day and the town is transformed into a giant, flour-based version of Skirmish, or some other of those 'weekend warrior' games.

The celebrations kicked off at around 5 am with chanting down at the Jokhang Temple. The chanting was performed by monks from an outlying monastery, who looked suitably solemn and wore the mandatory flowing red robes. It was the first visit to Lhasa for many of these guys. Chanting at the Jokhang Temple on the Dalai Lama's birthday was an immensely special privilege, and for most of them, a once-in-a-lifetime opportunity. Together with the throat-constricting smell of yak butter candles, it was like an interactive rendition of the *Baraka* soundtrack.

After the chanting in the central shrine finished, the doors to the rest of the Jokhang Temple were thrown open and all the Tibetans rushed off to their favourite buddha/thangka/shrine and made a special birthday offering. They lit candles, prayed and prostrated themselves in unimaginable and uncomfortable ways. After that, it was time for a big picnic down by the river at the Dalai Lama's former summer palace, Norbu Lingka.

Any other day of the year, Norbu Lingka is a peaceful collection of palaces, gardens and ponds. But on the DL's birthday it was transformed into a kaleidoscope of blankets, picnic hampers and bonfires, with children running around madly as only children under the age of five can. Adults sat in circles singing and eating and occasionally getting up to dance. It was like a big church picnic, but better. Here the faithful got to slowly write themselves off on chang, a tangy alcoholic drink made from fermented barley.

Unfortunately, I wasn't able to take part in this part of the celebrations. The Chinese army had blockaded the bridge crossing the Lhasa River with trucks and four-wheel drives, and stopped all foreigners from going any further. I contented myself with throwing flour at Tibetan families as they hurtled past on the weird three-wheeled tractor-with-trailer contraptions that most folk from Lhasa seem to gad about on.

Not every Tibetan headed down to Norbu Lingka. Hundreds of Tibetans stayed behind at the Jokhang Temple burning juniper bushes and prostrating themselves for most of the day. One old guy—a Khambas from Eastern Tibet, judging by the red yarn in his hair and the ornate dagger by his side—celebrated by leading a sheep on a rope around the Barkhor all day.

In the midst of all the celebrations, Chinese soldiers milled about nervously on street corners and outside Chinese businesses. With their truncheons, electrified batons and canisters of tear gas, they looked a right bunch of party-poopers, itching to step in as soon as anyone looked as if they were having too much fun. I was disappointed no one threw flour at them.

Without wanting to sound like one of the politically correct do-gooders I spent most of my time in Tibet making fun of, the most disappointing thing about spending the Dalai Lama's birthday in Lhasa was that the guest of honour didn't show. It would have been great to see the guy beaming as everyone sang, 'Hooray for Tenzin ... '. And I'm sure the Dalai Lama feels the same way. While it must be nice to have bands like the Beastie Boys organise benefit gigs for you—and supermodels like Cindy Crawford drop in for a chat—I'm sure if he had the choice, the Dalai Lama would prefer to spend his big day copping a face full of flour down in his old summer gardens at Norbu Lingka.

The next day all the Westerners in Lhasa would be heading off again, restarting the journeys they had put on hold for the birthday celebrations. I was heading north to Golmud. Others were flying to

Chengdu, but most were heading south towards Nepal. It was kind of sad, really. I'd been in Lhasa for close to a week and, despite the heavy presence of complete tossers, I had managed to make quite a few friends. There was the pretty Swiss girl who had flirted outrageously until her work chum from a foreign aid project turned up unexpectedly. There was the German who had shown me the way to the Pink Curtain, and Martin, the nightclubber from Melbourne determined to climb Mount Everest on a yak.

And you know what? I would also miss all the tossers in the dark corners of Tashi's. After all, I was heading into China proper. Who would I be able to incense now by loudly discussing my plans for printing a T-shirt that said 'Free Tibet with every purchase'?

CHAPTER SEVENTEEN

Chengdu

Soundtrack: That Chinese music that sounds like a cat being strangled

If you look at a map of China, Lhasa and Chengdu look enticingly close. As the crow flies, they are barely 1,200 kilometres apart. There's even a road heading east through Bayi, Rawu and Markam, where it splits into two—one fork heading east towards Chengdu, the other heading south to Kunming. But looks can be deceiving. For one thing, the road east was officially closed to foreigners. While that was not necessarily a problem—the Chinese are more likely to turn back someone trying to get into Tibet than someone trying to leave it—the state of the road was. My guidebook described it as the 'wildest, highest and most dangerous route in the world', and it was so bad that truck drivers refused to use it. The very real possibility of dying in a landslide, and the complete lack of transport anyway, meant that it would actually take longer using the road east than taking the more roundabout route north through Golmud.

Getting to Golmud was easy enough. There was a regular local bus that left Lhasa each day at 7 am and arrived at Golmud 36 hours later. The only problem, as far as I could see, was having to pay three times the price a local did for the ticket. Andy, a Chinese guy from Hong Kong, planned to travel to Golmud the same day as me and offered to buy me a ticket at the local price. The Chinese in Lhasa, not a sophisticated bunch at the best of times, seemed to think he was one of them. He bought tickets for two Israeli guys as well.

Of course, buying the tickets at local prices was the easy part. When we arrived at the station at 6.30 the next morning, the girl taking the tickets—wearing a blue uniform and a disposable breathing mask—refused to let us on board until we paid an extra 120 yuan for the 'foreigner supplement'. She eventually let us through, but at 7 am, when the bus was scheduled to leave, the bus driver discovered he had three foreigners on board and refused to leave until we paid him an extra 60 yuan each.

Andy suggested we pay it. He knew it would go straight into the bus driver's pocket, but he figured it would get the bus driver on our side and he would help us through the numerous checkpoints ahead. We would still be getting our ticket for considerably less than the foreigner price, so I handed over the extra cash. The Israelis, however, refused to pay the extra 60 yuan and called the bus driver all manner of names in Hebrew to boot.

It was quite an embarrassing scene. The bus driver took their bags off the bus. The Israelis threw them back on. The bus driver kicked their bags. The Israelis kicked his bus. The other passengers started to become agitated. They had settled into their seats and were anxious to head off on what promised to be a tortuous 36-hour journey. They started looking at me as if I had something to do with the delay. I shrugged my shoulders and pretended I didn't know them.

At 8.30 am the ticket clerk who had sold Andy the tickets turned up for work and got dragged into the dispute. Not surprisingly, he wanted to know where we had got our tickets. (He hadn't noticed Andy, who was sitting very quietly up the back, trying to remain inconspicuous.) I told him I had bought mine from someone at Tashi's. The Israelis, however, pointed the finger straight at Andy, and he was unceremoniously dragged off the bus.

At 9 am, two hours late, and a lot of testosterone later, I was forced to cough up an extra 60 yuan and Andy was let back onto the bus. The Israelis, however, were left behind. Even though they had eventually agreed to pay the extra 120 yuan, the driver refused to let them on the bus. I remember hoping—rather ungraciously— that their tickets were non-refundable.

The bus followed the Lhasa River along the valley out of town before climbing a narrow road into the mountains. At first, the mountains were dotted with whitewashed buildings and scraggly trees, giving the landscape an almost Mediterranean feel. But after traversing a high pass, we found ourselves travelling along a flat plateau backed by green rolling hills. Occasionally, in the distance, jagged peaks covered in pristine snow became visible through the clouds. Yaks and sheep grazed peacefully in the wide open spaces. It was a magical scene, spoilt only by the guy behind me talking constantly in a high-pitched voice.

That afternoon we passed the kind of vistas usually reserved for *National Geographic*: high summer pastures; dramatic barren land-scapes; a lone woman surrounded by a swirling flock of sheep. When the bus stopped for the driver to change a flat tyre, I lay waiting in the grass beside a small lake watching the clouds rush by. I felt as if I had found peace.

That peace didn't last long. Nasty black clouds soon rolled over the mountains, and the bus was trapped in a snow squall. The driver pulled over, waiting for it to pass. I remembered those stories my parents told me when I was a boy, about people getting caught in snowstorms and dying. The secret to surviving, they said, was not to fall asleep. I took comfort in the fact that it wasn't likely while old squeaky-voice kept nattering on behind me.

The storm soon passed, and the driver set off again. The road was slippery, which excited the boy racer instincts of the driver. He fishtailed the bus down the road, hooting and hollering and nearly wiping out the tractors and their rugged up drivers coming in the opposite direction.

After an evening meal of watery noodles in a garrison town not made any prettier by its covering of snow, we set off again along a road that had now deteriorated into a string of interconnected potholes. The bus lurched from one pothole to another with such violent intensity that passengers were tossed from their seats like rag dolls. I tried to sleep, but woke up gluggy-eyed to find that we were now travelling along what seemed to be a dry riverbed.

Dawn brought no respite. The scenery was bare and drab, and the road one long construction site. Armies of disheartened, grubby men and women toiled wearily repairing their assigned section of the road, stooping in the bitter cold. Beside them, oily machines spat out gravel and forty-four gallon drums of tar were heated on open fires. To the right of them was a flat monotonous desert, to the left the same. I don't know what these people had done to be sent to this hellhole, but whatever it had been, they didn't deserve this.

After a final checkpoint, the bus coughed and spluttered towards Golmud across a vast grey plain dotted with telegraph poles. In the distance, the chimney stacks of the potash mines that were the reason for Golmud's pathetic existence belched black smoke and flames into the sky. The bus limped into a ramshackle mechanic's shop, the bus terminal for this particular service. The other passengers headed off down a dusty road towards the train station, still a good two kilometres away. No one was staying in Golmud. There was no reason to; it was just a railhead to the rest of the country. I followed them, smiling and sweating, happy to be off the bus.

The station was a huge empty hall overlooking a huge empty square. A few optimistic souls had set up tables and were selling an assortment of stale biscuits and Chinese soft drinks. My footfalls echoed through the hall as I walked across the waiting room to the ticket window. With a combination of gestures, attempts at pronouncing Chinese and pointing to the appropriate Chinese characters in my Mandarin phrasebook, I asked for a ticket on the 2.45 pm train to Xining. The woman at the ticket office screwed her face up into the sourest expression possible and said 'méi yǒu', the Mandarin word for no.

Thinking that perhaps she had somehow misunderstood me—a reasonable conclusion, considering my Mandarin abilities—I went through the process more slowly and deliberately. Once again she shook her head and said no.

Andy had warned me about this on the bus. When faced with something out of the ordinary or something a bit too much like hard work, Chinese public servants will often say no. It's much easier than actually doing something, and if they get ticked off for it, they simply claim that they couldn't understand you. It was obvious that this woman just didn't want to go to the trouble of, firstly, finding out the cost of a foreigner ticket to Xining, and secondly, filling out the various forms needed to issue it.

There was only one way around this problem, and that was to make refusing to sell me a ticket more difficult than selling me one was. Now, luckily, this is something I do have a God-given talent for. When she refused to sell me a ticket for the third time, I stood my ground at the window and in pathetic, poorly pronounced Mandarin said, 'Where is the ticket office? Where is the ticket office?' over and over again. Eventually, she covered her ears, screamed and then issued me a ticket. At 160 yuan (the local price was 57 yuan), I kind of wished she hadn't.

Before I could get on the train, though, I had to run the gauntlet of scowling Chinese women in brown uniforms with red stars on their epaulettes. The first stood at the doorway to the platform, looking closely at my ticket, checking that I had been sufficiently ripped off before. Then she let me proceed to the only train at the station. Another woman, dressed exactly the same, and with a sour countenance not unlike that on girls' faces moments after I ask them to dance with me at discos, blocked the door to the train. After she had consulted with her twin sister guarding the door at the other end of the carriage, she grudgingly let me on board. Inside, a slightly less gnarly girl took my ticket, exchanged it for a plastic chit and led me to my compartment.

At first I thought the compartment was on fire, but once my eyes had adjusted to the haze I realised that it was smoke from the cigarettes of my fellow passengers. Five Chinese men of varying ages nodded and smiled—and one patted the empty seat beside the window and beckoned me in—before returning to their cigarettes and pipes. The youngest member of the group, a boy of ten, sat in the luggage rack, his feet dangling over the edge, smoking a roll-your-own of impressive proportions. I took a deep breath of air outside the compartment and took my place beside the window. There, barely visible through the smoke and centred above the window, was a non-smoking sign.

I had a momentary irrational urge to point to the sign and insist that they stop smoking. After all, I paid three times more for the trip than they did. But I realised fairly quickly that it would be a total waste of time. For one thing, they wouldn't understand my English, or my Mandarin for that matter. Nor was it very likely that smoking was actually banned on trains in China. The carriage was probably old European rolling stock, bought cheaply by the Chinese when it was deemed dangerous and unusable on the Continent, and had probably come complete with the signage.

It has also been my experience that smokers do not take kindly to non-smokers pointing out no smoking signs to them. I made that mistake on a bus from Dublin to London. I pointed out the sign to a guy and spent the next seven hours being harangued as a 'kangaroo fucker', albeit in a colourful Irish brogue. I decided to simply put up with it, just as I had in Turkey and Indonesia and every other place where 99 per cent of the population seem to have a two-packs-a-minute habit.

The train pulled out of Golmud at dusk. Within minutes we were shuffling across a grey, featureless plain backed by grey mountains that blended indistinguishably into the grey evening sky. A line of telegraph poles, silhouetted by what was left of the late afternoon sun, was the only distinguishing feature, but it soon disappeared into the murky evening, too. With nothing better to do, I clambered up into my bunk and fell asleep. It was the first time I had been horizontal in close to 48 hours. It was not a bad night's sleep, although I kept waking up and finding it hard to breathe. At first I rather fancifully thought it might have been altitude sickness— in the course of the journey the train had traversed passes over 5,000 metres high—but from the taste in my mouth, I knew it was the smoke.

The next morning I made my way to the dining car to escape the smoke. Along the way I was introduced to another startling Chinese custom—spitting. As part of their morning ablutions, most of the passengers were dredging up phlegm from the furthermost corners of their body and depositing it with a lazy aplomb on the floor, walls, doorways and windows of the carriage. They dredged with such intensity that I thought they were about to bring up yesterday's lunch, dinner and breakfast and a major organ or two. In the West, spitting is regarded as a somewhat unsanitary habit, but in China it is considered normal, and indeed essential to good health. (And with the country boasting the highest number of centenarians, who am I to argue?) At first I picked my way tenuously through the carriage, trying carefully not to let my foot fall in a pool of Chinese spittle, but it proved impossible. Instead, I careered through the carriages, slipping and sliding as if I was walking on ice.

The dining car, while spittle-free, echoed with an innocuous selection of bland Chinese muzak that warbled from tinny speakers. A smartly dressed man and woman joined me at my table. They were lawyers and could speak English perfectly. He was involved in commercial law and had been a guide with the Chinese Government Tourist Office. When the economy picked up he returned to the law, opening a practice in Lanzhou with a couple of his Beijing University mates. She was an assistant to a female judge. At first I couldn't quite ascertain what they had been doing together—were they colleagues or lovers?—but in the end I decided that it was work-related. I found it hard to believe that a couple would go to a potash mining town like Golmud for a dirty weekend. Regardless, he seemed particularly interested in the fact that I had just come from Tibet.

'You would have noticed that all the trucks and cars in Tibet are new,' he said, in a manner that made me feel I was in the witness box. 'That's because we're always giving them money. Any political agitation there is just another way to get more money out of Beijing.'

I didn't comment, but then I didn't need to; my learned companion was on a roll.

'What else is there in Tibet?' he asked rhetorically. 'Mountains! If it wasn't for the rest of China, Tibet would be really poor!'

I said that there must be something there—strategic borders, oil, wanton, easy women—otherwise the Chinese wouldn't be so keen to keep their hands on it. He changed the subject and asked me how I was finding China. I told him it was OK, but I was a little pissed off that I was charged three times the price for everything just because I was a gwailu.

'That's because they won't let us join GATT,' he said. 'As soon as the West accepts China, the prices will come down.'

I must have looked sceptical, because he continued with this theme.

'You know why Beijing didn't get the Olympics, don't you?' he asked. 'It was an OECD conspiracy. Not that it bothered us anyway.'

While I couldn't be sure about his OECD conspiracy theory, I knew the bit about the Chinese not being upset by the decision was ludicrous. I remember watching the announcement of the hosts of the Year 2000 Olympics on TV in London. (I'm embarrassed to say that when old Juan Antonio Samaranch said 'Shid-a-nee' it was one of the happiest moments of my life.) The Chinese delegates had broken down and sobbed. My new legal chum would not accept this.

'You are mistaken,' he argued forcefully. 'We are not emotional people.'

I knew what I saw, and was about to argue the point, but a young soldier walked by and the lawyer fell silent and pretended not to know me.

Just before Xining, the train skirted Qinghai Lake, the largest lake in China and home to Bird Island, a breeding ground for wild geese, gulls, cormorants, sandpipers and the extremely rare black-necked cranes. The lawyer pulled a pair of nifty combination bin-ocular/eye glasses from his briefcase. They looked like something you might order from an ad on the back of a comic—like a normal pair of glasses but with another panel in front with two milk-bottle bottom lenses that you could adjust. He looked out towards the lake, madly adjusting the specs for 10 minutes, then gave up.

'It is too hazy,' he said unconvincingly, knowing in his gut that the glasses were crappy and that he'd been ripped off. I knew then that he had just had his first real taste of capitalism. He went back to his carriage to sulk.

With the lawyer gone, the judge's assistant opened up and spoke to me.

'My employer went to Sydney for a Women's Law Conference,' she said quietly. 'She showed us pictures. So beautiful, so clean.'

Almost as if to emphasise her point, a man opposite us dredged up his lung and deposited it on the wall opposite. After it had slid to the floor, she continued.

'If it was up to me,' she said carefully, 'I would have given it to Sydney too.'

Not for the first time, I noted that most of the nicest people I met on this journey were women.

The Chinese are the first to tell you that the northwest is not the most attractive part of their country, and it seemed that Xining was keen to prove the point. You know when you are tuning your TV and you half pick up a signal, but it's grey and hazy and the colours are washed out? Well that's what Xining was like. There was also a dull, cold river rushing through the town and making a sound that was an awful lot like static. From what I could ascertain from the departure board—not much, as it was in Chinese characters—and from locals, who at least pretended they understood what I was trying to say from my phrasebook, there wasn't a connecting train to Lanzhou until the next morning. I had an afternoon and an evening to kill in Xining.

After nearly three days of solid travelling, I was exhausted. I stayed in the Yongfu Hotel, in a room overlooking the Huangshui River. The room had sky blue seersucker curtains and a matching bedspread, plus a bathroom and a TV. I switched on the TV and watched the English-language news. The highlight was a report about a restaurant in Beijing called 'Cabbages and Condoms'. Patrons ate bowls of stewed cabbage while flicking through leaflets on birth control and safe sex. Grisly footage of a vasectomy operation was played on TV monitors placed around the restaurant. The report finished with the manager assuring patrons that he had not put contraceptives in their meals.

I was surprised how much I enjoyed just *listening* to the report.

So very few people spoke the language in China that it was a rare treat to take in the Queen's English, no matter how poorly enunciated it was. In most countries I had travelled through, there seemed to be people around who could speak English—and at least one who actively wanted to. Similarly, in everyday travel situations, I always seemed to encounter ticket clerks and hotel managers who'd had enough contact with foreigners to pick up the phrases needed to facilitate the purchase of tickets or the securing of a room with an attached bath.

In China, however, hardly anyone speaks English—which, of course, is their prerogative, and quite understandable considering the brutal treatment the British dished out to them late last century—and in many ways it makes the country one of the most compelling and challenging to travel in. But that night in Xining, it just left me feeling worn out and isolated.

I was also feeling lazy, so I ordered a meal of fish (bony, as it turned out) to be brought to me from the kitchen below. (My *Lonely Planet* guide had described it as the best restaurant in town. Need I say more?) I even got the management to organise my train ticket to Lanzhou. It cost me an extra 10 yuan, but I didn't care. I was luxuriating in a lumpy bed that smelt of mildew rather than Marlboros.

A good night's sleep lifted my spirits. My train ticket appeared mysteriously out of the pocket of the manager as I checked out, and soon I was outside the station, running the gauntlet of a group of around 50 people doing Tai Chi with swords in the forecourt. Inside, the waiting room was clean, large and airy, with a Stalinist ceiling that seemed a mile away. It was dominated by a huge painting of Mao surrounded by cheerful ethnic minorities. I joined an orderly queue and shuffled along with the rest of the passengers past stalls selling food, cosmetics, books and shoes, and onto the train to Lanzhou.

As with the train from Golmud, the departure of the Lanzhou

Express signalled to the passengers that it was time again to dredge their lungs. The old man sitting opposite dredged with such ferocity that he sounded like an approaching jet. And when he spat, it whistled past my ear sounding like an F-15. Soon everyone else in the carriage joined in, and it sounded like a bombing raid over Baghdad.

The trip to Lanzhou, through dry, craggy mountains, was rather uninteresting. I passed the time talking to an Earnest Young English Speaker, Wenbin Deng, who had latched onto me not long after the train left Xining. He was from Jiangxi Province, in southern China, and I never did quite figure out what he was doing on a train in the northwest. I flippantly mentioned that I had never met a Wenbin before and he used that remark as a cue for a longwinded explanation of the meaning of his name. Wen meant culture. Bin meant bravery. He came from a small village where getting an education was difficult and rare. His parents hoped that naming him Wenbin would ensure that he would get an education as well as the courage to face any difficulties. In true Earnest Young English Speaker fashion, that was about as exciting as conversation with Wenbin got.

Things livened up when a soldier confiscated a box of peanuts from one of the countless hawkers who'd been passing through the carriage from the moment we had left Xining. They mainly sold food, magazines and ice cream, and although what they were doing was strictly illegal, Wenbin said that most had 'private connections' with the train guards, who turned a blind eye for a few yuan. This particularly unfortunate hawker—a chubby, cheerful, middle-aged lady—was obviously new to the game, and hadn't paid off the right person. She followed the soldier, laughing nervously, begging for her peanuts. The look on her face suggested that she could see her whole livelihood walking out on her.

An hour or so before Lanzhou, we came upon the Yellow River. It was swollen from the heavy rains that had fallen in the mountains, and was a dirty chocolate brown. I hadn't expected it to be yellow. I knew—well, I had read in my guidebook only minutes before—that it was named after the royal colour yellow because it, like royalty, was regarded as the source of life. The train followed it through tunnels and along cliff faces as it wound its way through the mountains.

At Lanzhou, my unilateral policy of being nice to Earnest Young English Speakers—no matter how boring or unbearable they are—paid dividends. Lanzhou was a big, ugly factory town trapped in a narrow valley. Smog hung heavily in the air and you could taste the carbon monoxide. I knew within moments that I didn't want to stay there and, as luck would have it, there was a train leaving for Chengdu that afternoon. There was a problem, though: trains leaving Lanzhou were heavily booked, and it often took foreigners 24 hours to get a ticket. I could try buying a ticket from a tout, but it was risky. My guidebook was full of stories of foreigners shelling out hundreds of yuan for a ticket they couldn't read and that only took them as far as the next station. In return for the kindness I displayed in talking to him, Wenbin agreed to buy me a ticket.

The ticket office at Lanzhou looked like the moshpit at a Pearl Jam gig—hot, sweaty and tightly packed. There was even a touch of crowd surfing. After buying a ticket, the only way back to the door and the station beyond it was to clamber over the top of the solidly packed crowd and hope they deposited you by the door with at least a little bit of dignity and the ticket you just bought. Wenbin dived into this mass of humanity as if he had been handed a special mission from God. He returned 45 minutes later, his hair mussed up and his clothes dishevelled, triumphantly holding a ticket.

'It is only a hard seat,' he said. 'There were no sleepers left. But I got it for the Chinese price.'

To show my gratitude, I gave him one of the cling-on koalas I carry around with me as a souvenir from my country and a small token of thanks for those who help me in my travels. I know it doesn't sound much, especially considering that Wenbin had just saved my sanity by talking to me in English—and a good $15 on the ticket as well. But believe me, in some countries they are quite the collector's item. I was careful to remove the 'Made in China' sticker before I gave it to him.

Even though Wenbin had thoughtfully gone to the trouble of reserving me a seat when he bought my ticket, I was not surprised to find my seat occupied when I boarded the train. In the developing world, seat numbers are still an alien concept. In most countries, this is not usually a problem. In fact, the 'mix-up' will often lead to experiences you would never have encountered otherwise. Chances are you'll become an honorary member of the family. They'll offer you food, a cup of tea and maybe even their daughter. There's always an ulterior motive, of course: they don't want you to get the guard, and they hope their generosity will move you to squeeze that little bit further across on the bench to let Grandma, Grandpa and the family goat squeeze in and ride for free.

Unfortunately, that wasn't the case on this train. Rather than a smiling granny loaded up with freshly steamed dumplings and a thermos of Chinese tea, my seat was occupied by a sharp-featured man with what seemed to be a permanent scowl and an unbending determination to be the rudest person in China.

'You just go 'way!' he snarled, in broken English. 'Not want you here. Somewhere else!'

Rather than becoming violent, I decided to play the dumb tourist and pretend I didn't understand a word he said. I smiled inanely, pointing to my ticket and then the seat as if it was all just some big misunderstanding that could be resolved with a smile. After pining to be able to communicate in English for so long, I was surprised how much pleasure pretending not to speak the language gave me.

'Go sit with peasants!' he spat. 'Over there!'

I smiled and nodded and continued to point at my ticket and the seat. Eventually, trembling with rage, he shifted just enough to let me sit down. I squeezed in, wiggling my backside to shift him aside further. He tried to hold his position, but my arse was bigger than his. I spread my legs and made sure I took up as much space as possible—all the while smiling, raising my eyebrows and nodding.

After half an hour, the elbowing began. He'd reach across the table in front of us to grab a cup of tea, and on sitting back would bring his elbows sharply into my rib cage. In return, I would rummage through my daypack, allowing my arms to flail about, sometimes catching him on the chin or, if I was really lucky, right on the nose. By early evening it had got to the stage where I was accidentally dropping my not insubstantial *Lonely Planet* China guidebook onto his groin. When it was time to sleep, I did so fitfully. I was afraid of what he might try.

I nodded off eventually, but after an hour of restless sleep I woke with a start, as my arm was being grabbed. At first I thought it was the sharp-featured one's grandmother, locking my arms behind my back so that her grandson could land a few blows into my midriff when I couldn't defend myself. But it was a young Chinese guy, neatly dressed in a Nike T-shirt and jeans.

'Can you speak English?' he asked excitedly.

When I said I could he became even more excited.

'Then you must come to our carriage!' he implored. 'There is plenty of room. You can even lie down on a seat and sleep!'

As I gathered my things to leave I 'accidentally' trod on my usurper's toes.

Li Yuan was a young university student returning to Chengdu after the summer holidays. He and his friends had commandeered an entire carriage and turned it into a fraternity house on wheels. Fresh-faced students—no doubt the privileged offspring of Party cadres and businessmen—were smoking, gambling, drinking and laughing raucously. At one end of the carriage a table had been set up for drinking games, and the floor around was littered with the bodies of students who had failed the test. A Buddha-shaped guy with spiky hair, round glasses that were far too small for his face, and an obviously huge capacity for alcohol sat behind the table undefeated and taunted the others into trying to beat him. When he spotted me, he lifted his arms triumphantly and chanted 'I love basketball! I love Michael Jordan!'

In other corners, students sat huddled over card games, with huge wads of yuan sitting in the prize pool. One group, perhaps the progeny of the new filthy rich capitalists of China, played for US dollars. All the while, other students ran up and down the corridor in their genuine Levis jeans, bare-chested and flicking each other with their genuine Hanes T-shirts. It was like the party scene in *Porky's*, but without the boobs. In fact, without girls at all. The Chinese one-child policy, and the Chinese preference for male heirs, meant that there wasn't a female in sight.

My long fair hair and general Western appearance caused a bit of a stir, and for a while I was the centre of attention. Each guy came up and practised his few words of English on me. They were like students the world over, interested in music, the latest Gameboy and girls. They wanted to know if I owned a dog—a major indulgence in China and a sign of immense wealth—and whether I had any sisters. I'm not sure what impressed them most—having two dogs or three sisters.

When I showed them pictures of my youngest sister, Melinda, they went into a chorus of yelping, cheering and wolf-whistling. The champion drinker left his post to have a look and then challenged me to a drinking game with Melinda as the prize. Melinda will be forever thankful that I cried off, citing an upset stomach. Instead, he took the photo and kissed it.

'I don't love basketball! I don't love Michael Jordon! I love *her*!'

That these guys were from the privileged classes of China was reflected in the fact that they were paying a little old guy to pick up after them and keep the carriage tidy. He also acted as security, stopping any unwanted passengers coming in when the train stopped at a station. Li Yuan called him a 'living Lei Fung' after the model soldier who appeared in all the Communist propaganda and was regarded as a model of hardworking decency. I had begun to despair of China, but Li Yuan's cynicism and open mocking of a Communist icon gave me hope for the place.

Outside, the scenery had changed too. Where it had been bleak and dry and barren before, we were now passing through rice fields and orchards and past mudbrick villages. This was a China more in keeping with the coffee table books of my childhood. When I was growing up, my Dad had a China fixation, and every birthday or Christmas one of us would buy him a book on China. He said he liked China because he admired the Chinese, although he never said exactly why. Being a short man, I think he saw the fighting spirit and attainment of independence of the vertically challenged Chinese as a one-fingered salute to all the tall people of this world. And secretly, I think he always wanted to go to China because he would be able to stand proudly on his two flat feet, not straining on tiptoes, and still see what was happening just ahead.

At about 10 pm, Li Yuan cleared a bench seat of students reading Chinese movie magazines and indicated for me to lie down. Using my camera bag as a pillow, I got myself into a comfortable position. I used a spare T-shirt to block out the light and my Walkman to block out the noise. I listened to one of my own compilation tapes—*Girls with Guitars*, an eclectic collection of guitar bands with female singers—and once again pondered my luck. Sure, I would wake up with a crick in my neck. But I could have ended up with broken bones if I'd spent the night rumbling with the agitated man down in second class.

When I woke up the next morning, my clothes were damp with sweat. I was certainly in another China now. The air was thick with humidity, and outside it was green and lush. The soil looked redder and more fertile, and the rivers were broad and deep. We passed waterfalls and houses with that darkened, aged look that comes from the black of mildew. Workers busily cleared landslides that had blocked roads. For the first time on the trip I felt I was beginning to make progress, and that home wasn't that far away after all.

After five days and 5,135 kilometres through the backblocks of China, I had finally reached Chengdu.

CHAPTER EIGHTEEN

Dali

Soundtrack: *1967–1970 (Blue Album)*—The Beatles

Chengdu is the capital of Sichuan Province, the largest and most
heavily populated province in China. It is a modern city of over
three million people, with wide tree-lined boulevards and soaring
glass skyscrapers. It is the major industrial centre of the southwest
as well as the region's administrative, cultural and educational
centre. Its affluence can be seen in the gleaming department stores
full of Japanese electronics and the latest Hong Kong fashions. The
day I arrived, it was also full of American college students trying
to get into Tibet.

It seems they had heard about Tibet on 'E! News' and had flown
to China in their summer break to witness the oppression first hand
and 'do their bit'. Nothing too risky, you understand—just empath-
ise with a local or two and hand out a few Dalai Lama photos then
fly out again with a few little trinkets secreted in their designer
packs to prove they'd been there. That was the plan. When they

got to Chengdu, these well-meaning college kids discovered that Tibet was 'officially' closed. In China, 'officially' closed means closed unless you go on one of the very expensive CITS tours. When I came upon the students, they were sitting in the restaurants angrily denouncing the oppression of their right to travel freely, while no doubt waiting for Daddy to come through with that extra money.

The students, and every other traveller in Chengdu, hung out in the hotels and restaurants facing the tree-lined footpath that ran along the Jin River between Renmin Nanlu and Xinnan Lu. They dined on sanitised Sichuan specialities from menus in English and sipped on ice-cold Coca-Cola. The Chinese nouveau riche of Chengdu raced up and down the dirty brown river in speedboats. Touts wandered from table to table, selling tours to acupuncture clinics or tickets to the Sichuan Opera—'Front row seats, backstage passes and English translations!' Others just practised their English. After spending close to a month in Tibet and the backblocks of northern China, I was surprised by how easy everything was. Travellers in Chengdu were virtually being spoon-fed a whole China experience.

I didn't stay long in Chengdu. To be honest, I felt like a pariah. I had made the biggest possible social faux pas in Chengdu—I had already been to Tibet. What's more, I wasn't all misty-eyed about the experience or about the fact I had been there on the Dalai Lama's birthday. As far as the college students were concerned, people like me didn't deserve to get into Tibet. The hostility was palpable. It got to the stage where I was convinced that when I walked along the Jin River, past all the restaurants, people turned their backs on me.

I decided to catch a train south to Panzhihua and then a bus to the mountainside village of Lijiang, in Yunnan Province. The ticket seller at the foreigner's window at Chengdu Railway Station told me that the soonest I could get a seat was in a week. A tout standing nearby whispered that a travel agent called John, in the arcade below the Traffic Hotel, could get me a ticket for the train leaving the next day.

John's office was the scruffiest in the arcade and consisted of a single chair and table and a beat up lounge for his clients to sit on. Scattered on the floor beside the couch were faded brochures on the various attractions of Chengdu, including the Panda Museum. The museum featured panda sculptures, panda bones, a collection of 'precious photos' and a display, which had the look of a school project, entitled 'Foreigners loving the Pandas'.

In the corner of the office there was some untidy bedding, from which John emerged, looking similarly dishevelled. He spoke perfect English, but he wasn't an Earnest Young English Speaker. He had learned English because it was a way to make easy money—lots of it. He promised to get me a ticket on the No. 93 Express leaving Chengdu at 9.15 pm, getting into Panzhihua at 10.30 the following morning. I imagined him down at the station with the other black marketeers swapping train tickets amongst themselves as if they were theatre tickets in New York or London.

'I'll give you a hard sleeper on tomorrow's Shanghai Express for a No. 145 Express to Wuhan stopping all stations to Chongqing.'

'You've got a deal!'

The tickets would be slapped down on the concrete floor, all within sight of the railway officials and the watchful gaze of a statue of Mao Tse-tung.

Whatever his methods—to be honest, I really didn't want to know what they were—John got me a hard sleeper on the next No. 93 and I was left with only a day to kill in Chengdu. I spent the day looking for the Panda Museum. The girl down at the CITS office had never heard of it, nor had she heard of Chengdu's other more famous attractions—Renmin Park and Wenshu Monastery. Instead, I wandered the streets and parks of Chengdu, hoping that I might happen upon a sign that said 'Panda Museum this way' or, at the very least, hear sounds that indicated that some intense panda loving was taking place nearby.

It wasn't my lucky day. I walked listlessly through glitzy arcades full of wide-screen TVs and along boulevards where men in uniforms dusted shiny new cars with feather dusters. The highlight of my day was buying pirate CDs of the Beatles' Red and Blue 'Best of' albums for $2 each. I also discovered that Chengdu wasn't as modern or progressive as I had first thought. There were still guys selling tiger paws as aphrodisiacs on the footpath, and the Chengdu public swimming pool wouldn't let foreigners in for a dip unless they produced a health certificate confirming that they didn't have AIDS.

It was dark when the No. 93 pulled out of Chengdu. The others in my compartment were already asleep in their bunks, cigarettes dangling precariously from their lips. Smoke lingered around the top of the cabin, lazily swirling in the breeze created by the fan when it occasionally spluttered to life. I had a bottom bunk this time, so the smoke was less intense. My greatest worry now was misdirected spittle from the top bunks. I lay on my side, leaving only my back exposed, and fell asleep.

When I woke up the next morning, the train was travelling through vibrant green rice paddies and thick stands of bamboo. Soon we made our way into lush green mountains, clinging to the mountainside along railway cuttings dripping with moisture. It was beautiful, enchanting. I almost expected to see pandas frolicking beside the tracks. These scenes of breathtaking beauty were often interrupted by the sudden appearance of a grubby, concrete town, built without any consideration of aesthetics, but they passed quickly and the greenness was upon us again.

Sometime during the night we had crossed the mighty Yangtze River. Apart from the odd grainy shot of the mighty river on a misty morning in one of my dad's coffee-table books, my dealings with the Yangtze River had been limited to the Monty Python sketch where English goalkeepers of the seventies recited poetry they had written about the Yangtze and how it had inspired them. The sketch ended with a football chant that began with 'We love the Yangtze, Yangtze Kiang' and ended with 'Yangtze is the river that we all support'. I found myself humming it.

With the Yangtze now behind us, and my last chance of seeing the great river now gone, I wandered down to the dining car for an early lunch. It was empty except for a group of angry staff in grubby white uniforms scowling at two Western girls who had been there since Chengdu. They had only been able to get a hard seat from the touts at the station, and were so horrified by the conditions in their allotted carriage that they had set up camp in the dining car instead. The Chinese staff were not amused.

'They keep telling us to go back to our seats,' said the American, a New Yorker called Ellen. 'But, hey, we've been ordering beers!'

'We even had a meal!' said Clare, the dark-haired Canadian.

'See that arsehole there?' said Ellen, pointing to a particularly surly waiter. 'He tried to charge us for sitting here. It's not like the place is full or anything.'

She was right. All the other tables were empty. I motioned for the waiter, and after he grudgingly come over, ordered a Coke.

'Now watch how long he takes,' said Ellen. 'You won't get that Coke for at least an hour.'

She was wrong. It only took him 45 minutes. But after putting it on the table, he stood there, motioning for me to finish it then and there and move on. I ignored him and took my time.

'Here, have some chocolate,' said the Clare. 'It's happy.'

I looked at her quizzically. The chocolate was a Chinese brand called Happy, but I didn't see the significance.

'If it ain't Happy, it's crappy,' the girls chirped in unison, before cracking up with laughter.

After wiping the tears from their eyes, they apologised for their temporary lapse of sanity. They had been travelling in China longer than I had, and it was starting to get to them.

'We've tried being nice,' said Clare.

'And we've tried speaking Mandarin,' said Ellen, showing me a beat up phrasebook with the most useful phrases marked with yellow highlighter. 'But it's like they can't be bothered.'

'At least we haven't been molested,' said Clare. 'Remember what it was like in Indonesia? We couldn't go 200 feet without getting our arses pinched!'

'Have you looked at yourself in the mirror lately, girl?' said Ellen, in a mock African–American accent. 'You ain't no Cindy Crawford no more!'

With that, both girls cracked up again, burying their heads in their arms and laughing until they were choking back the tears. The Chinese waiters looked on and tutted in disgust.

I stayed in the dining car with the girls until my destination, Panzhihua. They were heading further south, to Kunming and a plane home. As I left the train, they gave me a hug, and when I was on the platform, they threw me a bar of Happy chocolate from the dining car window.

'It'll help keep your spirits up,' said Clare.

I was a little overcome. I'd only known Clare and Ellen for a matter of hours and they were already sharing their precious stash of A-grade Chinese chocolate with me.

'Hell, it works for us,' said Ellen, sensing my emotion and lightening the situation.

As I thanked them, the train pulled away. I waved goodbye until the last carriage disappeared from sight.

I caught a dinted old bus that trundled through picturesque mountains covered in fir trees to Lijiang. Every hour or so the pristine mountain scenery was interrupted by a muddy town with a huge factory pumping toxic white foam straight into a river. I remember, when I studied Chinese history at school, seeing a photo of Mao

Tse-tung swimming in a river to prove that he was fit and healthy. It is obvious from the swirls and ripples around him that he had underestimated the rips in the river and his face had a forced smile that barely masked the panic. I always imagined that just beyond the frame of the picture was a boatload of Party cadres with out-stretched arms willing him to come aboard. As we passed these poisoned rivers, I wondered if Mao would still take a dip in a Chinese river if he were alive today.

The main bus station in Lijiang was a dusty hovel surrounded by concrete buildings; it successfully hides the fact that you've arrived in one of the prettiest towns in China. The station skilfully conceals the spectacular Jade Dragon Mountains to the north, and the dust and diesel fumes from the ancient buses cloak the fact that the air is crisp and clean. In fact, it is not until you struggle beyond the ugly urban sprawl—somewhere around Lion Hill—that you even notice the maze of windy cobbled streets and the ramshackle wooden buildings that make up the old town. It's also in this part of town that you'll first catch sight of the Naxi ethnic minority, descendants of Tibetan nomads who moved to these parts a few hundred years ago and have a penchant for wearing blue.

The Naxi are also famous for being one of the few matriarchal societies in the world. Women inherit all property, women run the judicial system and any children born are the responsibility of the mother. Even the Naxi language bears testimony to fact that it is the women who wear the pants in this society. If the meaning of a word needs to be enlarged, the word for female is simply tacked onto the end. Hence a *big* night out in Naxi is a *female* night out. The Chinese have tried to change this, of course, but any doubts you may have about the women still being in charge are quickly dispelled by a trip down to the markets in the old part of town. It's the women you'll see running all the businesses, playing hard ball with suppliers and buyers alike. It will be the women drinking tea and playing backgammon. And it's the women running the lucrative sidecar taxi services.

My first dealings with the female sidecar Mafia came when I wanted to go out to Baisha, a small village at the foot of the Jade Dragon Mountains, 12 kilometres from town. I found the drivers on the corner opposite the Mao statue. They lounged in the sidecars attached to their bikes—aviator goggles pulled up onto their white crash helmets—with practised looks of disdain on their face. When I approached them and asked to go to Baisha, they ignored me. Eventually, one tutted disapprovingly and indicated with a nod of her head that I should try the woman further down the queue.

I clambered into the sidecar, obviously made to Chinese dimensions, and sat there uncomfortably for 10 minutes with my knees under my chin. At first I thought we were waiting for more passengers, but when a little old lady who had been sitting on the pavement all along clambered on board I knew that I had been put in the sidecar for the amusement of all the other sidecar owners. The day's entertainment over, we set off down a bumpy dirt road, past rustic barns and into the Chinese countryside.

The ride was a short, but painfully uncomfortable, one through tiny villages and past cultivated fields of grain. I gripped the front of the sidecar tightly, but the suspension was such that on every bump, my legs and backside would be tossed violently into the air, clipping the head of the little old lady sitting behind me. When we finally reached Baisha, I watched what the little old lady paid and gave the driver exactly the same amount. She indicated for me to pay more, but I refused. She was furious, and started spitting and cursing. When I walked off she followed me, trying to run me over. I ducked off down a laneway and hid behind a pile of mudbricks until she gave up and drove away.

I had come to Baisha to visit Dr Ho, a Taoist physician who had achieved worldwide fame after he was eulogised and mythologised by the travel writer Bruce Chatwin. Dr Ho has the good luck of looking exactly like you might imagine a wise old Taoist physician would look like—white flowing beard, a wise old face and the mandatory white coat and hat, Red Cross and all. He has translated this image, plus the beautiful setting of his practice—beside a babbling brook lined with weeping willows—into a healthy business. He makes his living posing for photos, showing tourists his garden and musty old books about herbal medicine and then selling them packets of his special herbal tea.

Thanks to the incredible PR job Chatwin and subsequent writers have done, a lot of tourists come to Dr Ho expecting not only a cure for all that ails them, but the meaning of life as well. (There must be some void in our culture that sends people to the East looking for answers—I'd been stumbling upon these spiritual 'pilgrims' everywhere since India. More often than not, they seemed to have extremely well-paid jobs back in the West.) When all he does is dish them up a blend of herbal tea, they get a little upset. Some of the less gracious even claim he is a charlatan.

I have to say, I liked the guy. Even though he couldn't speak much English, I spent a few hours with him in his practice, watching him tend a constant stream of local villagers. They suffered everything from backache and rheumatism through to tinea and bronchitis, and Dr Ho treated each of them with respect and compassion. After ascertaining what ailed them, he consulted a variety of ancient leather-bound medical texts—stacked high on a bookcase groaning under their weight—and then mixed a treatment from the ingredients in an exotic collection of jars and beakers. More often than not, he refused to accept payment for his services. By paying a little too much for my satchel of herbal tea, I was subsidising the health and wellbeing of the good folk of Baisha.

As an outsider, I found it was best to treat a visit to Dr Ho like a visit to your grandparents. They make you a cup of tea, show you some old photos and then take you on a tour of their garden. Except with Dr Ho, the tea is herbal and supposedly medicinal, the old photos are yellowing press clippings, and the garden is full of plants that seem more suitable for a witches' brew than a Sunday roast. But I wouldn't call him a charlatan. After an afternoon with the guy, I tended to agree with John Cleese's assessment, scribbled in one of the older guest books—'Interesting bloke, crap tea.'

From Lijiang I caught a local bus bound for Dali, and spent eight hours in the company of Naxi women who seemed determined to prove that they could spit and smoke as well as the next bloke. The scenery was still distinctly Chinese, but there were hints of a more southern, tropical character—a rice paddy here, a water buffalo there. I was moving closer towards China's southern borders, from where I hoped to cross into Indochina and the rest of Southeast Asia.

I arrived in Dali at that time of the day when the sunlight gives everything a soothing golden hue. It was a pretty little place, on the western shores of Erhai Lake and backed by the imposing Cangshan Mountains. The old part of the town was all narrow streets, and the lake was dotted with ancient fishing boats with fishermen using cormorants to fish. In the middle of the lake was an island, crowned by a Chinese temple that looked as if it had been designed by the Disney Corporation. I had come to Dali because my guidebook described it as one of the few places in China where you could 'well and truly forget that you are in China'. After northern China and Chengdu, that sounded pretty good to me.

Dali was also a traveller's town, a scaled-down version of Kathmandu, with cafes playing Bob Marley and banana pancakes and lassis on the menu. Huguo Lu—the main street and nominated backpacker ghetto—was lined with restaurants and shops selling colourful ethnic clothes. The tailors in Dali, calling upon thousands of years of Chinese tailoring tradition, knocked up pseudo-Chinese outfits for a couple of dollars or so. And everywhere—eating in the restaurants or being measured up by tailors—there were travellers.

And not the type that haunted Chengdu waiting to get into Tibet, either—these were the types of travellers keen to drink and smoke and shag themselves senseless.

The keenest of them all was Gil. Gil was a shaggy-haired Israeli who was travelling the world to avoid doing National Service. In an ill-advised move I agreed to share a room with him so we could both save money. It was ill-advised because Gil had been travelling for quite a while—most of the time in China—and he hadn't had a shag.

'Peter, Peter, you don't understand,' he whined every morning. 'After six months the sap is rising.'

The sap may have been rising, but his standards weren't. As long as a person was a) female and b) breathing, Gil would try and charm them into bed. Even the rather plain girl in 2B across the hall, who wore stockings with the tops rolled down, sent Gil into a sexual frenzy.

'I want to roll her stockings all the way down,' he would say last thing each night. 'With my tongue!' It was an image I could well have done without, especially moments before I went to sleep.

I spent five days in Dali, doing nothing much other than eating steaks and drinking beer. I met a couple of English guys, John and Bill, and fell into a daily routine that consisted of moving from cafe to cafe, getting drunk and laughing at the latest shirt John had convinced a tailor to make for him. When things got really slow, we would also amuse ourselves with Gil's attempts to pick up women.

One Swedish girl told him that he didn't 'know how to treat a woman'. Seeing this as a challenge, he spent the next couple of days negotiating with one of the local Dai women for a crappy metal hair brooch that she assured him would capture the Swedish girl's heart. He presented it to her with a flourish, saying, 'I *never* disappoint a woman'. She gave him a kiss on the cheek. This partial success only served to frustrate Gil even more. He spent the rest of the night trying to pick up two lesbian English teachers who had come to China with the Voluntary Services Overseas. They were pale, bulky, hairy creatures who had used the VSO's 'right on!', politically correct attitude to get posted to the same village, and they weren't having a bar of him.

One night, after feasting on a Tibetan steak and one or three too many Chinese beers, we saw a tall, striking Dutch girl walk past the cafe in a slinky Chinese silk dress. She had obviously had a tailor run it up for her and thought she looked pretty damn hot in it. She did, so we all made a point of not looking at her; except Gil, of course. I joked that she was probably back at the tailor's insisting that he lower the neckline and tighten the waist. 'Only one guy looked at me,' I imagined her whining. 'An Israeli guy. And he looks at everybody!' Gil had the last laugh, though. I had to stay out late drinking beer at Jack's Cafe while he was back in our room shagging her. I decided then that it was time to move on. The next day I bought a ticket on the overnight sleeper bus to Kunming.

A sleeper bus is a distinctly Chinese phenomenon, and like the binocular glasses the lawyer had on the train to Xining, it *sounds* like a great idea. But also, like the binocular glasses, the practical application leaves a lot to be desired. The one I caught to Kunming was simply a bus with bunks, and had all the ambience of a mobile hospital. The only thing missing was the IV drip. To make matters worse, the bunks were only four feet long, and mine—a top bunk—was only centimetres from the roof. When I lay flat on my back, my nose was pressed against the roof. Now I don't know about your sleeping patterns, but I've never been one for lying flat on my back for nine hours at a time. I like to thrash about, flipping from side to side, knocking anyone unlucky enough to be sharing a bed with me unconscious. So it wasn't long before I was feeling extremely claustrophobic.

Luckily, there was an air vent above my nose. I pushed it open to give my nose an extra couple of centimetres and happily suffered the water that dripped in on my face from the heavy rain outside. The air was cool, and coupled with the humidity inside the bus, it soon formed condensation of the roof. If I held my nose in the right position, I found I could draw patterns in the condensation. When the road began winding I could just lie there and watch shapes form like a crazy sketchograph. Just for fun, I tried to write my name, but we hit a bump and I got a bloody nose.

It was still raining when the bus arrived in Kunming. Kunming was a smaller version of Chengdu—with high-rise buildings and stores selling appliances—but development was not yet as rampant, so there were still pockets of ramshackle wooden buildings and muddy lanes where butchers carved up buffalo carcasses on the street. The constant misty rain also gave the place a more compact feel, enveloping the skyscrapers and effectively cutting them off at the cloud line. It softened the harsher features, made the greens greener and gave the city a fresher, cleaner feel. Even the tacky space-age building with the giant dimpled golf ball on top looked OK.

I didn't plan to stay long in Kunming—it was just a stopover on my route further south through Yunnan province to an area called Xishuangbanna. This prefecture bordered both Laos and Myanmar (Burma), and was home to China's most colourful ethnic minorities—the Miao, Zhuang, Yao, Aini, Jinuo, Bulang, Lahu and Wa. The capital, Jinghong, sat on the Mekong River, a river that formed the border separating Laos from Myanmar and Thailand before skirting Cambodia and flowing into Vietnam. I had heard about a boat that left from Jinghong and travelled along the middle of the Mekong, in a no-man's-land between Laos and Myanmar, to Sop Ruak in northern Thailand. My plan was to catch it.

Well, that was my plan; like a lot of my plans, it was ill-conceived and hasty. It consisted of venturing further south into China when I should have been heading east to Hong Kong to get a Vietnamese visa for the more feasible plan of crossing from China into Vietnam. This 'alternative' plan of mine relied heavily on the existence of a boat that none of the guidebooks mentioned and that I had only heard about second- and third-hand. In fact, a girl from Hong Kong, who I'd met in Chengdu, had said that it was a fantasy boat, and that I was wasting my time.

That afternoon in Kunming I sat in a noodle shop and wrote down the possible areas in which this plan could fall over. In no particular order, they were:

> It didn't even exist.
> It did exist, but it only left once a month and I'd just missed it.
> It didn't take foreigners.
> It cost too much.
> It used to operate but the operators went out of business the day before.

Regardless, I decided to push ahead with the plan. I liked it because it got me out of China quickly. To be honest, travelling here had been hard work. Most of the people were unhelpful, I hated being charged three times the price for everything, the countryside was being fucked up at an alarming rate, and I had come down with a nasty chest infection courtesy of the charming habit of spitting. I was also tired. I wanted to get out of the country so badly that I was prepared to take the gamble.

I should point out that I did have my doubts about the existence of this boat. That's why I visited the Laotian consulate while I was in Kunming to get a Laotian visa. The consulate was in a room in one of the buildings that made up the Camellia Hotel, and consisted of a flag, a photo of the Laotian president and a desk with a neatly dressed middle-aged woman—the consul—sitting behind it. She spoke passable English and expressed surprise about the boat.

'The only way you can get into Laos is to fly,' she said. 'Our country is not completely open to tourists. I can issue you a seven-day transit visa. But only if you promise to fly to Vientiane. And once you get there, you can only stay in Vientiane.'

'Are you on the plane leaving Kunming tomorrow?' she asked.

I lied and said I was. I handed over $38 and she issued the visa immediately. It was probably a waste of money, but I had a feeling in the pit of my stomach that if there was a boat, it would somehow help if I had a visa of some sort. Besides, the writing was in Laotian and French. Maybe I could convince the Chinese it was a special 'down the middle of the Mekong' visa.

With my Laotian visa secured, and my spirits buoyed, I caught another sleeper bus to Jinghong, a large Chinese town that over-looked the Mekong. This bus was newer and the beds were longer, and after my trip from Dali, I had at least had the good sense to request a bottom bunk. We headed south on a dual-carriage express-way, deep into one of the most undeveloped regions of China. The road was smooth and wide and much too grand for the few cars and trucks that putted along it. Once again I found myself won-dering just what these Chinese folk were up to.

After a much more comfortable night's sleep, I awoke and lay in bed watching the subtropical scenery of vines and thick primary forest go by. The other passengers on the bus soon stirred and began their morning routine of spitting and coughing. They were all part of a Chinese tour group led by a pretty Chinese girl lying in the bed opposite me. Whenever I looked across at her she was reclining in her bunk and waving a floppy pink frankfurter sausage at me. It had a disturbing pink skin tone, so I simply smiled back nervously, afraid of where any other kind of acknowledgment may lead.

At a rest stop—a muddy bus station surrounded by mildewy stalls selling rotting fruit and warm cans of Chinese soft drink—she came over and spoke to me. Her English was perfect, and she spoke it in that sexy Asian–American accent that futuristic films like *Bladerunner* are convinced we'll all have by 2015.

'Are you not hungry?' she asked. 'I was offering you food on the bus but you didn't take it.'

Her name was Mae Ling and she was leading a group of 27 Chinese businessmen from Shanghai to Bangkok. After a few days taking in the Dai culture of Xishuangbanna, they were heading off down the Mekong by boat, carefully sailing in the no-man's-land between Laos and Myanmar, into northern Thailand. After hitting the bars and casinos in Chiang Mai, they would fly back to Kunming and then to Shanghai.

Fate had again smiled upon me. The mysterious boat down the Mekong *did* exist, and now I was in the company of a girl who was not only an employee of the company that ran it, but could speak perfect English as well. I very nearly laughed out loud in disbelief. The boat existed! I wish I'd taken the address of the girl from Hong Kong who had ridiculed me so I could write a letter to her and say 'Ha, ha' just like Nelson on 'The Simpsons'. I nearly knocked over a table of pineapples in my excitement.

As we stood in the muddy station, waiting for the other passengers to finish drinking tea or buy bags of rotting fruit, I told Mae Ling my story. I told her how far I had come and about my search for the boat—her boat. It was the sole reason I was in Xishuangbanna—to track it down and catch it. And now, now I had found it! Just as I was saying how I couldn't believe my luck, a troubled look came across her sweet face.

'I'm afraid you need a special permit from Beijing to travel on our boat,' she said sadly. 'And they only give the permits when you buy the tour. I think you also have to be Chinese.'

To be honest, I had suspected as much. Fate seemed to take great delight in dangling unobtainable treats in front of me and then snatching them away (incredibly cheap airfares usually, the last available seat being taken just moments before I call). I asked Mae Ling if there was any way she could get me on board the boat—

bribe her boss, hide me in her cabin, dress me up as a Thai prostitute—but she shook her head.

'No,' she said, sounding even more sad than before. 'It is too risky. If you were caught I would lose my job. It would be hard for me to find another.'

She scribbled something on a piece of paper.

'Here,' she said thrusting the note into my hand. 'Take this to CITS. It explains what you want to do. Maybe they can help you.'

The bus honked its horn and we all got back on board and into our beds.

By mid afternoon we were winding our way down a green misty mountain and into Jinghong. Jinghong was a seedy, sleepy, decaying town that was more Southeast Asian than Chinese. The air was thick with humidity. The mighty Mekong, a broad, orange-brown band, snaked through the town. The only incongruity—a sure sign of the touch of a Chinese hand—was the water slide amusement park beside it.

I stayed in a down-at-heel cafe–hotel down on Manting Lu, an area lined by restaurants and bars that offered meals and traditional Dai dancing to visiting busloads of Chinese tourists. At night the restaurants crawled with drunken Chinese businessmen staggering from one tribal minority dance show to another. That afternoon, in the broad daylight, with its gaudy hand-painted signs and heavy use of bamboo, the area had the feel of the girlie bar districts of Manila and Bangkok.

The next morning I went to the CITS office with the note from Mae Ling. The girl behind the counter was friendly, but she didn't know anything about the boat and suggested I try down at the docks instead. The 'docks', it turned out, were the banks of the river itself, and I spent the morning wandering up and down the muddy banks, from one dilapidated boat to another, asking their owners if they knew of a boat going to Thailand. They all shook their heads and moved away from me as if I were mad or, at the very least, in the early stages of rabies. One enterprising boatman—the owner of the most decrepit boat, incidentally—offered to take me for $1,500. If I had thought his boat had any chance of making the 260-kilometre journey, I may have given his offer some serious thought.

With my last hopes of getting a boat to Thailand dashed, I was faced with a dilemma. Did I venture towards Laos with a transit, fly-in/fly-out visa and try to get across a border I shouldn't even be at, or did I turn around and make the long trek back through Kunming to Canton and Hong Kong to get a Vietnamese visa? The fact that the Vietnam option would add another two weeks of travel in China made it trickier than it should have been. In the end, fate made the decision for me—the next bus to Kunming from Jinghong didn't leave until the next day, and a bus to Mengla, the town closest to the Laotian border, was leaving the bus station in 10 minutes. I bought a ticket for the bus to Mengla and jumped aboard.

The bus was ancient and decrepit—by far the worst bus I'd caught so far in China. The poor roads in Xishuangbanna had destroyed its suspension and rust had eaten away a fair amount of the body panels. A Chinese tourist who had travelled down from Beijing sat in the seat in front of me, hanging a white T-shirt he had just hand-washed, still dripping, from the luggage rack above my head. He spent the entire journey checking off each village on a map that lay on his lap. Whenever the bus passed something that I presumed the map notes as a point of interest—more often than not just an unusually shaped tree—he would turn around, point it out to me on the map and smile inanely. It didn't seem to worry him that I couldn't read Chinese and he couldn't speak English. As far as he was concerned, we were two tourists enjoying the whole ethnic minority experience.

I have to admit, it was probably one of the more interesting bus rides I had made in China. We were deep in the corners of southern China now, an area which had more in common with its Southeast

Asian neighbours than with its rulers in Beijing. The wooden huts that served as houses were raised off the ground, over corrals for pigs and buffaloes. Pretty girls washed themselves in waterfalls beside the road in bright, colourful sarongs. Buffaloes suckled their calves in the middle of the road. And all the while, we crawled along in the shadows of huge limestone cliffs covered in vines. As dusk fell, we passed a man herding a flock of ducks with a single bamboo rod. This bus journey was also one of my most eventful in China. One of the passengers spent the entire trip yelling at the driver. And when we hit a cow, a representative from every colourful ethnic minority within 50 kilometres, it seemed, popped up to survey the damage—much to the delight of the man from Beijing.

It was well after dark when we finally arrived in Mengla. Disappointingly, it looked like nearly every other Chinese town I had seen. The only distinguishing feature was a billboard poster of Bart Simpson lying on grass beside a river eating pineapples and melons. The bus driver thoughtfully dropped the Chinese tourist and me outside the only hotel in town. It was a tasteless chrome and glass monstrosity with fountains in the foyer that had long ceased to function.

I was not meant to be in Mengla. It was a sensitive border area that the Chinese preferred to keep foreigners away from. By rights I should have been rounded up by the local Public Security Bureau and run out of town. But it was late and the authorities had knocked off for the day. Even at the hotel, it was a bored night manager who checked me in, and he was too lazy to fill out the necessary forms. He wasn't even motivated enough to charge me three times the price, and instead put me in a room with the Chinese tourist and two other Chinese businessmen for only a handful of yuan.

The Chinese businessmen had just done their washing and hung it all around the room, and were about to head downstairs to the bar for a spot of karaoke. The Chinese tourist, keen to experience the whole Xishuangbanna experience, threw down his bag and accepted up their offer for us to join them. I declined. I wasn't in the mood to sing 'My Way'—the only song in English on offer in karaoke in these countries—with a gang of sozzled, middle-aged Chinese men who only spoke Mandarin. And besides, I had a spot of counterfeiting to do.

In a moment of madness—probably just after the Chinese tourist had pointed out the 'King of Tea Trees' to me on the trip to Mengla—I had decided to make a few pencil alterations to my Laotian visa. In the section that indicated what type of visa I had, the consul had written VTR, which I had taken to be the international flight code for Vientiane, and hence the only place I could enter. My cunning plan was to change it to VTR/R and argue with the border officials that the slash and the R meant I could cross into Laos by road. I spent half an hour practising the R in my notebook, until I was happy that it matched the R of the consul. As soon as I wrote it on the visa, I got paranoid—I ripped the page I had practised on out of my notebook and ate it. I slept uneasily that night, trying to convince myself that the worst they could do was send me back. Unfortunately, that was also my worse nightmare.

CHAPTER NINETEEN

Laos

Soundtrack: *Heaven Knows*—**Rick Price**

I had no trouble finding a van to the border early the next morning.
It was a Friday—market day in the village closest to the border
post—and there were at least ten vans heading that way. I sat in
the back of the worst of them, sharing a tattered bench seat with
colourful locals, hidden by their livestock and sacks of produce.
They all got off at a small village where other locals stood in the
mud bidding on a herd of buffalo in a roadside auction. The van
continued on for a couple of kilmetres to the border—a boom gate
in a muddy clearing in thick jungle.

As I approached the incomplete building that served as the
Chinese immigration and customs post, I was more anxious than I
had been at any time on the trip. At other contentious points—like
getting a visa for Iran or crossing from Nepal into Tibet—I had a
feeling, deep down inside, that I would succeed. But here on the
Chinese–Laotion border it was different. For one thing, it was a

restricted area and I was actually breaking Chinese law just being there. Secondly, I did not have a proper visa for the country I was trying to get into. And then there were the consequences. If I failed, it wasn't as if they'd just say no and send me on my way. They'd probably fine me and kick me out of the country as well. How would I get back into China and cross into Vietnam if my passport was stamped 'Never to Return'?

When the driver coughed and put out his hand for money, I realised I was procrastinating. It was something I have been doing since I was 15. Back then I'd dither over whether to ask Sandy Enright out. Sandy had blonde bobbed hair and dark brown eyes and was the prettiest girl I'd ever seen. I'd spend entire evenings imagining scenarios where I could ask her out. They all ended with her saying no, most often with her laughing. I worked myself into such a state that I never had the courage to ask.

At least in China I had the option of bribing my way across the border—something I'd never considered doing to get Sandy to go out with me. But bribing was something I was not altogether comfortable with. In fact, despite having travelled across Africa and South America, I had never bribed an official, and didn't really know how to go about it. Did I put the money in my passport and slide it across? Or should I just hand it over without saying anything. In the end, I put a 100 yuan note in my pocket and decided to play it by ear.

I entered the Chinese immigration and customs office and was greeted at the Arrival Check Desk by a sweet young Chinese girl with a natty blue uniform and a huge, toothy smile. She spoke perfect English and greeted me warmly and effusively. She listened intently and politely as I explained what I wanted to do. Then she nodded and gave me that concerned look that doctors give you when they are about to tell you that you have a life-threatening disease (or present you with their bill).

'I'm so sorry, but I cannot let you pass,' she said, with genuine concern. 'I am not authorised to allow a person from a third-class country to cross here.'

I expressed my surprise that Australia was regarded as a third-class country. I said I knew our economy was in a bad way, but I hadn't realised that the IMF had woken up to the fact yet. She explained that it was a matter of geography. Because we were in China, China was a first-class country. The country bordering China—in this case, Laos—was a second-class country. Every other country, regardless of its standing in OECD or in the FIFA soccer rankings, was regarded as a third-class nation. And at this border, Chinese law stated that only citizens of first- and second-class countries could cross. Taking a gamble that this particular border—deep in the south of China—didn't have open and trouble-free communication with head office in Beijing, I told her that the law had changed.

'The Laotions wouldn't have given me this otherwise,' I said, pointing to my freshly altered Laotion visa.

She faltered for a moment, taking my passport and looking closely at it. Just as I thought she was about to weaken, she shook her head.

'No. I'm sorry. I'm afraid you will have to go back to Kunming and fly.'

When she mentioned the word 'fly', I flinched and shuddered quite noticeably. If reason wasn't going to get across, perhaps a chronic case of overacting would. It worked, because she asked me if I was OK. I was thinking on my feet now, not sure what I was doing or how far I could take it. I put on the most pained expression I possibly could.

'My father was killed in a plane crash,' I said solemnly, pretending to be holding back the tears. 'In . . . Australia. When . . . I was . . . ten.'

She was horrified. When I was sure I had her complete attention, I continued.

'I haven't been able to fly since,' I said in a voice that sounded as if it had been deadened by decades of sadness. 'If you look in my passport you will see that I have come all this way from London without flying in a plane.'

I finished that sentence with a sob. I just wish the whole thing had been videotaped, because I'm telling you, I would have been a shoo-in for an Oscar at the Academy Awards that year. She put her hand on my shoulder and comforted me. Then she called her boss over and spoke to him in a hurried whisper, both of them casting furtive glances in my direction as I pretended to be wiping back the tears. She told me to sit down and rest and they disappeared into another room.

I sat in the vinyl lounge chair for what seemed an eternity, watching young children playing outside by squirting each other with muddy water from syringes. My hopes and moods changed as regularly as the cast on 'Neighbours'. I consoled myself by thinking that it was a good thing they were taking so long. It meant that my plea was getting full and thorough consideration. Just as I let this thought lighten my mood, I thought of a worse, but more probable, reason for the delay. They were trying to ring Beijing to find out about the new law! They would find out I had lied, and their bosses would remind them that I wasn't meant to be there in the first place, something that had obviously been forgotten in the excitement of the tale about my father's death.

Nearly three hours later, the girl returned to the room, smiling sweetly. My passport had been stamped and she had filled out all the paperwork for me. All I had to do was sign the forms. I thanked her by saying 'Máfan nǐle', a Chinese phrase that means 'sorry for being so much trouble'. She smiled sweetly again.

'You've been no trouble at all.'

My acting must have been better than I'd thought. I suppressed my natural urge to punch the air and holler, and instead decided to honour the memory of my 'dead' father by walking calmly past the boom gate and to a small auto-rickshaw waiting on the other side. After negotiating a price with the driver—a little more than I would normally have paid but, hey, I was in a generous mood—I set off down a skinny dirt road through the jungle towards Laos.

Considering that I only had a transit visa—and a criminally falsified one at that—crossing into Laos at the border post of Boten was surprisingly easy. The young immigration official on duty that day had been taught English by an Australian man down in Vientiane, and greeted me like a long-lost friend. He stamped me into Laos without even appearing to look at my visa. He was too busy practising his English idioms.

'My name is Mr Bounmi,' he beamed, shaking my hand vigorously. 'My English has gone to the dogs, but if there is anything I can do to help you, please feel free to ask.'

I asked Mr Bounmi if he could kindly tell me how I could get to northern Thailand. I had planned catch a boat straight through to Thailand and didn't have a scrap of information on Laos.

He beamed a smile that said he had been waiting all his life to perform such a task, and quickly searched his desk for a piece of paper and a pen. As villagers waiting to cross into China shuffled uncomfortably from foot to foot, he drew a crude map of the route from the border to Pakbeng, a town on the Mekong where I could catch a boat to Thailand. It listed the major towns and the distance between them in kilometres. He even wrote a special message in the corner in Laotian telling whoever read it that I was his friend and should be given every assistance in getting to Thailand.

'If you follow this map,' he said proudly, 'You will be in northern Thailand in two days!'

Much to the dismay of those waiting to cross, Mr Bounmi then locked the door and indicated for me to follow him to the market stalls just down the dirt track.

'Listen to me rabbiting on,' he continued. 'You must be hungry enough to eat a horse.'

After shouting me a plate of noodles and limp vegetables, he helped me change money by introducing me to the stallholder who offered the best exchange rates. He arranged a lift with a ute to Muang Xai, the first big town, once again making sure that I was charged the local rate, and bought me warm Coke to drink while I waited for the van to leave. He waved as we drove off, inexplicably singing the chorus of the Rick Price song 'Not a Day Goes By'. I wondered if the locals who had been trying to cross into China were waiting back at the immigration post with a noose and a burning desire to string him up.

I sat on a wooden bench in the back of the ute with a dozen or so Laotians who looked at me with a mixture of fascination and fear. One small child, sitting on his mother's lap, screamed and turned, sobbing into his mother's breast whenever he looked at me. Others admired my backpack, tugging on the straps and kicking it as if it were a car. They had obviously not seen anything like it— or me—before. I suddenly felt that my journey was an adventure again.

Mr Bounmi's map indicated that there was a customs post 18 kilometres down the road where I would have to stop. After half an hour or so down a bumpy road and past thatched huts, we reached it. It was a low, white, concrete building at the bottom of a hill, and next to it, in a huge clearing, were hundreds of new Japanese and Korean cars. They were parked in neat rows, were all the same charcoal grey, and still had plastic protecting the seats and the interiors.

Inside the building, a clutch of customs officials in grey uniforms were measuring towels that a Chinese woman was bringing into the country by the sackful. The guy with the ruler barked out the measurements to a guy with a calculator who figured out how much duty should be charged. It must have been steep because the Chinese woman was wailing and tearing at their uniforms, imploring them not to charge her so much. They spotted me but, with a couple of bags of towels yet to be measured, they just waved me away. The driver of the ute grabbed my arm and dragged me away before they changed their minds.

The road to Muang Xai went through high rolling hills covered in poppy plants. The plants were harvested by Hmong tribespeople, and for the next 100 kilometres, we travelled through their lands. When the van passed through villages and people caught sight of me, they screamed. It struck me that tourists trekked for weeks in northern Thailand to see what I was seeing from the back of the van and that the hill tribes they saw were nowhere near as untouched as this. For the first time in a long while, certainly since entering China, I was experiencing a real thrill from travelling.

The only other vehicles we passed on the road were trucks taking scrap metal to China. The scrap metal they carried was 'war surplus', old bomb casings from the two million tonnes of bombs that were dropped on Laos during the Vietnam War. Some of these bombs had been dropped in anger—the US accused Laos of harbouring the VC—but a lot were just excess bombs dumped on returning from sorties over Vietnam. In the sixties and early seventies, more bombs were dropped on Laos than were dropped on Europe during the whole of World War II. That's the equivalent of a plane-load of bombs every eight minutes every day for nine years. Those bombs cost the US taxpayers more than $2 million a day. I found it a brilliant irony that the Laotians were now making a quick buck flogging the bombshells to the country the US had been trying to keep in check.

Muang Xai was an ugly scar on the stunning countryside that surrounded it. It sat on the junction of one road running south from China towards Pak Mong and another that ran west from the Vietnamese border to Pakbeng and the Mekong River. The plain, brown buildings and functional utilitarian feel of the place reflected its status as a crossroads town. Its only redeeming feature was the market, a lively, colourful affair selling the usual assortment of

Chinese crap, including towels, as well as fresh produce like limes, papaya and honeycomb. It was too late to continue to Pakbeng, so I stayed the night.

My hotel room was bare and dusty, but the bed was comfortable and the overhead fan worked. That night a wild thunderstorm hit the town so hard that the electric lights flickered and the windows shook. The thunder grumbled and then cracked, continuing to reverberate for minutes around the surrounding hills. Then came the rain, so fat, heavy and intense it was as if the clouds—like the US bombers decades before—wanted to dump their load as quickly as possible and move on. I went to sleep that night excited that I had finally made it out of China, and revelling in the conceit that I was in a truly turbulent place.

It was still raining heavily the next morning. In a gesture of kindness, the driver of the van I caught to Pakbeng let me ride in the cabin with him. I remember thinking that it would never have happened in China—unless, of course, huge amounts of money had changed hands. I shared the cabin with two little old hill tribe women resplendent in their intricate black and blue dresses. They spent the first half-hour of the journey staring at me, trying to figure out what tribe I belonged to.

The road out of Muang Xai passed through cultivated fields and villages of raised bamboo huts. Most of the huts seemed to have bomb casings as foundations, protecting the wood from termites and stopping it from rotting. As we passed, some of the more observant villagers spotted me riding in the cabin. Some stared wide-eyed and pointed, unable to speak from shock. Some had the presence of mind to smile and wave. But more often than not, those who spotted me simply screamed.

At last the rain stopped, and I could see clearly out the windscreen again. Before me now was a *National Geographic* vista of northern Laotian life—small boys sitting beside the road with rifles, toying with the corpses of rat-like creatures they had just shot; a family riding in a cart being pulled by an albino buffalo; and men returning from the poppy fields for lunch with their ploughs, shaped like harps, slung over their shoulders. At one point, the van had to swerve to avoid hitting an elephant that charged out of the jungle with a group of laughing boys on its back.

Soon the villages became less frequent, and the road wound its way up into the mountains. The road here was narrow and wet, and constantly fought a losing battle with lush jungle that threatened to swallow it whole. Huge multi-coloured butterflies floated across the road in the sun, and I saw more birds that morning than I had in my entire time in China. The stench of the jungle was strong here— putrid and pungent, filling my nostrils with the smell of a last great wilderness.

Just before lunch, we reached Pakbeng. Pakbeng was a collection of wooden houses and shops lining a road on a hill overlooking the Mekong River. At the end of the road was a bend in the river that acted as a port for the assortment of wooden houseboats, longboats and speedboats that plied the river north to Chiang Kong in Thailand or south to Luang Prabang and Vientiane. It was a pleasant enough town, in a down-at-heel, steamy kind of way, but no one on my ute was staying. Within minutes of arriving they were being led by touts to a string of longboats waiting to take them up the river to Thailand. Two guys in the back, eager to get the best spot, had put on life jackets as the van drove into town.

Mr Bounmi had been as good as his word. If I had wandered down to the dock and jumped into one of the longboats heading north, it would indeed have taken me only two days to get to Thailand. I would be on the well-worn banana pancake trail, travelling easily south through Thailand and towards Malaysia, Singapore, Indonesia and home. But another idea was forming in my mind and niggling at me. I still had five days left on my visa. Things had gone smoothly to this point—what if I travelled south along to the Mekong to the old imperial city of Luang Prabang and then on to the capital, Vientiane? That way I could cross into Thailand over the new Friendship Bridge, paid for and built by the good old Australian taxpayer.

It meant staying the night in Pakbeng. There were no boats heading south until the next day. I stayed at the Soukchareun Sarika, a wooden hotel on a steep cliff overlooking the river and the port. The hotel itself was nothing to write home about, but its toilets were extraordinary. They were at the back of the hotel, overhanging the cliff, and had fantastic views over the Mekong as it swept south towards Luang Prabang. I've read in a guidebook since that it's 'probably the best view from a bathroom in the whole of Laos'. I'd go as far as saying that you'd be hard pressed to find a better view from a bathroom anywhere.

The next morning there was a knock on my door and a small boy indicated that I should come down to the dock where a speed-boat was leaving for Luang Prabang. It was long and slender, with a chunky engine that took up most of the boat, leaving room for only four passengers. We weren't allowed to board until we had donned a life jacket and crash helmet, and soon I knew why. After letting the boat drift out to the middle of the river, the engine bur-bling like a senior citizen eating custard, our driver gunned the boat with such ferocity that my head snapped back and hit the guy sitting behind me.

It felt as if we'd been sucked into a Nintendo 64 game called Mutant Mekong River Racers, and our driver was determined to get the highest score. He banked the boat heavily into river bends, spraying water into the overhanging jungle, dodged skilfully through treacherous whirlpools and rips and skirted submerged logs with protruding branches that looked unnervingly like the arms of a drowning man. At one point he skidded over a mid river sandbank and we became airborne. I don't think it helped us go any faster. I just think he liked hearing the engine go 'rrrrreeeeeeee!'

We continued on our way, roaring past slow wooden houseboats and ignoring women standing on the bank waving catfish at us, and reached the clearing that served as Luang Prabang's speedboat dock in the record time of 2 hrs: 13 min: 28 sec. The driver approached the steps as recklessly as he had approached the rest of the journey, powering through an arc that sprayed water over the lichen-covered steps leading down to the river.

A small van waited by a small wooden pagoda covered in vines and, for a small amount, the driver agreed to take me and the other three passengers to Luang Prabang. The centre of town was still a good eight kilometres away down a dirt road that passed under the canopy of ancient trees and alongside wats (temples) displaying an eclectic mix of Thai, Burmese and Khmer influences. When we finally reached Luang Prabang, I realised why the speedboat had dropped us so far from the town centre—Luang Prabang is such a sleepy town, they wouldn't have been able to handle the noise.

Now I want you to imagine the opening scene of a Hollywood blockbuster—a re-make of *The King and I*, perhaps, with Martin Scorsese directing, just as he did in *Kundun*, and with a similar budget. We open on a quiet, exotic city on a misty river. Overlooking the town, and crowned by a golden pagoda, is a hill covered in lush green vines and trees as old as time. From the hill, the town stretches lazily over a block or two, and is dotted with French colonial buildings with shutters and tiled roofs covered in moss. On the neat but dusty streets, colourfully dressed locals stroll lazily past vendors selling delicious fruits. From a vantage point high above the town, the camera spies a line of orange-robed monks leaving their monastery with their alms bowls, and it follows them as they go from one delicately carved wooden house to another, begging for food. And, while we can't smell—this is the movies, after all—we know the air is thick and sultry with the smell of rotting leaves and deep, rich soil. That, my friends, is Luang Prabang.

Luang Prabang was the royal capital of Lane Xang, the land of a million elephants, and with its natural beauty and embarrassment of magnificent temples is a designated UNESCO World Heritage Site. I was enchanted with the place the moment I saw my first wat—its high, pointed, layered roof sweeping elegantly towards the ground—and got my first smile from two pretty girls with long black hair and long, tapered, silk skirts. It had that potent mix of timeless elegance and spirituality that travel brochures like you to believe exists in all of Southeast Asia.

I stayed in a guesthouse in an old colonial building that looked as if it hadn't been painted since the French had been kicked out. The paint was peeling, the rooms were damp and musty and the shutters on the windows were broken and crooked. But the owner was always ready with a cup of hot tea and the verandah on the second floor proved the ideal place to watch the slow, sleepy world of Luang Prabang pass you by. At night I wandered into town and ate strange hotpot meals that made my mouth go numb while giggling girls attempted to play Rick Price songs on a wooden xylophone. (For a lightweight Australian purveyor of soppy love ballads, Rick was getting a lot of attention in Laos.)

Nothing happened while I was in Luang Prabang. And for all I knew, nothing happened anywhere else in the world either. I was in a corner of the planet that the rest of the world had simply passed by. I guess that's what I liked so much about the place. I was able to spend my days in Luang Prabang aimlessly, more often than not climbing up Mount Phousi to Wat Chom Phousi and just watching the city below. Then I'd wander down and buy a delicious French roll with a mysterious spicy filling from a smiling girl under an umbrella before going back to my room for an afternoon nap.

Any doubts I may have had about Luang Prabang being a town where time had stood still were dispelled when I spotted an old Holden Belmont panel van. Now the Belmont was an Australian motoring classic, and hadn't been built since the late sixties.

'Very good car!' said the owner, slapping the bonnet. 'Very strong. No trouble 30 years. Please send more.'

I would have stayed longer in Luang Prabang. Hell, if I could have, I probably would have spent the rest of my life there. But after three days I realised that my visa was about to expire and I made half-hearted enquiries down at the dock about boats heading south to Vientiane. I was genuinely disappointed when the master of the port told me there was a wooden cargo boat loaded with small Japanese sedans leaving the next morning at 8.30. I was devastated when the captain told me he'd take me on board as a passenger. The only piece of good news was that it was a slow boat and would take two days to get to Vientiane.

If Luang Prabang had looked beautiful the first time I saw it, it was stunning the morning I left. Mount Phousi was shrouded in mist and a light rain fell, giving the city a clean, fresh feel.

The boat was in effect a wooden barge, and it was returning its cargo of Japanese cars to Vientiane after the Chinese had refused to take them at the Chinese border. They sat in a neat row at the front, covered by a huge canvas tarpaulin, and taking up most of the space on the vessel. At the back of the boat was the raised bridge, where the captain stood behind an old wooden wheel and negotiated the tricky eddies and currents of the Mekong. Behind the bridge (in fact, still part of it) was a small wooden shack—a kitchen, and a toilet hanging off the back over the river. This boat would be my home for the next two days. It was also home for the captain's wife, his three-year-old son and his ageing father.

The day was slow and peaceful. The captain's wife spent the day cooking and playing with her young son. The captain's father, like all retirees who have passed on businesses to their sons, spent his time chastising his son and, I imagined, saying things like, 'If I was still in charge, we'd be in Vientiane now, you great pillock!' I spent the day on a mat listening to my Walkman, eating the snacks the captain's wife laid before me, drinking Chinese tea and watching Laos pass me by. By the time we reached Pak Lai, just as the sun was setting over the thickly wooded mountains, I'd almost forgotten all about Luang Prabang and the fact that I only had one day left on my visa.

The river was too treacherous to negotiate in the dark, so the boat anchored overnight at Pak Lai. Pak Lai was another sleepy town of raised wooden huts and dusty stores that seemed to sell only canned meat and plastic cups. Its distinguishing feature was an abandoned fairground with a rusting ferris wheel covered in vines. I ate a meal of soggy noodles in a cafe that played country and western music louder than it ever should be played, and watched monks in orange robes walk by, their steps in time with the plonk, plonk, plonk of the bass line. I retired to the boat, spending the night swatting off mosquitoes that I was certain were laden with malaria and/or dengue fever.

We left Pak Lai at dawn and made our way slowly down the Mekong to the stretch of the river that formed the border with Thailand. It was here that the fundamental differences between the two countries were most apparent. On one side was Laos, one of the most undeveloped countries in the world, covered in the thick, untouched rainforest. On the other, Thailand, a country developing at breakneck pace, totally cleared of jungle and dotted with cultivated fields surrounded by trees planted in neat rows. Twenty years ago, on this same stretch of river, you would not have been able to tell the two countries apart. Now, with its asphalt roads, international issue reflective yellow road signs, and bungalows with corrugated tin roofs, Thailand looked just like Queensland.

Soon we reached the most treacherous part of the Mekong, a stretch of river booby-trapped with shoals and sandbanks and hidden rocks and known for its fluctuating currents and vicious eddies. In Laotian legend, this part of the river is inhabited by a giant river serpent that feeds on unwary river craft, sucking the blood of their passengers as well as pulling out their hair and extracting their teeth. The captain's wife made a shrine of flowers and fruit, lit an incense stick and started praying.

The captain, meanwhile, turned the wheel wildly, trying to keep control and steer the boat through. His father shouted and pointed at rocks and submerged logs, admonishing his son for the foolhardy path he had chosen. After an hour, the most treacherous section had been passed and the captain's wife threw a garland of flowers into the river. The end of the rapids was marked by a smile from the captain's father and a temple in a cave on the side of the river where a Buddha statue looked out serenely across the Mekong. A line of monks had just finished visiting, and they were filing down the stairs into a boat.

With the rapids successfully negotiated, the boat was carried quickly but calmly down the river towards Vientiane. The river was calmer here, and the deep blue sky above was streaked with wispy white clouds. It was the last day on my visa, and I was hoping to reach Vientiane in time to cross into Thailand. But soon the clouds took on a pinkish hue and I realised we would be lucky to reach Vientiane by dark, and that I may have to spend another night on board. As it was, we arrived at Vientiane's northern jetty just as the last of the light was fading.

Saying farewell to the family proved to be more emotional than I imagined it would be. The captain shook my hand vigorously, and his father did too—he was a little gruffer, to be sure, but his handshake was firm all the same. The captain's wife gave me a hug, and when I presented her with a 'cling-on koala', she imme-diately gave it pride of place in her little shrine. I caught a van into the centre of Vientiane with a tear in my eye. It was too late to cross into Thailand, so I found a room just down from the Nam Phou Fountain on Manthatourath Road. As I slept in a bed with a mosquito net, my Laotian visa officially expired.

The next morning I wandered the quiet, empty streets of Vientiane and decided it was the most laid-back capital city in the world. It was a beguiling mix of French colonial charm and Southeast Asian ambience, a place where you could count to ten between passing cars. The town centre was full of enchanting cafes where croissants and jam and the best coffee in Asia were served by smiling waiters. And when I visited the department of immigration, expecting to be chastised, told to leave the country immediately or thrown into jail for overstaying my visa, I was given a cup of tea instead.

'Don't worry,' said the guy in charge. 'You can stay as long as you like. They'll just charge you $5 for each extra day you stay.'

After checking out Vientiane's version of the Arc de Triomphe— smaller, much less traffic—I decided to visit the Revolutionary Museum. It was housed in an old French building that used to house the highest-ranking French official in Laos. Now it was full of photos and artefacts depicting the fall of the colonialists and their brutal ways.

I liked the idea of a Revolutionary Museum. Would it be more 'out there' than other museums? Did it display its photos and artefacts in new and innovative ways? Or did it venture down even more radical paths by not displaying anything at all? As usual, my imagination was way ahead of itself. The only thing revolutionary about the Revolutionary Museum in Vientiane was that it was so ordinary and still had the hide to charge $5 to get in.

As it was, I didn't get beyond the entrance. When the girl taking money discovered I was Australian, she insisted on introducing me to an Australian woman working for the museum as part of an Australian aid project. The woman's name was Nancy, and she was from Sydney. Her brief had been to teach the Laotians preservation techniques, but on arriving she found out that no one even knew exactly what the museum had. Now she worked out of a low white building at the back of the museum—just past five giant stone jars from the Plain of Jars archaeological site that were scattered around the lawn—cataloguing the collection.

'The French were given the project first,' she explained. 'But they were freaked out by all the propaganda saying what bastards they are. They love us Aussies, though, especially Rick Price.'

Bloody Rick Price. It seemed I couldn't go anywhere in Laos without hearing about one of Australia's blandest troubadours. I told Nancy how Mr Bounmi had serenaded me at the border with 'Not a Day Goes By', and about the Rick Price xylophone instrumentals in the restaurants of Luang Prabang, and asked her what the fuck was it about the Laotians and Rick Price?

'I'm not sure, but he may have played here when the Friendship Bridge opened,' she said. 'You haven't got a copy of *Heaven Knows*, have you? The director of the museum has been hassling me for it for months. Wants to give it to his daughter for her birthday.'

Nancy took me back to the museum and showed me her favourite exhibits. They included soil samples from all the different provinces, an elephant carved from a single log and a display of Lego blocks entitled 'Modern Lao educational techniques'. When she found I'd actually paid, she got the girl at the ticket office to give me back my $5. A bunch of Laotian guys stood around near the entrance trying to flick each other on the backside with their upturned hands. They were Nancy's protégés.

'The hardest part of the job is trying to get these guys to be serious,' she said, laughing. 'On my first day they left a human tongue in my drawer.'

That was nothing compared to what they did to the little old museum guard. He was old enough to be an exhibit himself, and he bore the brunt of most of their pranks.

'Most of the time they just handcuff him to poles and steal his whistle,' she said. 'But they know he always sneaks a nap around three o'clock, so they sometimes set the alarm off then.'

Apparently the guys thought it was a great laugh seeing a decrepit old man running up the stairs of the museum, huffing and puffing, pulling on his pants. I left the museum pleased that I had at last found a museum with a sense of humour. It *was* a revolutionary museum after all.

I spend two more days in Vientiane doing, well, nothing. I had planned to visit the morning markets down at Thanon Lane Xang, but by the time I finished my coffee and croissants in a cafe on Chao Anou Road, the morning was over. I did spend one afternoon wandering around Wat Sisaket, the oldest wat in Vientiane, but my plan to visit Wat Pha Kaew just across the road was postponed indefinitely when I was waylaid by a bunch of monks and invited to join them for a cup of tea. I began to understand a joke a waiter had told me in a cafe: the PDR in the country's official name—Laos PDR—didn't stand for 'People's Democratic Republic', it stood for 'Please Don't Rush'.

Australia has close ties with Laos—we built the port at Luang Prabang and Nancy was in Vientiane as part of a foreign aid project—and by the end of my stay I started to understand why. While the Thais—and to a lesser extent, the Vietnamese—are gung-ho capitalists in the US tradition, the Laos are more laid back, like us. Their most important source of foreign exchange doesn't come from hard work and entrepreneurial spirit, it comes from receipts they get from planes flying overhead between Bangkok, Tokyo and Hong Kong. With 80 international flights each day, at $300 a pop, they rake in a cool $8.5 million a year for just being there. And let's face it, you can't get more laid back than calling your currency the kip.

I guess that's why I didn't begrudge them the so-called Friendship Bridge that Australia built for them. The 1.2 kilometre bridge spanning the Mekong was opened in April 1994 and was financed with over $30 million from Australia. That the bridge was a big

deal can be seen in the fact that you can still buy the special com-
memorative edition of the *Vientiane Times* celebrating the event on
the streets of Vientiane—and by the fact that when I finally left
Laos (three days after my visa had expired), the immigration guy
at the Friendship Bridge stamped me out of the country without
question.

When I walked over the bridge my tax dollars had helped build,
I was sad to leave. After the hospitality I had enjoyed, I decided
that a bridge was the least we could give them. If they'd just get
over their Rick Price fixation, I'd even go as far as saying that Laos
was my favourite country in the world.

CHAPTER TWENTY

Ko Phangan

Soundtrack: *No Limit*—2 Unlimited

Nong Khai, the Thai town on the opposite side of the river, was larger and busier than Vientiane, but had none of the Laotian capital's peaceful charm. Instead of orange-robed monks and revolutionary museums, it had traffic and pollution and air conditioned stores selling furry steering wheel covers. I bought a ticket on the overnight train to Bangkok, and spent the rest of the afternoon holed up in a restaurant beside the railway tracks, drinking Pepsi and watching the Thai version of 'MTV'.

The train to Bangkok left on time and was modern and clean. I had splashed out and treated myself to a sleeper berth. It was only second class, but the sheets were crisp and each bunk had a little curtain that you could pull across for privacy. I slept until 4.30 the next morning when the cleaning lady came along as we passed Bangkok Airport and hustled me out of bed. It was still dark outside, but floodlit construction sites were already abuzz with activity. Skyscrapers were being thrown up at a rapid rate and khlongs (canals) were being filled to make way for freeways. I spent the rest of the trip to Bangkok's Hualamphong Station pondering how quickly things were changing.

I caught a tuk-tuk to Khao San Road, the traveller's ghetto in Banglamphu. Tuk-tuks are three-wheeled bug-shaped taxis that dart around Bangkok like evil little ladybirds, poisoning the city with their gases. I don't generally use tuk-tuks when I'm in Bangkok; I much prefer to use the ferries that ply the canals or the buses that service everywhere else. But at 5 am, those options weren't available. Regardless, I was alarmed to notice that, even before dawn, the traffic had almost become gridlocked.

It was too early to go looking for a room, so I got the tuk-tuk to drop me off outside the Hello Restaurant. A Spanish guy and his Thai girl stumbled up to me, supporting each other, and asked me if I knew a guesthouse nearby where they could go and fuck. Further along Khao San Road, down the police station end, two drunken Westerners fell out of a tuk-tuk and collapsed onto the footpath. In the doorway of the Hello Restaurant a group of Thai girls offered me some pink pills for 120 baht. Apart from that, Khao San Road was as quiet as a churchmouse.

As the only 24-hour restaurant on the Khao San Road strip, the Hello Restaurant was jumping. Each of the dark wood-panelled booths—their tasteful white laminex tables grubby with cigarette ash and spilt food—was full of travellers in various stages of drunkenness and stonedness. Most sat bleary-eyed, their heads in their hands, waiting for a coffee or some breakfast to revive them. One couple waiting for a bus to the airport (judging by the packs around them) sat groping each other, stopping periodically to flick through the holiday snaps they had just had developed.

I found a room in a guesthouse in one of the lanes that ran off Khao San Road. I threw my bag on the bed, and after a quick shower to wash the off the sweat that was already forming on my brow, I went for a walk down past Wat Phra Kaew and the Grand Palace, on to Chinatown and then up Silom Road. It was three years since I had been to Bangkok and the changes were quite staggering. The economic boom was at its peak and there were no signs of the impending crash. The city was a huge construction site—office towers were popping up like oversized mushrooms, and concrete flyovers for freeways were snaking their way through the city like spaghetti. Alarmingly, Thai architects seemed to be in a competition as to who could design the high-rise building that looked most like a penis.

The pollution had got worse, too. A thick brown smog hung over the city, and walking the streets was enough to give you a headache. In an attempt to counter the lethal quantities of carbon monoxide they were breathing, the traffic cops wore white plastic breathing masks which—together with their matching white plastic helmets—made them look like the stormtroopers out of *Star Wars*.

A new consumerism was also evident. Billboards advertised clean three-bedroom terraces in estates on reclaimed rice paddies on the far-flung edges of the cities, and the parking lot of Chulalongkorn University looked like a luxury car yard. Up on Silom Road and in Siam Square, sparkling new department stores enticed Thai consumers with goods from all over the world. The Zen World Trade Centre on Ratchadamri Road captured the new mood of Thailand in a promotion that featured a Thai goddess with many arms, each holding a different shopping bag.

But Khao San Road had hardly changed. It had always been a shopping mall for backpackers. There were banks to change your money, travel agents to arrange your onward journeys, photo labs to develop your holiday snaps or to sell you film, and restaurants to feed and water you. And, of course, between the shops and spilling out onto the road itself were hundreds of tiny stalls—most no more than rickety wooden trestles—selling ethnic clothing, Thai trinkets, music tapes, pirate electronics and fake Rolex watches.

It always amazes me, wandering around these stalls, just what rabid consumerists backpackers really are. You'll see long-haired guys who refuse to pay an extra $2 to travel second class on a train happily spending ten times that on a silly hat or a ridiculous shirt. And tanned girls who'd rather get bitten by bedbugs than pay a bit extra for a much nicer room are quite willing to spend the equivalent of a month's wages for a bottle of Chanel No. 5 and a Gucci T-shirt. And you'll see confirmed tightwads throwing money around on Rasta bead bracelets, music tapes and Calvin Klein undies. I guess I shouldn't talk. In one afternoon alone I bought two cotton shirts covered in Buddhas, two pairs of Levis 501 copies for $7 apiece, and a T-shirt with the Coca-Cola logo on it in Thai. I also bought two tapes—*Thirteen* by Teenage Fanclub, and *His 'n' Hers* by Pulp—and had my ears pierced again.

One thing *had* changed in Khao San Road—the restaurants along it had started showing videos. They listed the videos they were playing on blackboards out the front, luring patrons in with promises of *Pulp Fiction* with their pineapple lassis. The TV monitors were always at the back of the restaurants—away from the harsh glare of the sun—so everyone sat with their backs turned to the street. I didn't like it. To me it spoiled what is one of the great delights of dining on Khao San Road—sipping on a cold drink and watching the passing parade of people wearing the silly clothing they had just bought.

Those readers eager for salacious tales involving girls, balloons and unusually propelled darts will be disappointed to know that I didn't visit Patpong Road—the infamous stretch of girlie bars and nightclubs between Silom and Suriwongse Roads. I'm afraid I'd done all that before. I'd been lured into a girlie bar by a menu promising an array of exotic acts involving every known piece of cutlery and an unopened bottle of Coke—and I had nearly come to blows with the proprietor when he moved a palm tree to reveal a sign saying that there was a 200 baht door charge instead of the free admission I'd been promised. I'm pleased to say, I learnt my lesson.

It all happened on a night I was meant to catch up with my friend Sean outside of King's Castle II, one of the more seedy bars on the strip. (Look for the huge neon sign featuring a King of Hearts, you can't miss it.) The place was full of red-faced Germans with tiny topless Thai girls sitting on their laps. Each girl wore a numbered plastic badge pinned onto her Lycra bikini briefs. One, a waitress, came and asked if she could help. When I told her I was looking for my friend, she replied, 'I can be your friend!' It was a pretty tempting offer from a topless girl with the most fantastically pert breasts I'd ever seen. However, Sean and his friend arrived, and we spent the rest of the night going from bar to bar, all the bars having names like the Pink Panther and the Big Banana Bar. When Sean's friend noticed the numbered plastic badge on the Thai guy smiling at him as he stood at the urinal, we had the good sense to call it a night.

No, this time I was just passing through Bangkok. I didn't visit the floating markets. I didn't go to Wat Po (or any other wat, for that matter). Nor did I check out the Royal barges. I had done all that on my first visit to Bangkok. There was no reason for me to visit them again. But there was one thing I did have to do before I left Bangkok. I had to visit my grandfather's grave. He was a gunner in a Lancaster bomber that was shot down over Burma in October 1944, and he was buried in Kanchanaburi—130 kilometres west of Bangkok—in an Imperial War Graves cemetery near the bridge over the River Kwai.

It is a story that would make a great Hollywood movie, with someone like Brad Pitt playing the role of my grandfather. A dashing young serviceman, off to serve his country, discovers his young wife is pregnant. During his training, first in the icy snows of Canada, and then the scorching sun of Egypt, a daughter is born. He writes every day, sending photographs of himself and of his mates mugging it up in front of the Sphinx. And in return he gets letters from his wife and photographs of his tiny daughter—my mother. One night, in a bombing raid designed to destroy the Death Railway that the Japanese are building from Burma into Thailand, his plane is shot down. The War Office contacts the wife to tell her of the tragedy, but their letter is unclear and seems to indicate that her husband's body has not been found. She never remarries. Instead, she holds onto the slim hope that he may have survived and will come stumbling out of the jungle and back into her arms one day.

We never talked about my grandfather's death. My mother started crying whenever he was mentioned. We had been shown his name on the roll of honour down at the War Museum in Canberra, but that was about it.

I caught a bus up to Kanchanaburi and from there, a small van to the outskirts of town where the Imperial War Graves cemetery was situated. The cemetery is a credit to the Imperial War Graves Commission and the people they employ. It is an oasis of orderliness and tranquillity in an area that is at best dishevelled, at worst, decrepit. With its well tended gardens, freshly mown lawn and thousands of clean, polished plaques, each representing a lost soul, it is a fitting tribute to the men who gave their lives in that war.

I made my way to the caretaker's cottage at the side of the cemetery. The friendly caretaker showed me a book—*The War Dead of the British Commonwealth and Empire 1939–1945*—that listed where my grandfather was buried. It also threw light on the mystery about whether his body had ever been found.

'See this entry here?' the caretaker said, pointing to the word 'Coll.' next to my grandfather's name. 'It means he is in a collective grave. They found his body, but could not distinguish it from all the others on the plane.' It was a horrible thought, but at last the mystery was solved.

My grandfather was buried in grave 4, row G. I approached the plaque with some trepidation. Two young Thai guys with long hair, keen to practise their English, spoke to me as I passed.

'You have friend here?' they asked.

'My grandfather,' I replied.

'Ooh,' they said solemnly. 'Take it easy, man.'

I had never known my grandfather, and nor had my mother. Yet after years of looking at his photos, I felt I knew him. And, somehow, I knew I liked him. He looked intelligent and sensitive, and there was something—perhaps a twinkle in his eyes—which suggested he saw the world in a cock-eyed fashion. Basically, he seemed to be the epitome of everything I would like to be.

When I found his plaque, the same as all the others, what I felt most was sadness. It was a simple plaque of blackened brass, like all the others in the endless rows around it. Below an RAAF emblem, in raised gold lettering, it said, '421 757 Warrant Officer J.K.S. Radnidge 6th October 1944 Age 25. His duty fearlessly and nobly done. Ever Remembered.'

I wondered how things might have been different if he had lived. What sort of life would my mother have lived? Would she be the same person if she'd had a father around? If he'd been any sort of judge of character, he certainly wouldn't have let my mum go out with my dad. I also wondered what he would make of this trip, or indeed my penchant for long journeys. I kind of figured he'd understand. It was pictures of him in exotic locales—in front of the Sphinx in Egypt, in particular—that had stirred my urge to travel. The rest of my family was quite content to stay at home.

I picked some flowers from the garden amongst the headstones and laid them on my grandfather's plaque. After a moment of silence, I turned and left. A woman who worked there, seeing me spend some time at the grave, went across and polished the plaque with a shoe shine brush, knocking the flowers off in her attempt to make it shiny. I caught the bus back to Bangkok, an even longer journey in the peak hour traffic. The visit to my grandfather's grave had taken up a whole day, but it was something I'd had to do and it had been worth every minute.

>>>

That night I caught an overnight train south down the Thai isthmus to Surat Thani. My plan was to go to Ko Phangan, a small island off the east coast, for the monthly Full Moon Party. It was an indulgence that would eat up precious time, but I justified it by telling myself that if the hippies were around today, they would be there, in droves. The ticket, a second class sleeper that included the cost of the ferry ride from Surat Thani to Ko Samui and Ko Phangan, cost only 459 baht, then around $20.

The train left Hualamphong Station just after 9 pm. It was identical to the train I had caught from Nong Khai, right down to the aqua blue colour scheme and curtain for the bunk, except for one thing: I had been the only foreigner on the Nong Khai Express, but this train was packed with us. My carriage had its own cabin attendant, a tiny man dressed in a neat blue uniform, who went from passenger to passenger asking if they would like anything to eat. He handed me a menu, written in English, headed 'Good Food for your Health', that listed every deep-fried dish imaginable, and was guaranteed to give any National Heart Foundation a heart attack.

The large number of foreigners on the train also meant it was crawling with cops. They constantly patrolled the carriages in their brown uniforms and reflector aviator glasses, their hands ever ready over their shiny silver guns. They looked quite menacing, but spent most of the time looking under the seats. The carriage attendant, seeing my alarm, felt moved to comfort me.

'Don't worry, they're not looking for drugs,' he explained, 'They are looking for slitherers.'

Slitherers, apparently, were thieves who shimmied up and down the aisles at night on their stomachs, stealing things out of backpacks as their owners slept. The Southern Express provided rich pickings, so I was glad I had the upper bunk.

The upper bunk didn't have a window, though, so my trip south from Bangkok was largely an audio one: the suction sound and then the whoomph of a train passing in the opposite direction; the echoing roar when we crossed a metal bridge; the squeal of brakes as we approached a station; and station announcements in Thai.

The train arrived at Surat Thani at dawn. The attendant moved through the carriage shaking sleeping foreigners awake and telling them it was time to get off. I clambered off the train and onto the tracks, and followed a rabble of foreigners through a hole in a chain wire fence then onto a fleet of modern coaches waiting on the other side. The coaches drove through narrow dusty streets to the docks, where a boat waited to take us to the islands.

The boat was large and relatively modern, but it looked as if it had already endured a hard life. The varnish on the railing had cracked and flaked off, and there were black stains around the diesel exhaust pipe. The state of the lifesaving equipment suggested that maintenance had been, at best, cursory. The seats in the lower lounge filled quickly, so passengers and their backpacks began to fill the decks, sitting on the cracking fibreglass roof and standing three-deep on top of the lifesaving capsules. Soon every part of the boat was covered with backpackers in various shades of brown and stages of world-weariness. From the dock, it would have looked almost Biblical—a football crowd walking on water.

I grabbed a spot on top of a pile of backpacks on the upper deck. By the time the boat finally set sail, the morning sun was high enough to start frying those of us on the roof. I arrived in Ko Phangan, three hours later, an unnatural shade of red.

During the trip, a number of locals moved about the crowded decks showing off photo albums, touting the various guesthouses and bungalows on the island. The photos seemed to have all been taken on crappy instamatic cameras that turned what was probably a lovely beach into a blue-grey stretch of sodden sand. The bungalows appeared to be a similar blue-grey, as were the restaurants, the food and the smiling guests and staff. I remember thinking that they would be better off not showing the photos at all. Everyone on board had a picture of a palm-fringed beach paradise in their minds. If I was a tout I'd say, 'You know that picture of paradise you have in your mind, the one created by a glossy expensive brochure back in your home country? Well, it's just like that.'

The touts were wasting their time with me. I was heading to Bottle Beach, a secluded beach on the north of the island that could only be reached by boat. A Swedish girl in Bangkok had told me about it, capturing my imagination with tales of warm, balmy nights in rustic cabins overlooking a moonlit bay. Of course I failed to consider that I would be there on my own and that all that seclusion could get a bit boring. In my mind's eye, I was there with her.

The port of Thong Sala gave no indication that Ko Phangan was an unspoilt paradise full of beaches and coves, all lined by the mandatory coconut trees and attractive bungalows. It was an ugly collection of restaurants and shops selling swimsuits and other beach needs. A pack of open-backed utes waited to ferry arriving backpackers to their chosen beach and bungalow. Although the Full Moon Party was still a good eleven days away, most people were heading for Hat Rin, the most developed and crowded beach on the island, the beach where the party was actually held. The only other people heading for Bottle Beach were two English girls, Jill and Emma, from Sheffield. The van drove us along a dusty road across the island to Ban Thong, where a motorised dugout canoe took us down the coast to Bottle Beach.

My guidebook said that Bottle Beach—Hat Khuat, to give it its proper Thai name—was undeveloped. That was an understatement.

The beach consisted of three sets of bungalows. That's all. Nothing else. One set of bungalows on the north end of the beach. Another set on the south end. And a set in the middle. The guy piloting the boat beached it in front of the middle set of bungalows. So that's where I stayed. And so did the English girls.

My bungalow was a thatched hut that looked straight out over the bay. On the verandah there was a hammock where I could kick back and listen to my Walkman or read a book or just watch girls in bikinis walking by. The beach was outside my door, the water a few steps further. Just 100 metres away, a restaurant served delicious meals and ice-cold beers. If the mood struck me, I could walk along the beach to the other bungalows and sample what their restaurants had to offer—freshly caught lobster or steamed perch, perhaps. And the weather? The weather was perfect.

So how did I pass eleven days in this tropical paradise? Well, it went something like this. Sleep until 10. Have breakfast. Lie on beach listening to Walkman. Have lunch. Sit at table under palm tree in front of restaurant ordering beer, chicken salads and tropical fruit. Return to room to read, swinging in hammock on balcony of bungalow. Have afternoon swim. Meet Jill and Emma outside restaurant and decide which of three restaurants to give our custom to that evening. Go to restaurant. Return to one of two bungalows and drink beer while listening to music and staring out to moonlit sea. Go to bed. Repeat eleven times.

My favourite part of the day was our afternoon beer. We'd sit at a table under a palm tree, our feet in the sugar-white sand, and make up names for all the other guests on the beach. There was John Boy, a guy who looked like he was from 'The Waltons'. There was Quentin, a guy whose hair was receding in a Tarantino manner. And there was Uma. The girls were particularly cruel in their comments about Uma. She kind of looked like Uma Thurman—hence the name—and wore tiny cut-off shorts, a tight Lycra top with exposed midriff, and long purple Doc Martin boots.

I'd join in and make fun of her inappropriate beach gear, but in all honesty, I quite fancied her. I didn't dare tell the girls that, though.

I listened to just two tapes during my stay at Bottle Beach—*Thirteen* by Teenage Fanclub and *His 'n' Hers* by Pulp—and both soon became intimately entwined with the smell of suntan lotion and chicken salad. Songs like 'Radio' and 'Escher', from *Thirteen*, captured the daytime ebullience of having a laugh, drinking beer and longing for Uma. *His 'n' Hers*, particularly 'David's Last Summer', captured that time between dusk and going to bed—the sensation of things winding down, but with the hint of possibilities still hanging in the air. The cheesy mix of the whole album also captured the inherent tackiness, shallowness and unreality of a holiday on a Thai beach. Even now, I can put on either of those albums and be immediately transported back to Bottle Beach. Which, I'm sure you'll agree, is not a bad thing.

The night of the Full Moon Party came around and a special longboat was arranged to take the Bottle Beach partygoers down to Hat Rin. We clung to the sides as the motorised dugout canoe ploughed through waves turned an enchanting tone of silver by the full moon above us. The hour and a half ride down the coast to Hat Rin was both beautiful and terrifying.

Even before we rounded the last cape before Hat Rin we could see a light in the sky like the glow from a small city. There was also a hum of music—all different types—mixing together into an indistinct babble. Occasionally, one beat or riff or snatch of vocals would break through and, for a few seconds, have a life of its own. The excitement in the air was tangible, rippling through the water and through every passenger.

As we rounded the cape, we were presented with a sight that was a crazy mix of the Riviera and pure southern Thailand. The bay was filled with all kinds of water craft, most of them ferrying passengers across from Ko Samui for the night. They ranged from the long, pointy speedboats that roared in and out, dropping off the more affluent tourists, to the more utilitarian longboats that dropped off an altogether scruffier clientele.

Hat Rin was going off. The beach was littered with thousands of people drinking and smoking and doing whatever else it was that got them off. Behind them, stalls lit by hurricane lamps sold T-shirts, batteries, fluorescent necklaces, food and drinks, including a rather interesting speed punch. A constant stream of people wandered along the sand past these stalls, sampling the punch and then sampling the music on offer. Further back, the more permanent bars and clubs of Hat Rin played their usual musical selection—Bob Marley, Tracy Chapman, Creedence, The Doors, that sort of thing. Their only concession to the techno intruders was to play *No Limit* by 2 Unlimited every now and then.

At various points along the beach, visiting DJs had set up mobile sound stages on the sand, offering hard-core techno to hard-core dancers. It was an interesting sociological exercise to note the different dance styles at each sound stage. They seemed to be divided along national lines and I offer here my notes from the evening—in the interests of greater human understanding, of course:

European (esp. Italian)
Music: Pumping
Dress: Lycra bicycle shorts
Dance style: Aerobics work out
Drug of choice: Speed
Distinguishing features: Periodic clenching of fists and rapid pumping of arms in front of chest. Often punctuated by a primal 'whoah!'

English
Music: Laid back
Dress: Classic hippie or Ibiza bare midriff

Dance style: Lots of floating hand movements and stroking of faces
Drug of choice: Ecstasy
Distinguishing features: Compulsion to make boxes, big or little, with hands

Australian
Music: Not fussy
Dress: Boardies
Dance style: Depended on state of inebriation (the further gone, the more likely to resemble a chook flailing about with its head cut off
Drug of choice: Beer
Distinguishing features: Total lack of coordination and tendency to fall over after each attempt to dance

After midnight, I sat on a large rock at the southern end of the beach. From here I could survey the whole beach. It looked like an orgy—a clambake on ecstasy, a gathering of Gidgets on acid. Every now and then, someone would let off a firework, lighting the sky with a shower of red or green or yellow, and prompting a communal 'aaahh' from the throng below.

I could also spot the heavy police presence. Some were highly visible, moving through the crowds in their drab brown uniforms, occasionally checking people's bags. Elsewhere, undercover agents were infiltrating groups and entrapping people by offering to sell them drugs. The word on the beach was that there was a British film crew there to film the hedonistic delights and, afraid that the word would get back to the UK that this was a liberal, anything-goes scene, the Thai Government wanted to send out a tough message. The rumour was that over 100 people had been arrested already.

The party reached its zenith at dawn, just as the sun peeped over the horizon. It was a wild pagan ceremony now, like one of those 1950s B-grade *Lost City of Atlantis* flicks—people in various stages of undress rushing into the water, dancing frantically at the sun. One English girl—who had drunk a little too much speed punch, if you ask me—rushed up and down the beach, yelling, 'Face the light! Face the light and pretend you're a cat!'

Elsewhere, people were hugging and stroking each other's faces and saying things like 'Peace and love' and 'You're wonderful!' Their eyes were like pinpricks and they were chewing gum frantically. But it was a brilliant moment—thousands of people silhouetted against the morning sun, dancing in their own inimitable fashion, whacked on their own type of drug. When the English girl with the feline fixation went up to a Thai policeman and pawed his face, purring 'Meow, meow, I am a cat', I was glad I'd stayed straight.

CHAPTER TWENTY-ONE

Malaysia–Singapore–Indonesia

Soundtrack: The Oils, Chisel, and a little bit of INXS

Most travel books give you the impression that every step of a journey is an adventure, every day an introduction to interesting new people and amazing new sights. In fact, most travel writers would like you to believe that there is never a dull moment. Which, of course, is an utter load of crap. There are some parts of a trip that you want to pass through as quickly as possible; at the end of these parts, you have nothing more to show than the kilometres covered. This part of the journey was like that for me.

I caught an overnight boat back to Surat Thani from Ko Phangan with Jill and Emma, the two English girls. The boat journey was notable for only two things: it got there without capsizing, and the good folk from the *Guinness Book of Records* weren't waiting when it arrived to give it an award as the world's slowest boat journey over 145 kilometres. The van ride from Surat Thani across the Thai–Malaysian border to Penang was similarly uneventful, unless you regard driving over the world's third-longest bridge as one of life's defining moments. Even Penang, a colourful island city steeped in ancient Chinese culture and architecture, left me a bit cold.

But my journey through this part of the world was not without its moments. I had an interesting conversation with the owner of a gold shop in Georgetown about the delicate relations between Australia and Malaysia. He apologised for his Prime Minister, Dr Mahathir—who had made inflammatory comments about my country—by saying that he was 'an emotional man', and he expected me to return the favour and apologise for our former Prime Minister, Paul Keating, calling Mahathir recalcitrant. It was something I was disinclined to do. That comment, on the eve of an APEC meeting in Japan, had the rather wonderful effect of sending millions of Australians scurrying to their dictionaries to find out exactly what 'recalcitrant' meant. (In case you're still wondering, it means obstinately disobedient, objecting to restraint.) Besides, I agreed with Keating.

The night I spent at the Reggae Club in Penang with Emma and Jill wasn't bad either—mainly because it involved the consumption of many free beers. They were given to me by British sailors who were on leave and keen to score with the girls. They plied me with beer until I passed out on the rattan floor. I woke up the next morning with a dozen Bob Marleys looking down on me and the sound of 'No woman, no cry' ringing in my ears. Rather alarmingly, I was convinced I had spoken to Jah.

That I was out of sorts couldn't be denied. I had been on the road for seven months now, and I was feeling a little jaded. It was time to put some heavy-duty kilometres behind me. If I wanted to realise my dream of travelling overland from London to Sydney without flying, I'd have to get to Timor before the winds changed.

If I didn't, the yachts—my best chance of crossing the last 483 kilometres across the Timor Straits—would have stopped sailing to Darwin for the season.

Proof that I was out of sorts was evidenced by the way I chose to get from Penang to Singapore. Instead of slowly making my way down the Malay Peninsula in a decrepit bus—calling in at Rantau Abang to see the turtles, or popping into Melaka to check out the Portuguese ruins—I caught an overnight Super Luxury VIP express bus straight through to Singapore. With its ultra-wide, velour covered, reclining seats—so big and luxurious that there were only twenty-four on the entire coach—it was the closest thing to flying I'd done on the entire trip. Nor was it particularly hippie-like.

I justified my decision to take the bus by the fact that hippies had never spent much time in Malaysia either. To put it bluntly, they weren't welcome. An official government regulation at the time banned hippies from staying in the country. It read: 'If you are found dressed in shabby, dirty or indecent clothes, living in temporary or makeshift shelters you will be deemed a hippie. On being deemed a hippie, your visit pass will be cancelled and you will be ordered to leave Malaysia within 24 hours, failing which you will be prosecuted under immigration laws. Furthermore, you will not be permitted to enter Malaysia again.' In the mid seventies this regulation was used as a pretext to round up and deport Westerners living in the popular hippie communes in the kampong at Batu Ferringhi and Bahang Beach on Penang and from the Tanjung Kling Beach centre near Melaka. Most of the hippies only stayed in Malaysia as long as I did.

The saddest moment of this part of my trip was saying goodbye to Emma and Jill. In the short time I had known them, they had become quite good friends. I would particularly miss sitting around with them and slagging off everyone who walked by. Judging by the gift they presented me with as I got onto the bus, they would miss me too. It was a necklace with a polished stone pendant, engraved with a Chinese proverb. It read: 'The tongue is the only tool sharpened through use.'

I arrived in Singapore at 8.00 the next morning. The bus terminated near Raffles, the legendary colonial hotel and the only building in Singapore with any sort of old-world charm. I made my way along the neat, clean streets to a hostel in an apartment block opposite a shiny new department store with a multiplex cinema and a Burger King. I decided that Singapore was like those architect-designed houses you see in magazines like *Vogue Living*. It looks very nice, and everything is in its place, but you wouldn't want to actually *live* in it.

Singapore had taken a much more, well, Singaporean approach to the problem of hippies than the Malaysians had. They'd let them in, but only if they got a haircut. In the seventies, squadrons of barbers waited—at the airport, the causeway to Malaysia and the ports serving Indonesia—to give anyone with hair over their collar a complimentary short back and sides. A hippie was given the choice of losing his hair or not entering Singapore at all. Not surprisingly, most decided to give Singapore a miss.

Since then, Singapore has become even more sterile and over-regulated. The massive fines for littering, chewing gum and forgetting to flush the toilet are just the most obvious examples of the Singaporean government's treating its people like naughty school children. I know it's easy to take cheap shots at Singapore, but really, the country is a little too conscientious for its own good. Consider the evidence that presented itself to me in the two days I was condemned to stay there:

> A state-sponsored 'Most Courteous Bus Driver Competition'.
> Omnipresent posters featuring a cartoon lion saying, 'Let's be more courteous to each other.'

> Government-issued Singaporean flags hanging from the apartment blocks facing Malaysia across the causeway.

> A guy whipper-snippering the construction site of a new flyover to make sure it was neat and tidy.

> The cheesy government-sponsored posters proclaiming the joys of family life.

The posters were perhaps the most damning evidence of Singapore's slide into national Nerdism. In nurturing a race of sober, conscientious workers who dressed neatly and took great pride in their personal hygiene, the Singapore government had also created a race of people who had forgotten to procreate.

The posters featured scenes of happy family life—feeding the orang-utans at the zoo, mum getting a birthday cake from her children, three kids jumping on the bed with mum and dad—and were prominent in every subway station and covered walkway. 'Kids make you see how happy life can be!' they screamed. Others were even more heavy-handed with the saccharine. 'So much fun, so much laughter,' they beamed. 'So much love for ever after! Why wait? With a family, life's great!'

At least the Singaporeans had emotionally progressed; now they were at least in a position to actually have kids. The last time I'd visited Singapore, the same government department had been using posters to encourage Singaporean males to get themselves a partner. It seemed that Singaporean males were too busy working to get girlfriends, so the government organised singles' cruises and parties to help them meet girls. I still have photos of the posters. One featured a middle-aged matron introducing a young Singaporean man to a Singaporean female, the caption reading: 'It's only an introduction. The rest is up to you.' The new poster campaign seemed to suggest that now they needed help with the rest.

I didn't stay long in Singapore—just long enough to have a Big

Mac with fries and call my mum from the new general post office. Within 48 hours of arriving I was leaving again, heading off to the less civilised shores of Indonesia. I caught a boat from the docks at the squeaky clean World Trade Centre. It was a boat journey from the first world to the third, passing super tankers and modern freight ships that milled outside Singapore, and then the wooden kampongs of Tanjung Pinang in Indonesia.

Tanjung Pinang is the principal town of Insular Riau, a collection of Indonesian islands that lie scattered in the equatorial waters between Singapore and Jakarta. Three hundred years ago, the area was the heart of the Malay civilisation, with its rulers holding sway over much of Malaysia and Indonesia. Not that I'd get much chance to discover what was left of that golden era amongst the filthy streets and shabby wooden houses of Tanjung Pinang. Fate decided to smile kindly on my plan to get to Timor quickly—the monthly Pelni liner to Jakarta was leaving that night, and even at such short notice I was able to get an economy class ticket. I'd have to wait for some other time to check out the intriguingly named Bong's Homestay mentioned in my guidebook.

Pelni is the national shipping company of Indonesia, with over 70 cargo and passenger ships connecting the country's major and provincial harbours. Most of their ships should have been sold for scrap metal years ago, but some, like the one I was catching to Jakarta, are modern, German-built vessels with standardised and reasonable fares. The KM *Lawit* left from Kijang Harbour—not far from Tanjung Pinang—and would sail through the night, arriving in Jakarta some time after lunch the next day. Judging by the seething mass of Indonesians assembled on the dock with their household contents piled up around them, buying the ticket had been the easy part.

Boarding a Pelni liner is a bit like competing on 'Gladiators'. But instead of swinging on ropes or dodging giant padded poles, the challenge is to negotiate a steep gangway, seething with people, without falling into the water below. While you won't find any thick-necked Gladiators in tight leotards trying to block your progress, similarly built Pelni officials will try their hardest to make sure you fail to get aboard.

I plunged into the melee and failed to get on board on my first two attempts. I was thwarted by a pack of garlic smugglers, their sacks bursting with cloves of garlic, who were determined to stay ahead of me. My third attempt looked doomed, too—I had stumbled about halfway up the gangway and had to duck away from the fist of a Pelni officer as it whistled past my face, forcing me into the back of one of the smugglers. Just I was being sucked back into the crowd and back towards the dock, I grabbed onto the railing and deftly manoeuvred my way to the top of the gangway. A friendly Pelni official took my ticket and asked, 'Ekonomi, or would your prefer to sleep on the deck outside the bridge?' I looked at the scrum of Indonesians clawing their way towards the bowels of the boat and Ekonomi, and decided on the deck outside the bridge.

The deck outside the bridge was covered and although a sign just in front of it said that no passengers were allowed past this point, it was packed with backpackers who had decided to camp here rather than face the horrors of the Ekonomi decks below. Some played cards. Others listened to their Walkmans. Most, however, slept—covering themselves against the cold of the night with their grubby sleeping bags. The crew, including the captain, stepped over comatose travellers and picked their way through their backpacks without comment or complaint.

During the course of the voyage to Jakarta, the deck outside the bridge became a tiny community—a traveller's ghetto where people shared tatty vinyl mattresses (salvaged from the Ekonomi deck below) and passed around joints. People took turns going down to the kitchen for the complementary meals of fish head and rice, secure in the knowledge that their possessions were safe. Guys with long hair and wearing baggy pants sat strumming guitars while their girlfriends braided their hair. When another girl, her nose pierced and her breasts swinging freely under a skimpy tie-dyed singlet, moved amongst us offering to massage our shoulders, I remember thinking that this is what it must have been like on the hippie trail.

In fact, the whole scene was reminiscent of the hippie communities Paul Theroux described in *The Great Railway Bazaar*—the colourful clothing, intricate amulets and tanned bodies were definitely all on display. He had been quite dismissive of the hippies and their free and easy ways. He condemned them for escaping society and then forming similarly strict hierarchical communities themselves. But, after 18 hours on the deck just outside the bridge, I must say that it's a lifestyle I could become quite accustomed to.

Sadly, at 3.00 the next afternoon it was all over. The KM *Lawit* made its way through Jakarta Bay and pulled alongside Tanjung Priok dock in the east of the sprawling city—and I caught a bemo straight to the Pulo Gadung, the bus terminal that serves the buses heading east to Bali. A bemo is a Japanese van used to convey people from one point to another in Indonesia for a fixed, and often negligible, price, but unlike most Japanese vans, bemos have the capacity to fit entire football crowds inside them, and are not considered to have reached their prime until they are rusted, dented and only firing on two cylinders.

The bemo dropped me off a couple of hundred metres from the terminal. It would have taken me all the way in, maybe right up to the door of my bus, except that the entrance was blocked by the smouldering shells of three burned-out buses. A large number of police and army officers swarmed around what was left of the buses, supervising ancient fire engines trying to hose down the flames, and holding back curious onlookers. I wondered what had happened. Was it an accident? An act of terrorism? Or the result of the student protests that were breaking out in various parts of the city? Before I could ask, I was hustled along to a hole in the compound wall by a policeman wearing a white vinyl belt and aviator glasses, and pointed towards the buses going to Bali.

In keeping with the generally self-indulgent tone of this section of my journey, the bus I caught to Bali was a super luxury coach with velour seats and air conditioning. But this being Indonesia, the seats were broken and the air conditioning didn't work. It was also packed with enough people to fill Wembley Stadium, as well as their sacks of produce and assorted poultry. Alarmingly, one of the roosters chose to perch on the headrest of my seat. As we inched our way through the gates and onto the street—past the bulldozers pushing the remains of the buses into the open canal running beside the road—I took solace in the fact that, unlike everyone else on the bus, I had a whole seat to myself. A couple of hundred metres from the terminal, however, just out of sight of the police and the army, the bus stopped to pick up another passenger. He was young, sweaty and sooty, and smelled suspiciously of petrol—and he squeezed in beside me.

The guy introduced himself as Budi. He was a student at Jakarta's Universitas Indonesia. And as if in answer to an earlier question, he told me he had been involved in the torching of the buses and was sensibly leaving town for a while.

'It was an act of revenge,' he explained. 'Our friend was killed in an accident caused by the bus driver's stupidity. The company refused to compensate for his death so we burned their buses.'

The bus to Bali was an overnight one, so most of the journey passed in darkness. Java was little more than a blur of roadside trees and faceless concrete towns illuminated by the headlights of oncoming traffic. I slept fitfully, woken constantly by either the driver swerving violently to avoid head-on collisions or (less often) the rooster ruffling its feathers above my head. At still other times I was woken by Budi dribbling on my shoulder. When we reached the ferry that took us from Banyuwangi in Java to Gilimanuk in Bali at dawn, I was glad to be able to stretch my legs.

The trip from Gilimanuk to Denpasar was a reminder of why

Bali remains so popular with tourists. We passed red-brick temples topped by ornate stone gargoyles, fluorescent green terraced rice paddies, picture postcard beaches with palm trees tumbling onto the beach and beautiful smiling women in sarongs carrying fruit on their heads. The world's leading design company, if given an unlimited budget and a brief to create the perfect tropical island, would be hard pressed to do better. But then you reach Denpasar—a dirty, polluted, concrete hovel of a city that challenges every no-name town in Indonesia in unlikeableness—and you realise that not everything is perfect in paradise. And after that, you reach Kuta. It's good preparation, really.

Kuta was once a small, sleepy village where folk just ate tropical fruit and performed rituals. Now it's a maze of narrow and grimy roads lined with shops selling loud batik clothing, leather goods of dubious styles and crappy painted wooden carvings of frogs sitting on lily pads, fishing. In small, dingy restaurants, silly Western women with braided hair (and old enough to know better) sit groping pretty Balinese boys. Elsewhere, passing packs of drunken Australians stagger from one bar to another.

I met one of these drunken Aussies at a place called Koala Blue. After close to seven months, I was hanging out for an Australian beer, and figured that a bar with the word 'Koala' in its name would be able to help me. It did. The trouble was, it was also 'helping' a dozen other visiting Australians. The drunkest was an engineer called Aussie Mick. He worked for BHP in one of the mines in Western Australia's isolated northwest and wore the standard Aussie-in-Kuta uniform of shorts, a singlet and rubber thongs.

'Bali's closher to me than Perth,' he slurred. 'Pluth ish cheapa to get pisshed 'ere. I come up 'ere every 'oliday.'

Mick was typical of the Aussies in Kuta. He ate in a place called Norm's that offered 'fuckin' good tucker', and drank in the inappropriately titled Manhattan Bar, where he could watch the progress of the West Coast Eagles in the AFL match of the day beamed in via satellite. (The Manhattan also boasted the largest spa pool in Australasia and real 'home style' roast dinners cooked with real Aussie Gravox. As the sign proudly proclaimed, the cooks at the Manhattan 'don't know what coconut oil is ??!!'.) At night you'd find Mick propping up the bar at Koala Blue or going on one of Kuta's organised pub crawls that boasted 'Avoid hangovers—stay drunk!'

While I was in Kuta, I came up with a list of other things to avoid while you are in Kuta:

> Avoid getting your hair braided. It is not a good look, especially if you have a receding hairline, as I do.

> Avoid making appointments you don't intend to keep with hair braiders. You may think that they won't recognise you amongst the hundreds of other tourists, but they will. When it comes to remembering faces, Balinese hair braiders are Mensa material. You'll spend the rest of your stay in Kuta ducking beads and dodging elastic bands.

> Avoid making eye contact with copy-watch hawkers. Even a casual glance will result in the unwanted purchase of a fake Rolex, maybe even a dozen.

> Avoid buying batik shirts. The Indonesians themselves have trouble carrying them off. What chance do you think you have?

But there is one thing I suggest you *don't* avoid in Kuta—the cassette shops. They are huge, bright stores with walls lined with cassettes of every artist you could ever imagine and some you couldn't. Bali used to be a haven for pirate cassettes. They were illegal, poorly made copies of popular artists, with crappy photocopied artwork that always mixed up the track listings. Sometimes they got them wrong altogether. Many a Beatles fanatic visiting Bali has bought a copy of the *Revolter* cassette thinking they've found a long-forgotten masterpiece. Then the major record labels decided to counter piracy by releasing the same albums on better quality cassettes—complete with the original artwork—at the same price. The result is a great chance to supplement the tired bunch of tapes you've been listening to on your Walkman for months.

While most of the cassettes on offer are heavily skewed towards visiting Australians like Aussie Mick—they're the perfect place to complete your Cold Chisel or Midnight Oil collection—you can occasionally find a few gems. I found a copy of *Don't Smile* by a Swedish band, This Perfect Day, months before it came out back home, for example. But you can also find some horrors. I bought *Girl Power*, by Shampoo, on the strength of the cover alone. (Did you know it came out in Asia a good year or so before it came out anywhere else?) It had a really dreadful, shouty version of 'I Know What Boys Like' on it that almost ruined my trip. The original, by The Waitresses, was one of my favourite songs when I was growing up. It was a lot slyer, and is probably the reason I still have a bit of a fixation for waitresses in ultra-short skirts who chew gum in a bored yet salacious manner.

Despite the siren call of the cassette shops, I actually spent most of my time in Bali down at Benoa Port. It was home to the Bali International Yacht Club and a 1,000-rupiah (50c) bemo ride from Denpasar's Tegal bemo terminal . It was where every ocean-going yacht in Bali arrived and anchored and my guidebook suggested that it was a great place to find a ride on yachts heading south to Australia. Well, it's not. Not while I was there, anyway. I went out to the port every day for a week and wandered around the marina looking for yachts heading south to Australia without any luck at all. It got to the stage that the bemo drivers knew me by name. 'No luck today, Mr Peter?' they'd say when I eventually gave up and sat in their bemos as they waited for more passengers before heading off. In the end, the harbourmaster felt moved to have words with me. I was becoming a nuisance, he said. There were no yachts heading to Australia. And if they were, they'd all be going via Timor. Why didn't I go down to Kupang and bother the harbourmaster down there?

He was right. While it would have been great to get a yacht, the longer I waited in Bali, the more chance I had of missing out altogether. It was time to head east again.

Nusa Tenggara, the chain of islands that stretch eastward from Bali, includes some of the most beautiful and untouched islands in Indonesia. For the adventurous traveller they offer an endless selection of unspoilt beaches, traditional cultures and rugged volcanoes. One could spend months wandering around soaking up the sights. I passed through it in two and a bit days on a bus. These are my impressions from the bus window:

Lombok

Time spent there: 8 hours.

Description: Smaller, drier Bali, but without the tourists.

Highlight: Guys in conical hats fishing under shadow of dry volcano at Labuhan.

Go back factor: Low. Maybe higher around the Gili islands.

Sumbawa

Time spent there: 33 hours including 8 hours sleeping on locked bus at Bima and another overnight stay in shitty losmen (family run guesthouse) near harbour at Sape.

Description: Green rice fields, rolling hills, volcanic

ridges, picturesque bays, crappy concrete towns. A bit
of everything, actually.

Highlight: Spending the night in a locked bus at Bima
and getting small children to pass me food through an
opened window.

Go back factor: Low. Higher if guaranteed no forced
sleeping on buses.

Komodo

Time spent there: 0 hours. Passed by on ferry.

Description: Dry, brown island dotted with dark green
trees.

Highlight: Borrowing binoculars from dorkish Korean
tourists in futile attempt to spot legendary Komodo
dragons. Only indication of presence of said dragons is
a group of tourists on hillside with long zoom lenses
and the carcass of a goat.

Go back factor: Medium. High if vicious dragon attack
on tourists guaranteed.

Western Flores

Time spent there: 17 hours.

Description: Pretty, green part of the island, dotted
with volcanoes.

Highlight: The coolest looking volcano, spotted at
dawn with clouds like pink GT stripe behind it. Smoke
coming out of an open gash on the side also
impressive.

Go back factor: High.

My long bus journey through Nusa Tenggara ended, appropriately
enough, in Ende. Ende is the capital of Flores and is situated almost
exactly in the middle of the island. It's a laid-back town, set on a

lovely bay and surrounded by steep volcanic peaks. Sukarno, who led Indonesia to independence in 1945, lived here when he was exiled by the Dutch in 1934, and even though it is the major administrative centre of the island, the town still has the feel of a backwater. Boys played soccer on a dusty pitch surrounded by frangipani trees and overlooked by crumbling colonial villas. In the centre of town, shops selling ikat rugs, shawls and blankets were left unattended as their owners slept under trees nearby.

When I arrived in Ende I was presented with two choices: wait three days until the scheduled ferry left Ende for Kupang in Timor or go down to Ipi Harbour and see if there were any other boats going. Impatient sod that I am, I went down to the harbour. As luck would have it, a ship bound for Atapupu, a small town halfway up Timor, was in port loading cargo. Better still, the captain said that he would take me across for only 20,000 rupiah ($10). As it would be leaving before dawn the next day, he suggested I stay the night on the boat, so I arranged to return later that evening with my bag.

It had taken me 12 days to get to Ende from Singapore. I'd travelled on four boats, four buses and countless bemos and vans. Now Timor was a mere 240 kilometres away across the Savu Sea. For the first time for a long time, luck seemed to be on my side; the end was near.

CHAPTER TWENTY-TWO

Dili

Soundtrack: *Let Love In*—Nick Cave and the Bad Seeds

I returned to the docks at Ipi Harbour at the appointed time and
found the KM *Ratu Rosari*—anchored 200 metres off shore. It had
finished loading and was waiting until dawn before setting sail for
Timor. A man fishing from the dock saw my distress, and after
handing me his rod and disappearing into the dark, soon returned
with a canoe to paddle me across the still water to the boat. It was
a magical moment—the water gently lapping against the canoe—
spoilt only by the loud easy-listening music blaring from the boat.

After yelling for attention for a good ten minutes, a crew member
finally spotted the canoe and lowered a small ladder for me to climb
up. He pointed to a spot on the open deck—just in front of an old
Toyota Landcruiser and amongst the colour TVs, rice colanders,
rattan chairs and a single mountain bike—where I could spend the
night. I laid out my sleeping bag, made a pillow out of a towel and
had one of the best night's sleep I'd had in a long time.

I woke the next morning to the sound of the diesel engines starting. It wasn't quite dawn, but I could make out the pink streaks of
the rising sun behind the silhouetted cone of Ipi volcano. When we
set off, passing dugout canoes full of fishermen and their nets, I
felt, for the first time in Indonesia at least, that I was setting out on
a grand adventure. In my mind's eye, I was Errol Flynn on a schoo-
ner sailing the South Sargasso Sea.

The boat made good time, but even so, it took us most of the
day to get across to Atapupu. I spent the day under the canvas
cover, watching the crew feed and water thousands of tiny chicks
in boxes and cages. The young mechanic sat reading the manual
for the engine. I asked if there was a problem, but it seems he was
just being conscientious. The boat tracked along the coast of Flores
before turning right and heading straight for Atapupu.

Lunch was served in a small area at the back of the boat. It was
here, over a bland meal of rice and fish, that I was befriended by
the First Mate. He was playing a submarine game on his Gameboy.
He was a round, slow-moving man with large, bulging, hooded eyes
that blinked in slow motion. After lunch, he invited me to his cabin.
It was a small room, just down from the kitchen, with a sign saying
'Muslim' over the door and a beautiful shell hanging on the door.
The room was clean and homely. Beside the neatly made bed there
was a short-wave radio and an old photo of himself with an old
European priest in a ridiculously loud batik shirt. He also showed
me photo of a Swedish girl called Erin who had spent ten days on
the boat. When I went to leave, he grabbed my arm and looked
earnestly in my eyes.

'I am alone, but not lonely.' He held my gaze until he was sure
I understood what he said. It was obviously very important to him.

The KM *Ratu Rosari* arrived in Atapupu just after 4 pm. Atapupu
is one of Timor's busiest cattle ports, but seemed equally capable
of handling a cargo of small poultry. Within seconds of docking,
an army of Indonesians in faded blue uniforms appeared from

nowhere to help unload the ship. I walked beside whitewashed concrete warehouses, past a smiling policeman at the gate and onto the
road.

The road was the main east-west road between Kupang and Dili,
but it was little more than a single-lane ribbon of asphalt. Atapupu
was the midpoint between these two cities, and was little more than
a line of dusty shops and restaurants and trees with their trunks
painted white. I waited in the shade of the largest one and wondered
which way I should go.

The sensible option was to head west to Kupang. It was the major
port in these parts. If there were any boats heading to Australia,
that's where they would be going from. But to the east was Dili,
and East Timor, a place etched deep into every Australian university
student's consciousness. It was tempting to head there, to see first-
hand what John Pilger had been going on about, but it was a
restricted area, and there was every likelihood I would be turned
back anyway.

In the end, the decision was taken out of my hands. After waiting
for half an hour without a single vehicle passing, a shiny new Dai-
hatsu Feroza four-wheel drive heading towards Dili stopped in front
of me. A well-dressed Indonesian leant across his driver and asked
if I wanted a lift to Dili.

The guy's name was Ratu, and he was an engineer from Java,
working for a company in Dili. As part of the relocation package,
his kids were sent to an exclusive boarding school and he got a
house in Dili with maids and a brand new car, complete with driver.

The road followed the coast, passing through dry stony plains
backed by dry stony mountains. Haggard looking people scratched
out a living drying salt and keeping skinny, bony cattle in corrals
made from sticks or stones. To me they looked rather sad, but Ratu
thought otherwise.

'Can you believe that twenty years ago these people were
walking around in bark clothes?' he said. 'There were no roads, no

schools. Indonesia has been very good to these people!'

It reminded me of the line about Tibet spun by the Chinese lawyer on the train from Golmud. I couldn't see how the Indonesians had helped these people in the slightest. But I bit my tongue. The car was air conditioned and I was enjoying the most comfortable ride I'd had in Indonesia.

The conversation turned to where I would be staying in Dili and, after consulting my guidebook, I gave him the name of the cheapest place in town.

'Oh no! You cannot stay there,' he insisted. 'The company I work for owns the Hotel Dili. You can stay there . . . for free!'

We passed through the military roadblock that marked the border between West and East Timor with a minimum of fuss. This is where I probably would have been dragged off the bus and sent back to Kupang if I'd been on my own. But as I was with Ratu, I was waved through into the troubled East Timor province with what almost amounted to a smile.

The Portuguese influence in East Timor was immediately apparent. The ruins of the fort that once marked the border looked just like the ruins of forts in old Portuguese colonies throughout Asia and Africa—dark and mildewed but with a kind of friendliness that Spanish, English or Dutch forts couldn't (or didn't want to) achieve. Within minutes of entering an ex-Portuguese colony, it always strikes me that the Portuguese seemed more interested in achieving a certain quality of life than in building empires.

This attitude was immediately apparent in Dili. The heart of the town was its sleepy seaside promenade, a long, sweeping waterfront lined with huge, shady waringin trees. Old Portuguese buildings with terracotta-tiled roofs and white stucco walls overlooked the bay, and the town was dotted with shady squares. On the beach, fishing boats were dragged ashore and fishing nets repaired in a scene that wouldn't have looked out of place on Portugal's Atlantic coast. But perhaps the most lasting legacy from the Portuguese is the siesta that closes the town between noon and 4 pm.

Naturally, we pulled up outside the Hotel Dili just after three. The reception desk was unattended, and we stood there for a good half hour, ringing the bell and listening to the clock tick. In the end, Ratu gave up and we sat and read old, faded magazines until four, when the front desk clerk, refreshed from his sleep, returned to duty.

'As you can see, the Timorese still have much to learn,' said Ratu, as he signed a form for my room. 'But I'm sure your room will be fine.'

It was. It was large and airy and had a bathroom and a walk-in wardrobe. There was a phone on a table beside the bed and it was air conditioned. It was by far the best room I'd stayed in on my trip. And when I looked at the room rates posted on the back of the door, I discovered it was also the most expensive. I was glad I wasn't paying. Ratu was as good as his word. I spent the next three days at the Hotel Dili, taking all my meals there and having my laundry done. And I didn't have to pay a single rupiah.

I spent most of my time in Dili just walking along the promenade or sitting in the restaurants that lined the squares, falling into the rhythm of the town. But after the first day, I began to sense a tension underneath the laid back, easygoing exterior. I started to notice the armed Indonesian soldiers on every corner and the choppers that took off and landed from the military airport in the middle of the town all through the day. Down by the Mercado Municipal, a charming Portuguese market building opposite the town's busiest roundabout, there was a whole Indonesian regiment sitting in covered army trucks as if they were waiting for something to happen. The Indonesians claim that the East Timorese asked the Indonesians to liberate them. Judging by the heavy military presence in Dili, it was something they still needed reminding of.

I also noticed a lot of long-haired men in tattered clothes hanging around on the streets of Dili. Most were half-castes, and with their exotic Eurasian looks, I fancifully imagined that they were Fretilin guerrillas down from the mountains on a little R and R. They were mostly left alone—ignored by the Indonesian soldiers and passed without acknowledgment by the people of Dili going about their daily business. They had a proud and defiant stance, however, and I couldn't shake the feeling that they were more than just the town beggars.

On my last day in Dili I ventured down to the docks to see if there were any boats heading to Australia. With a bit of luck I could avoid going to Kupang altogether. The only boat in town was unloading crates of Tiger Beer from Singapore and after it had unloaded it was heading back to Singapore. The harbourmaster said they hardly ever loaded boats going to Australia. They all left from Tenau Harbour in Kupang. He suggested I would be better off trying there.

The next morning I caught the 6 o'clock bus to Kupang. It was a hot, eleven-hour journey through dry, brown mountains covered in stark, leafless trees. The scenery was oppressive and morbid, almost evil, and seemed to be sucking the life out of the people trying to scratch out an existence there. I spent the journey listening to a tape I'd bought in Bali, *Let Love In* by Nick Cave. It was the perfect soundtrack to the stifling scenes passing me by as the bus coughed and spluttered and ground its way amongst the mountains. When Nick snarled 'Do you love me?', it was if he was the land and the question was directed to God. And I can only say that the answer from the big fella upstairs was a resounding 'No!'.

Kupang is the commercial and administrative centre of the whole Nusa Tenggara region of Indonesia. As the bus wound its way towards the city, Kupang looked almost pretty. Set in hills and spilling down to the sea, it seemed to abound in pleasant, wide streets, neat government buildings and relatively well-tended gardens. But down near the harbour, in the centre of town, where brightly coloured bemos congregated with their tinny sound systems blaring, it was just another shitty Indonesian town.

I decided to stay at the Sea Breezes Homestay, a decrepit hotel on the interestingly named Jalan Ikan Tongkol (Tuna Fish Street). The rooms were pokey, with crumbling plaster, and there was a half-hearted attempt at a psychedelic mural in the bare reception. But it was right near the Kupang Yacht Club, which was where I hoped to find a yacht bound for Australia.

The hotel's owner, Abdul, was pissed already, and sat behind a desk chewing betel nut and spitting it into an old artillery shell. He had long, permed hair pulled back into a ponytail, and spoke with an annoying over-the-top Aussie accent peppered liberally with obscenities. I asked him if he knew of any boats going to Darwin.

'Mate, you're gonna have to bloody well go to fuckin' Teddy's,' he slurred. 'If there's any of the fucking yachties in town, that's where they'll be. Getting pissed!'

He laughed as if that was the funniest thing he had heard all day. From the little I'd seen of Kupang that day, it probably was. He offered to take me there and motioned me to follow him. Just outside the marina compound he stopped, straightened himself and looked at me seriously.

'You'll buy me a fuckin' beer, won't ya?' he asked.

I nodded.

'Well what are we fuckin' waiting for?' he said, slapping me on the back.

Teddy's was a bar in a thatched hut surrounded by wooden outdoor tables and chairs, just behind the marina at Kupang Yacht Club. Abdul was right. It was full of drunken Aussies from Darwin, looking for cheap sex with the ageing slappers who ambled between the tables. The women all wore skimpy lycra outfits and laughed and joked as they moved amongst the men, bending over enough to make sure the guys got a good look at their cleavage. It was a scaled-down, low-rent version of the girlie bar scenes of Manila and Bangkok.

The Aussies all looked the same—middle-aged men in shorts,

long socks and T-shirts stretched taut over huge beer bellies. They sat at the bar, clutching stubbies of beer in neoprene stubbie-holders bearing salacious slogans from pubs and nightclubs in Darwin. They all looked older than their 40 or 50 years, thanks to the harsh sun of the Top End and excessive alcohol consumption. Even worse, there wasn't a single yachtie amongst them. They were just washed-up emotional wrecks who had flown in to buy what they couldn't get back home.

When I was at the bar buying beers, I asked the barman if he knew of any yachts heading to Darwin. He shook his head.

'No, the wind's just changed,' he said. 'They're all coming up here now. You should have been here a couple of weeks ago.'

Noticing my crestfallen look, he handed me a piece of paper.

'If you want to write a note asking for a ride, I can stick it up here on the bar if you like,' he said. 'Any boats that come in, they'll see it. They always come here first.'

I scribbled a pathetic plea saying that my last hope of achieving my dream rested upon some kind-hearted captain and that I could be contacted at the Sea Breezes Homestay. One of the Aussie drinkers, his face redder and blotchier than the others, tapped me on the shoulder—with a little more strength than he intended, I'm sure—and looked at me earnestly.

'The crocs are nesting high in the Top End this year,' he slurred.

I looked at him quizzically.

'Means there'll be a big wet,' he continued, waving his free hand above his head for emphasis. 'A *big* wet! If you know what I mean!'

I didn't. But before I could ask him what that had to do with the possibility of my finding a yacht, he slumped on the bar as if giving me that piece of information had drained him of what little strength he had left.

The next morning I went to the Pelni office. I had heard lots of rumours about a Pelni service to Darwin on my way across Indonesia. And so had the guy at the counter.

'There is talk of starting a boat to Darwin,' he said, 'but there are no concrete plans. Try down at the harbour at Tenau. There are always cargo boats going to Australia. You might be able to get a passage with them.'

Tenau Harbour was about eight kilometres from town—a picturesque bemo ride along the coast past thatched huts and palm-fringed beaches spoilt only by the inordinate amount of rubbish on the sand. The bemo driver dropped me off at the boom gate in front of the port. I startled two security guards sleeping in the security box.

Once they shook off the effects of their slumber, they were like a hyper Laurel and Hardy. Each tried to outdo the other by impressing me with his limited English and super-friendliness.

'A cargo ship left for Port Hedland this morning!' the first quipped.

'But another leaves for Darwin next week,' chimed in the other. 'Perhaps you can go on that!'

'You must go to Perkins Shipping Company in town!' said the first.

'Yes! Yes!' interrupted the other, shoving a piece of paper he'd been busily scribbling on into my hand. 'Here! Here's their address!'

'They're Australian!' said the first. 'They are sure to help you!'

Then they waved down a bemo for me and spoke to the driver in Indonesian.

'He will take you straight to the office of Perkins,' said the first.

'And don't pay him more than 5,000 rupiah!' said the other.

As I drove off, they stood outside their office, waving goofily.

'Goodbye, Mr Peter!' they yelled in unison. 'And good luck!'

The Perkins Shipping Company was in a neat office on a hill overlooking Kupang. The manager—an Australian—was overseas, so his Indonesian offsider, Pieter, was in charge. He was a jovial friendly guy, but his news was not good.

'Yes, we have boats going to Australia,' he said. 'In fact we have one going to Darwin next week to pick up cattle. But I'm afraid I cannot let you aboard. Australian union regulations!'

Apparently the cargo boat was only allowed to carry a certain number of people. If they let me aboard, one of the crew members would have to stay behind. The other problem was that the boat wasn't registered or insured to take passengers. I would have to say that I was a crew member. But as an Australian, I would have to be in a union. And to join the union I would have to be in Australia. There seemed to be no way around the problem.

'It is the Australian unions that have destroyed your dream,' he said. 'In fact, they are destroying your country.'

Warming to the theme, and sounding very much like a spokesman for Australia's waterfront reforms, Pieter continued.

'Many years ago you were worried about the Communists in Australia,' he said, 'but look, with all your social security, Australia is the most Communist country in Asia!'

Then he changed tack. Now he was anticipating the line of the immigration spokesman for Australia's One Nation Party.

'It is the refugees who cause all your problems,' he said. 'All you get is the scum. You should screen your immigrants! Intellectual Asians should be allowed in to develop northwest Australia.'

He also had views on our defence expenditure.

'Why spend $300 million on an advanced warning system when you could spend that money developing the Nusa Tenggara region of Indonesia as a buffer zone!'

Afraid that he would turn into Fred Nile or the moral majority next, and start complaining about the corrupting influence of the Sydney Gay and Lesbian Mardi Gras, I turned the conversation back to other possible ways of getting to Australia.

'Why don't you try the Indonesian fishing ships?' he suggested.

'They are always fishing illegally in your waters, and they often camp in deserted bays in the northwest of Australia. Maybe one of them will drop you off on a deserted beach somewhere.'

Taking me to a map on the wall, he pointed to Roti Island, a small island off the tip of Kupang.

'Most of the fishing boats come from here,' he said, pointing to villages on the southern coast of the island. 'Go to the villages and ask around. You may be lucky.'

It was a long shot. I didn't particularly like the idea of being stranded on a beach somewhere off the Kimberley, trying to catch fish with my bare hands and eating them raw just to survive. But I thanked him for his help anyway. The way things were shaping up, it could be my best chance.

That night I went to Teddy's to check if anyone had responded to my notice. The barman shook his head and said that I shouldn't hold my breath. I was contemplating changing the notice to include the words 'Will pay handsomely' when I was cornered by a drunken Aussie. He asked me what part of England I was from, and didn't seem particularly perturbed when I told him I was from Sydney. It seems he just wanted someone to talk to.

'I'm in town to get married,' he slurred. 'Let me buy you a drink!'

I knew I was in dangerous territory. A drunk. A story. A beer. But before I could extricate myself, the barman had opened a stubbie and placed it in front of me.

'Yeah, an Indonesian girl,' he said, getting all misty-eyed. 'So tight I can hardly get me dick in!'

I spluttered, choking on my beer.

'Not like those Aussie girls, eh?' he said, slapping me on the back as if I was his closest confidant. 'I stick my finger in and tell her I'm just making it bigger!'

I never quite know what to do in these situations. Should I get all indignant about this guy speaking about women in such a demeaning manner and storm off? Or should I join in and secure an evening of free beer for myself? That night I sat meekly drinking my beer, hoping that if I kept quiet and didn't encourage him, he would just shut up. It didn't work.

'Did I tell you about the first time she gave me a head job?' he asked, shaking his head and smiling at the memory of it. 'When I started moaning she ran off, frightened. Thought there was something wrong with me!'

I felt like telling him there was something wrong with him. It can't be natural to have an uncontrollable urge to tell complete strangers the intimate details of your life.

'I could never marry an Australian girl,' he said. 'Always telling *you* what do. I prefer it the other way!'

I spotted Abdul staggering in and used him as my excuse to extricate myself from this living *Penthouse* Forum page. I didn't like Abdul, and I didn't like listening to his fake Aussie accent, but it had to be better than listening to this guy.

I told Abdul about the fishing boat plan and asked him what he thought. He was not impressed. One of his best friends was the captain on an Indonesian fishing boat.

'That cunt's always getting caught by the Australian Navy,' he said. 'He just tells the bastards that he didn't know he had strayed into Australian waters, that it was all a big fuckin' mistake. How's he gonna explain having a fuckin' Aussie on board?'

Abdul was right. No Indonesian fishing captain in his right mind would take an Australian passenger on board. It would mean landing on Australian soil, not just fishing in Australian waters. If he got caught, his boat—his livelihood—would be impounded and burnt. (The Australian government had just made quite a show of torching captured Indonesian fishing boats on a deserted beach near Darwin.) And he'd probably end up in an Australian jail.

Yet another plan scuttled. I'd only been in Kupang for two days and I had received more conflicting stories, followed more false leads and heard more outright lies than Mulder and Scully do in an entire season of 'The X Files'. But no matter which way I looked at it, the bottom line remained the same: there were no boats—not any I could catch, anyway—going from Kupang to Darwin.

Only 483 kilometres separated me from my homeland and my dream of travelling overland from London to Sydney without flying. After getting through Iran, after getting into Tibet, after talking my way across the Chinese–Laotian border, I fell at the last hurdle.

I would have to fly to Darwin after all.

CHAPTER TWENTY-THREE

Kakadu

Soundtrack: *All I wanna do*—Sheryl Crow

I knew I was home the moment I arrived at Darwin International Airport. Even in the tropical far north, the customs and immigration hall had a distinctly Australian look about it. You could see it in the counters, designed by committee to be bland and non-confronting. You could sense it in the air conditioning, set to a level determined by extensive research to provide maximum comfort. You could read it in the government literature, translated into every language on the planet. You could even smell it in the disinfectant, chosen because its aroma offended the fewest people. But the biggest giveaway was when I noticed that all the immigration officers were wearing long socks with their tailored shorts.

Margaret Thatcher once said that Australians should be bloody thankful they were colonised by the British and not by the Spanish or any of the other superpowers who'd been sniffing around the coastline in the late 1700s. Her point, I think, was that the British endowed their colonies with infrastructure that would stand them in good stead for the way the world developed and a language that became the international language of business and diplomacy. As an Australian, I know they left us with something else, something a little less useful: a meddlesome, well-meaning bureaucracy, hamstrung by its own attempts to be politically correct.

Of course that day I found it all strangely reassuring. I had grown up with Australian bureaucracy and had adopted the distinctively Australian approach to it—I ignored it. It didn't *really* affect my life, and if some government official in some sterile office in Canberra got off on creating these bizarrely inoffensive environments, well that was his problem. Like all Australians, I had also learnt to take a similarly blasé approach to the draconian immigration and customs forms I had to fill in every time I came back into the country. In the section that asked me if I was on drugs, had TB, had a criminal record or had ever been accused of being of unsound mind, I simply ticked 'no'. If I could give one piece of advice to international visitors to Australia who are freaked out by these forms, it would be this: don't admit to anything.

I spent my first night back in my country of birth in a dorm full of Swedes, Americans, Brits and Germans in a hostel called Ivan's on Mitchell Street. The hostel was an old motel—each dorm a room where the beds had been ripped out and replaced by bunks—and it had a swimming pool and a restaurant that sold $2 roast dinners and cheap beer. At midnight the air conditioner in my room caught fire and we all milled around the pool until the smoke cleared.

I spent the next day wandering around Darwin. It's a small, neat town with pastel-coloured government buildings and a brand new cultural centre. It had malls and ATMs and pubs that had familiar beers on tap. Everywhere I looked, I came upon reminders that I was in my homeland—a Coles New World Supermarket here, a Lowes Menswear there, even all the banks. In all the time I'd spent away, I never expected to get all sentimental and nostalgic over a National Australia Bank logo.

From Darwin, my plan was to head south to Alice Springs and Adelaide, then west to Sydney, my home. Before I left Darwin, though, I really wanted to visit Kakadu National Park. For Australians, Kakadu is a place that resonates with both natural and cultural significance. It was one of the first places in Australia to achieve a world heritage listing *and* most of *Crocodile Dundee* was filmed there. It is also a place that resonates with romance. When I was at university, many a relationship blossomed under a hand-painted sign crying 'Export Fraser, not uranium'. The mining of the park was *the* big protest issue on campus. Now that it seems the Federal Government will allow the Jabiluka mine to go ahead, it will probably have the same resonance for a whole new generation.

The trouble is, Kakadu is also huge. At over 19,000 square kilometres, it's one of the biggest national parks in Australia. Elsewhere in the world, such vast areas and distances aren't such a problem. There seem to be human settlements everywhere and there always seems to be a bus or a van or a bicycle to take you there. But in Australia, there are lots of huge empty spaces. And a lot of places are hundreds, sometimes thousands of kilometres from even the slightest hint of civilisation. Kakadu National Park is one of those places. If I wanted to see even a fraction of the wonders it had to offer, I'd have to take a tour.

And I'm not a great tour taker. I guess I baulk at having someone tell me what to do. But in the end I swallowed my pride and decided to go on an all-terrain four-day eco-tour to Kakadu. The brochure assured me that they only conducted small group tours with an emphasis on the flora and fauna of Kakadu. It claimed that even if I wasn't someone who usually 'did' tours I would enjoy the eco-tour because it was aimed at the adventure traveller looking for an 'experience', not just a sightseeing trip. What's more, my guide would be well-versed in all aspects of Kakadu's unique environment, and dedicated to educating visitors about Kakadu whilst preserving it for all to enjoy.

I regretted my choice the moment Dave, the tour leader, turned up at Ivan's at 7 am in his white Toyota Landcruiser troop carrier. As I took my place on the bench seats that lined the side of the car, I noticed two things that immediately disturbed me. Of the nine of us on the tour, I was the only one who wasn't a German, and secondly, the other eight were couples.

Dave was a bit of a worry, too. Although he looked the part in his khaki shorts and Akubra hat, he had an earnestness that bordered on the pathological. Everything along the side of the road was described in painstaking detail, from road signs to telegraph poles, right down to why a particular mix had been used for the asphalt on the road. My fellow travellers loved it. I seemed to be on a school excursion that only the nerds had been invited on.

Our 45-minute extended stop to look at the termite nests that dotted the countryside along the road to Kakadu was the perfect example of the purgatory to which I had been condemned. I'd always thought the idea of a two metre high termites nest was pretty cool. But after a cursory explanation of why they built them so high—termite mounds are ingenious constructions oriented to avoid the full heat of the sun and, a piece of trivia, they always face magnetic north—I was ready to take a few photos and move on. The Germans, however, wanted to know more.

'So vot you are saying,' said Hans, the tall one and the designated spokesman for the group, 'zey verk on an almost hierarchical level, ja?'

It got worse when we crossed the Alligator River.

'Vhy are zey called ze Alligator River ven zey are full of crocodiles?' asked the Germans.

'Two theories,' said Dave, warming to the challenge. 'One is that the naval officers charting this area confused the crocs with American alligators. The second is that the name comes from the HMS *Alligator*, one of the ships that surveyed the estuaries of Van Diemen Gulf in 1837.'

Regardless of which theory you subscribe to, the East Alligator River also marks the boundary of Kakadu National Park, and a sign beside the highway announces the fact. To be honest, it didn't look that different from the open grassy woodlands we'd been driving through since Darwin. The swampy wetlands I always associated with Kakadu didn't appear until we had crossed the two branches of the Wildman River. By that time, thanks to the endless questioning of the Germans at each stop, it was late in the afternoon. We set up camp beside a peaceful billabong at Mardugal in the last rays of the afternoon sun.

The Germans set about pitching their tents in the same detailed manner in which they had asked questions, brushing the ground clear of any stones that could cause discomfort during the night and scouring the trees overhead to see if there were any branches that might fall during the night.

'Hans was nearly killed by a falling branch in the Daintree,' explained Helga when she caught me shaking my head in disbelief. I doubted, however, that even that would have shut him up.

After our camp was ready, Dave drove us eight kilometres down a dirt track to Cooinda and Yellow Waters billabong. I don't want to appear a nationalistic Aussie—God knows we're world leaders in the sport—but Yellow Waters was one of the most beautiful places I have ever visited. It was a vast wetland, a waterway snaking its way through waterlilies and bull rushes, dotted with delicate white flowers and hundreds and thousands of water birds. As the sun sank lower over a distant line of eucalypts, the sky turned every shade of orange imaginable, before deciding on a dark tangerine with rather audacious slashes of pink. The sun finally disappearing behind the trees was the cue for the magpie geese and egrets to flap lazily in silhouette into the night. The signs warning about the dangers of crocodiles were the only discordant note, giving the place a sinister feel.

Just as the orange was fading towards darkness, another Landcruiser troop carrier—a little more beat up and ill-kempt than ours—drove recklessly into the car park and screeched to a halt. A bunch of equally ill-kempt backpackers piled out, led by a tour guide who looked like a cross between Crocodile Dundee and Sir Les Patterson.

'I told you we'd miss the sunset, you bunch of pissheads,' he yelled. 'Get yer arses into gear. Tomorrow, no beer until after lunch!'

'Pisspot tours!' hissed Dave. 'Or, as we like to say, Kakadu by the carton. British backpackers, mainly. The amount of beer they consume, I'd be surprised if they even remember they were here!'

The backpackers from Pisspot Tours at least looked like they were having fun. They staggered down the boat ramp—a can of Victoria Bitter in each hand—and splashed about in the water. They either didn't notice the crocodile warning sign or were too sozzled to care. The Germans shook their heads, tutting and sneering in a manner they usually reserved for those countries in the EU that can't meet the monetary requirements of the EMU. Dave gathered us together and hustled us off to our Landcruiser, trying to protect us from their bad influence. The Germans were happy to leave, but I couldn't help looking over my shoulder, watching the others and wishing I was on their tour.

The next morning I woke early and walked down to the billabong near our campsite. It was calm, and a mist hung over the still water. A few birds croaked at each other. It was a magical moment of solitude that was spoiled too soon—two of the Germans powerwalked by, obviously doing their daily exercise.

'You should be careful near ze water!' they warned. 'Ze crocodiles may be hungry, ja?'

I thanked them, but inside I was muttering, 'I should be so lucky!'

The itinerary on our first full day in Kakadu saw us visiting the Aboriginal rock paintings at both Ubirr and Nourlangie Rock. Ubirr featured the famous X-ray style of Aboriginal paintings as well as paintings detailing first contact with white men. The invaders were painted with firearms and axes as well as with their hands in their pockets. I liked the fact that, to the Aboriginal artists at least, pockets were as much a notable difference in the newcomers as the ability to shoot and kill. From here we drove to Nourlangie, where we clambered up the huge rocky escarpment onto the ridge that was famous both for its spectacular view over the park towards Arnhem Land and because it was the spot where Paul Hogan twirled the bullroarer in *Crocodile Dundee*.

Next we cantered along the half kilometre circuit to the Aboriginal art sites at Anbangbang Shelter and Anbangbang Gallery. The gallery was brought to world attention in 1962 by David Attenborough, and is famous especially for its painting of Narmarrgon, the Lightning Man, a cool looking guy with lightning zapping between his head and feet, and stone axes poking out of his head, knees and elbows. It also featured paintings of a couple of other Aboriginal spirits and family groups of men and their wives heading off to a ceremony. It was hard to look at these pictures and not feel you were looking at something from the dawn of time.

'So how old iz zees pictures?' asked Hans.

'Well, the paintings can't be dated exactly,' said Dave, 'but the evidence suggests that some paintings could be more than 20,000 years old, making them some of the oldest human works in the world.'

The Germans nodded and aaahed and seemed genuinely impressed.

'But why are zey so bright?' asked Hans, not convinced.

'Oh, the Aborigines still touch them up,' explained Dave. 'Sometimes they add new paintings. See that one over there? It was painted in 1985.'

Hans was outraged.

'They are not old, zen. Zey are only as old as ze last time zey were touched up!' he said indignantly.

'If they didn't touch them up they would have disappeared centuries ago,' argued Dave. 'They get damaged by water and before they got rid of the buffaloes up here, they'd come and rub against them!'

Hans was not to be swayed. I wondered how he would have reacted if he had found out that the Aborigines sometimes mixed washing powder into the paint to make the whites whiter. Dave continued to argue the case for touching up, saying they did the same thing in the Sistine Chapel. The discussion was cut short when the drunks from Pisspot Tours turned up at the gallery.

'Look!' yelled one, pointing at Namarrgon the Lightning Man. 'It's an Abo Power Ranger!'

On our second day in Kakadu we drove along a bumpy, sandy road through stands of eucalypts to Jim Jim Falls. Here the sheer majesty of the towering sandstone escarpment and thundering waterfall left the Germans awe-struck, and shut them up for a while. From Jim Jim Falls we floated on air mattresses through the gorge to Twin Falls. The Germans approached the whole exercise with typical Teutonic precision and were soon stroking in swift methodical time as Hans barked 'Links, links, links, recht, links . . .' In true Australian fashion, I just lay back and let the river take me along to Twin Falls.

Twin Falls was a natural amphitheatre of tranquillity and gorgeousness. Below the falls and to the right was a sandy bar where we pulled up our mattresses and lazed about, our feet still dangling in the water. Dave pointed to a spot 25 metres up the canyon.

'See that grey line there,' he said. 'That's the water level in the wet season.'

It was extraordinary. In another month or two this whole area would be covered by enough water to swallow up a 20-storey build-ing. It was hard to comprehend the transformation that would take place. At the moment, we could still float around gazing up at the walls of the canyon, listening to the thundering of the waterfall that, according to Dave, was only operating at a fraction of its capacity.

Just after lunch, Dave led us up a path beside the waterfall. After scrambling over rocks and under eucalyptus trees for 40 minutes, we came to the top of the falls. From here we could look down upon the pool below or up the gorge and across the enormous plains and escarpments of the park. For a fleeting moment it was as if we were the only people in the world, forgotten souls in a huge vast land. Then, at the far end of the escarpment, we saw nine shapes floating towards the waterfall. At first I thought it might have been crocodiles, but it turned out to be more exciting than that.

'It's ze drunks!' spat one of the Germans. 'Zey have invaded our paradise again!'

By the time we made our way back down to the lagoon, the Pisspot Tours brigade had arrived and were lounging around the sandbar or floating listlessly on their air mattresses, with a can of beer resting on their bellies. (They had devoted one whole air mat-tress to transporting an esky full of beer.) They were surprisingly subdued. Most it seems, were nursing hangovers.

'What's it like up there?' one inquired.

'Pretty good,' I answered nonchalantly. I wanted to say how wonderfully spectacular it was, but I didn't want to appear as dorky as the rest of my group.

'I'll have to take your word for it,' he moaned. 'I can hardly take a piss today I'm so buggered.'

'Yeah, I know how you feel,' I answered unconvincingly. I wished I was too buggered to take a piss as well. And I wished I was on a tour where the only question being asked was 'Where's the beers?'.

'Want a beer?' he asked, as if he'd read my mind.

I would have loved to join in, but I had to decline. Dave and the Germans were packing up in disgust. I felt like someone who had been accepted into the cool group at the school dance just as his parents turned up to take him home.

'Nah, I gotta go,' I said, motioning towards the Germans with upturned eyes. 'Maybe some other time.'

When he answered, 'Yeah, whatever', I knew I'd been written off as just as big a loser as the rest of my group. Not for the first time, I cursed going on a bloody politically correct eco-tour.

On our final morning in Kakadu, we returned to Yellow Waters to take a boat cruise on the billabong. All the tour groups in Kakadu—including Pisspot Tours—took the cruise in a big aluminium vessel that could take 30 or 40 people at a time. The tour guides used the cruise as a chance to take a break; they let the guide steering the boat do all the talking and answer all the questions. The Germans, being Germans, hurried aboard to get the best seats, up front.

'Entschuldigen,' one asked the guide, slopping on sunscreen and then spraying himself with insecticide as he spoke, 'will zis tour be going clockvise or anti-clockwise?'

'I dunno, mate,' said the guide. 'We just go up that way, turn right and then chuck a uey.'

The German looked up at the sky, calculating the path of the sun's trajectory, then chose the seats on the right-hand side of the boat, figuring that that side would get the least amount of sun. There wasn't enough room for me, so I went and sat with the drunken Poms. They were sitting in the hottest and least protected part of the boat, using the cruise as an opportunity to work on their tans. Beside them they had their trusty esky full of ice-cold beer.

The boat cruised through spectacular wetlands, past nesting birds and through fields of lily pads. The highlight of the cruise was spotting a giant croc, four metres long, sunning itself on the bank. When it opened its mouth everyone gasped, and enough film was exposed to keep Kodak in business well into the next century. Even Hans was momentarily lost for words. The only ones not impressed were the drunken tourists from Pisspot Tours. They'd stopped at Adelaide River Crossing on the way to Kakadu and had seen the world famous jumping crocodiles.

'They were fookin' brilliant, mate,' one of them said, with a thick cockney accent. 'They jump out of the water like a pair of performing dolphins. You gotta see it, mate!'

After the cruise, we were heading back to Darwin. I asked Dave if we could stop at Adelaide River Crossing and check out the famous jumping crocodiles on the way back. It wasn't part of our tour, but I hoped Dave would accommodate my whim.

'I'll ask the others. If they're willing, we'll stop,' he said.

'Nein, nein,' said Hans, ever the leader. 'Ve vill not be party to such cruelty. Ve came to Kakadu to see nature in its natural environment. Not to zee some animals performing like zey are in ze circus!'

And so disappeared my last chance of a little bit of politically incorrect fun in Kakadu.

CHAPTER TWENTY-FOUR

Uluru

Soundtrack: *The Right Time*—Hoodoo Gurus

I travelled the 1,500 kilometres from Darwin to Ayers Rock via Alice Springs in a Coaster driven by Jason, a 24-year-old guy from the western suburbs of Sydney. The Coaster was part of a service offered by a chain of backpacker hostels in the Northern Territory. They recognised that a lot of backpackers didn't want to simply barrel down the Stuart Highway to Alice Springs on a Greyhound bus. They wanted to barrel down the Stuart Highway *and* visit places like Katherine Gorge, Mataranka Springs, Tennant Creek, the Devils Marbles and Ayers Rock along the way. Instead of one day, the trip took five—but that included a two-day side-trip to Ayers Rock. As an added bonus, the trip also included 'expert' commentary from Jason.

I was the only other Australian on the bus. The other 15 passengers were a motley collection of backpackers, Europeans mainly, who had come to Australia to escape the approaching winter. They were so different from one another that I wondered how the whole concept of the European Union continued to work. Within a day, the passengers had settled into three distinct groups, largely along national lines—Germans, Italians and Brits. Two Danish girls joined the British contingent, as did Sylvia, a German who was shunned by the main German group because she actually had a sense of humour. Naturally, as a colonial, I was part of the British group.

The divisions between the groups were mostly linguistic, but they were territorial as well. The bus was carved up like Europe at Yalta after World War II. The Germans took the front of the bus, talking amongst themselves and asking Jason questions incessantly. The group of young Italian girls annexed four seats in the middle, laughing amongst themselves and swapping Walkmans. The Brits took the rest, lounging around the back of the bus sleeping, drinking and taunting the Germans about the 1966 World Cup.

The division also manifested itself in the tapes each group chose to play on the bus's cassette player. At first, Jason put his own music on. He had a collection of classic rock not dissimilar from the tripe played by radio stations—Pink Floyd, Creedence Clearwater Revival, The Rolling Stones, and The Beatles—that he liked to play as he drove through what was essentially an endless stretch of red dirt and rocks. But distances being what they are in the Northern Territory, it didn't take long for him to go through all his tapes. On the second day he foolishly agreed to let us take turns and put our stuff on.

It was not one of Jason's better ideas. The Germans played Celine Dion, the Italians played crappy Euro-cheese. The British contingent—buoyed by the heady days of Britpop—insisted on playing Oasis, Blur and Pulp. Each choice caused a commotion of complaint and moaning from the other two groups, which did nothing to foster a spirit of goodwill amongst European nations. It also got dangerous. When one of the Brits nearly sent us careering off the side of the road in an attempt to reef out a Celine Dion cassette from the cassette player, Jason brought peace to the bus by pretending that the cassette player was broken.

The first major town we came upon after leaving Darwin was Katherine. This spot first came to prominence when an Overland Telegraph Office was built there in 1871. Not that Jason told us that. Nor did he tell us that the town was the headquarters of the School of the Air, the unique radio service that provides lessons for children isolated on the huge cattle stations in the Northern Territory. I found out all that in my guidebook. The only time Jason said anything of note was when he asked us what sort of beer we wanted to buy from the town's supermarket (before we headed east for 30 kilometres off the Stuart Highway to Katherine Gorge). I decided to make a note of all the interesting facts Jason forgot to tell us and number them.

Katherine Gorge is the main attraction in the Nitmiluk National Park. It's actually 13 different gorges cut into the sandstone by the Katherine River. The gorges are separated from each other by rapids which form divides of rocks and boulders when the water level drops in the dry season. The river is 11 kilometres long, and in the wet, when the river is in full flow, it can rise as much as 18 metres. The walls of the gorges are the red weathered sandstone common in these parts and, while not as high as some of the areas in Kakadu, are every bit as spectacular.

Important fact not imparted by Jason No. 3: The traditional owners of Katherine Gorge, the Jawoyn, believe that the gorge was formed in the Dreamtime when an ancestral goanna-person came here to eat insects and was speared to death. It was his bleeding that created the river.

We camped overnight at Katherine Gorge and the next morning, as part of the Coaster service south, we hired canoes to take a closer look at the gorge. It wasn't long before the divisions within the group became apparent again. The Germans took their time, gazing up at the sheer sandstone walls and marvelling at their beauty. The Italian girls reached the first rapids, decided that dragging the canoes over the rocks was too much like hard work, so gave up, and swam and sunbaked there. We of the British contingent, a competitive bunch, decided to race. By the time we reached the fourth gorge we were too buggered to continue, and were content to laze on some rocks in the sun. Ian, a guy from Finsbury Park, found a high ledge and soon we were all doing bombs into the water.

That afternoon Jason drove us to Mataranka, 103 kilometres further south. On a Northern Territorian scale it was just down the road and, after setting our tents up in the neat campground, we made our way to the springs for a swim. The springs were the closest thing to a perfect oasis I have ever seen—a clear crystal pool, spa warm, and surrounded by palm trees. They were also therapeutic, soothing the aches and strains brought about by racing the canoes in the gorge. The only blight was the hundreds of fruit bats that hung in the tree screeching and using the area below the trees as a urinal. Sylvia swam over to the ledge I was sitting on and sat beside me.

'It is so beautiful here,' she cooed, 'We have nothing like this in Germany. You are so lucky to be an Australian.'

The fact was, Sylvia had as much chance of coming back here as I did. It's not as if Sydney is just down the road. I was going to comment on this—and the smell of bat piss as well—but decided to simply smile instead.

Important fact not imparted by Jason No. 47: Next to our camp-site at Mataranka—I probably passed it on my way up to the shop to buy an ice cream—stood a replica of the hand-hewn Elsey Homestead used for the film We of the Never Never.

The next day we were to put some serious kilometres behind us. We broke camp early and headed south towards Daly Waters and Tennant Creek on a straight, sealed road across dry, dusty plains. The journey was largely uneventful except for a squabble that broke out between the Brits and the Germans over Kraftwerk—the Germans claimed that they were the pioneers of the whole Electronica genre, and the Brits disagreed, arguing (unconvincingly) that it was guys like Gary Numan who had led the way. Jason effectively killed the argument stone dead when he said that they were all wrong—it was an Australian haircut band called Real Life who had started it all with 'Send Me An Angel'.

By lunchtime we had reached Daly Waters and the Daly Waters Pub. In fact, they were one and the same. The Daly Waters Pub was built in 1893 and serves as the bank, post office and police station for the small community around it. The Coaster had barely come to a stop outside it when we were greeted by one of the inhabitants, a young guy in dirty jeans and boots and a beat up Akubra hat.

'G'day,' he said, in the broadest of accents. 'Don't just sit in the bus. Come and drink some piss!'

He introduced himself as Troy—a name which seemed strangely inappropriate for the Australian outback—and said he worked on a cattle station a couple of hundred kilometres away. I think he fancied his chances with the girls—especially the two Danes—because he made quite a show of helping them off the bus and leading them into the pub. When he spotted my long hair he feigned disgust.

'Where are you from? Woodstock?' Then he laughed. 'Get a haircut!'

Inside the pub he shoved two other cowboys off some stools, dusted the stools off and presented them to the girls. It seemed he was in Daly Waters for a big rodeo in two days' time.

'I was saying to me mates,' Troy explained, 'I reckon I'm a pretty good chance at the bucking bronco.'

The backpackers, particularly the Germans, lapped it up. They had now met a genuine Aussie, their own Crocodile Dundee. The rest of us Aussies were just wusses from the cities, he said. It's stockmen like him who are the *real* Aussies. At first I thought Troy was putting it on, exaggerating, acting out a part and giving the tourists what they wanted. But after a while, I came to the conclusion that Troy may well have been 'fair dinkum'.

The pub was definitely fair dinkum. At various points around Australia you'll find Aussie theme pubs full of franchised Australiana and built in the grand Australian architectural tradition of the outdoor dunny. But they are just cartoon caricatures. The Daly Waters Pub was the real thing. The back wall, just behind the pool table, was covered with stubbie coolers from all over Australia. Over the bar there was a mounted cow pat with the inscription 'Genuine NT bullshit', and a collection of posters and stickers full of the sort of sophisticated humour Australia has become famous for. My favourite was the picture of a caterpillar mounting a crinkle-cut fry. The chip had a caption that said 'Cut it out, arsehole. I'm a French Fry!'

After we had finished our mandatory beer, we ate lunch on the tables outside—basically some sandwiches thrown together with what was left in the eskies. Troy came over to see what we were having and turned up his nose.

'Call this food?' he sniffed. 'Are you vegies or something?'

Spotting me again, he pointed an accusing finger.

'It's you bloody long hairs, innit?' he accused. 'You've probably even got lentils.'

After his tirade he sat down at the table and put his beer down. When he was sure he had the attention of all the girls, he started a little story.

'On the station,' he said softly, 'we have five rump steaks each and a whole wad of onions . . .'

We were rescued from more of this by one of the Germans, who spotted a galah drinking beer out of a can. All of a sudden Troy wasn't the most interesting Australian oddity any more.

After lunch we left Daley Waters for the Devils Marbles. As we wandered back towards the Coaster, a coachload of Australian pensioners arrived, and Troy abandoned us to try his Aussie charm on them.

'These are the people that built this country!' Troy called back to the Danish girls. Then he returned his attention to the pensioners and began his spiel, albeit altered slightly.

'G'day,' he said to them, using his broad accent again. 'Don't just sit in the bus. Come and drink some . . . um . . . have a tipple!'

The old ladies with wisteria hair tittered.

Important fact not imparted by Jason No. 79: Daly Waters was an important staging post in the early days of aviation. Amy Johnson landed here, and it was also used by the Queensland and Northern Territory Air Service, the fledgling airline that later became Qantas.

According to Aboriginal legend, the Devils Marbles, giant spherical boulders perched atop a slight ridge, are in fact eggs laid by the Rainbow Serpent. After seeing them that afternoon, silhouetted against the setting sun, I could tell it must have been a bloody big snake. I clambered amongst them, posing for the inevitable photos where it looked like I was stopping them rolling away—right up there with the shot of me holding up the Leaning Tower of Pisa—before returning to our campsite to drink copious amounts of alcohol around a spluttering fire.

We spent the next day travelling across flat red desert to Alice Springs. We stopped briefly at a roadhouse where Aborigines sold boomerangs and corroboree sticks and refused to have their photos taken, and then at the monument marking the point where the Tropic of Capricorn crossed the Stuart Highway. After travelling

around the Equator and seeing a number of monuments thrown up
to celebrate it in various corners of the world, I was keen to see
how my country celebrated this cartographical oddity. I am pleased
to say that it was done with style and dignity. Better still, the most
interesting aspect of the monument, a goat symbolising the Capricorn astrological sign, had been desecrated in a peculiarly Australian
manner. Some wag had painted Ronald McDonald with his clown
pants around his ankles doing unnatural things to the poor creature.
I was so impressed that I got Sylvia to take my photo next to it.

After spending the night in a backpacker hostel in Alice Springs,
we headed off on our complimentary two-day side trip to Ayers
Rock, 445 kilometres away. Ayers Rock—or Uluru, as its traditional owners, the Anangu, prefer to call it—is regarded as one of
the natural wonders of the world. Rising dramatically from the flat,
red expanse of the landscape around it, it is 348 metres high,
1.3 kilometres long and has a circumference of over 8 kilometres.
In many ways it's just a bloody big rock. But for a bloody big
rock, it has quite a hold on the Australian national psyche.

I remember when I was in Year 12—probably only six months
after I'd got my driver's licence—I had a hare-brained idea to drive
to Ayers Rock and back during the Easter holidays with a class-
mate called Andy Barton. I don't know where the idea came from—
maybe we'd seen some documentary on TV—but it grabbed our
imaginations and wouldn't let go. We made the mistake of telling
Mr Purvis, our Ancient History teacher, about our plan, and he said
we were mad. He even threatened to tell the principal if we went
ahead with it. I'm not sure now what it had to do with the principal,
but it must have been a pretty convincing argument because we
gave up the idea of going. It was either that or we simply did our
sums and realised that we couldn't afford the petrol needed for the
5,500 kilometre round trip.

The next time Ayers Rock entered my life was in 1980, when
Lindy Chamberlain cried 'A dingo's got my baaaby!' Lindy was

the wife of a Seventh Day Adventist minister, and it wasn't long before the whole nation was convinced that she, not a dingo, had killed her baby Azaria. Seventh Day Adventism being something of a fringe denomination, the media was soon full of all kinds of fanciful suggestions—the name Azaria meant 'sacrifice in the desert'; the Chamberlains had a tiny black coffin in their garage; all Seventh Day Adventists kill their newborn babies.

I had been brought up as a Seventh Day Adventist, so I knew that a lot of what the media was saying was a load of hysterical crap—well, the one about them killing their newborn anyway. To be truthful, Seventh Day Adventism is just your average Protestant religion, but it holds its church services on Saturday and has a strong emphasis on health issues. The coffin they found in the Chamberlains' garage was in all likelihood part of one of the anti-smoking campaigns the church is always running. (If you ever get the chance to go along to a Seventh Day Adventist anti-smoking program, do. It's worth it just to see Smoking Sam, a dummy that smokes cigarettes. He has two glass jars filled with cotton wool as lungs, and they turn black after just one cigarette. It certainly had an effect on me. I've never smoked a single cigarette in my life.)

Still, it was a lot of fun to see how the Seventh Day Adventists reacted to the whole situation. They started a legal fighting fund and tried to counter a lot of the misinformation appearing in the press. But to be honest, I think they secretly loved it. By their interpretation of the Bible, they were the 'true church', and in the days of the end—the Second Coming, that is—the true church would be persecuted. The whole Azaria Chamberlain kerfuffle could have meant Jesus was about to show.

Of course, I was only seeing this from the outside. I had left the church and gone 'worldly' three years earlier—defying my parents and going to the 1977 Grand Final replay between St George and Parramatta. (God must have been less concerned than my parents by my indiscretion because my team, St George, won 22–0.) My parents stopped making me go to church and I only attended irregularly, and that was to see my friends and meet girls.

But in my mind, Azaria—and Australia's morbid fascination with her disappearance—was inextricably linked to Ayers Rock and served to strengthen its hold on the nation's psyche—and mine as well.

When I first set eyes on Ayers Rock late that afternoon, it did not disappoint me. It looked exactly like it does in the photos. No, it was better than the photos. Photos don't capture the awesome size or the brooding silence. Ayers Rock was actually better than I expected. Years of travel have taught me that this is a very rare phenomenon indeed. The Little Mermaid in Copenhagen was smaller than I expected, and, disappointingly, only a metre from shore, so every Italian tourist could jump on her and fondle her breasts. Trevi Fountain was less lavish. Only two other wonders of the world have also lived up to the hype: the Pyramids in Egypt and the Taj Mahal in India.

Jason parked the Coaster in the car park at the sunset viewing area on the west side of the Rock. Although sunset was still a good hour or so away, the car park already looked like Woolworths on a Saturday morning. The perimeter fence was lined with people waiting, resting their zoom lenses on the wooden posts. Other more adventurous souls set up tripods on the roofs of their cars. Some, in panel vans, lowered the back door and lay in the back just watching. A lot of people obviously wanted a soundtrack for the occasion—the car park was a cacophony of Mozart, Yothu Yindi, Midnight Oil, Icehouse and, frighteningly, Michael Bolton. I was just thankful that no one was playing 'Solid Rock' by Goanna. Then I really would have lost it.

I'd seen the time-lapse photography of the Rock changing colour—as has anyone who has ever seen any nature program on Australia—but nothing really prepares you for the occasion. It's as if God is trying out a series of colour swatches to see what colour goes best with the blue sky and the red earth. The sun finally sank below the horizon, leaving the sky a deep blue-black and the Rock nothing more than a brooding silhouette.

On the way back to the campground at Yulara, the tourist complex 18 kilometres from the Rock, we stopped to get our nightly case of beer. As Jason and I walked towards the bottle shop, an Aboriginal man appeared out of the bushes and offered us $100 to buy him a case of beer.

'You can keep the change, brudder,' he slurred. 'Just get us a case, VB, Foster's, I don't care.'

Jason brushed him aside and walked quickly into the bottle shop. I couldn't believe he let such an easy moneymaking opportunity slip.

'Not worth it,' he explained. 'If you get caught it's a massive fine, maybe even jail. It's illegal for the Aborigines to buy grog.'

I didn't know that. I would have been tempted to take up the guy's offer. I christened the advice *Useful fact imparted by Jason No. 1*.

The next day we woke at 5 am and climbed Ayers Rock. Jason explained the significance of the route the climb took; how it followed the path the Mala men (ancestors of the traditional landowners) had taken when they planted a ceremonial pole on the top of the Rock, when they first arrived from the west. He explained that the Anangu regarded the Rock as sacred, and would prefer that people didn't climb. Some of the Germans looked a little uneasy, but in the end no one in the group decided against climbing. It was just something we all felt compelled to do.

It was still dark when we began the climb, and the chain handrail marking the start of the climb—and the steepest part of the ascent— glowed in the moonlight in the hour before dawn. The path to the cairn that marks the highest point of the Rock is 1.6 kilometres long. But it is the first 500 metres that are the hardest—an almost vertical climb up smooth rock. Beyond that, the path became easier

380 THE WRONG WAY HOME

to climb and the white dotted line (it looked like the dotted line on coupons) was also easier to follow. Ours was the first group to start the climb, and soon Sylvia, Ian and I forged ahead, keen to get to the cairn before anyone else.

Soon we were making our way across the top of the Rock. It wasn't as smooth and flat as it looks in the photos; it is a series of ridges and valleys, dips and ravines. If it wasn't for the white line, you could very easily get lost and maybe even tumble over the edge. It was also windy and bitterly cold.

We reached the cairn just as the sun peaked over the horizon in the east. To be honest, the view from the top was nothing compared to the view of the Rock from the ground. But there was something overwhelmingly spiritual about watching the land come to life from the highest part of its dry heart. Sylvia, Ian and I danced a little jig, not unlike the drunken circle dance at the party all those months ago in Clapham.

CHAPTER TWENTY-FIVE

Sydney

Soundtrack: 'Knuckle Too Far'—James

I left Alice Springs on a McCafferty's bus bound for Sydney via
Adelaide. The sensible thing to do would have been to break the
journey in Adelaide, but after eight months on the road, I was tired
and I wanted to get home. I'm sure my mother was also rather keen
to put an the end to the whole charade of pretending not to know
where I was and that she wasn't worried about my wellbeing.

The road south out of Alice Springs was straight and unremark-
able, the landscape as flat and sparse as anything I had seen in the
Northern Territory. Remarkably, after the bus crossed the South
Australian border, everything became even bleaker and sparser. It
was flat, an incredibly *flat* flat—broken only by the odd commu-
nications tower—and I was overwhelmed by the vast emptiness of
my country. Like 95 per cent of Australians, I am a coastal dweller.
I always kind of had an idea that there was this huge sullen nothingness over my shoulder, brooding behind my back. But in a city,

with the coast on one side and a mountain range on the other, I could kid myself that everything was neat and controllable.

Soon the sun set and a full cheddar-yellow moon rose, illuminating the vast open plains. I stared out of the bus window, taking stock of my life, listening to my Walkman. As often happens, the scenery, the moon and my mood synchronised perfectly with the song playing—'Knuckle Too Far', by James. I should warn you, it's not the sort of thing you want to be listening to when you are returning after a long journey to no house, no money and no job. The bass line begins softly, like a heartbeat pulsating in time with the moon, and the mournful lyrics are all about staying on the road too long. That night it made me panic.

Just before midnight—still 935 kilometres north of Adelaide—the bus reached the opal mining town of Coober Pedy. Now Australians get very patriotic about opals. They haven't got the crisp clarity of diamonds, they don't stir your soul the way a well-cut emerald will—as far as I can see, they are just milky white stones with a few specks of colour in them—but they can only be found in Australia, and as far as Australians are concerned, that makes them the best damn stones in the world. Coober Pedy is also an underground town—the incredible heat on the surface forces the inhabitants to seek relief underground. For an underground town, though, there seemed to be an awful lot of stuff above ground—a hotel, a supermarket, a bakery and even a pizzeria.

The bus made a rest stop at the town's Italian pizzeria (John's Pizza) and was met by a scruffy bloke touting for the town's hostel. He gave a little spiel about the underground dorms and a few of the backpackers—Scandinavians, judging by their socks and sandals—followed him into town in the crisp midnight air. The rest of us went into the pizzeria to wait as the driver ate the medium super supreme that would sustain him until Adelaide.

A group of young Aboriginal girls sat outside the pizzeria eating pizza. Their entertainment for the night was to say hello to everyone as they entered and then laugh raucously when they answered back. My hello threw them.

'You're from Australia!' they said, astonished.

'Yep.'

'Whereabouts?'

'Sydney.'

'Well, we're from Coober Pedy,' said the most precocious, laughing like it was the funniest thing anyone had ever said. When the bus left, they waved goodbye and most people on the bus felt compelled to wave back, which made them laugh even more.

From Coober Pedy the bus barrelled down the Stuart Highway, passing road trains five trailers long. When I woke up, we were in Adelaide. As you would expect of a city with the nickname 'the city of churches', Adelaide was neat and green and very much the model of respectability.

I am always surprised how much (and how many) towns and cities live up to my preconceptions of them. Superficially, at least, they seem to match the urban myths. This was particularly true as the bus continued towards Sydney from Adelaide, making its way northeast towards the Hay Plain and NSW. Griffith, out on the Murray Irrigation Area and on the outskirts of the Hay Plain, gave off the appropriate aura of an area steeped in crime and nefarious drug dealing. The bus stopped late at night in a dingy diner that looked like something out of middle America, peopled with the sort of low-life losers you see in any Coen Brothers movie. Canberra, well, it was as sterile and boring as you'd imagine a totally planned city populated nearly exclusively by public servants would be.

My *Lonely Planet* guidebook on Australia reckoned that Australians hate Canberra because of school excursions. I disagree. I think Canberra is actually the *perfect* school excursion destination. You get to see the few interesting things in Canberra while you are young—the War Memorial, the National Art Gallery, Parliament House—and hence have no reason to ever go back there. It's not as if there's a great pub or club scene to lure you back. In fact, the only thing in Canberra that would lure anyone over 18 back is the burgeoning pornography industry.

After Canberra, the bus rejoined the Hume Highway, the main road connecting Sydney and Melbourne. It's a rather boring expanse of divided motorway where the monotony is broken only by the occasional giant service station or McDonald's. 'Progress' has seen the highway barrel through former farmland, bypassing towns and robbing the local businesses of passing trade in the process. But it's not just the locals who have been robbed. The bypasses have short-changed travellers as well. The Goulburn bypass now circumvents the Big Merino, a giant concrete ram as big as a house. And the Marulan bypass has removed the uniquely Australian Big Pavlova from all but the most pernickety tourist itinerary.

By mid morning the bus was nearing the outskirts of Sydney. I tried to approach Sydney like I did Budapest or Esfahan or Lhasa— as someone arriving for the first time—but I couldn't. The bus was approaching Sydney through its southwestern suburbs, the area of the city where I grew up, and it wasn't long before the landmarks of my misspent youth were popping up everywhere.

The first came on the outskirts of Campbelltown, 55 kilometres from the centre of the city, when I spotted the turn-off for the Menangle River. The Menangle River holds a special significance for me because it was there that I got to kiss Simone Hofmeyer — for the first (and only) time. Simone was an exotic Scandinavian– South African mix, with porcelain skin and an accent that melted your heart—and quite frankly, I had been smitten with her for a couple of years. I'm sure Simone doesn't remember much of the night, though. She passed out in my arms, drunk on Blackberry Nip. Even now, a glass of Ribena always reminds me of what I missed out on.

The next landmark of my youth, a more painful one, was the bunker. The bunker was a concrete building on top of a hill about two kilometres away from my high school. Once a month, our PE teacher would make us run there and back, as some kind of sick torture. After the first 500 metres you would get the idea of sitting under a tree, resting until the idiots who went all the way there came back past the tree again, then joining up and running back to the gym as if you had gone the whole way. The trouble was, the bunker was right next to the freeway, so our teacher would drive there and wait up the top, ticking your name on the roll as you arrived. He was a sick man, our PE teacher. Not only did he get us to run up steep hills and back, he also liked to make us run along gym mats as the rest of the class threw medicine balls at us.

After the bunker, the other landmarks of my youth came in quick succession:

Liverpool: the record shop where I'd listen to LPs while I was waiting for my bus. It was where I bought my first single, 'Ballroom Blitz' by The Sweet, and had my first introduction to Punk and New Wave, Elvis Costello's *This Year's Model*, still one of my favourite albums ever.

Burwood: the first place I lived after leaving home, a little old wooden house owned by Hugo the Yugo. It was my first year at university and it soon degenerated into 12 months of sleeping in, watching telly, and staying up late drinking.

Parramatta Road: the used car yard where I bought my first car. It was a burnt orange Datsun 120Y coupe with a go-fast stripe down the side.

Broadway: Sydney University, my old uni, where I eventually made an attempt to study properly. I started with law, but eventually graduated with a BA and a career-oriented medieval history major.

Then the McCafferty's bus pulled into a parking bay under the giant sandstone arches of Central Station and we had arrived in Sydney proper. The Opera House and the Harbour Bridge—the high-profile icons of my city—were a couple of kilometres north, hidden by a forest of skyscrapers. I got off the bus and, amongst the tanned Europeans, waited for my pack. They were excited about being in a new city and, no doubt, a little daunted by the prospect of changing money and finding somewhere to stay and eat.

I had been like that too—in Prague, in Tirane, in Varanasi and in countless other cities and towns—but now, my journey was over. Twenty-five countries, 13 boats, 34 buses, 16 trains, 21 mini vans, six car rides and one solitary flight later, I was finally—and rather suddenly, it seemed—home. It had taken me eight months to do it— the same amount of time it used to take the convicts to come by boat when they were transported from England—and I too had travelled from London to Sydney the hard way. I found a public phone nearby and rang my mum to tell her that I had arrived home safely. Even though it was a local call, I don't think she quite believed me.

At the end of it all, I am pleased to report that in many ways the old hippie trail is alive and kicking. Well, in spirit, anyway. Brad the Pervert was still having sex until his penis dropped off. In Darra you can still buy cheap hash—maybe not for the same price as a packet of crisps, but for no more than the cost of a loaf of bread. And the backpackers in India and Thailand still have the same penchant for colourful clothes and tacky amulets. More importantly, the old hippie maxim of peace, love and understanding lives on in the generosity of people like Martina in Zagreb, Skender in Gjirokaster, Fatty in Bam and the Afghani consul in Peshawar.

And if I hadn't been desperately broke, I'm sure I would have turned around and gone back the other way, there and then.

home

The Wrong Way Home
Slide Show

Thanks to the wondrous phenomenon that is the Internet, you're all cordially invited to the slide show about my trip from London to Sydney at **www.petermoore.com.au**.

It's on 24-hours-a-day, 365-days-a-year. And it's just like the slide shows you had to endure as a kid—lots of poorly composed, blurry photos of people and places you don't really care about—but at least at this one you can turn it off with a click of the mouse.

To help keep you entertained, I've also added some other features to the site, like a currency converter that tells you just how many Laotian kip you get for your hard earned cash, and an advice section where travellers can leave or find up-to-date tips on the countries covered by this trip. If you feel so inclined, you can also send me an email and tell me what you thought of the book.

So, I'll see you there, shall I?

Just don't forget to bring the sherry and sponge cake.